T0274644

ADDICTION

WHAT EVERYONE NEEDS TO KNOW®

ADDICTION
WHAT EVERYONE NEEDS TO KNOW®

SUZETTE GLASNER

OXFORD
UNIVERSITY PRESS

OXFORD
UNIVERSITY PRESS

Oxford University Press is a department of the University of Oxford. It furthers the University's objective of excellence in research, scholarship, and education by publishing worldwide. Oxford is a registered trade mark of Oxford University Press in the UK and certain other countries.

"What Everyone Needs to Know" is a registered trademark of Oxford University Press.

Published in the United States of America by Oxford University Press 198 Madison Avenue, New York, NY 10016, United States of America.

© Suzette Glasner 2024

All rights reserved. No part of this publication may be reproduced, stored in a retrieval system, or transmitted, in any form or by any means, without the prior permission in writing of Oxford University Press, or as expressly permitted by law, by license, or under terms agreed with the appropriate reproduction rights organization. Inquiries concerning reproduction outside the scope of the above should be sent to the Rights Department, Oxford University Press, at the address above.

You must not circulate this work in any other form and you must impose this same condition on any acquirer.

Library of Congress Cataloging-in-Publication Data
Names: Glasner, Suzette, author.
Title: Addiction : what everyone needs to know / Suzette Glasner.
Description: New York, NY : Suzette Glasner, [2024] |
Series: What everyone needs to know |
Includes bibliographical references and index.
Identifiers: LCCN 2023057395 (print) | LCCN 2023057396 (ebook) |
ISBN 9780190946555 (hardback) | ISBN 9780190946548 (paperback) |
ISBN 9780190946579 (epub) | ISBN 9780197768747
Subjects: LCSH: Alcoholism. | Substance abuse—Prevention.
Classification: LCC RC565 .G54 2024 (print) |
LCC RC565 (ebook) | DDC 362.292—dc23/eng/20240209
LC record available at https://lccn.loc.gov/2023057395
LC ebook record available at https://lccn.loc.gov/2023057396

DOI: 10.1093/wentk/9780190946555.001.0001

This material is not intended to be, and should not be considered, a substitute for medical or other professional advice. Treatment for the conditions described in this material is highly dependent on the individual circumstances. And, while this material is designed to offer accurate information with respect to the subject matter covered and to be current as of the time it was written, research and knowledge about medical and health issues is constantly evolving and dose schedules for medications are being revised continually, with new side effects recognized and accounted for regularly. Readers must therefore always check the product information and clinical procedures with the most up-to-date published product information and data sheets provided by the manufacturers and the most recent codes of conduct and safety regulation. The publisher and the authors make no representations or warranties to readers, express or implied, as to the accuracy or completeness of this material. Without limiting the foregoing, the publisher and the authors make no representations or warranties as to the accuracy or efficacy of the drug dosages mentioned in the material. The authors and the publisher do not accept, and expressly disclaim, any responsibility for any liability, loss, or risk that may be claimed or incurred as a consequence of the use and/or application of any of the contents of this material.

Paperback printed by Sheridan Books, Inc., United States of America
Hardback printed by Bridgeport National Bindery, Inc., United States of America

To my mom and dad, who instilled the compassion, perseverance, and sense of purpose that drive me to help people change their lives.

CONTENTS

FOREWORD

Addiction: What Everyone Needs to Know is quite simply one of the most engaging, informative, and practical books on addiction that I have ever read. As an addiction researcher for the past 45 years I have reviewed all kinds of books about addiction. Many were scholarly tomes dedicated to providing researchers with the latest scientific findings. Others were personal chronicles of an individual's or a family's struggles to overcome dependence on alcohol and/or other drugs. The scientific books were of course essential—the facts contained in them formed the foundation of what we know. Yet, so many of the scientific findings described were simply not available to most of the public. Similarly, the personal accounts of overcoming addiction and achieving recovery were often deeply motivating, but often very personal and thus not broadly relevant to the large population of those affected.

What I have rarely read during my career is a book designed for the very large number of individuals, families, and communities who need accurate, practical information and sensible guidance on basic questions that will inform immediate, critical decisions on what to do. Some of the most basic of these questions are:

- "Is my child/partner/friend addicted—how can I tell?"
- "What does addiction do to the body and brain—what causes the seemingly uncontrollable urges to use?"

- "Is marijuana addictive—why does it seem safe to use?"
- "What can I do—are there any effective medications or therapies that reliably work to treat addiction?"
- "Is there life after addiction—what is 'recovery' and is it attainable/sustainable?"

I too have asked these questions when dealing with addiction in my own family, or when asked for my opinion by friends and colleagues facing the same problems. So many times I thought , . . if I am supposed to be an expert, and I don't have clear answers to these fundamental questions—how can a school teacher, or a policeman, or a business executive make informed decisions that will profoundly affect their futures?

I wish I had had Doctor Suzette Glasner's book, *Addiction: What Everyone Needs to Know*, to help my own decisions and to provide practical guidance for all the families, healthcare providers, and policymakers who asked me for advice over the years. The questions posed above are the focus of many of the chapters of her book. The answers provided within those chapters are simultaneously scientifically accurate and also practical and constructively motivational. Dr. Glasner knows the science through her years in addiction research at UCLA, and she has applied the most important and effective parts of that science in her years of clinical practice. She has clearly profited from her experience, blending the clinical science with common sense in a very fluid and engaging writing style.

As importantly, Dr. Glasner has provided a realistically optimistic portrayal of the road from addiction to recovery. Unlike so many of the TV and internet advertisements for addiction treatments, Dr. Glasner does not indulge in impossible promises of cure—just the facts coupled with sound, realistic clinical guidance. The book makes clear something that is so difficult for those in crisis to see: that there *are* effective medications and therapies available to treat addictions, and that recovery is an attainable, sustainable result of science-based, comprehensive continuing care. In short, the book conveys realistic hope without minimizing or exaggerating the struggles.

So, for all these reasons I am very grateful to Dr. Glasner for this contribution on both a personal and professional level. Finally, I have a very readable book I can recommend to patients and parents, physicians and clergy, attorneys and judges, teachers and employers who have exactly the same important addiction questions and concerns addressed in this book. Dr. Glasner has masterfully combined her decades of work in research, clinical care, and teaching into an exceptionally clear and direct discussion of the most important questions affecting addicted individuals and their families.

A. Thomas McLellan, PhD.,
Emeritus Professor of Psychology in Psychiatry,
University of Pennsylvania, and former Deputy Director
of the White House Office of National Drug Control
Policy under President Barack Obama

Part 1

WHAT DOES ADDICTION LOOK LIKE?

1

INTRODUCTION

HOW CAN THIS BOOK HELP YOU UNDERSTAND ADDICTION?

What you will learn from this book

- The symptoms, diagnosis, and causes of addiction
- How to know when professional help is needed to address addictive behaviors
- The effective medical and psychological treatments for addiction
- Behavioral techniques that help manage addiction and prevent relapse
- How treatments and lifestyle changes can be tailored to a person's unique characteristics, symptoms, and life situation

Alisa, 42, found herself in an emergency room in southern California, with no recollection of how she had gotten there. Her problem started many years earlier when, bored and unsatisfied in her marriage and role as a stay-at-home mother of two school-aged children and feeling isolated from her close family in Boston, she began drinking alcohol just to "have fun" and be social. She had found some friends, mostly other moms from her children's elementary school, with whom she could go out for drinks and enjoy herself. Over time, she developed a habit of going out to run errands once her kids were settled in and doing their homework after school, and would stop into a local bar by herself to have a few drinks before going home. Tension began building in her marriage when she took hours to come home from "running errands" in the evenings, at times arriving noticeably intoxicated after having driven herself home. When she and her husband Jay were at social functions where alcohol was being served, Alisa spoke increasingly loudly and somewhat angrily. Not surprisingly, the more often Jay had to try to slip out of parties and other gatherings unnoticed with Alisa, the more he dreaded these events. After a while, she began attending them without him.

Her problems escalated when she blacked out at a bar one night while on a "girls' trip" to the desert with a few of her friends. When she woke up in the emergency room, Alisa was told that her friend Beth had brought her in after she lost her balance in the bathroom of the bar and started vomiting and passing out intermittently. Her friend was worried that if she took her back to their hotel room, she might vomit in her sleep and something bad could happen to her. Alisa's doctor in the emergency room diagnosed her with an alcohol use disorder and provided some referrals to residential treatment programs for addiction where she could be evaluated more thoroughly for alcoholism. In the meantime, he suggested that she try attending an Alcolics Anonymous (AA) meeting for support and advised her to stop drinking.

When Alisa returned home, her husband told her that he had thrown out all the alcohol in the house and that her drinking had to stop. "I made a huge mistake," she said to her husband, "but does that mean that I'm an alcoholic and I can never ever drink again?" "Why would you ever *want* to drink again, Alisa?" he shouted angrily. "If you don't stop, our marriage will never make it." Even though her drinking had caused her some stress and embarrassment, quitting altogether sounded like the last thing she wanted or needed to do.

What do you need to know to help someone with addiction?

This book will equip you with factual information about addiction and its treatment, with the assumption that those who are affected, either directly or indirectly by this illness, are better positioned to accept, live with, and cope effectively with it, with the relevant knowledge on hand. For someone in Alisa's situation, and for those who love or care about her, some of the important questions to gain understanding and take steps to address the problem are:

- What are the symptoms of a substance use disorder?
- Where does social/recreational substance use end and substance use disorder begin?
- What caused this illness, and how long does it last?
- How does one know when a relapse is imminent?
- What triggers relapse once a person is in recovery?
- What can one do to minimize the chances of relapse?
- Are there different medication and/or therapy treatments for addictions to different types of substances?

By the time you've reached the end of this book, you will have answers to these questions, along with a more thorough understanding of addiction and its treatment.

Is there hope for recovery from addiction?

Substance use disorders affect at least one in every seven American adults.[1] Like Alisa, those who suffer from addiction (which is a severe substance use disorder) experience many difficult problems in their family, social, and work lives. People with addictions to alcohol and drugs are also at high risk for physical health problems (e.g., cardiovascular illness, liver disease, and infectious diseases), mental health disorders (e.g., depression, anxiety, and psychosis), and suicide. Thankfully, despite the widely held belief that addiction is a lifelong illness from which people don't recover, the scientific data on treatment for alcohol and drug use disorders suggest the opposite—there *is* hope for recovery. With psychological treatment, and in many cases medications, it is possible to return to a normal life, free from the once devastating consequences of alcohol and drug use. These treatments make it possible not only to reduce and/or eliminate alcohol and drug use from one's life, but to prevent relapses (or contain them so that they don't spiral out of control or last for a long period of time); cope effectively with environmental and psychological triggers; and function well in important life roles at work and home. If you or someone you love is in the throes of an addiction, this may be difficult to imagine, but a wealth of scientific research, coupled with the inspiring true stories of people who have struggled through addiction and its treatment, speaks to the potential for a rewarding life in recovery.

Who is this book for?

Whether you have already come to recognize that you have an alcohol or drug use disorder, are becoming concerned that you might have one, are worried about a friend or family member who may have or definitely has one, or are considering embarking upon a career in substance use or addiction treatment, this book will help you understand the disorder and learn how it can be treated effectively. In the chapters that follow, you'll find current information on the defining features of alcohol and drug addiction, its causes, its medication and psychological (also known as "behavioral") treatments, and the lifestyle changes that can aid both short- and long-term recovery. Naturally, these treatment approaches should be adapted to the unique circumstances in an individual's life and work best when they are tailored to each person. In other words, not every scientifically based treatment works for every person with an addiction. In this book, you will learn more about how an individual with addiction can discover the treatment approach that is the "right fit" to facilitate success in their recovery.

In my clinical practice, I have found that the early stages of coming to recognize an alcohol or drug use disorder bring about many questions and anxieties. Those who suffer from addictions and their family members tend to find information about the causes, symptoms, behavioral patterns, and effective treatment options very reassuring. Because the illness of addiction is, by definition, characterized by a loss of control over one's behavior, the way it unfolds in a person's life can be quite unpredictable. This unpredictability can lead a person with addiction and their loved ones in and out of "crisis mode" as the drug or alcohol use disorder takes hold and leads them to act in ways that are uncharacteristic of the person they once were. For Alisa and Jay, understanding how chronic alcohol use affects the brain and behavior, and how treatment that brings about changes in alcohol use can stabilize the brain's functioning and lead to other positive behavioral changes, could have been quite helpful to inform next steps for Alisa and her family. Without this information, it was challenging for Alisa to understand the rationale for changing her drinking.

Why do people return to substance use even after it causes problems?

After some self-reflection, Alisa realized that despite her initial reluctance to quit drinking she shared her husband's concerns about what had happened in the desert. Though she knew it wouldn't be easy, Alisa decided to try to spend the next month alcohol-free.

Weeks went by and, to her husband's great relief, Alisa stayed sober. It wasn't until Jay went out of town to a conference that something inside of her began to shift. Her children were at school and she was feeling bored and a little lonely. "I've been doing so well," she thought. "It's a beautiful day out, it would be nice if I could just go out to lunch at my favorite outdoor restaurant and have a glass of wine with my meal." One drink led to many, and later that night when her husband discovered that she had returned to drinking, the tension at home became palpable once more. Logically Alisa knew that alcohol was creating problems in her life, and drinking wasn't a good idea. But her body and mind seemed to be telling her otherwise.

Alisa's story is not as unusual as it might sound. Because she didn't fully understand the nature of her alcohol use disorder, she was of the mindset that getting sober might be a matter of pure willpower. She didn't realize how progressive the illness of alcoholism is, or why the ER doctor felt that she met criteria for this disorder. She wasn't aware of the warning signs of relapse either, so as she was confronted with them, she walked straight into a trap; her illness enticed her with the notion of drinking a single glass of wine, which she had intended to be the end of it—yet it was just the beginning.

Understanding the biological causes of addiction, including the way in which it can affect decision making, can help to clarify why, despite knowing how destructive alcohol had become to her important relationships and her overall functioning, Alisa continued to feel preoccupied with a desire to drink.

"No one understands": How do common misconceptions about addiction affect the recovery process for individuals and families?

After trying unsuccessfully on her own to stop drinking over several months, Alisa entered outpatient treatment, where she attended one-on-one and group therapy and learned quite a bit about her alcohol use disorder. An addiction medicine doctor prescribed a medication called Naltrexone to help curb alcohol cravings and prevent relapse. Following treatment, Alisa spoke with a few close friends about her diagnosis and treatment. They were supportive, but some of their comments made her feel a little uneasy. One friend doubted her diagnosis: "You just need to learn to control yourself a little better when you drink, you've always been a lightweight," and "maybe you're just going through a mid-life crisis!" This led Alisa to wonder if her husband's response to her "crisis in the desert" *was* somewhat exaggerated, and she was just going through a tough time in her life.

Alisa's husband seemed to be walking on eggshells around her. Jay's intentions were coming from a caring place, but he seemed to be constantly scrutinizing her for signs that she would drink or had been drinking. When her mood was even slightly unhappy or irritable he would ask her if she was going to see her doctor soon, and if she thought that the therapy was "working." He asked her almost every day if she had taken her medication, and it felt somewhat intrusive. What neither of them fully understood was that rebuilding trust in a marriage or other close relationship(s) is a very normal part of recovery that doesn't resolve itself overnight, and, as you'll learn in Chapter 11, sometimes marital or family therapy can help.

People who have little experience or knowledge of addiction and its treatment may make many incorrect assumptions about it and may not know to talk about it in ways that are helpful, leading them to say and do things that feel alienating and annoying to a person who is struggling with addiction and initiating a plan of recovery. Many people erroneously view addiction as a reflection of poor choices or a moral failing, leading them to make critical and judgmental comments. They may view a person with addiction as overly fragile. Because trust has been eroded between the person with addiction and their loved ones, they are likely to question that person about their follow-through with their treatment plans (whether that means attending treatment or self-help groups, taking medicine, or a combination of these things). They will often be quick to jump to conclusions about relapse based on very slight changes in one's mood or behavior.

Despite many decades of research that has clearly established addiction as a chronic brain illness with genetic and biological underpinnings, the stigma attached to this disease is far from gone. This is something that a person who suffers from addiction can both defy and accept—while it is worth the effort to share with others one's knowledge about addiction as a chronic illness to promote their compassion and understanding, not everyone who views addiction as a reflection of poor choices will be willing to see a different perspective. Consulting with a health professional with expertise in addiction treatment can be helpful to make these conversations easier.

What can recovery look like?

Alisa's first year of recovery was quite challenging, but now, one year later, her life has changed for the better in many ways. A few months into sobriety, she was diagnosed with depression, and she began taking Celexa (an antidepressant). With the depression symptoms under control, she found that the desire to drink did not come up as frequently or intensely. The boredom and loneliness that used to trigger her appeared to be partly influenced by her low mood and inability to enjoy things, both of which are symptoms of a depressive disorder. She had not realized this, and thought that she was just a person without enough sources of joy and pleasure in her life, which was partly why she turned to alcohol.

Alisa and Jay have found their way back to a healthy marriage. They began seeing a couples' therapist with specialty training in addiction, and after about three months of counseling they felt that things were back on track in their relationship. The therapist helped them learn how to communicate about Alisa's recovery in ways that were constructive and mutually supportive. Jay learned how to "check in" with Alisa in a non-intrusive way, giving her the space and independence she needed to rebuild her confidence while respectfully and caringly holding her accountable for the commitments she had made to her continuing recovery. With time, Alisa came to accept that his fears were pretty normal, and that the longer she sustained her sobriety, the more of the "old Jay" she began to see—relaxed, trusting, and optimistic about their future. Together, they learned about the warning signs of relapse and how to discuss concerns that either of them might have if some of these signs were to come about. Alisa continued to attend individual therapy on a weekly basis, and she gave her therapist full permission to speak to Jay about her treatment if needed. Overall, the key to their marriage surviving Alisa's alcoholism was the mutual agreement they shared to be open about her recovery, coupled with the skills they both acquired in therapy about how to communicate about her alcoholism and recovery without stirring up conflict.

Finally, and perhaps most importantly, Alisa is coming to terms with the idea that her alcohol use disorder is a chronic illness, while at the same time realizing that this doesn't mean that it will always be a "front and center" issue in her life. She has come to recognize that, by remaining vigilant about her recovery, she can *manage* this illness and live a fulfilling life. She is learning that managing it simply means staying consistent with her treatment, prioritizing her health and well-being (both physical and mental), and tuning into any relapse warning signs that she or her trusted loved ones might notice. With these practices in place, she doesn't need to worry about the alcoholism taking her life over again.

Looking forward: How to use this book

This book is divided into four sections. In Chapter 2 in this section, "What Do Addiction and Recovery Look Like?" you'll learn about the symptoms of a substance use disorder both from the perspective of the individual who is suffering from it and those who are close to that person. Expanding upon Alisa's story, you'll become familiar with the behaviors that tip off loved ones as an addiction is developing and progressing, and how a person who is living with alcohol or drug addiction may come to recognize what is happening to them and develop a desire or intention to change. In terms of prevention, Chapter 2 also describes how a person who is vulnerable to addiction can become self-aware, notice their own warning signs, and prevent the illness from developing and/or worsening. Chapter 2 also goes into depth about genetic, biological, and environmental risk factors for addiction. This chapter offers answers to the often-asked questions about whether addiction is a choice or a reflection of moral weakness, providing detailed explanations of the basis of our scientific understanding of addiction as a brain illness.

Part 2, "How Do Alcohol and Drugs Affect the Brain and Behavior?" describes the health effects of alcohol and other drugs with addiction potential, including marijuana, stimulants, and opioids, along with tobacco, nicotine, and e-cigarettes. In this section, you'll learn science-based information that clarifies common myths and misconceptions about alcohol and drugs, such as the idea that there are certain types of addictions that people can't recover from (e.g., addiction to methamphetamine). Common questions about various substances (e.g., is marijuana addictive?; are e-cigarettes and vaping safer than smoking?) are addressed so that you can become more comfortable thinking through and talking about these issues with others, whether you're contemplating your own decisions to use or avoid these substances, or helping to keep others informed when they are thinking about or actively using them. Part 3 contains a wealth of information about various types of psychotherapy approaches, along with a summary of the evidence for their effectiveness in ameliorating different types of addictions. This section also discusses medications for treating addictions to various substances (particularly alcohol and opioids, for which we have the most developed and well-studied set of FDA-approved medication treatment options). In this section, you'll also gain an understanding of how they work at a biological level to affect addictive behaviors. You'll learn about the conditions under which different types of medications might be recommended by a physician or other licensed provider who prescribes medication. You will develop strategies for evaluating, as a consumer, the quality of a treatment program for alcohol or drug addiction. In addition, you'll find a description of the reasons behind the devastating rise in overdose deaths both from opioids and other substances, along with lifesaving strategies to prevent overdose fatalities. Finally, Part 4, "Addiction and Recovery Long Term: The Prognosis Can Be Great" focuses on the prognosis of those with substance use disorders long-term, the practical implications of understanding addiction as a chronic illness (e.g., what that means about how long and what type of treatment is needed over the course of one's life), how to prevent relapse, and finding meaning in life while living with a substance use disorder.

2

WHAT DO ADDICTION AND RECOVERY LOOK LIKE?

What is addiction? What's the difference between addiction and substance use?

People experience addiction in different ways, and the specific symptoms, substance(s) used, complicating conditions (e.g., psychiatric or medical illnesses that are present at the same time), and life impact of these symptoms are important considerations when forming an approach to treatment.

Kevin is a 44-year-old man who has been working as an assistant producer for a television show for over six years. Kevin has been struggling with his addiction to an opioid painkiller, oxycodone, for over 10 years now. Having been through multiple treatment episodes, Kevin's longest period of sobriety was two years. He relapsed three years ago, after he and his girlfriend of many years broke up and she moved out, which led him to feel depressed and lonely. Since that time, he has been alternating between periods of heavy oxycodone use and unsuccessful attempts to detoxify and quit on his own. As his addiction has worsened, despite great efforts to "keep it together," Kevin's co-workers and supervisors have noticed that the quality of his work is not what it once was. He also became more and more depressed and isolative each time he returned to oxycodone use, and though he recognized that using was leading him to a very dark place emotionally, he found himself continuing to use anyway. For Kevin, the process of coming to recognize that he needs professional help to detoxify from oxycodone has taken years. "I'm finally starting to see that this addiction is bigger than me," he related to his doctor. "I can't fight it on my own anymore."

In this book, you will notice that two different terms are used to describe people with problematic alcohol and/or drug use: *substance use disorder* and *addiction*. The term *substance use disorder* is a recognized psychiatric diagnosis that appears in *Diagnostic and Statistical Manual of Mental Disorders, Fifth Edition, Text Revision* (DSM-5-TR), a manual for the assessment and diagnosis of mental disorders, guided by the American Psychiatric Association. Professionals with expertise in diagnosing and treating addiction usually think of a substance use disorder as a set of symptoms indicating problems related to the use of alcohol or drugs, which are present at the same time over a specified time period. Why do we distinguish between an addiction and a substance use disorder? According to the DSM-5-TR, substance use disorders fall into one of three categories, according to the severity of the symptoms a person is experiencing: (1) mild, (2) moderate, or (3) severe. Although "addiction" is not a formal DSM-5-TR diagnosis, scientists and practitioners generally think of addiction as a severe substance use disorder. If you are new to all of this terminology, you probably have lots of questions, such as: How long does it take for someone to progress from a "mild" to a "severe" substance use disorder? Do most people who start out with a mild disorder eventually become addicted? How does a doctor distinguish between the mild, moderate, and severe categories? Which of these categories of substance use disorders need to be treated? You might have more questions about treatment, which will be addressed in Chapters 10 through 12. For now, we'll begin with a deeper dive into the diagnosis.

How does a health practitioner distinguish between the mild, moderate, and severe categories?

To understand these distinctions, let's begin with understanding what qualifies as a "substance use disorder." The core feature of a substance disorder is a progressive loss of control over the use of alcohol or another substance. There are 11 symptoms described in the DSM-5-TR, and the mild/moderate/severe designation reflects the number of symptoms a person suffers from. This tells a treatment provider how serious the loss of control is and how impactful drug or alcohol use has become on a person's life, including their ability to function and their well-being physically and psychologically. A *mild* diagnosis is given when two or three symptom criteria are met. When four or five symptoms are present, a *moderate* diagnosis is indicated, and when six or more symptoms are observed, the diagnosis is considered *severe*. There are a variety of symptoms that people experience when they are losing control over their use of alcohol or drugs. Any combination of these symptoms can be present in a person with a substance use disorder.

What Is Addiction?

- A set of symptoms that go together, reflecting that a person has lost control over their use of alcohol or drugs.
- People with addiction don't all experience the same symptoms.
- Symptoms can be physical, such as experiencing discomfort when the effects of a drug wear off.
- The person may have difficulty controlling how much or how often they use alcohol or drugs, with repeated failed attempts to stop or cut back.
- Use of alcohol or drugs causes problems in important areas of life (such as work or relationships).
- Alcohol or drug use causes or worsens physical or emotional health problems.
- Despite the problems caused by using alcohol or drugs, people with addiction continue to drink or use the substances anyway.

What are the physical symptoms of addiction?

There are two core physical symptoms of a substance use disorder: tolerance and withdrawal. When *tolerance* is present, a person will find that they need to use more and more of the substance to achieve the same effects on their mind and body, or that the amount that they have been using doesn't seem to impact them in the same way any longer. For example, if a person drinks alcohol to relax and take their mind off things, they may find that at first, they would experience a release of tension after two drinks. If the person develops tolerance, then they may notice that the effect of alcohol is no longer apparent after two drinks, but maybe requires three or four. Alisa, whose alcoholism we discussed in Chapter 1, could consume large quantities of alcohol once she had developed a high degree of tolerance. The same pattern emerges with drugs; a person with tolerance needs to take them in increasing amounts to feel the same high or rush that felt so good in the beginning. Kevin's use of oxycodone followed this pattern, ultimately making it very difficult for him to quit on his own.

Withdrawal is a set of physical symptoms that can emerge over time and are apparent as the effects of the substance begin to wear off. Withdrawal symptoms vary in nature, depending on the particular drug that is used. For alcohol, as an example, the classic "hangover" symptoms are in fact alcohol withdrawal signs, including nausea, vomiting, shakiness, insomnia, head-ache, and anxiety or nervousness. One of the ways a person can come to recognize that they are experiencing withdrawal symptoms is when they find themselves taking the substance in efforts to alleviate these uncomfortable symptoms. You've probably heard of the saying, "Take a hair of the dog that bit you," a common phrase people use to describe why they may drink when they're hung over the next day. Have you ever wondered where that saying comes from? It is based on the medieval belief that, if a person was bitten by a rabid dog, applying the same dog's hair to the infected wound could heal it. When extended to curing a hangover, the advice was, "After a debauch, take a little wine the next day."[1] We now understand that this approach to self-medicating withdrawal symptoms, when done *repeatedly*, is a sign of loss of control over substance use.

A third symptom that can have both physical and psychological components is experiencing *cravings* for alcohol or another substance. A craving is a strong urge or desire to drink or use drugs, which can present itself in different ways. Some people experience cravings physically; they may feel tension or a sensation in a particular part of their body (e.g., in their stomach or their chest). For others, a craving can present itself as a thought, which for some people, feels intrusive or unwanted, such as "I need it," or "I can't get it out of my head." Cravings are a newer part of symptoms of a diagnosable substance use disorder, as they were added to the fifth edition of the DSM in 2013. This was largely because those who treat addictions felt that the effective treatment of cravings, potentially with medications, could be an important strategy for helping people recover from addiction.[2]

What are the behavioral symptoms of addiction?

Apart from the physical symptoms of tolerance and withdrawal, and the physical and/or psychological experience of cravings, there are several behavioral symptoms that reflect a loss of control over one's use of drugs or alcohol. These can fall into three categories. First, *impaired control* over one's use of alcohol or drugs can become apparent in a few ways:

1. When a person makes rules for themselves about drinking or using drugs (e.g., planning to drink or use only on certain days, or in particular amounts), only to end up breaking them, this is a sign of impaired control over substance use. We saw this in the case of Alisa, who tried to drink casually while her husband was out of town, but she wasn't able to stick to it and found herself exceeding her planned limits and drinking to intoxication.
2. Spending increasing amounts of time either acquiring substances, using them, or recovering from their effects is

another indication that control over use is slipping away. If you think about it, most people don't intend to devote most of their time to a habit that doesn't have tangible benefits, and if anything has gradually mounting costs, personally and otherwise. But when an addiction begins taking on a life of its own, the affected person's life becomes dominated by the need to drink or use drugs. This need begins to actively take center stage as it pushes other important needs aside.

3. Finally, a clear sign that a person is losing control is when they try repeatedly to cut back or stop drinking or using drugs and are unable to, or if they are frequently preoccupied by a desire to do so but are not able to make it happen. For example, Kevin tried several times to "self-detox" from oxycodone, attempting to quit over a period of days, but found that time after time, the withdrawal symptoms were so unbearable that, by day four or five, he caved and ended up relapsing. Kevin was clearly struggling with a frequent desire to stop using oxycodone, and despite his repeated efforts he was not able to sustain abstinence from it.

The second category of behavioral symptoms is quite easy to recognize: *risky use.* A person who is engaging in risky use of a substance does things that are not safe when they are under the influence of alcohol or drugs. For example, they drive or do other things (such as swimming or taking a bath) that are dangerous while they are intoxicated. A person who repeatedly engages in risky use behaviors often does so despite knowledge that their behavior could have serious health or personal consequences. For example, risky use can (and often does) lead to legal problems, such as receiving a citation for driving under the influence (DUI). For an individual with a substance use disorder, having received a DUI may act as a deterrent to drinking and driving for a period of time, but as the substance use disorder progresses or worsens, the behavior often repeats itself. Repetition of risky behaviors can lead to more difficulties, as loved ones become frustrated, disappointed, and even hopeless about the prospects of recovery. And legal problems may intensify, leading to both financial and emotional strain for the individual and their family.

Finally, a third domain of symptoms comprises *social problems*. Although the term "social problems" sounds like it refers to relationships we have with one another, it is actually much broader than that. It's about the way a person functions as a citizen in our society, which involves not only maintaining important interpersonal relationships, but also the ability to contribute meaningfully to society by being productive (either academically or at work or in the community). When a person is functioning well socially, they participate in activities that promote their own physical and emotional well-being. This can involve a wide variety of healthy behaviors, including exercise, pursuing hobbies that they enjoy, learning new skills, or improving existing skills in areas of life that are meaningful to them. When a person's social well-being is good, they generally meet, and at times may exceed, expectations around school or work performance (of course, even in a very healthy person, this can depend on how inspired they are by their school and work pursuits!). People who display healthy social behavior spend time with their loved ones and make efforts to feel connected, which not only includes family but may also involve maintaining friendships. When a person's drug or alcohol use affects their ability to be productive, this is a reflection of an illness developing or existing (i.e., a substance use disorder). Sometimes this means that the quality of a person's work academically or at their job has diminished, but it can also be reflected by inconsistent attendance or punctuality at work. These patterns begin to appear when a person's use of alcohol or drugs, or their need to recover from episodes of using them, interferes with their ability to follow through with commitments and function in various roles and responsibilities in life. These same types of patterns of inconsistency, unreliability, and altered performance can be observed in a person's relationships with family members, children, co-workers, and friends. A person with a developing substance use disorder may become distant from loved ones and friends, showing up less frequently at social gatherings, or attending but not acting like their "usual self."

When diagnosing a substance use disorder, a doctor or other clinician will evaluate whether there is evidence of social problems resulting from repeated alcohol or drug use. As described above, social problems can be reflected in one of two ways: (1) repeatedly failing to fulfill one's responsibilities at work, school or home; and/or (2) progressively reducing one's involvement in other things that once took priority (e.g., spending less time with friends or loved ones, disengaging from hobbies or other healthy activities, such as exercise). For Kevin, social problems became apparent as his work quality declined, and his supervisor noticed this change. We have been discussing various difficulties that can emerge when a person begins to lose control over their use of alcohol or drugs, affecting the individual's physical, social, and emotional health. A final and important symptom of a substance use disorder is when a person continues to drink or use drugs even after they've experienced worsening of physical or psychological problems that are linked with alcohol and drug use. This was apparent in Kevin's case, as his depression continually worsened when he was using oxycodone, which he recognized. Still, he couldn't hold himself back from continuing to use it.

The DSM-5-TR Criteria for Substance Use Disorders

Pharmacological Symptoms

- May include tolerance, or needing to take increasing amounts of a substance to get the desired effects.
- May include withdrawal, or uncomfortable symptoms when a substance wears off.
- Cravings can be present in between periods of substance use.

Impaired Control

- Drinking or using drugs more than planned.
- Unsuccessful efforts to cut back or stop.
- Spending a lot of time acquiring, using, and/or recovering from the effects of alcohol or drugs.

Risky Use

- Drinking or using drugs in situations that are dangerous.

Social Problems

- Use of alcohol or drugs interferes with a person's ability to function at work or at home.
- Activities that improve a person's well-being are given up because of alcohol or drug use.
- Despite the problems caused by using alcohol or drugs, people with a substance use disorder continue to drink or use the substances anyway.

Severity

- Substance Use Disorders are classified as mild, moderate, or severe.
- These categories are based on the number of symptoms observed (mild = 2–3, moderate = 4-5, severe = 6+)
- Severe substance use disorders are often referred to by treatment providers as "addiction"

What does addiction look like?

If you know or love someone with an addiction, it may look something like this. Drinking or using drugs was once casual and fun, but at some point, maybe all of a sudden or maybe very gradually, it's like a switch went off. Being around that person when they were drinking or using just wasn't the same. It became harder to connect with that person. Negative and at times frightening things would happen when they were drinking or using drugs. Maybe they got into arguments or fights with other people. Maybe they started to black out or forget what they had said or done when they were high or intoxicated. They might have lied to you to conceal their use of alcohol or drugs. Maybe the person was arrested or got into some other kind of trouble in relation to drinking or using drugs. Perhaps being around the person became stressful or embarrassing when drinking or using was part of the picture. They may have started to neglect or avoid certain people or important responsibilities because of drinking or using drugs. They may have become isolated or distant from loved ones. Many of these behaviors would seem out of character. Once that line is crossed, when social or recreational drinking or drug use transforms to addiction, there are many ways in which a person might change their demeanor or behavior. In most, if not all cases, these changes reflect the core struggle of the nearly 20 million Americans who suffer from addiction: a loss of control over use.

Is it usually obvious to other people when someone has an addiction?

Just as a person can function—at least to a point—with undiagnosed hypertension, diabetes, and a whole other host of chronic illnesses, the same is true of certain people with addictions. The amount of time that can lapse from when a person begins to display addictive behaviors, to when they come to believe that they can't get themselves under control on their own, can vary widely from one person to another—sometimes this realization comes quickly, whereas at the other extreme, in some people it can take many years. Even when both the person and their loved ones agree about drug or alcohol use having become problematic, depending on their understanding of the problem and its treatment, the need for a medical and/or psychological intervention may not be entirely apparent.

How do people recover from addiction?

Despite common misconceptions that addiction cannot be overcome by most people, decades of scientific research have shown that the various treatments that are available for substance use disorders are, indeed, effective. But it's not an easy road. Because addiction leads to changes in the brain that affect impulse control, decision making, and psychological well-being, simply changing or removing the presence of a drug from the body isn't enough to make a person well again. The road to recovery often has detours (like slips or relapses) and unanticipated twists and turns (such as mental health problems emerging in the process). For these reasons, the path to long-term success will differ from one person to another. For some, stable recovery is achieved after more than one attempt to change and/or more than one episode of treatment. Setting the expectation that recovery takes time can be helpful not only to a person who is trying to overcome addiction, but to their friends and loved ones, who may assume that a person will come out of 30 days of treatment "back to normal." What many people don't realize is that for most, those first 30 days are just the beginning of the recovery journey, and setbacks are a normal part of the process.

The good news is that people with addictions have more pathways to recovery than ever before. Medications are increasingly accepted as a treatment approach, psychotherapy has a rich scientific literature supporting its effectiveness, and the way in which these treatments are delivered is rapidly evolving, with data from randomized clinical trials showing strong support for telemedicine as an option for those who prefer it or have difficulty gaining access to in-person care.[3,4]

How many people receive treatment for their addiction?

You might be surprised to learn this fact: of the nearly 44 million people in the United States who need treatment for a problem with alcohol or drug use, only about 3 million receive treatment in a specialty addiction treatment setting.[5] That leaves over 90% of those who would benefit from treatment without the help that they need to overcome their problem. This is unfavorable for the full spectrum of problematic alcohol and drug use—for those with a developing, mild, or moderately severe problem, treatment could prevent escalation into a full-blown addiction. For those who suffer from severe addictions, particularly in the wake of the opioid overdose crisis, treatment could literally be lifesaving. For those whose life meaning and purpose have been lost to the pursuit of alcohol and drugs, treatment provides a chance to rebuild a rewarding and fulfilling life.

Why are the majority of those who need help left untreated? There are three primary reasons: most commonly, approximately 40% of those who need help but are not treated don't feel ready to stop drinking or using drugs. Among about a third of those who don't receive help, the primary barrier is the cost of care and/or the inability to access care. Finally, a smaller subset of individuals who are left untreated don't realize that they have a problem.

Does substance misuse always progress to addiction?

Many people, including those who have not yet been diagnosed with a substance use disorder, find themselves uncertain as to whether they really have a problem with alcohol or drugs. You may wonder whether having one "bad" episode of alcohol use when you drank too much and did things you might regret means that you have a diagnosable alcohol problem, or what it means if you had one episode like that followed by a month or longer of very little drinking before you had another problem related to your drinking.

One of the keys to understanding substance use disorders is to think in terms of a progressive problem that develops over time, with repeated episodes of *misuse*. In fact, all substance use disorders begin with signs of *misuse*, which is the use of alcohol, illegal drugs, or prescribed medications in ways that are harmful to ourselves and/or to those around us. But misuse is not the same as an addiction, and it does not mean that addiction is inevitable. Substance use and misuse are widespread problems, with 60 million Americans having reported binge drinking in the past year and over 61 million having used an illicit or non-prescribed drug in the same timeframe.[6] Misuse, in which health or social problems emerge—either immediately or over time—as a result of substance use can lead to serious consequences, including arrests or legal problems resulting from driving under the influence, automobile crashes, suicide attempts and fatalities, and even overdose deaths. If left unaddressed, substance misuse, when repeated over time, *can lead to* a substance use disorder, a diagnosable illness that, as we've discussed above, can lead to health problems and difficulties in daily functioning, and may require special treatment to resolve.

How many people who misuse alcohol or drugs have a diagnosable substance use disorder?

To place the question of substance misuse versus substance use disorder into context, consider these figures: less than one-third of those who reported binge drinking in 2019 had a diagnosable alcohol use disorder.[7] Similarly, of the 11 million people who admitted to having misused heroin or prescribed opioids in the past year, 2.5 million met criteria for an opioid use disorder. That said, the vast majority of social and health problems related to alcohol and drug use occur among those who are not addicted. For this reason, world leading experts in prevention, treatment, and public policy relating to addiction suggest that reducing substance misuse in the general population is critical to reducing the harms and costs associated with substance use in America.[8]

Addiction is not an inevitable outcome for those who progress from substance misuse to a substance use disorder. Addiction is a chronic and severe form of a substance use disorder, whereas some people can experience mild and temporary substance use disorders. In fact, it is estimated that the most severe symptoms of addiction will develop in approximately 10% of those who are exposed to drugs with addiction potential.[9]

What makes someone more or less likely to develop an addiction?

A person's vulnerability to developing addiction is dependent on many aspects of their family and personal history, including genetics, mental health problems, and features of their environment. To predict how likely a person is to develop an addiction, you would need to consider what we call *risk* and *protective* factors. A *risk factor* is something that makes a person more susceptible to developing addiction. The greatest risk factor for addiction is genetics, which determines 40% to 70% of a person's vulnerability to develop a substance use disorder. However, there are risk factors other than genetics that are quite influential.[9] These include influences in the person's immediate environment, such as:

- Easy access to alcohol and/or drugs
- Facing a great deal of family conflict

Personal risk factors can also affect the likelihood that a person will develop an addiction, and may include:

- A history of substance use and/or mental health problems in a person's immediate family
- Personal history and/or current struggle with a mental health disorder
- Having experienced trauma, abuse, or neglect
- Exposure to violence

For young people, risk factors in addition to those noted above may include:

- Exposure to heavy advertising of alcohol or other substances
- Living in neighborhoods and/or going to schools where drinking and drug use is common
- Little parental monitoring
- Minimal involvement in school

There are also "buffers" or protective factors that may act to reduce the likelihood that a person, even when they have some risk factors, will ultimately become addicted to alcohol or drugs. For young people, these include:

- Parents' frequent supportive monitoring of their adolescent children (i.e., knowing their whereabouts, friends, and activities)
- Involvement in school

Additional buffers for individuals of all ages are:

- Availability of and involvement in healthy recreational and social activities (e.g., sports, community group activities)
- Developing good, healthy coping skills

Another important scientifically based fact about addiction vulnerability is that age matters, with adolescence and young adulthood especially critical phases of life. Those who get through their adolescent years without developing a substance use disorder are unlikely to become addicted to alcohol or drugs later on in life.[10,11]

The Adolescent Years and Addiction

Why are adolescents so vulnerable to developing addiction? Studies show that brain development is not complete until sometime between age 21 and 23 among women, and between age 23 and 25 among men. When people use alcohol and drugs prior to that time, they can have powerful effects on undeveloped brain circuits, increasing the likelihood that the young person will develop addiction later on in life. The prefrontal cortex is one of the last areas of the brain to fully mature, and this region, often referred to as the "CEO of the brain," controls many important adult functions, including logical reasoning, controlling one's impulses, and healthy decision making. On the other hand, the limbic region, which controls emotions, develops earlier. As one psychologist described, it is as if the teenager has a fully functional car accelerator, but the brakes have not been installed yet (p. 72).[a] When a teenager is experiencing high emotions or intense peer pressure, the underdeveloped "brake" may become overwhelmed by the "accelerator" in the brain, leading to unhealthy decisions. With all this in mind, it is not surprising that adolescence is the age that is associated with the highest risk for developing a substance use disorder, and 85% of those who meet criteria for a substance use disorder in their lifetime do so during adolescence. This makes the teenage and young adult years the most important targets of prevention and early treatment/intervention efforts.

---

[a] Walsh D. (2004). *Why Do They Act That Way? A Survival Guide to the Adolescent Brain for You and Your Teen*. New York: Free Press.

Can addiction be caused by environmental factors, such as stressful life changes, job difficulties, or financial problems?

These are extremely important questions. Indeed, there has been a growing awareness of what scientists call *social determinants of health*, which are an individual's personal circumstances that can affect their health and well-being. These circumstances not only influence how susceptible a person is to developing an addiction, but also how likely they are to receive and benefit from treatment. It is estimated that, of all the changeable contributors to health and wellness, about 50% are related to environmental, social, and economic circumstances.[12,13] Most scientists would doubt that personal circumstances such as economic hardship or the absence of family or social support alone would cause addiction without the contributing influences of genetics and biology. However, we can say with reasonable certainty that stressors such as financial difficulties or family conflict could increase the chances that an individual could experience a new or worsening substance use disorder. These stressors could also influence the timing of what we refer to as the "onset" of a substance use disorder (or when in life it begins). A person's life circumstances can also influence the likelihood that they will relapse after treatment has ended. Understanding how these conditions are tied to a person's drinking or drug use can help a doctor, counselor, or other healthcare professional to decide what types of treatment and/or other services could be most helpful to enable that individual to overcome an addiction.

What kinds of environmental stressors or personal circumstances are especially influential?

Stressors related to economic stability, such as employment status, access to nutritious food, and safe housing have been found in studies to influence the likelihood and severity of problems with alcohol and drugs, as well as the chances of treatment success for individuals with addiction.[14] For example, in the context of the COVID-19 pandemic, people whose employment was negatively impacted (e.g., those who experienced decreased pay or job loss) were more likely to drink alcohol more frequently and/or heavily,[15] and those who experienced financial strain struggled with more problems related to their alcohol use.[16] Another set of life circumstances that can influence the likelihood of addiction and recovery is the quality of a person's social life. Healthy social relationships can offer protective financial and emotional resources, making help and support for problematic substance use and/or mental health issues more accessible.

On a related note, a person's ability to access quality healthcare can affect the timely diagnosis and treatment of their substance use disorder. Being unable to access care, whether because of a lack of health insurance coverage or unaffordable costs of care, is the reason that one in three people who need treatment for a substance use disorder report that they did not receive it.[17] Being able to access care is tied to several other personal life circumstances such as education and the physical environment where an individual lives; for example, people who have access to quality education and achieve higher levels of educational attainment generally live longer and suffer from fewer health problems,[18] and those who live in safer and more cohesive neighborhoods are more likely to be able to access the care that they need.[19]

Part 2

HOW DO ALCOHOL AND DRUGS AFFECT THE BRAIN AND BEHAVIOR?

3

WHAT DOES ALCOHOL DO TO THE BRAIN AND BEHAVIOR?

How does alcohol affect people? Do its effects vary from person to person?

Drinking alcohol is an integral part of social life all over the world. People drink to socialize, celebrate, and unwind. One of the interesting facts about alcohol is that people vary widely in the way that they respond to it. Alcohol has many known effects on the brain, which is why it makes us feel and act in certain ways when we drink, but the *way* that alcohol affects the brain and the *extent of its impact* on the brain is not the same for everyone. Some of the factors that determine how alcohol affects different people include the following:

- How much and how often one drinks
- Age when a person started drinking and how long they have been drinking
- Age and gender
- Current physical and mental health status
- Genetic background and family history of alcoholism

In general, when a person drinks, alcohol enters the bloodstream almost immediately, and the initial effects are experienced within as little as 10 minutes.[1] Typically, as you drink increasing quantities of alcohol, the concentration of alcohol in your bloodstream, known as your blood alcohol concentration level (BAC), increases, and the higher your BAC is, the greater the range and intensity you can experience of alcohol's effects on the brain, body, and behavior. Intoxication is usually a two-phase process: first, you feel relaxed and perhaps exuberant, giving way to positive social and emotional experiences. In the second phase, you may feel hung over, exhausted, and/or depressed, or in the case of having consumed larger quantities of alcohol, you could experience vomiting and loss of consciousness.[2]

How does age impact drinking?

Age is an important factor when considering how alcohol affects the brain and body. This is especially true for people who begin drinking at a young age, as well as those who develop problematic drinking habits in older age. Young people whose brains are still developing are more likely to transition from experimenting with alcohol and other substances to developing an alcohol or substance use disorder. In fact, according to a large survey that followed young people and tracked their alcohol use and related problems over time, 45% of those who started drinking alcohol prior to the age of 14 grew up to have an alcohol use disorder, compared to 10% of those who started drinking after they turned 21.[3] Looked at in a slightly different way, in terms of how age relates to the risk of progressing from social drinking to problematic drinking or even alcoholism within a decade, similar results were found. Those who started drinking at an early age were more likely to have an alcohol use disorder within 10 years of initiating alcohol use.

Not only does alcohol use at an early age predict the development of alcohol-related problems, but at the other end of the age continuum, alcohol misuse in older age is concerning because of the negative impacts of alcohol use on the aging brain. Americans are getting older, with nearly a third of women and a quarter of men age 55 and older, and current research shows that they are drinking more. By 2050, nearly 1 in 5 Americans will be 65 or older, compared to 1 in 7 now. At the same time, adults over the age of 60 are drinking more across the board, and women over the age of 60 are showing increased binge drinking. You might wonder why this change in alcohol use among older people is important, and that is a great question! Recent research using brain imaging scans over the course of 14 years to study the effects of alcohol on the brain found that, over time, various structures in the brain showed evidence of shrinkage among those who had alcohol use disorders. These effects were especially pronounced for those who were 65 or older, and the effects of aging on important areas of the brain that control what is known as "executive functioning" occurred more rapidly among adults with alcohol use disorders in this age group. Executive functioning refers to our essential cognitive abilities, such as planning and organizing a course of action, controlling our impulses, and exercising good judgment. Although the normal aging process involves changes in the frontal cortex, which controls executive functioning, this aging process is *accelerated* for those who have an alcohol use disorder, including those whose alcohol-related problems developed later in life.[4]

Why are older people drinking heavily, and why is it worrisome?

As people age, they become vulnerable to depression and other psychological struggles. For an older person who already has an existing alcohol use disorder, in between drinking episodes the effects of alcohol withdrawal on their mood and emotions can be compounded by the psychological challenges that are brought on by the aging process. In this situation, an aging person may turn to alcohol to self-medicate. Over time, this both makes the alcohol use disorder worse and can intensify the very negative emotions that the person is trying to suppress or avoid by drinking.

The Cycle of Drinking to Self-Medicate

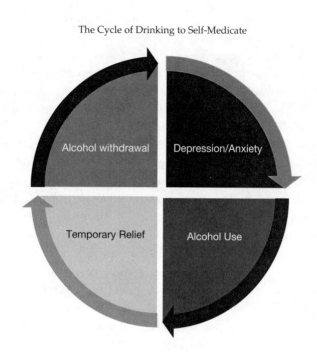

Apart from the effects on the aging brain, the body's ability to metabolize alcohol changes as people age, so that alcohol can remain in their system for longer—and for some, alcohol affects their thoughts, feelings, and behaviors more intensely than it used to. This increases the risk of harms from alcohol, such as accidents, falls, and injuries. In addition, because many older people take medications that don't mix well with alcohol, the risk of complications from combining alcohol with other chemicals is higher in this age group.

How does gender affect the brain and body's response to alcohol?

Although men generally drink larger quantities of alcohol than women, drink more often, have higher rates of alcohol use disorders, and are more likely to engage in risky behaviors when under the influence, women who drink heavily are more susceptible to a variety of alcohol-related health problems.[5] One of the main reasons that women's biological response to alcohol is different from that of men is because, when a person drinks, the rate at which their blood alcohol level rises depends upon how much body water they have. Because women weigh less than men on average, and for each pound that they weigh, they have proportionally less water in their bodies than men do, their blood alcohol concentration becomes higher, faster. So, if a man and a woman drink the same amount of alcohol, the woman's blood alcohol concentration will be higher, placing her at greater risk for health complications from alcohol use. Studies have shown several key differences between men and women in alcohol use and misuse patterns, rates of alcohol use disorders and related psychological and behavioral problems, and effects of alcohol on the brain. We review these differences in further detail below.

Collectively, studies of the health effects of alcohol show that compared to men, women:

- are more vulnerable to long-term effects of alcohol on their health;
- experience alcohol-related medical problems sooner after developing an alcohol use disorder;
- die of chronic alcoholism at a younger age than men with alcoholism;
- have greater risk of developing severe alcoholic liver disease;
- develop *cardiomyopathy*, a disease of the heart muscle that makes it harder for the heart to pump blood to the rest of the body, after fewer years of drinking and smaller amounts of alcohol consumption, compared to men; and
- experience brain changes (e.g., loss of brain volume) and cognitive problems from alcohol at a faster rate than men.

The risk of breast cancer among women who drink alcohol is also 5% to 9% greater among those who drink one alcoholic beverage a day, compared to those who are non-drinkers,[6] and for every additional drink they consume on a daily basis, their risk increases further.

Women and men also differ in terms of the specific aspects of their personal, family, and medical history that place them at risk for alcoholism.[7] For women, research has found that there are 3 predictors that are related more strongly to developing an alcohol use disorder than they are for men:

1. Family history of alcoholism
2. Experiencing an anxiety disorder early in life
3. Addiction to nicotine

For men, characteristics that predict a stronger risk of alcohol use disorder include:

1. *Novelty seeking,* a personality trait involving tendencies to seek out new experiences that create intense emotions. These experiences often involve risk-taking.
2. Behavioral and emotional problems in childhood and adolescence, involving disregard for and aggression toward others. When formally diagnosed, these patterns of emotional and behavioral problems are known as Conduct Disorder.
3. Childhood sexual abuse
4. Loss of a parent
5. Low self-esteem
6. Dissatisfaction with one's marriage

You might be wondering why it is useful to know what the different predictors of alcoholism risk are for men and women. If you or a loved one is involved with alcohol in a way that concerns you, then having some idea of the types of personality characteristics, personal experiences, and genetic vulnerabilities that place a man or woman at especially high risk for developing problems can inform the steps that you take next. In Chapters 9 and 10 we will discuss specific actions you can take to find professional help to either prevent escalation of a problem with alcohol or treat an existing one.

The reasons that men and women drink alcohol and re-lapse to alcohol use after periods of sobriety also differ. While women are more likely to drink heavily when they experience unpleasant emotions such as depression, when in conflict with other people, and as a way of reducing tension, men more often report that they use alcohol to enhance pleasant emotions and when they feel social pressure to drink.[8] Along these same lines, when women relapse to alcohol use after treatment, it is more likely to be related to unpleasant emotions, whereas men are more vulnerable to relapse when they encounter so-cial pressure.[9,10]

How common are alcohol-related health problems and alcoholism?

Health problems arising from alcohol and deaths that result from misuse of alcohol are rising in America. As the director of the National Institute on Alcohol Abuse and Alcoholism, George Koob, Ph.D., said, "It's the addiction that everyone knows about, but no one wants to talk about."[11] Dr. Koob is trying to change this, along with the broader community of scientists and practitioners who are working tirelessly to better understand and more effectively treat alcoholism. Understandably, discussions about problematic alcohol use have taken a back seat as the opioid overdose crisis made headlines several years ago and continues to impact the United States in profound ways. Nevertheless, many people don't re-alize (1) how common alcohol use disorders are, including the fact that there are seven times more people affected by alcohol use disorders than opioid use disorders, and (2) how this ill-ness affects the health of the brain and body. Americans are suffering from increasing harms related to alcohol use, ranging from emergency room visits to hospitalizations and deaths. Approximately 29 million adults in the United States suffer from an alcohol use disorder, a number that is likely rising in the wake of the COVID-19 pandemic. In fact, studies suggest that 1 in 4 people (approximately 23%) began drinking more during the pandemic.[12] Research has also shown that many people around the world openly attribute their increasing use of alcohol during this time to the stress and emotions brought on by the COVID-19 pandemic.[13,14,15] These observations are concerning, since drinking to cope with negative experiences increases the likelihood that a person will develop an alcohol use disorder. Some of those who are at the greatest risk of turning to alcohol or other substance use as a means of coping with the stress, loneliness, and isolation brought on by the pandemic are individuals who have suffered from mental health issues in the past, and those who have a history of problematic alcohol or other substance use.

Because alcohol misuse is one of the leading preventable causes of death, contributing to more than 3 million deaths worldwide each year, having an understanding of the drinking habits that increase the risk of developing an alcohol use disorder, as well as the signs and symptoms of an emerging or diagnosable disorder, can be helpful to inform the decision to work toward cutting back or quitting, and/or seeking professional help to enable you or your loved one to do so.

How do I know if I or someone I care for is at risk for alcohol-related health problems?

Scientists have debated for many years about how to define problematic alcohol use, or use patterns that you should be concerned about in terms of both physical health implications and possible development of a drinking problem. The first thing you need to know is how to "count" your drinks to see where you stand on the current guidelines and recommendations. These guidelines, which have come together after many years of scientific research, come primarily from two organizations that have been heavily involved in research on problem drinking and alcoholism: the National Institute on Alcohol Abuse and Alcoholism, and the Substance Abuse and Mental Health Services Administration.

You might find the definition of what constitutes "1 drink" a little bit surprising, as many people find that it takes less alcohol than they thought, and that once they count the number of drinks they typically have on an occasion or even throughout the week, their patterns reflect drinking more "heavily" compared to the way that they viewed themselves. This is part of the reason why it is so helpful to be familiar with the limits of alcohol use that we understand to be safe for overall health. If you or your loved one can stay within those limits without a struggle, that's an indication that you don't have a problem with alcohol use. If controlling your drinking enough to stay within the non-risky range is difficult, then you probably need some professional help. One thing we know about treatment for alcohol use disorders is that, despite the fact that most people who receive help do benefit from it, less than 10% of those who need help with their drinking problem actually receive it. Let's take a look at what safe or "non-risky" alcohol use looks like, and how to measure whether you are staying within those guidelines based on your drinking patterns.

What is "a drink"?

Before we consider how many drinks you can have to stay within a range that is consider safe from a health perspective, you need to know how to count your alcoholic beverages. It isn't as easy as it may sound, because the amount of liquid in your wine glass or beer bottle is one piece of relevant information, but it doesn't tell you all that you need to know to count accurately. You also have to take into consideration, when counting your drinks, how concentrated your beverage is with alcohol. In the United States, we define a "standard drink" as a beverage that contains 14 grams of alcohol, or a little more than half an ounce (0.6 fluid ounces) of alcohol.[16] If you look at Figure 3.1, you will find that drinks of different sizes contain the same amount of alcohol. All three of the drinks pictured

What Is a Standard Drink?

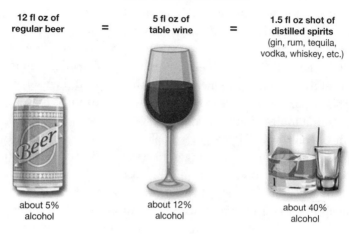

| 12 fl oz of regular beer | = | 5 fl oz of table wine | = | 1.5 fl oz shot of distilled spirits (gin, rum, tequila, vodka, whiskey, etc.) |

about 5% alcohol   about 12% alcohol   about 40% alcohol

Figure 3.1 What is a Standard Drink?

Source: NIAAA (2020)

have the same amount of alcohol, even though they are quite different in size.

The best way to find out how much alcohol is in a beverage you're drinking is to check the label on the bottle. Although not all beverages are required to display their alcohol content, many do, and it is usually displayed as alcohol by volume; for example, on a bottle of wine, you may see it expressed like this: 5% alc/vol. If you pay close attention to the differences in alcohol concentration between certain kinds of beverages, you might realize that some are more similar to one another than you might have thought (e.g., light beer and regular beer have very similar alcohol content). If you are trying to calculate how many drinks you consume on a typical occasion or over the course of a week, here are a few guidelines on the quantities you will find typically in different types of containers:

- 12 ounce bottle of regular beer = 1 drink
- 16 ounce bottle of regular beer = 1.3 drinks

- 22 ounce bottle of regular beer = 2 drinks
- 40 ounce bottle of regular beer = 3.3 drinks
- 750 ml bottle of wine = 5 drinks
- A shot (1.5 ounce) of 80-proof distilled spirits = 1 drink
- A mixed drink or cocktail = 1 or more drinks
- A "half pint" of 80-proof distilled spirits (200 ml) = 4.5 drinks
- A "pint" or "half bottle" of 80-proof distilled spirits (375 ml) = 8.5 drinks
- A "fifth" of 80-proof distilled spirits (750 ml) = 17 drinks

Since malt liquor is higher in alcohol concentration than regular beer, each of the size containers of regular beer described above will correspond to a greater number of drinks. Drink calculators that can quickly provide information about how strong your mixed drink or cocktail is, and/or how much alcohol is in different size containers, can be found on the National Institute on Alcohol Abuse and Alcoholism's *Rethinking Drinking* website: https://www.rethinkingdrinking.niaaa.nih.gov/Tools/Calculators/Default.aspx.

This website also has calculators that can tell you how many calories you consume from alcohol beverages each week, month, or year; the amount of money you spend on alcohol; and how much alcohol it takes to move your blood alcohol concentration beyond the legal limit.

How do we define moderate drinking?

Health care providers and scientific experts in addiction tend to classify alcohol use—some people are "social drinkers" who consume alcohol from time to time, some are moderate drinkers, and others are heavy drinkers who likely have an alcohol use disorder. So, how do you know where you fall? The guidelines for moderate alcohol use are different for men and women, since, as we reviewed earlier, they metabolize alcohol differently, with smaller quantities leading to higher blood alcohol levels in women compared to men. Moderate alcohol use is defined as follows:[16]

- Up to 1 drink per day for women (not to exceed 7 drinks per week)
- Up to 2 drinks per day for men (not to exceed 14 drinks per week)

The potential health benefits of moderate drinking has been a subject of debate for quite some time. Several studies have shown that moderate alcohol use is associated with good health, especially in relation to heart attack and stroke risks. Much of this research comes from epidemiological studies, which have found that in Western countries where chronic illnesses such as coronary heart disease, stroke, and diabetes, are among the primary causes of death, alcohol is protective against mortality, especially among middle-age and older men and women.[17] These studies, combined with results showing that alcohol increases "good" HDL cholesterol and can reduce the presence of proteins in the blood, such as fibrinogen, that are involved in the formation of blood clots and make heart attacks and stroke more likely, support a role of moderate alcohol consumption in reducing these health risks. Research has also shown that drinking is correlated with a lower risk of developing Type 2 diabetes, along with other common health difficulties such as gallstones. That said, the relationship between moderate alcohol use and chronic diseases is complex, as not everyone who drinks experiences health benefits from it. According to a recent study of alcohol use and its relationship to diseases among over 1 billion people across the world, recommendations for safe and potentially beneficial amounts of alcohol consumption should be based on age and geographical location, with those *under the age of 40* subject to the strictest guidelines. This younger group was not only found to be susceptible to health risks and harms associated with drinking (such as motor vehicle accidents, suicides, and homicides related to alcohol use), but alcohol use did not benefit their health or lower their risk of chronic diseases. On the other hand, those aged 40 or older without underlying health conditions may see benefits including reduced risk of cardiovascular disease, stroke, and diabetes, from a limited quantity of alcohol use (i.e., between 1 and 2 standard drinks per day).[18]

While keeping in mind the potential health benefits of drinking small to moderate quantities of alcohol for certain people, it is important to keep in mind that those benefits not only vanish if a person who is drinking alcohol moderately transitions to heavy alcohol consumption, but they are replaced with a range of potential health risks, which, if alcohol use cannot be controlled, can lead to devastating outcomes. These risks are described in more detail in the section further below on alcohol and health, and can include severe liver disease, high blood pressure, and traffic accidents.

What constitutes heavy drinking and binge drinking?

For some, the meaning of "moderate drinking" is a bit confusing. Do these guidelines mean that a woman who has eight drinks a week is an alcoholic? What about a man who usually has two drinks with dinner but sometimes ends up drinking 3 or 4? The answer is not black-and-white, but there are two things to consider when addressing these questions: first, although a person can exceed these amounts from time to time without developing full-blown alcoholism, drinking more than these quantities poses health risks, one of which is developing an alcohol use disorder. Second, there are two alcohol use patterns that are often observed among those with alcohol use disorders: *binge drinking* and *heavy drinking*, so knowing what these terms mean can help you evaluate whether your drinking habits or those of someone you care about are a cause for concern.

How is binge drinking defined? The National Institute of Alcohol Abuse and Alcoholism defines binge drinking as a pattern of alcohol consumption that brings a person's blood alcohol level up to 0.08% (or 8 grams per deciliter) or higher.[16] Studies suggest that typically, this occurs among *men after 5 or more drinks* are consumed, and *for women, after 4 or more drinks* are consumed within a 2-hour period.[19] The Substance Abuse and Mental Health Administration (SAMHSA), a branch of the US Department of Health and Human Services that is devoted to reducing the burden of substance use and mental illness, defines binge drinking similarly—5 or more alcoholic drinks on the same occasion for men, and four or more drinks for women. The "same occasion" means that the drinks were consumed either one after the other in a very short time, or within a few hours of each other. If you have consumed alcohol in these quantities and timeframes at least once in the past month, then by SAMHSA's definition, you have engaged in binge drinking.

What about heavy drinking? Heavy drinking is a close relative of binge drinking, defined by the National Institute on Alcohol Abuse and Alcoholism as more than four drinks on any given day for men, or more than three drinks for women. According to SAMHSA, heavy drinking is defined directly by how often a person *binge drinks*, so anyone who has met the criteria for binge drinking on five or more days within the past month is considered a heavy drinker.

Binge Drinking: How Common Is It?

Studies show that 1 in 4 adults binge drinks,[a] consuming around seven drinks during a typical binge episode.[b] As you can see from the chart below, the majority of those who binge drink are between the ages of 18 and 34, but there are still quite a few people who are 35 and over who drink in binge patterns. In fact, people who are 35 and over consume more than half of the 17 billion total binge drinks that are consumed by adults each year. Though those who are 65+ are the smallest group shown in the figure, there is a concerning increase in binge drinking among this group in recent years.

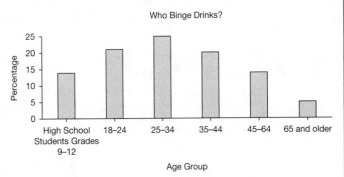

Source: Centers for Disease Control, 2022[c]

Binge drinking among young people is also very concerning. Most people under the age of 21 who drink alcohol report binge drinking, and often do so in large amounts.[d,e] Binge drinking is also twice as common among men, as compared to women.

---

[a] Substance Abuse and Mental Health Services Administration. (2021). *Key substance use and mental health indicators in the United States: Results from the 2020 National Survey on Drug Use and Health* (HHS Publication No. PEP21-07-01-003, NSDUH Series H-56). Rockville, MD: Center for Behavioral Health Statistics and Quality, Substance Abuse and Mental Health Services Administration. Retrieved from: https://www.samhsa.gov/data/

[b] Kanny, D., Naimi, T. S., Liu, Y., Lu, H., & Brewer, R. D. (2018). Annual Total Binge Drinks Consumed by U.S. Adults, 2015. *American Journal of Preventive Medicine, 54*(4), 486–496. https://doi.org/10.1016/j.amepre.2017.12.021

[c] Centers for Disease Control and Prevention. (2022). Binge drinking. Retrieved from: https://www.cdc.gov/alcohol/fact-sheets/binge-drinking.htm#print on August 13, 2023.

[d] Esser, M. B., Clayton, H., Demissie, Z., Kanny, D., & Brewer, R. D. (2017). Current and Binge Drinking Among High School Students— United States, 1991–2015. *MMWR. Morbidity and Mortality Weekly Report, 66*(18), 474–478. https://doi.org/10.15585/mmwr.mm6618a4

[e] Substance Abuse and Mental Health Services Administration. (2020). Report to congress on the prevention and reduction of underage drinking. Available from https://store.samhsa.gov/sites/default/files/pep21-03-11-002.pdf

What's so bad about binge drinking and heavy drinking?

It's not at all uncommon, and plenty of people who don't have alcoholism binge and/or drink heavily from time to time.[20] According to research, the downside of these drinking patterns really comes down to health and safety risks. Though most people who have had lots of heavy drinking experiences that were not "scary" or life threatening may be reluctant to believe that something bad could happen to them as a result of binge drinking, below are the most common and concerning health risks that have been studied:

- Every 45 minutes, someone in the United States dies in a motor vehicle accident involving a driver who was impaired by the effects of alcohol.[21]
- Binge drinking places people at risk for *alcohol poisoning*, which accounts for six fatalities daily in the United States.[22] The more a person drinks, the higher the risk of death from alcohol poisoning.
- Binge drinking increases the likelihood of developing an alcohol use disorder.[23]
- Studies support a strong connection between binge drinking and violence. Alcohol use is common among perpetrators of violent crimes, including homicide, assault, robbery, and sexual offenses.[24]
- Alcohol intoxication and alcoholism both increase the risk of suicide.
- People who binge drink are more likely to engage in unsafe sexual behavior, which increases the risks of contracting sexually transmitted infections and unintentional pregnancy.[25]
- When alcohol enters the bloodstream quickly, as it does when someone binge drinks, "blackouts" are more likely, in which there are gaps in a person's memory for events that occurred while they were intoxicated.
- Unintentional injuries including falls, burns, drownings, and other potentially deadly consequences of heavy alcohol use are more likely in the context of binge drinking.[26]

New Research: "High Intensity Drinking"

Recent research has identified a severe form of binge drinking that is most commonly observed among college students.[a] This pattern, termed "High Intensity Drinking," is defined as consuming twice the amount that is considered binge drinking, within a short timeframe—for women, that's eight or more drinks on a single occasion, and for men, it's 10 or more drinks. Because this can cause a young person's blood alcohol concentration to spike quickly, the potential health and safety consequences are especially concerning.

---

[a] Patrick, M. E., & Azar, B. (2018). High-Intensity Drinking. *Alcohol Research*, 39(1), 49–55.

How do you know when you or someone you care for has an alcohol use disorder?

If you or someone you care about has an alcohol use disorder, all the symptoms that you or your loved one experience point to a single underlying problem: a loss of control over alcohol use. How that is expressed may differ widely from one person to another, and the time it takes for a person's drinking to progress to a point where they have lost control will also vary between individuals, but the end result is the same. Control becomes increasingly untenable, not only over drinking itself, but the expanding impact of drinking on important aspects of life, including a person's capacity to be dependable both personally and professionally, and their physical and mental health and well-being. As you'll see in the following case study, this dynamic unfolded quite gradually for Paige, but at a certain point the progression of her alcohol problem accelerated, leading her to recognize that she desperately needed help.

Paige is a 31-year-old woman who works for her family's restaurant business. Paige began drinking alcohol, smoking marijuana, and experimenting with other drugs like cocaine and ecstasy when she was in high school, but after emerging from that phase, she found that she preferred mostly to drink. As a high schooler, she had a lot of freedom—probably too much so, as her parents were both heavy drinkers and were often busy working at the business. When Paige was in her 20s, her dad became very ill and sadly, he died at the age of 51 from pancreatic cancer. In her late 20s, Paige became more involved with alcohol, finishing out her evenings with a few cocktails, which progressed over the course of a few years to two or more bottles of wine. She noticed herself gaining weight and feeling pretty down on herself overall, and the drinking was wearing her down physically. Overwhelmed and exhausted from the ups and downs of drinking heavily each night and waking up hungover and stressed each day, Paige decided it was time to stop drinking already. But when she tried, she was overcome with very powerful urges to drink that she just couldn't get rid of unless she satisfied them, at least with a couple of cocktails. She felt really out of control. She didn't even enjoy drinking or feel relieved or relaxed by the effects of alcohol like she used to, but yet, she couldn't stop herself. Feeling alone and a little hopeless, she called a friend of hers who was a psychotherapist and asked her if she had any suggestions about where she could go for help.

Paige had developed many signs of an alcohol use disorder. She was vulnerable to this problem to begin with, since she appeared to have some risk factors for addiction. First, we know that she had a genetic vulnerability to addiction, given that both her mother and father suffered from alcoholism. Second, she had a history of trauma, having lost her father at a relatively early age. In terms of the specific symptoms we observed, the first was apparent when she experienced *tolerance* to alcohol, since we know that she increased the number of drinks she was consuming from a few cocktails to a few bottles of wine each night. She also had symptoms of alcohol *withdrawal*, which she experienced as hangovers in the mornings. One of the telltale signs of withdrawal and increasing dependency on alcohol is when a person uses alcohol in an effort to reverse the symptoms, which Paige began to resort to as her hangovers intensified. In addition to these physiological symptoms, important parts of Paige's life became *negatively affected by her drinking*, including her physical well-being. Not unlike many people who seek out treatment for an alcohol use disorder, Paige had a *strong desire to control her use of alcohol*, and she tried to do so, but *she was unable to.* She also struggled with *cravings* when she tried to take breaks from drinking. Finally, she began experiencing some physical symptoms that were worsened by her use of alcohol, including weight gain and the effects of frequent hangovers, but *she continued to drink anyway.* Adding the number of symptoms Paige was experiencing (each of which are italicized), her total is 6, which would lead to a diagnosis of a *severe* alcohol use disorder. Though it might sound like a hopeless predicament, people do recover from severe alcohol use disorders with treatment. Paige is giving herself the opportunity to heal by seeking treatment. In Part 3 of this book, we will explore in depth the different types of treatment that could be helpful to Paige.

What are the treatments for alcohol use disorders?

As you will learn more about in Chapters 10 and 11, there are two different types of treatment for alcohol use disorders: behavioral treatments and medications. There are three currently approved medications in the United States to help people change their drinking, stop drinking altogether, and/or prevent relapse to drinking after a period of abstinence. These medicines can be combined with behavioral treatment, or they can be used as a stand-alone treatment approach. As an added layer of support, self-help or mutual-support groups such as Alcoholics Anonymous (AA) can offer peer-led guidance, mentorship, and support for people who are in recovery from an alcohol use disorder.

Fortunately, most people with alcohol use disorders can benefit from some form of treatment, including those with a severe form of the illness like Paige. Studies show that about one-third of people who are treated for problems with alcohol use achieve full remission from their alcohol use disorder (i.e., they become symptom-free) 1 year later. Many others are able to reduce or control their drinking and report fewer problems related to their use of alcohol.[11]

4

WHAT DOES MARIJUANA DO TO THE BRAIN AND BEHAVIOR?

What is marijuana, and how widely used is it?

After alcohol, marijuana is the most commonly used "psychoactive" drug (meaning, a drug that affects one's mind or mental state) in America, especially among young people. Nearly 12 million young adults reported using marijuana in 2021,[1] and in 2020, annual use reached its highest level among college students in over three and a half decades, with 44% of participants in a national survey that included 1,550 individuals reporting having used it in the past year (compared to 38% in 2015).[2] In addition, a growing number of teens are using marijuana on a daily basis.

Also referred to as pot, weed, dope, or cannabis, marijuana is the dried leaves, flowers, stems, and seeds from the *Cannabis Sativa* or *Cannabis Indica* plant. With the expanding legalization of marijuana for medical or adult recreational use across the United States over recent years, you may be hearing about different compounds and products made from marijuana, some that are addictive or mind-altering, and some that aren't. This can be confusing, but the first fact to familiarize yourself with to make it easier to understand is that there are different chemical compounds in the marijuana plant. Tetrahydrocannabinol (also known as THC) is one of these compounds and is mind-altering, causing a person to feel high when they use it.

Cannabidiol (also known as CBD) is a chemical compound in the marijuana plant that affects a different part of the nervous system than THC and does not make a person feel high.

How does marijuana affect the brain?

Marijuana has both short- and long-term effects on the brain. In the short term, when a person smokes marijuana, THC quickly passes from the lungs into the bloodstream. The blood then carries the chemicals to the brain and other organs throughout the body. The way that marijuana is taken will affect the amount of time it takes for a person to feel high. For example, when marijuana is eaten in the form of "edibles," the body absorbs it much more slowly than if it is smoked. It can take an hour or even longer to feel the effects of marijuana when it is eaten, whereas smoking marijuana leads a person to feel high within minutes. For those who use edibles, this can lead to unintentional ingestion of large quantities of marijuana, because they continue to eat it in greater quantities while they think that it isn't working. Consuming large amounts of marijuana in this way can release toxic levels of THC into the bloodstream, which can lead to very unpleasant and dangerous effects on the brain, such as psychosis.

Apart from eating and smoking marijuana, each of which can be done in various ways (for example, there are several methods of smoking, including the use of hand rolled cigarettes or "joints," blunts, pipes, and bongs), there is one other way of ingesting it which has been used more over the past several years: vaping. The use of vaporizers enables people to bypass smoke inhalation, instead inhaling a *vapor* containing marijuana's active ingredients. Part of the appeal of vaping marijuana, especially for young people, is that it is less obvious than other combustible methods of smoking it, since vaporizing marijuana does not produce the pungent odor that smoking a joint or bong would. However, one source of serious concern about the practice of vaping marijuana is that some people vaporize *marijuana extracts*, such as hash oil or wax, and the THC concentration of these extracts can be 4 to 30 times greater than that of dried cannabis.[3,4] This not only poses higher risk of developing an addiction to marijuana but also, with higher potency, there is a greater likelihood that a person will experience adverse physical and/or psychological effects of marijuana use.

What is the endocannabinoid system?

We all have a cell-signaling system in our bodies called the endocannabinoid system, even if we don't use marijuana or cannabis (see Figure 4.1). This system regulates many bodily functions, including how a person feels, moves, and reacts. The natural chemicals our bodies produce that interact within the endocannabinoid system are called *cannabinoids*, and, like THC, they influence a person's important feelings and behaviors. So,

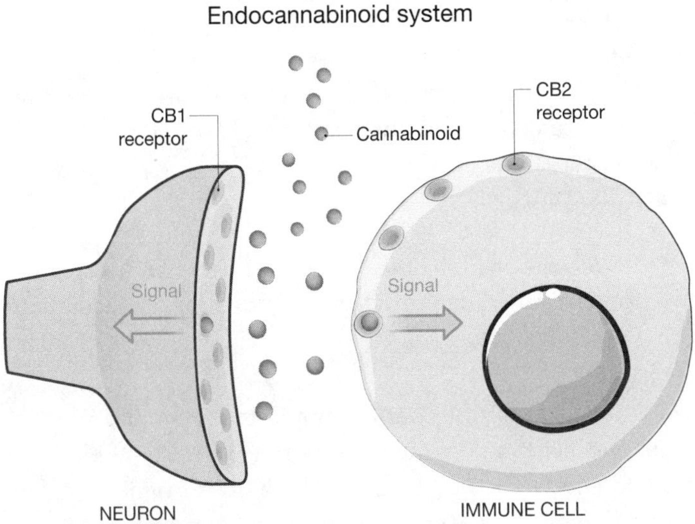

Figure 4.1 The Endocannabinoid System

see https://www.istockphoto.com/vector/endocannabinoid-system-gm1317749811-405087328

Source: Designua/Shutterstock

to understand how THC can affect a person physically and/or emotionally, we look to scientific studies of how THC interacts with our endocannabinoid system. Our endocannabinoid system extends through many parts of the body, including our brain, nerves, skin, and immune system, to name a few.[5] When a person uses marijuana, the THC they take in activates specific brain cell receptors in the endocannabinoid system that normally react to natural THC-like chemicals. By over-activating the parts of the brain that have the highest numbers of endocannabinoid receptors, THC produces an experience of feeling "high." At the same time, because these receptors are located in various parts of the brain and body, people who use marijuana experience not only that "high," but a whole range of other effects on their mood, movement, memory, senses, and grasp on reality. Specific effects may include:

- Problems with thinking and problem solving
- Difficulty remembering things
- Altered and/or intense sensory experiences (for example, seeing brighter colors)
- Altered perception of time (for example, feeling that time is passing more slowly than it really is)
- Increased appetite
- Mood changes
- Anxiety
- Psychosis (in high doses and/or with regular use of high-potency marijuana), which may include hallucinations and delusions

These are some of the short-term effects of marijuana on the brain and behavior. In the long term, studies show the most notable effects on cognition, or the ability to think and process information, as well as learning and memory.[6] This is especially problematic for teens, whose brains are not yet fully developed. Marijuana use has been shown to interrupt brain development in young people in some ways that are not certain to recover, even after quitting.[7] For example, in one study, researchers followed over 1,000 individuals from birth to age 38 and tested their cognitive abilities first in their early teens, before exposure to marijuana, and again at age 38, after some of them had established a pattern of regular marijuana use.[6] This study found that, while those who did not use marijuana showed an increase in their IQ over time, a loss of IQ points was observed among those who had a cannabis use disorder. Decreases in IQ were the most pronounced for those who had a cannabis use disorder that began in adolescence, and those for whom the cannabis use disorder persisted over several years. In fact, those who initiated their use of marijuana in adulthood did not experience a decline in their IQ in relation to persistent or chronic use. People who knew the study participants well were also interviewed as part of this research, and those who were familiar with participants who used marijuana persistently over time shared that they had observed attention and memory problems. This study highlights just how vulnerable young people are to the effects of marijuana on the developing brain. Although some studies suggest that cognitive functioning can recover after a person quits using marijuana,[8] whether full recovery occurs may depend on various aspects of one's personal history and marijuana use patterns (e.g., how often and how heavily they use marijuana, how old they were when they started). Generally, the risk of long-term cognitive problems from marijuana use is highest among those who initiate use at an earlier age and use more heavily and frequently.[9]

What are the health risks of marijuana use?

Figure 4.2 describes the effects of THC on the areas of the brain where high numbers of cannabinoid receptors are found. Some of the THC effects described do not appear "risky" from a health standpoint—for example, the effect of marijuana on the nucleus accumbens, which controls motivation and our experience of natural rewards such as food and sexual activity,

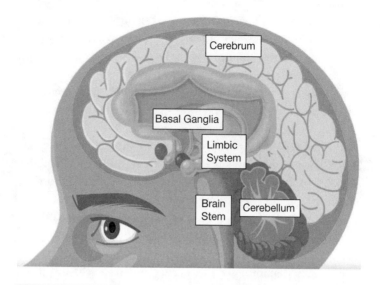

Brain Structure	Normal Functions	THC Effects
Cerebrum	The cerebrum powers our ability to think, plan, solve problems, and make decisions. It also processes information from our senses, allowing us to see, feel, hear, and taste.	Cannabis can disrupt thinking, attention, and decision making. It can alter our senses, and in some people, it can lead to psychosis symptoms, such as hallucinations and delusions.
Basal Ganglia	Involved in motor function, cognition, and emotion, as well as how the brain responds to rewards.	THC increases the amount of dopamine in the basal ganglia. Studies show that dopamine helps the brain remember and repeat behaviors that are rewarding. This can ultimately lead a person to become addicted to cannabis after using it regularly.
Limbic System	A group of structures (including the amygdala and hippocampus) that are involved in processing emotions and memories.	When THC attaches to receptors in the amygdala, it can cause fear and anxiety. THC can also interfere with the function of the hippocampus, leading to short-term memory problems.
Brain Stem	In charge of functions our body needs to stay alive – breathing, heart rate, and digestion.	Prescription medications with small amounts of THC can help relieve nausea for people with cancer who are receiving chemotherapy. However, frequent use of cannabis products with higher quantities of THC can sometimes lead to excessive vomiting that can require medical attention. High amounts of THC can also lead to increases in heart rate.
Cerebellum	Involved in balance and motor coordination, as well as perception of time.	Cannabis can impair a person's coordination and sense of time.

Figure 4.2 Marijuana's effects on the brain

Adapted from NIDA, 2024 (accessed at https://nida.nih.gov/themes/custom/solstice/interactive/cannabis/)

is to make a person feel euphoric or really good. It would be natural for you to wonder how and why this, and several other effects of THC described in this figure (e.g., anti-nausea effects), would be negative.

The fact is, though some of the short-term effects of THC on the brain and behavior pose risks to health and safety (for example, slowed reaction time can be dangerous in a variety of contexts, such as when driving), the effects of THC are not all negative. Health risks and complications associated with marijuana use become more likely with heavy and frequent use, which can lead to: (i) progressively more intense and harmful effects on the brain and behavior (for example, anxiety that worsens and leads to paranoia and psychosis), and (ii) reversal of some of the beneficial effects of use (e.g., anti-nausea effects subside and a person becomes severely and persistently nauseous). These risks fall into physical and mental health categories, which are summarized below.

What are the physical health risks of marijuana use?

Smoking or vaping marijuana can irritate the lungs, leading to frequent, often daily bothersome symptoms such as coughing and phlegm, as well as a higher risk of lung infections and illness. While the risk of lung cancer is not higher among those who smoke marijuana according to research,[10] concerns have emerged regarding the impact of smoking and/or vaping tobacco or marijuana on potential complications from COVID-19,[11] including becoming sicker and developing pneumonia.[12]

What are the mental health risks of marijuana use?

In the long term, use of marijuana is linked with certain mental health problems, including depression, anxiety, and psychosis. People who are vulnerable to mental health problems, either because of genetics or other reasons, are at especially high risk of experiencing psychiatric illness alongside marijuana use.[13] For example, *psychosis*, a mental state that reflects loss of touch with reality, can occur in different forms in someone who has used marijuana: (1) a person can experience *hallucinations*, which means that they see or hear things that are not really there; and (2) a person can show signs of *paranoia*, which is an extreme form of anxiety in which a person becomes very distressed due to the belief that other people are trying to harm them or give them a hard time, when this is not actually true. As paranoia progresses it can lead to *delusions*, which are untrue ideas that a person believes so firmly that even if shown evidence that disproves them, the person will persist in believing them, which affects their behavior and ability to function in important ways. For example, Maria—a 23-year-old woman who had been smoking marijuana since the age of 13, and in the past four years was smoking about three times a day—developed paranoid delusions that her family was trying to hurt her.[14] At the same time, she began hearing voices that were telling her that she was going to die. She had never heard these voices before, and the delusions and voices went on for two days before she went to the hospital. At the hospital, she described the profound fear and anxiety that the delusions were causing her, even though they really did not make any logical sense. She said, "I believed that people were trying to hurt me. My mother was doing usual things. She was telling me to go to the kitchen. Why would my mother keep telling me to go to the kitchen? It makes no sense. I must be bugging out. I know my mother would never hurt me. Something is wrong with me . . . I'm so scared." Maria had a history of psychiatric illness, having been diagnosed with depression and post-traumatic stress disorder (PTSD) when she was 15. She also has a genetic predisposition to psychiatric illness, as her parents both suffer from mood disorders—her mother has depression and her father has bipolar disorder. These aspects of her personal psychiatric history and genetics set the stage for a psychotic episode after prolonged and heavy marijuana use. In fact, current research shows that, compared to people who have never smoked marijuana, those who smoke high-potency marijuana on a daily basis are five times more likely to develop psychosis.[15]

Like Maria's experience, most commonly, psychotic reactions to marijuana are short term but very unpleasant, having been described as "hearing voices, becoming convinced that someone is trying to harm you, or that you are persecuted."[16] These transient but intense experiences have been reported by one in seven people who use marijuana.[17] But some people who are vulnerable to more serious psychotic illnesses can begin experiencing symptoms when they are using marijuana, and then the symptoms can take on a life of their own, "converting" to a chronic psychotic disorder such as schizophrenia. In fact, adolescents who use marijuana have two to three times the risk of later developing schizophrenia compared to those who do not use marijuana,[18] and studies describe marijuana as one of the strongest *preventable* sources of risk for a later diagnosis of a chronic psychotic illness.[19] This is especially true when marijuana with high levels of THC is used.[20] Scientific experts suggest that vulnerable children and teens, especially those who have family members with a history of psychosis, should be educated about these risks and strongly advised to avoid marijuana use.

Is marijuana addictive?

In Chapter 2 we discussed substance use disorders and how they are diagnosed. As a quick refresher, a substance use disorder is a condition in which a person progressively loses control over their use of a drug, leading to health problems that affect one or more important life areas (for example, their social life, work performance, or mental or physical well-being). Some people are more surprised than others to learn that repetitive use of marijuana can lead to a diagnosis of a cannabis use disorder, just as chronic use of stimulants such as cocaine can lead to a diagnosis of a stimulant use disorder. This notion of an addiction to marijuana may not be intuitive for a number of reasons. First, unlike many other drugs such as cocaine or opioids that people tend to associate with addiction, marijuana is typically not perceived as a "hard drug." Many people don't readily imagine that taking a drug like marijuana, which may affect a person's mental state or behavior in ways that seem more subtle (for example, by making a person feel calm and mellow) than what you might observe with other drugs like cocaine or methamphetamine (which amp people up and may make them act in ways that are more obviously "abnormal") could lead to an syndrome of addiction. These are reasonable points . . . so, how do we understand marijuana as an addictive substance? How do we know that it is addictive, and how is addiction to marijuana different from other types of drug addiction?

It is important to recognize how marijuana and the ways in which it is used have changed and evolved over the past several decades when considering its potential to be addictive. Because they contain higher levels of THC, the strains of marijuana that are currently available are more potent than ever before. In fact, according to data on the THC content in seized samples, marijuana potency has more than doubled worldwide, and more than quadrupled in the United States,[21] where THC content in cannabis plant material products sold on the streets and in cannabis dispensaries ranges from 25%–35%, and cannabis "concentrate" products contain up to 85% THC.[22] This is important because marijuana with higher THC concentration increases the risks associated with its use,[23] including addiction. Other ways in which the use of marijuana has evolved is through the increased availability of different ways of ingesting it, such as vaping and edibles, both of which can lead to exposure to high levels of THC. For those who are new to marijuana use, exposure to such high THC levels may lead to more rapid toxicity and harmful effects, which may explain the increase in emergency room visits related to marijuana use.[24]

Can chronic use of marijuana lead to a cannabis use disorder?

The short answer is yes—a cannabis use disorder, ranging from mild to severe, can develop when someone uses marijuana repeatedly over time. You may recall that in our discussion of substance use disorders in Chapter 2, we highlighted the differences in severity that people experience, ranging from mild to severe. An addiction is a severe, extreme form of a substance use disorder, and while there is evidence that some people do experience addiction to marijuana, as is true of other drugs to which people can become addicted, many with cannabis use disorders have mild or moderate symptoms. For example, a person with mild symptoms may find that they are using increasing amounts of marijuana even though they didn't plan to, and are experiencing some psychological or physical effects of marijuana that are undesirable, such as a lack of motivation to do things that are important to them. They might feel that they want to stop or cut back on marijuana use but are having a hard time doing this successfully. A person with these symptoms may be able to mostly live a normal life but is having some marijuana-related problems that create conflict and/or discomfort. As this disorder progresses, living a normal life can become more difficult, and addiction can develop, but it is not inevitable. People who are affected by a cannabis use disorder may or may not suffer from the extreme disabling symptoms that we observe in people who struggle with addiction. However, even with mild or moderate symptoms, a cannabis use disorder can be disruptive enough in a person's life that treatment becomes necessary to enable one to return to functioning as they normally would. Treatment of a cannabis use disorder, especially for a person who is vulnerable to addiction, can help prevent the progression of a mild disorder into a severe one. Let's look at an example of how someone with moderate symptoms of cannabis use disorder is affected.

Richard is a 28-year-old single man who broke up with his girlfriend about six months ago and moved from the East Coast to Hollywood, California, to pursue a career in the music industry. He found a job working in a music production company, and things were off to a fine start, but he found himself feeling a little down and periodically quite irritable with other people. Feeling the pressure of getting closer to age 30, as his close friends from college were beginning to settle down and start families, he began exploring online dating, but it wasn't going so smoothly. He just wasn't connecting with anyone, which was not only discouraging, but it was causing him to feel pretty lonely. Richard had been smoking pot on a daily basis since he was 19, and he didn't think much about it. He went to see a therapist to address his mood and irritability, and to explore why it was so hard for him to find a girlfriend. When they started talking about his last girlfriend, Rose, he began seeing connections that he hadn't considered before, between his use of marijuana and some of the difficulties he had been experiencing.

He and his girlfriend had broken up because she felt that he wasn't really "present" and connecting with her. She said that he often seemed "checked out" and that when they did communicate, he was frequently irritable and short with her. He went from being a very sociable person to someone who preferred to stay home, smoke weed, and relax on a Friday or Saturday night, and this bothered Rose. As Richard explored his lack of emotional connection with Rose, he began to think more about his connection to things that he had once been passionate about, like his career. Though he had found a job that was generally in his area of interest, he was not especially excited about the job, and he was not making a great effort to work his way up to his "dream job" as a producer. This was not really like him, as he had always been a pretty goal-driven person. As he thought more about his life, he realized that he had become somewhat isolated and a little depressed, and one of the few things he really looked forward to each day was coming home and smoking pot to unwind. In fact, every day, he would start thinking about and looking forward to smoking pot a couple of hours before he would get off work. "There has to be more to life than this," he thought.

Richard's story is not unusual. He came to treatment for some problems that he didn't initially even consider could be related to his use of marijuana. His mood and irritability may have been brought on by intermittent withdrawal from marijuana, but he had not yet connected the two. Being "checked out" and distant from his girlfriend, which is partly what caused them to break up, was a byproduct of spending much of his time at home high. But now, even when he wasn't high, he was not easily connecting with other people, something he had not experienced before in his life. In fact, he came to realize that he was losing his connection with his own aspirations. Though not especially bothersome, he was noticing daily cravings for marijuana a few hours before he got off of work, and he was finding himself avoiding social activities so that he could stay home and smoke weed, a pattern that had started when he was living with Rose.

Richard had moderate symptoms of a cannabis use disorder, including cravings for marijuana, symptoms of marijuana withdrawal (such as irritability), relationship problems with Rose that resulted directly from his use of marijuana, and spending less time doing things that he used to do for fun (like spending time with his friends) because of his increasing use of marijuana. Although Richard was not initially looking for treatment to address his marijuana use, current trends indicate that more and more people are recognizing that marijuana is causing problems for them and seeking help for this reason. In fact, the demand for treatment for cannabis use disorder is higher than for any other substance except alcohol.[25]

What is the scientific evidence that suggests that marijuana is addictive?

There are several lines of evidence that have led scientists to understand marijuana as an addictive drug. First, epidemiological research, which studies the incidence, patterns, and causes of disease conditions, has shown that people who use marijuana (1) report similar types of problems to people who use other addictive drugs, (2) enroll in treatment for their problems with marijuana at rates that are similar to those observed for other drugs, and (3) experience comparable rates of relapse to marijuana use after treatment, just as those who are treated for other drug use disorders such as cocaine.[26] Second, like other drugs that are more commonly thought of as addictive (such as opioids and alcohol), studies have documented a clear withdrawal syndrome that is experienced by people who use marijuana frequently when they stop using it or attempt to cut back. Third, in recent years more people have sought out psychological or behavioral treatment for problems related to their use of marijuana. Let's take each of these sources of evidence and understand them a little bit further.

Are the problems experienced by people who use marijuana similar to those that affect people who use other drugs? The 11 symptoms (described in Chapter 2) that people can experience when they develop a substance use disorder represent the most common problems we see among people who use drugs that have the potential to be addictive. Because of scientific evidence that people who use marijuana can develop these same general symptoms, the criteria for diagnosing a cannabis use disorder are essentially the same as those for other drugs such as opioids and tobacco.[27] Part of the controversy about whether marijuana is addictive centers around the belief that among people who use marijuana, these symptoms (or having enough of them to warrant a diagnosis of a cannabis use disorder) are rare. Although this was the case 25 years ago,[28,29] as more people have initiated marijuana use over the past few decades, the rate at which people experience related symptoms and problems has changed substantially. According to recent national data from studies of more than 36,000 Americans, between 20 and 30% of marijuana users develop a cannabis use disorder.[30,31,32] People who start using marijuana prior to the age of 18 are especially vulnerable to developing a cannabis use disorder, according to research showing that they are four to seven times more likely than adults to have a future diagnosis.[33] Nearly a quarter of those with a cannabis use disorder have severe symptoms, many of whom are not able to function in *any* important life role, including work. While there are many people who have mild or moderate symptoms of cannabis use disorder, for those who have severe symptoms the illness can impact a person's life profoundly.

Is there such a thing as marijuana withdrawal? Scientists working closely with people who use marijuana over the past few decades have discovered a marijuana withdrawal syndrome, experienced by 47% of people who regularly use marijuana when they abruptly stop using it, or when they cut back after a prolonged period of regular and/or heavy use.[34] Symptoms can include grouchiness or irritability, anxiety, insomnia, low appetite, restlessness, and depressed mood, along with a range of physical symptoms such as abdominal pain, sweating, fever, chills, or headache. These symptoms usually are most intense during the first week after stopping marijuana use but can last for up to a month.[35,36] Marijuana withdrawal symptoms are not typically as severe as those suffered by people who are in opioid or alcohol withdrawal, probably because THC leaves the body slowly.[37] However, they are uncomfortable enough that many who experience these symptoms report distress and have difficulty functioning in their normal daily activities.[38] In addition, some of these symptoms, especially depression and anxiety, can make it difficult to quit and are part of the reason that people relapse when trying to quit or use marijuana less.[39,40]

New Research: For Teens, Cannabis Is Nearly as Addictive as Opioids

According to recent research, the rate of addiction to cannabis among teens is on par with prescription opioids.[a] Based on data collected through national surveys, within a year of trying cannabis for the first time, nearly 10.7% of adolescents between the ages of 12 and 17 met the criteria for cannabis addiction, and using cannabis increases the risk that they will later become addicted to other substances. Among adolescents in that same age group who experimented with prescription opioids, a little over 11% became addicted within a year. These rates were nearly double those of people who started using cannabis and prescription opioids in their early adulthood (i.e., at or after age 18), highlighting the profound vulnerability of people who start using drugs at an early age to developing problems related to their substance use, especially addiction.

[a] Volkow, N. D., Han, B., Einstein, E. B., & Compton, W. M. (2021). Prevalence of Substance Use Disorders by Time Since First Substance Use Among Young People in the US. *JAMA Pediatrics, 175*(6), 640–643. https://doi.org/10.1001/jamapediatrics.2020.6981

How do the rates of treatment and relapse for cannabis use disorder compare to those of other substances?

According to the past 20 years of scientific research, the problems that people experience when they develop a severe cannabis use disorder are more similar to other drug use disorders than different. In fact, the reasons that people seek treatment for their marijuana use are similar to those for other drugs such as alcohol and cocaine, and include having trouble functioning in important areas of life (for example, missing school, work, relationship, and family problems), feeling guilty about using marijuana, financial difficulties, low energy and self-esteem, sleep and memory problems, dissatisfaction with life,[41,42] withdrawal symptoms, and perceiving themselves as unable to stop.[43]

Not unlike other severe addictions, people who are interested in changing their heavy cannabis use are unsuccessful when they try to reduce or stop using on their own.[44] Despite several well-established effective psychotherapy approaches to helping people use cannabis less heavily and/or frequently, the majority of those who undergo treatment have difficulty sustaining abstinence from cannabis over the longer term. In clinical trials evaluating some of the most effective behavioral treatments for cannabis use disorders, when abstinence is measured week after week through urine drug screens, evidence of "continuous" or sustained abstinence over time is observed in approximately 20% of individuals.[45] While many more achieve reductions in how often and how heavily they use marijuana, the science on treatment for marijuana use disorders lines up with what has been observed across many studies of those who are in recovery from alcohol, tobacco, stimulant, and other addictions—both the early phases of quitting and efforts to stay quit are challenging and typically involve multiple "slips" or relapses followed by extended and repeated treatment episodes before success is achieved.[46]

Is marijuana a gateway drug?

While marijuana use can precede the initiation and/or worsening of problems with other substances, marijuana as a gateway to other substance-related problems probably isn't the "whole story." Indeed, studies have shown that use of marijuana is likely to come before a person uses and/or becomes addicted to other drugs.[47] In a large national study in which people were followed over several years to see how their use of alcohol and drugs changed, those who were using marijuana at the start of the study were more likely to develop an alcohol use disorder within three years than individuals who were not using marijuana.[48] Other studies have shown that the earlier a person begins using marijuana, the more vulnerable they are to becoming addicted to other substances later in life.[49,50] This supports the idea that marijuana use at a young age can mark the start of progressive use of and loss of control over substances. Animal studies have found a biological explanation for this predictable sequence of drug use: the brain circuits that are involved in making a person feel the "rush" or high from some of the first typically used drugs like nicotine or marijuana become "primed," leading a person to feel an even *more* intense or pleasurable high from other drugs like cocaine.[51]

Even though marijuana use can come before experimentation with "harder" drugs, there are a few things we have learned through addiction science that paint a more complicated picture than a simple theory of marijuana as a gateway drug. First, marijuana is not the only drug that leads to the use of other addictive substances. Alcohol and nicotine are also often "beginner" drugs that open the door to use of other harmful drugs. According to one study, in 2012, nearly 90% of American adults ages 18 to 34 who had ever used cocaine had smoked cigarettes prior to trying cocaine.[52] Second, the majority of those who use marijuana do *not* in fact go on to use more addictive drugs.[53] So, as an alternative to a simple gateway theory, scientists have proposed that: (1) marijuana is one contributor to the problematic use of alcohol and/or other substances later on, making the use of other drugs more likely when combined with other risk factors for addiction (such as being in a social environment where others are using alcohol or drugs, psychological problems such as trauma, and family history or genetic vulnerability to addiction); (2) people who are vulnerable to developing addiction are more likely to initiate use of readily available substances like marijuana or nicotine, and their social interactions once they begin using these make them more likely to progress to using other substances. These possibilities are based on the idea that there are shared root causes (both genetic and environmental) that increase not only the likelihood that a person will become involved with marijuana use, but also increase their risk of using other drugs.

Medical and recreational use—is it safe, and does it work?

As policy changes across America have increasingly legalized marijuana for medical and/or recreational use, attitudes and perceptions about marijuana have shifted over the past two decades, with a growing majority of Americans favoring the use of marijuana for medical purposes. As marijuana has gained greater societal acceptance, an increasing majority of both adolescents and adults have come to view it as a relatively harmless drug.[54] Understanding the health and safety risks that are posed by marijuana use (especially heavy and regular use) as well as its potential for therapeutic benefits is important, given the stream of anecdotal and often inaccurate or incomplete information that is widely distributed through social media and other popular media outlets.[55]

As reviewed earlier, marijuana poses a variety of health risks, especially to younger people whose brains are still developing. Because of the adverse and potentially long-lasting effects of marijuana on cognitive development and abilities, including memory and judgment, regular use by teens can have an impact on their future pursuits and achievements, well-being, and health. Also, though many people believe that marijuana is not habit forming, studies have consistently shown that it is addictive, with nearly a third of those who use it experiencing a cannabis use disorder,[21] and those who begin using it early in life have a greater likelihood of becoming addicted to other drugs later on. For those who develop an addiction to marijuana, there is a risk of experiencing a withdrawal syndrome,[56] with many of the withdrawal symptoms overlapping with symptoms of depression and anxiety disorders. Although most people are aware that widely used drugs like opioids and alcohol can cause withdrawal, knowledge of marijuana withdrawal is not as widespread,[57] and those who use marijuana to self-medicate symptoms of depression and anxiety may be doing so without the benefit of complete information about the potential risks and benefits.

Which cannabis-based compounds are FDA approved?

Even though many states permit marijuana to be dispensed for medical purposes, and anecdotal reports of therapeutic benefits of marijuana-derived compounds are accumulating, the US Food and Drug Administration (FDA) has not approved "medical marijuana,"[52] and there is very little known about the long-term effects of using it, especially for vulnerable individuals with pre-existing health conditions (e.g., cancer, conditions such as AIDS that compromise the immune system, or cardiovascular and neurodegenerative diseases). That said, there are certain formulations of THC that have been approved by the FDA for the treatment of nausea among those with cancer who are undergoing chemotherapy, and to stimulate appetite for individuals with AIDS who suffer from wasting syndrome. These medications, dronabinol (Marinol) and nabilone (Cesamet) are taken orally in pill form. Other marijuana-based medications use cannabidiol (CBD), a chemical found in the marijuana plant that does not have the rewarding effects that make a person feel "high" like THC. Currently there is one CBD product that has received FDA approval for the treatment of two rare, severe forms of epilepsy. This medication, Epidiolex, contains a purified form of CBD and is taken as a liquid. Though this is the only CBD-based product that has gained FDA approval, various other medications that either contain CBD or a combination of THC and CBD are being investigated in clinical trials. One such medication that has been widely used in the United Kingdom, Canada, and several European countries is Sativex, a mouth spray that is used to treat pain and tightness or stiffness in muscles, known as spasticity, among people who suffer from multiple sclerosis.

Surveys have shown that many people use medical cannabis to treat depression and anxiety.[58] Those with PTSD also turn to cannabis-related products to alleviate their symptoms. Looking closely at the science on medical cannabis as an alternative to psychiatric medications, several reviews have failed to find evidence that cannabinoids are effective as a treatment for anxiety or depressive disorders,[9,59] although studies to further evaluate potential therapeutic benefit for psychiatric illnesses that can be difficult to treat (such as PTSD) are ongoing. Although chronic cannabis use among Americans with depression nearly tripled over the past decade,[60] research has shown that, among those who suffer from mental health problems, the use of cannabis can actually worsen depression, anxiety, PTSD symptoms, and overall psychological well-being over time.[61,62] When surveyed about how cannabis use affects psychological symptoms, less than half of those who use medical marijuana for this purpose report that it provides symptoms relief,[63] and some experience "rebound" anxiety after they discontinue their use of medical marijuana.[64] This is likely a result of cannabis withdrawal; thus, an important piece of knowledge for those who seek relief from depression and anxiety symptoms by using cannabis is the possibility that a cannabis use and withdrawal cycle can develop over time. When this happens, a person can wind up "chasing" these symptoms by using cannabis, and because of the short-term relief that it provides, they may not realize that a longer-term problem with withdrawal symptoms can emerge. This withdrawal syndrome, which includes anxiety and depressive symptoms, may worsen the very symptoms they were chasing.

Risks of Marijuana Use

Physical Risks

- Those who smoke or vape marijuana are at higher risk of developing lung infections and lung illness.
- The acute, short-term effects of marijuana on blood pressure increase the risk of heart attack.
- Marijuana use can cause dizziness when a person stands up, increasing the risk of fainting or falling.
- A few studies have linked marijuana use in adolescence with increased risk of testicular cancer in young adult males.

Cognitive/Brain Effects and Safety

- Marijuana use can impair judgment, motor coordination, and reaction time.
- In combination, these problems can impair a person's ability to drive safely.
- Studies show that marijuana increases (sometimes doubling or more) the risk of being involved in vehicle crashes.

Psychological Risks

- Development of a cannabis use disorder, and/or an addiction to cannabis.
- Marijuana withdrawal syndrome.
- Psychiatric complications of marijuana use, including depression, anxiety, and psychosis.

What are the available treatments for cannabis use disorders?

Research over the past several decades has supported the use of various behavioral or psychotherapy treatment approaches for cannabis use disorders, which will be described in greater depth in Chapter 11. As there are no FDA-approved medications to help people change their use of cannabis, behavioral treatment is currently the gold standard, and scientific research has shown that those who received evidence-based behavioral treatment for cannabis use disorders (including relapse prevention, contingency management, and motivational interviewing or a combination of these approaches) fared better than 66% of those who were in a control or comparison group, such as a waitlist for treatment or "usual care,"[65] Those with cannabis use disorders often have a long history of using cannabis by the time they seek out treatment; studies show that on average those who pursue professional help to change their use of cannabis have used regularly for more than a decade and have tried unsuccessfully to stop around half a dozen times.[42,52] It is not uncommon that people who struggle to control their use of cannabis have overlapping problems, either with addiction to alcohol or other drugs, or with their mental health, and in some cases both. If you or someone you care about who uses cannabis also has a mental health disorder (such as a mood or anxiety disorder), it's important to know that getting quality care for the mental health problem (which typically consists of medication, psychotherapy, or both) can help make it possible to change a person's excessive cannabis use.

The behavioral treatment approaches with the most consistent evidence for their effectiveness in changing a person's use of cannabis are the following:

- *Cognitive-behavioral therapy*, which teaches people strategies to identify and change thought and behavior patterns that perpetuate the cycle of problematic cannabis use.
- *Contingency management*, which involves frequent monitoring of a target behavior (e.g., cannabis use) using objective ways of measuring it (e.g., urine testing). Immediate rewards are provided for progressing toward the desired outcome (i.e., reductions in or abstinence from cannabis use).
- *Motivational enhancement therapy*, an approach to helping a person develop or strengthen their commitment to changing their use of cannabis or other substances.

Combining the above three approaches leads to the best treatment outcomes,[66] and these behavioral treatments can be successfully delivered either in person or using virtual platforms, with therapies delivered primarily through web access in combination with limited counseling showing some of the best success rates for those who are trying to remain abstinent from cannabis use.[67]

5

WHAT DO NICOTINE AND TOBACCO DO TO THE BRAIN AND BEHAVIOR?

America has come a long way since the 1960s, when 42% of the population identified as regular smokers; at the time, smoking was widely accepted, and little was known about its future health impacts. As evidence revealing the adverse health consequences of smoking and exposure to secondhand smoke mounted, Americans' attitudes and beliefs about cigarettes shifted dramatically. Today, though there is still room for improvement, the prevalence of smoking is half of what it was five decades ago, at about 22%.[1] In 2019, the US Food and Drug Administration raised the legal minimum age for sale of tobacco products, including cigarettes, cigars, and e-cigarettes from 18 to 21 years. Tobacco use continues to be the leading cause of preventable death in the Unites States, with the most vulnerable individuals to tobacco-related diseases being those who struggle with poverty, other addictions, and mental health difficulties.

What is the relationship between tobacco and nicotine?

Tobacco is a plant with leaves containing the highly addictive chemical known as nicotine. Once harvested, tobacco leaves are dried, aged, fermented, and processed in a variety of ways before being put in tobacco products. These products can be:

- *smoked*, in cigarettes, cigars, bidis, kreteks, pipes, or hookah (water pipe);
- *applied to the gums*, by dipping, using chewing tobacco, snuff, and snus;
- *inhaled* or sniffed (snuff can be used in this way).

There are many potentially harmful chemicals apart from nicotine that can be found in tobacco or created when tobacco is burned, particularly in cured tobacco leaves, which may contain many cancer-causing ingredients. In fact, an estimated 7,000 chemicals are found in smoke from combustible tobacco products.

Different Ways Tobacco Products Are Used

There are many ways in which tobacco is used; here you can find descriptions of some of the terms used to describe the various delivery methods:

- **Bidis** are small, thin, hand-rolled cigarettes that may be secured with a colorful string at one or both ends. They are imported to the United States from India and other Southeast Asian countries. Some bidis are flavored (e.g., chocolate, cherry, mango), while others are unflavored. Smoke from a bidi contains 3 to 5 times more nicotine than a regular cigarette, increasing risk of addiction and other health complications.
- **Kreteks** are also referred to as "cloves" or "clove cigarettes." They are imported from Indonesia and contain a combination of tobacco, cloves, and other additives. Regular Kretek smokers have 13 to 20 times the risk of developing lung abnormalities compared to nonsmokers (Nuryunarsih, 2021).

  Because bidis and kreteks have higher concentrations of nicotine, tar, and carbon monoxide compared to conventional cigarettes, they are not safe alternatives to conventional cigarettes. Kreteks are now prohibited from being sold in the United States.
- **Hookah** is a type of water pipe with a smoke chamber, a bowl, a pipe, and a hose, which is often used to smoke flavored tobacco. Also known as *narghile*, *argileh*, *shisha*, or hubble-bubble, the myth behind the hookah pipe is that it is a cleaner, purer, and safer way to use tobacco. The fact is that hookah still delivers nicotine to the

---

brain and body, and studies show that those who use hookahs inhale 100 to 200 times the volume of smoke in an hour-long hookah
session than they would by smoking a cigarette (CDC, 2021).

- **Snuff** and **snus** are two forms of smokeless or noncombustible tobacco. Chewing tobacco and snuff are the two main forms of smokeless tobacco that are used. Dry snuff is loose finely cut or powdered
dry tobacco that is usually sniffed through the nostrils. Snus is cut
tobacco that is either loose or inside of a small pouch and placed
inside of the mouth.

[a] Nuryunarsih, D., Lewis, S., & Langley, T. (2021). Health Risks of Kretek
Cigarettes: A Systematic Review. *Nicotine & Tobacco Research: Official Journal
of the Society for Research on Nicotine and Tobacco, 23*(8), 1274–1282. https://
doi.org/10.1093/ntr/ntab016
[b] Centers for Disease Control and Prevention. (2021). Hookahs. Retrieved
from: https://www.cdc.gov/tobacco/data_statistics/fact_sheets/tobac
co_industry/hookahs/index.htm#:~:text=In%20a%20typical%201%2Dh
our,nicotine%20of%20a%20single%20cigarette. on 2023, November 18.

How does nicotine affect the brain?

Cigarettes have been referred to as a "very efficient and
highly engineered drug delivery system,"[2] the reason being
that when tobacco is smoked, nicotine rapidly reaches peak
levels in the bloodstream and makes its way into the brain.
On average, a smoker takes in between 1 and 2 milligrams
of nicotine every time they smoke a cigarette. Since it takes
about 10 puffs to finish a cigarette, a person who smokes half
a pack (or 10 cigarettes) daily takes in 100 "hits" of nicotine
to their brain every day. People who use nicotine without
smoking it (e.g., those who use smokeless tobacco) can take
in as much nicotine as a cigarette smoker, but the difference
is that it reaches peak blood levels and the brain more slowly,
since it has to be absorbed by mucous membranes in the
mouth first. Even after tobacco is removed from the mouth,
nicotine continues to be absorbed into the bloodstream, and
it stays in the blood longer for those who use smokeless tobacco than for smokers.

After exposure to nicotine, the adrenal glands are stimulated, and adrenaline (also known as epinephrine) is released. This, in addition to activation of the brain's reward pathways, causes a person to feel nicotine's stimulating effects, which include a rush of pleasure and an increase in blood pressure, respiration, and heart rate.

You may have heard that nicotine is highly addictive, and there are biochemical reasons why that is true. First, like other "harder" drugs like cocaine and heroin, nicotine causes increased amounts of the chemical dopamine to be released in the brain, and dopamine regulates feelings of pleasure. Second, there are other chemicals contained in tobacco smoke such as acetaldehyde, which can magnify the effects that nicotine has on the brain. Third, although nicotine rapidly enters the brain within 10 seconds of inhalation, those effects, along with the pleasure they produce, vanish quickly. This leads the smoker to continue dosing to maintain those rewarding effects and prevent themselves from experiencing withdrawal symptoms.

What are the symptoms of nicotine withdrawal?

The experience of withdrawal can be part of the cycle of addiction to any substance. When a person uses a substance like nicotine, which is dosed repeatedly throughout the day with every puff of a cigarette that is taken, the brain becomes accustomed to those stimulating "hits" of nicotine occurring at regular and frequent intervals. When a person stops using cigarettes, the brain becomes confused, and this can make a person feel sick. This experience of feeling sick when you stop using nicotine is the withdrawal syndrome from the drug. It can happen in between smoking cigarettes throughout the day—acting as a cue that it's time to smoke again—or when a person tries to quit smoking. In both scenarios, the symptoms are so uncomfortable for a person who is addicted to nicotine that they may find themselves smoking even though the rational part of their brain told them not to. The symptoms of nicotine withdrawal include:

- Cravings for nicotine
- Feeling angry, frustrated, or irritable
- Insomnia, or difficulty falling or staying asleep
- Trouble concentrating
- Feeling restless
- Feeling depressed or anxious
- Increased appetite

Less common symptoms of nicotine withdrawal can include headaches, dizziness, fatigue, coughing, mouth ulcers, and constipation.[3] Typically, these symptoms are the most severe during the first week after quitting, especially the first half of the week, but after that, over the course of a month, they improve steadily. In some less typical cases, nicotine withdrawal symptoms can persist for months.[4]

What are the health risks of nicotine and tobacco use?

Though one might think that the use of nicotine itself leads to health problems, it is actually the chemical additives that are the most hazardous to one's lungs, cardiovascular system, and other vital organs. Being a smoker can lead to chronic and life-threatening illnesses, including lung cancer, chronic bronchitis, and emphysema.[5] By placing a person at higher risk of heart disease, those who smoke are more vulnerable to acute health consequences of an unhealthy cardiovascular system, such as stroke and heart attacks. Those who use smokeless tobacco are at increased risk for cancer, and in particular mouth cancers. In addition, despite the myth that there are certain ways to use tobacco that are less likely to lead to health difficulties (e.g., hookah smoking), the risk of diseases resulting from smoking are increased regardless of how tobacco is used. Other diseases that are linked with smoking include Type 2 diabetes, pneumonia, cataracts, and leukemia. For pregnant women, smoking increases the risk of pregnancy and birth complications, including miscarriages, stillborn or premature infants, or infants with low birth weight. In addition, children born to mothers who smoked during their pregnancy are more vulnerable to experiencing learning and behavioral problems.

Secondhand smoke exposure (also known as *passive smoking* or smoke you don't mean to breathe in) also poses health risks, causing over 41,000 deaths annually. People are exposed to secondhand smoke either from the burning end of a cigarette or other tobacco product, which is known as *sidestream smoke*, or the smoke that is exhaled by another person, known as *mainstream smoke*. Sidestream smoke poses a greater risk to a bystander's health than mainstream smoke, because this type of smoke has a higher concentration of nicotine and cancer-causing chemicals. When a child or an adult are exposed to secondhand smoke, this can lead to health problems including lung cancer and heart disease. The most vulnerable group from a health perspective are children, who can suffer from a host of problems when they live with parents or relatives who smoke, including:

- Getting sick more frequently
- Lung infections such as bronchitis or pneumonia
- Increased likelihood of coughing, wheezing, and shortness of breath
- Sudden infant death syndrome
- More frequent ear infections

An additional risk that is more commonly observed among children is nicotine overdose, or harmful and/or potentially lethal symptoms that result from a toxic reaction to ingesting the drug. There are a few ways that this can happen when a child is living or spending time around people who use tobacco products: children can accidentally chew nicotine gum, or patches that are used to help people quit smoking, or they can drink e-cigarette liquid. If a child or adult is suspected to have ingested nicotine in any of these ways and is experiencing symptoms such as difficulty breathing, vomiting, fainting, headache, weakness, or a change in heart rate, immediate medical attention is needed.

6

WHAT DOES VAPING DO TO THE BRAIN AND BEHAVIOR?

As a relatively new but very popular way of using nicotine, especially among youth, many people lack accurate information about what vaping is, what the risks are, and how it can affect health and well-being. This is a good time to equip yourself with knowledge, especially if you or someone you know is a parent, as the most recent research shows that 2.5 million young people admit to having used e-cigarettes in the past 30 days, and nearly one-third say that they have been using them daily.[1] Now regarded by many as a "youth vaping epidemic,"[2] vaping devices have become the most commonly used form of nicotine among young people in America.[3]

What is vaping and how is it different from an e-cigarette?

Vaping devices are what people use to inhale or breathe in an aerosol. The aerosol usually contains nicotine, flavorings, and other chemicals. Vaping is made possible by the use of vaping devices such as an *e-cigarette*. There are many vaping devices, differing in appearance. Some of them look just like regular cigarettes. Sometimes referred to as "cig-a-likes," these are often marketed to "beginner" vapers as an easy initial transition from cigarette smoking to vaping. E-cigarettes can also look like cigars or pipes. Other, more discreet devices look nothing like a cigarette—they have been designed to appear like commonly used objects such as pens, USB flash drives, car keys, Apple watches, and can even be concealed inside hoodies and inhaled using a device that appears just like hoodie strings. And since these devices don't have a bad smell, unlike regular cigarettes, they are very easy to disguise, making them easily marketable to teens and adolescents. There are over 460 different e-cigarette brands, and though they may differ in appearance, they all generally work the same way: they are battery-powered devices that heat liquids containing nicotine, flavorings, and other chemicals, to form an aerosol that is inhaled by the user (whom we will call the "vaper"). According to some studies, teen vapers often don't realize that the aerosol they are inhaling contains nicotine, and instead think that they are inhaling only the flavorings.

E-cigarettes typically have four parts (see Figure 6.1):

1. The cartridge: this holds the liquid (also known as *e-liquid* or *e-juice*) that, when heated, will become an aerosol for the vaper to inhale.
2. The atomizer: this is a coil that heats the e-liquid or e-juice, transforming it into an aerosol (or tiny airborne droplets).
3. Sensors: e-cigarettes rely on sensors to turn them on.
4. The battery: A rechargeable lithium-ion battery provides a current that is powerful enough to heat the atomizer to 400° Fahrenheit in a matter of seconds.

E-cigarettes have many names, which are worth familiarizing yourself with so that you can follow what is going on with a young person who may be using them; some of the commonly used names include:

- E-cigs
- Juuls
- Pens

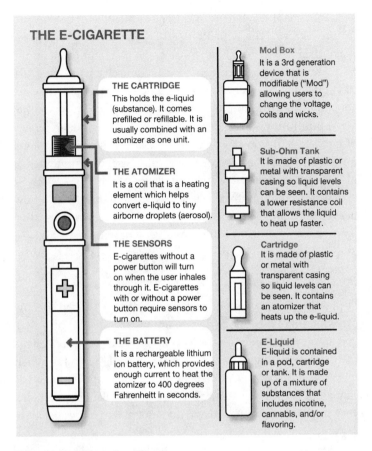

THE E-CIGARETTE

THE CARTRIDGE
This holds the e-liquid (substance). It comes prefilled or refillable. It is usually combined with an atomizer as one unit.

THE ATOMIZER
It is a coil that is a heating element which helps convert e-liquid to tiny airborne droplets (aerosol).

THE SENSORS
E-cigarettes without a power button will turn on when the user inhales through it. E-cigarettes with or without a power button require sensors to turn on.

THE BATTERY
It is a rechargeable lithium ion battery, which provides enough current to heat the atomizer to 400 degrees Fahrenheitt in seconds.

Mod Box
It is a 3rd generation device that is modifiable ("Mod") allowing users to change the voltage, coils and wicks.

Sub-Ohm Tank
It is made of plastic or metal with transparent casing so liquid levels can be seen. It contains a lower resistance coil that allows the liquid to heat up faster.

Cartridge
It is made of plastic or metal with transparent casing so liquid levels can be seen. It contains an atomizer that heats up the e-liquid.

E-Liquid
E-liquid is contained in a pod, cartridge or tank. It is made up of a mixture of substances that includes nicotine, cannabis, and/or flavoring.

Figure 6.1 The Anatomy of an e-Cigarette

Source: CDC, 2022

- Vape pens, dab pens, and dab rigs
- E-hookahs
- ENDS (Electronic Nicotine Delivery Systems)
- Vaporizers
- Tank systems
- Mods (customizable, more powerful vaporizers)
- Mod pods

Unfortunately, what many vapers may not know is that use of Juuls and other high-nicotine e-cigarettes contain nicotine salts that enable high concentrations of nicotine to be released in aerosol form. These nicotine salt-based forms of e-cigarettes make them easier to inhale, more appealing, and more addictive. Vapers do not necessarily pace themselves and their use of vaping devices according to the amount of nicotine they are consuming—for example, they may or may not be aware that a 200-puff Juul pod contains the amount of nicotine in a pack of cigarettes. If you or someone you know is vaping, asking questions about the type of device they use, their knowledge of how concentrated the nicotine in their delivery system is, and how frequently they use it can provide insight into how heavily they are using nicotine and how much awareness they have about the extent of their involvement with it.

Do people vape substances other than nicotine?

Depending on the type of vaping device that is used, people can vape either nicotine or delta-9-tetrahydrocannabinol (THC), and some will vape both. As you are probably aware, THC is the main active ingredient that makes people feel high when they use marijuana. Another substance that can be vaped is cannabidiol (CBD), a chemical in the *Cannabis* plant that contains very small amounts of THC and does not make people feel high.

How are substances like THC, CBD, and nicotine inhaled when a person is vaping?

An *e-liquid* (which can also be referred to as e-juice or vaping juice) is stored in the part of a vaping device that is called a pod, cartridge, or tank. This e-liquid can contain a mix of substances including nicotine, THC, CBD, flavorings, and/or other solvents. Below (illustrated in Figures 6.2 through 6.5) is a list of the ways in which e-liquid can be stored and released, depending on the specific vaping device:[4]

- Cig-a-like: The e-liquid is contained in a disposable device, so there is no tank, pod, or cartridge.

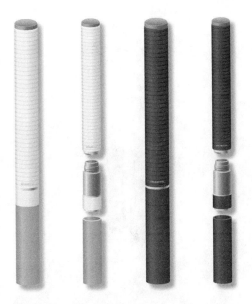

Figure 6.2 Cig-a-Like
Source: CDC, 2023

- Battery pen: The e-liquid is contained in a prefilled or refillable cartridge.
- Pod mod: The e-liquid is contained in a prefilled or refillable pod, which can also be called a pod cartridge and/or may contain nicotine salts.
- Vaporizer, dab rig, or dab pen: By applying noncombusting heat, vaporizers can convert dry herbs, wax, and oil into an aerosol, which releases their active substances (such as THC) in a form that the vaper inhales. Marijuana herb, hash oil, and dab wax are used with vaporizers.

Speaking of dab wax, what is dabbing?

First, let's clarify what dab wax is—this is a *marijuana extract*, which contains a concentrated oil from the marijuana plant (see Figure 6.6). Dab wax and other extracts are much

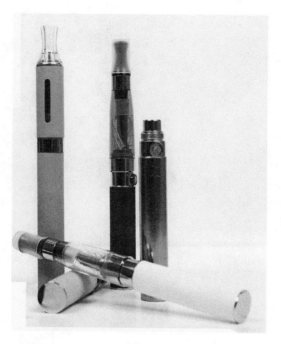

Figure 6.3 Battery Pen
Source: CDC, 2023

stronger than dried marijuana, containing more than 80% THC, compared to regular marijuana which has 25–35% THC content.[6] *Dabbing* is when people smoke or vape marijuana extracts.

When vaping dab wax, the vaper takes a small amount or "dab" of wax, puts it on the end of a vaping device called a "dab rig," heats it with a flame, and finally, inhales the aerosol that is produced in this process. Dab wax also has some nicknames, including:

- Butter
- Batter
- Diamonds

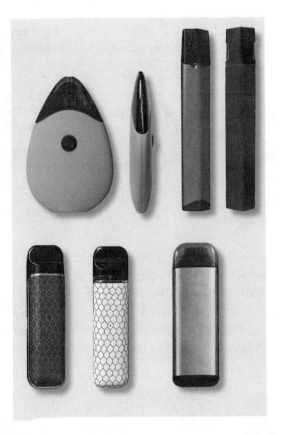

Figure 6.4 Pod mod
Source: CDC, 2023

- Resin
- Sauce
- Shatter

There are numerous health risks tied to dabbing, including inhalation of pesticides and other poisonous solvents that, in more than 80% of marijuana extracts, can be left over from the extraction process.[5] The risk of developing addiction to marijuana also increases when marijuana extracts such as dab

Figure 6.5 Vaporizer, Dab Rig
Source: CDC, 2023

wax are smoked or vaped.[6] One study found that using "dabs" caused people to build up a higher tolerance to THC and more withdrawal symptoms when they cut back or stopped using marijuana, compared to dry marijuana.[7] As we reviewed in Chapter 2, tolerance and withdrawal are physical symptoms of a substance use disorder. Despite these potential problems,

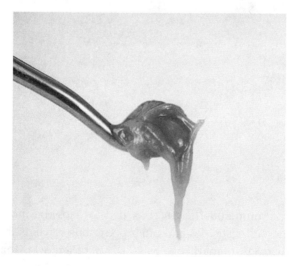

Figure 6.6 Marijuana Concentrate
Source: CDC, 2023

marijuana concentrates are becoming more popular among recreational marijuana users. Dabbers are more likely to use these concentrates out of "curiosity" and a desire to experiment, according to a large national survey, though those who dab regularly also express that they are worried about their marijuana use.[7] Sharing information about the risks related to vaping these concentrates could be helpful to people who may unknowingly experiment with these addictive substances.

What is dripping?

Dripping is an increasingly popular way that people use e-cigarettes and is different from dabbing. Dripping is when people produce and inhale vapors by placing e-liquid drops directly onto heated atomizer coils. When asked why they use e-cigarettes to drip, teens in a large national study said that it creates thicker clouds of vapor, gives them a stronger throat hit (a pleasurable feeling experienced when the vapor causes their throat to contract), and makes flavors taste better.[8] The risks of dripping are largely unknown at this time, though a few studies have shown that heating e-liquids at high temperatures can expose those who drip to toxic chemicals in the vapors, including formaldehyde and acetone.[9,10]

How does vaping affect the brain?

Much like regular cigarettes, the effects of vaping on the brain have to do with the delivery of nicotine into the bloodstream. Once nicotine is absorbed from the e-liquid in an e-cigarette, it travels through the body and stimulates the release of certain brain chemicals, including epinephrine and dopamine. The release of epinephrine (which is also known as adrenaline) causes the nervous system to speed up its activities, causing rises in blood pressure, heart rate, and breathing. The release of dopamine that is triggered by nicotine is what makes it so pleasurable that some people find themselves wanting to experience it over and over, leading to addictive behavior. The stimulating and pleasurable effects of nicotine on the brain are experienced almost immediately when a person smokes or vapes, which is partly why e-cigarettes, like any other delivery method for taking nicotine, are highly addictive.

What are the health risks associated with vaping?

Though our understanding of the health effects of vaping is only beginning to evolve, perhaps the most concerning risk of vaping is its potential to lead to nicotine and even other drug addiction. The risk for drug addiction results from priming the brain's pleasure pathways; by activating these areas of the brain, vaping creates a powerful memory of how good it feels when our pleasure chemicals (such as dopamine) are released in large amounts. This places a person at higher risk of using and becoming addicted to other substances that lead to similar feelings.

The other main health risk of vaping is that it exposes the vaper's lungs to a variety of chemicals, of which the health effects of repeated exposure are not well understood. These chemicals come from various sources: some are added to the e-liquids, some are produced when the e-liquids are heated and vaporized, and some are toxic particles from the devices themselves.[3] Although the specific chemicals may vary depending on the type of vaping device used, some of the concerning compounds apart from nicotine that can be ingested include flavoring such as diacetyl, a chemical linked to serious and potentially fatal lung disease; volatile organic compounds such as benzene, which is found in car exhaust; and toxic heavy metals such as nickel, tin, and lead.[11] Exposure to aerosols from vaping can cause tissue damage and inflammation,[12] and diminishes the ability to fight infections.

Apart from the potential long-term adverse health effects of becoming addicted to nicotine and being exposed to toxic chemicals, since August of 2019 nearly 3,000 reports of serious lung injuries associated with vaping, including some resulting in death, are currently being investigated by the Food and Drug Administration (FDA) along with the Centers for Disease Control and Prevention (CDC).[13] The investigation has revealed that the majority of the vaping products linked with these cases contain THC, the psychoactive ingredient in marijuana that makes people feel high when they use it. The CDC also reported that many of the THC-containing e-cigarette or vaping products that were linked with these lung illnesses were acquired from family, friends, or in-person or online dealers. Another compound that has been strongly linked to the lung injury outbreak is Vitamin E acetate, which is used as an additive or thickening agent in some vaping products. Vitamin E acetate is also added to some vitamin supplements and skin creams. While it doesn't appear to have harmful effects when swallowed or used topically in such products, inhaling this substance may be harmful to a person's lungs.[14] With this knowledge, the CDC and FDA have made a number of recommendations to help people avoid developing lung injuries or complications, and to prevent related deaths:

- Do not use vaping products that contain THC.
- Do not use THC-containing vaping products from informal sources such as family, friends, or dealers.
- Vitamin E acetate should not be added to any e-cigarette or vaping products.
- Do not add *any* substances, like THC or other oils, to vaping products.
- No vaping product has been FDA-approved for therapeutic uses. If you wish to use THC for a medical condition, consult your healthcare provider.
- E-cigarette or vaping products should not be used by youth or pregnant women, regardless of whether they contain nicotine, THC, or both.
- A person who chooses to use these products should monitor themselves for symptoms such as cough, shortness

of breath, and chest pain. Seek prompt medical attention if any health concerns arise after using a vaping product, either by contacting one's primary care provider, going to the emergency room, and/or contacting poison control at 1-800-222-1222.

Fortunately, since the widespread release of information about the potential causes of this lung illness outbreak among vapers, there has been a decline in cases, which is thought to have resulted from increased public awareness of the dangers of vaping THC-containing vaping products, along with removal of Vitamin E acetate from some vaping products and law-enforcement actions related to illicit products.

Is vaping a "gateway" to other substance use?

Since e-cigarettes are so popular among young people, with more high school students now vaping than smoking regular cigarettes, concerns are mounting about what this means for the future of our young people. Will they later turn to regular cigarettes, or even other addictive drugs? Or is vaping one of many experimental behaviors that occur during a transient phase of youth?

As research accumulates on this topic, it has become clearer that using nicotine at a young age can have a lasting impact on future health-related behaviors, and that vaping can serve as an introduction to other nicotine products and drugs of abuse over time.[14] According to a series of recent studies, teens who vape are at greater risk of switching over to regular cigarettes; for example, high schoolers who use e-cigarettes are seven times more likely to smoke regular cigarettes six months later, compared to those who do not vape.[15] Since the brains of young adolescents are still in the process of development, introducing nicotine to their brains' reward systems can have long-term effects on their behavior. Not only are adolescents and young adults at greater risk for the development of nicotine addiction, but early exposure to nicotine can lead to mood disorders and permanent lowering of impulse control. This, combined with the tendency to experience other drugs as more pleasurable after nicotine exposure has occurred, is partly why young people who have used nicotine may be vulnerable to addiction to other drugs, such as cocaine and methamphetamine.[16]

Can vaping help you quit smoking? A summary of the current evidence

Because e-cigarettes emit fewer toxic substances than combustible cigarettes, they have been touted as safe alternatives to smoking, and even as agents for smoking cessation. Scientific support for these assertions is mixed. When regular smokers switch to vaping as a complete replacement, evidence suggests that indeed, vaping devices may be a less harmful mode of nicotine delivery than combustible cigarettes. However, we don't have enough data concerning the safety of e-cigarettes to refer to them as "safe alternatives," and we know that nicotine is highly addictive regardless of how it is delivered. In regard to the use of vaping products for the purposes of smoking cessation, scientific support is inconclusive. One study that followed more than 800 vapers who were attempting to quit cigarette smoking found that only 9% had stopped using combustible cigarettes one year later.[17] Another study of vapers across 28 European Union countries found that use of e-cigarettes was linked to *lower* rates of quitting cigarette smoking and *greater* frequency of combustible cigarette use, compared to those who did not vape or use e-cigarettes.[18] In contrast, a recent review of 78 studies found that e-cigarettes were more effective than nicotine replacement therapies in promoting quitting.[19] Although more research is needed to draw conclusions about whether vaping nicotine can be helpful as a harm-reduction tool for those who are trying to quit smoking cigarettes, the most straightforward approach for anyone who would like to stop smoking is to use one of the seven quit aids that have been approved by the FDA and demonstrated over many years of research to be safe and effective. To develop skills to manage urges or temptations to smoke and help maintain your quit status over the long term, combining one or more of these quit aids with behavioral or psychological treatment can be highly effective. In Part 3 we review available and scientifically based treatments for addiction and will describe these available options.

What are the available treatments for tobacco cessation?

Thankfully, there are very effective treatments that are relatively easy for smokers to access. These include both medications (many of which are available over the counter) and behavioral therapy (with many programs available over the internet through websites and/or virtually delivered coaching programs). Studies have shown that the most successful approach to tobacco cessation is the combination of medications with behavioral counseling,[20] more so than either of these approaches on their own. In Chapter 12 we will take a closer look at the full range of treatment options for smoking cessation.

7

WHAT DO STIMULANTS DO TO THE BRAIN AND BEHAVIOR?

What are the most commonly used stimulants?

The group of drugs known as psychomotor stimulants include cocaine, methamphetamine, and prescription stimulants. *Cocaine* is a highly addictive, illicit stimulant drug that is made from the leaves of the coca plant from South America. *Methamphetamine* is an illicit synthetic stimulant that, like cocaine, is powerfully addictive. Unlike cocaine, methamphetamine is chemically similar to amphetamine. Generally, prescription stimulants containing amphetamine are used as medications to treat attention deficit hyperactivity disorder (ADHD) and narcolepsy, which is a medical condition in which a person experiences overwhelming daytime drowsiness and sudden attacks of sleep. Methylphenidate (trade names, for example, include Ritalin and Concerta) is one type of prescription stimulant, and amphetamines (trade names, for example, include Adderall and Vyvanse) are a second, both of which are widely prescribed in the United States.

Why are current stimulant use trends so dangerous?

The second decade of the 21st century gave way to rising rates of stimulant use and addiction, a trend that has continued into the past several years. Unfortunately, the concerning trends in cocaine and methamphetamine use are very closely linked with the opioid epidemic, and are claiming an increasing number of lives.[1] Fentanyl, a synthetic opioid that is 50 to 100 times more potent than morphine, has made its way into the cocaine and methamphetamine supply, produced and transported to the United States via Mexican cartels. Stimulants have become widely available and inexpensive, with variable quantities of fentanyl mixed into them. With fentanyl driving the rise in overdose deaths over the past handful of years, its combination with stimulants is now fueling a "sub-epidemic" among those who use cocaine and/or methamphetamine, for whom overdose rates are sharply increasing. In fact, studies show that some people who suffer from opioid addiction have switched to using methamphetamine because they fear that the opioids they are taking may contain fentanyl. Without awareness of the potential for methamphetamine to be laced with fentanyl, those who make this opioid-to-stimulant transition may be heading down a path to accidental overdose despite efforts to avoid it.[2]

The Lethal Combination of Stimulants and Fentanyl

Large amounts of methamphetamine and cocaine that are trafficked into the United States and sold on the streets contain fentanyl. Why is this so deadly?

- Fentanyl is a very powerful opioid, and like other opioids, it can suppress the respiratory system, making a person unable to breathe.
- When a person's breathing slows down or stops as a result of a fentanyl overdose, they can develop hypoxia, a condition involving reduced oxygen supply to the brain. This can lead a person to enter a coma, sustain permanent brain damage, or die.
- A person who takes opioids regularly may develop tolerance to many of its effects, including its effects on breathing. This means that over time, they are able to take progressively larger amounts of opioids without experiencing depression of their respiratory system.
- However, a person who buys cocaine or methamphetamine that is laced with fentanyl often does not know that fentanyl has been added to it, and because their body has not developed tolerance to

this drug, they may be especially vulnerable to the effects of fentanyl on their respiratory system. This makes them more likely to experience a lethal overdose.

- People who use stimulants like cocaine or methamphetamine are often unaware of the dangers of fentanyl overdose.

What is cocaine and how do people use it?

A fine, white, crystal powder, cocaine (Figure 7.1) is referred to as "blow" or "coke" and is typically snorted through one's nose, and sometimes rubbed into the gums. Cocaine can also be converted to "crack," which is a rock crystal form (also known as "freebase cocaine") that varies in color from yellow to pale rose or white. This highly potent form of cocaine is then heated and smoked. Commonly known as "crack" because of the crackling or popping sound made when it is heated, the purity of this form is considered very high, and it reaches the bloodstream much more rapidly when smoked compared to snorting the powder form. A smaller subset of people who use cocaine dissolve and then inject it. Another form that people

Figure 7.1 Cocaine
Source: Adobe Stock

sometimes inject is a combination of cocaine and heroin, known as a "speedball."

In general, when drugs are taken in a way that leads them to reach the brain more rapidly, because of the immediacy of the "rush" or high that a person experiences, the urge to repeat use of the drug is more powerful. For this reason, the method of taking a drug has a lot to do with how rapidly a person may become addicted to it. Like other drugs, among people who use cocaine, the highest risk is to those who *inject* it, because this is the quickest way for it to reach the brain and affect a person's feelings and behaviors. Not only does the high occur almost immediately, but it is both intense and relatively brief, lasting for less than 15 minutes. The urge to re-experience the rush can be overwhelmingly strong, since it feels so amazing, and yet that feeling fades away quickly. Second to injecting it, smoking cocaine (i.e., in the form of crack) is the next most addictive method, producing a high that lasts for 10 minutes or less. When snorted, the rush will last anywhere from 15 to 30 minutes. As a person's addiction progresses and they develop tolerance to the effects of stimulants, they often transition from snorting it to smoking or even injecting it, as the longing for a more intense and rapid rush intensifies.

Does the way you take cocaine make a difference in its health effects?

The long-term health effects of using cocaine also differ according to the method a person uses to take it. For example, those who *snort* cocaine may lose some of their sense of smell and can suffer from nosebleeds, frequent runny noses, and difficulty swallowing. On the other hand, people who *smoke* cocaine mostly experience respiratory problems as a result, including asthma and coughing, and they are more susceptible to respiratory infections such as pneumonia. For those who inject it, the greatest risks are related to contracting infectious diseases, which can result from sharing needles and include HIV and Hepatitis C, as well as infections to skin and tissue around the area where they inject the drug, including abscesses and cellulitis. An *abscess* is a painful collection of pus under the skin, caused by a bacterial infection. In a person who injects drugs, this happens when bacteria enter the body through an unsterile needle or unclean skin. Treating the abscess includes draining the abscess and taking antibiotics. *Cellulitis* is a common and potentially serious bacterial infection in the skin, occurring when a crack or break in the skin allows bacteria to enter. A person with cellulitis will have a swollen, red, affected area that is usually painful and hot to the touch. This condition, if left untreated, can be life-threatening, because the infection can spread to the lymph nodes and bloodstream.

What does it mean when a drug is "cut" with another substance?

You may have seen or heard references to illicit drugs being "cut" with other drugs or substances. This means that the drug is being mixed with another substance in efforts to dilute it; this way, the product is bulked up before it is sold, increasing profits. Usually, what is referred to as the "cutting agent" (or substance that is mixed with the drug being sold) physically resembles the drug it is being mixed with, so that the consumer can't tell that the drug has been diluted with something else. Cocaine, for example, would typically be "cut" with another white powder, such as a sugar or starch. Another substance that cocaine is often cut with is lidocaine, a local anesthetic. Since cocaine naturally has an anesthetic effect on mucous membranes, it is known to numb the gums when placed directly on them. Since lidocaine has stronger anesthetic effects than cocaine, a person who is buying cocaine might sample it by putting some on their gums, and if it is cut with lidocaine, they might assume that the powerful numbing effect reflects that the cocaine is of very high quality.[3] Several other numbing cutting agents are used for the same effect, including benzocaine, procaine, and tetracaine.

Many cutting agents that are used to dilute a drug and increase profits are pretty harmless, and beyond being irritating to one's nose, their effects are not noticeable. However, there are cutting agents that prolong and intensify the effects of illicit drugs, which are sometimes referred to as *adulterants*, and these can be harmful and even lethal. Banned for human consumption by the Food and Drug Administration (FDA), the two most commonly found adulterants in cocaine are levamisole and phenacetin. Levamisole, found in more than 80% of seized cocaine coming into the United States,[4] is a drug used in the farming industry to treat worm infections, a common problem in livestock. The combination of cocaine with levamisole can cause organ malfunction in the heart, lungs, and brain, and has been linked to fatalities.[5] Mixing cocaine with levamisole can also cause severe skin infections, as well as adverse reactions including nausea, vomiting, fever, dizziness, and confusion. Phenacetin, a frequently used crack cocaine cutting agent, is a pain reliever and fever-reducing medication that was taken off the market many years ago because it was found to be carcinogenic and was linked with other health complications, including kidney failure. Cocaine cut with phenacetin is associated with a range of negative effects, including low blood pressure, loss of consciousness, heart failure, and death.

Finally, cocaine may be laced with other illicit drugs to increase the effects of both substances, which most commonly include:

- Fentanyl
- Heroin (known as a speedball)
- Marijuana
- Hash
- LSD (acid)
- PCP

Since fentanyl can be fatal in extremely low doses, cocaine cut with fentanyl can lead to overdose and death. Even a tiny

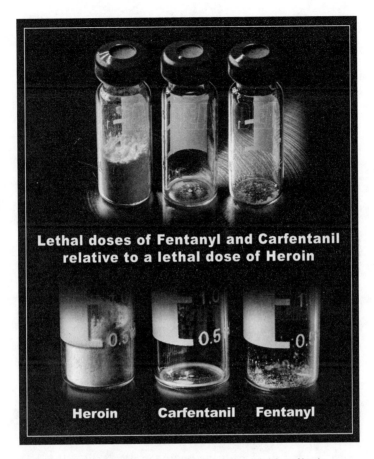

Figure 7.2 Lethal doses of fentanyl and carfentanil relative to a lethal dose of heroin
Source: DEA, 2021

amount of fentanyl, as little as 2 milligrams (the size of two grains of salt), is a fatal dose for most people (Figure 7.2). During the extended period of isolation due to COVID-19, a dramatic increase in overdose deaths connected to fentanyl-laced drugs was documented.[6] As an example, San Diego County was hit hard in the first half of 2020, with the fentanyl overdose cases more than doubling in comparison to 2019. According to District Attorney Summer Stephan, "dealers continue cutting various illegal drugs with fentanyl and now more than ever it's a recipe for death. The public needs to be aware of the danger of using any controlled substance even if packaged like a harmless medicinal pill. Higher overdose numbers tell us there's likely more product on the street in San Diego that may be laced with deadly fentanyl. I'm urging you to share this potentially life-saving message with your loved ones today."[7] Not unlike other geographic areas across the nation, counterfeit pills marketed as oxycodone (also known by the trade name OxyContin, for example) and/or alprazolam (also known by the trade name Xanax, for example) accounted for the majority of fentanyl-related overdose deaths in San Diego in 2020.

"While buyers may think they're getting cocaine, oxy or Xanax, in reality they're playing a high stakes game of Russian roulette," said United States Attorney Robert Brewer. "When it comes to fentanyl, there's no truth in advertising and you can forget about quality control. Hundreds of unknowing buyers end up ingesting a deadly dose of fentanyl, which has left scores of grieving San Diego families in its wake this year."

> According to Dr. Glenn Wagner, San Diego County medical examiner: Years ago when we saw a death from fentanyl toxicity, it was usually someone misusing an excess of their legally prescribed medicine; but today almost all of the fentanyl deaths that we see result from people that have taken counterfeit pills sold illegally as oxycodone or alprazolam (but containing fentanyl instead of the other drugs). These pills are deadly and even just part of one pill kills.[7]

How does cocaine affect the brain and behavior?

The reason that cocaine is so addictive is because the short-term effects of it are intensely pleasant. It makes people feel very happy, energetic, and alert. Some people find that it helps them get things done efficiently. These pleasant feelings are the result of cocaine's effect on our natural brain chemical, dopamine, which is released when we experience positive emotions such as joy and pleasure (Figure 7.3). Normally, our brain cells communicate with each other to trigger the release of dopamine. One cell releases the dopamine, and the next cell "receives" it, causing a person to feel those pleasant sensations and feelings. Then, whatever dopamine is left in the space between the cells gets recycled back into the cell to be used later. Cocaine use interferes with that recycling process, so that the extra dopamine in between those cells accumulates. When the reward center in the brain is flooded with these unusually large amounts of dopamine repeatedly, the brain begins to adapt, and the intensely pleasurable feelings that were once brought on by all this excess dopamine begin to diminish. When that happens, the dose of cocaine that once made a person feel really amazing doesn't do much anymore, and they have to take progressively larger doses for the brain to react the same way. This is how cocaine addiction develops, and explains why you might hear about people with addiction trying to "chase that first high." It becomes more and more difficult for the brain to come back to that first high, and as that happens, and a person uses larger amounts of cocaine, both the experience when high and the aftereffects of that can become very unpleasant.

You might be wondering how the experience when a person is high on cocaine, a drug that is known for making people feel happy and even euphoric, can become unpleasant. If you think about the psychological experiences a person might have while taking a stimulant as ranging from mild to extreme, it will be easiest to picture how this could happen. Let's say someone uses a small amount of cocaine and it makes them feel happy, talkative, and energetic. That would be a somewhat mild and very positive psychological reaction. Now, let's say they take a little more and they begin to feel not only intensely happy but also excited and very alert. This might be a moderate psychological reaction that is mostly positive, but imagine if they took more. What would *extremely* alert feel like? It might make

Some drugs target the brain's pleasure center

Brain reward (dopamine pathways)

How drugs can increase dopamine

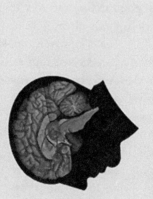

While eating food

While using cocaine

These brain circuits are important for natural rewards such as food, music, and sex.

Typically, dopamine increases in response to natural rewards such as food. When cocaine is taken, dopamine increases are exaggerated, and communication is denied.

Figure 7.3 How drugs affect the brain's reward system

Source: NIDA, 2020

a person notice things they wouldn't otherwise; for example, they might pick up more intensely on the way other peoples' facial expressions appear. It might also make them hear sounds around them more clearly or loudly. Intensifying these types of sensations is not always pleasant. Hearing loud sounds could be irritating, and being more tuned in to people's facial expressions while on a mind-altering substance might lead a person to misinterpret these expressions. Maybe someone who's very serious could seem upset or hostile. As a person's sensations and perceptions become more intense, they can become irritable, and even paranoid. Some of the symptoms reported by people taking large amounts of cocaine include anxiety, restlessness, irritability, panic, and paranoia.[8]

The aftereffects when using cocaine heavily can be unpleasant as well, and because of cocaine's short *half life* (that is, the time required for half of the drug to be cleared from the body), which is about 90 minutes,[9] withdrawal symptoms can begin a short time after a person's use of cocaine. The initial withdrawal experience is known as "the crash," a period of hours to several days involving symptoms that include:

- Feelings of exhaustion
- *Hypersomnia,* or excessive sleeping
- Absence of cocaine cravings
- Feeling sad or down
- Increased appetite
- Restlessness
- Irritability

Though there is some debate concerning the length of time it takes for cocaine withdrawal symptoms to resolve, a syndrome lasting for up to 10 weeks has been described,[10] with symptoms similar to "the crash" including:

- Feeling lethargic
- Anxiety

- Difficulty sleeping
- Strong urges or cravings to use cocaine
- Feeling moody or rapidly shifting emotions
- Trouble concentrating
- Depression
- Irritability

People with a history of clinical depression are more vulnerable to developing withdrawal symptoms, with studies showing that they are five times more likely to experience a withdrawal syndrome compared to those who don't have a history of depression[11] and tend to experience more intense cravings when in withdrawal,[12] posing greater challenges to addiction recovery. Since dependence on other substances, such as alcohol, is quite common among people who use cocaine,[13,14] discomfort can be magnified when withdrawing from multiple substances (e.g., cocaine and alcohol) at the same time.

What Are the Signs that Someone Uses Cocaine?

If you are concerned that a loved one may be using cocaine but are not sure, pay close attention to the following signs:

- Talking or moving very fast
- Shaking and twitching
- Not eating or sleeping very much
- Mood shifts between seeming very happy and acting angry or nervous
- The person goes through periods of time (e.g., days) when they seem tired and sad
- Nosebleeds (this is often a sign of using cocaine by snorting it)
- He/she has a constant runny nose
- Marks on the person's arms (this is a sign that they are injecting the drug)

Can you overdose on cocaine?

The overdose risk from cocaine is real and unfortunately increasing, as the most recent estimates show that over 24,000

Americans died from cocaine-involved overdose in 2021.[15] This follows a trend that started in 2010, when overdose deaths involving cocaine increased by more than 60% despite the fact that cocaine use was declining overall.[16] Studies have found that opioids have a central role in these rapidly shifting overdose trends,[17] which occurred alongside a growing supply of heroin and illicitly manufactured fentanyl in the United States.[18] Since fentanyl and its analogs (such as carfentanil, acetylfentanyl, butyrfentanyl, and furanyl fentanyl) are highly potent, with almost immediate effects on the brain and body (i.e., within 60 seconds), someone who either intentionally or unknowingly uses cocaine and fentanyl in combination would be very susceptible to the sudden respiratory depression (or slow, ineffective breathing) that can result from opioid use and overdose that can ultimately lead to death. As you'll learn in Chapter 12, having naloxone readily available, not only for people who primarily use opioids but also for those whose "drug of choice" is cocaine, is becoming increasingly important as a way of reversing the lethal effects of overdose.

What is methamphetamine?

Methamphetamine can take three forms, which differ mostly in their appearance and purity. The three main forms are:

- Speed (powder)
- Base
- Crystalline (ice or crystal)

Chemically similar to amphetamine, methamphetamine has an appearance as a white or yellow powder that resembles cocaine, although it can also be in pill form. This powder or pill form is commonly known as *speed,* and is generally low in purity (10% to 20%).[19] People usually take speed by sniffing it through their nose (i.e., "snorting"), swallowing it in pill or tablet form, or dissolving it in water or alcohol and injecting it. *Base* is another form of methamphetamine, often described as a damp or oily substance with a white to yellow or brown powder. It can have a "toffee-like" appearance and is also referred to as "paste," "pure," and "wax." This form has greater purity than speed, though not by a lot—whereas speed has been described as 10%–20% in purity, base is thought to be around 20%. Although some people swallow base, it is more typically injected.

Also known as "crystal meth," the purest (around 80%) and most potent form of methamphetamine has a translucent to white crystalline appearance and looks like shards of glass or shiny, white or bluish-white rocks (Figure 7.4). Crystal meth has various street names, including *ice, crystal, d-meth, glass, Tina, and blue,* and is typically smoked or injected. When smoked, usually a glass pipe, or less commonly a bong or water pipe, is used. Crystal meth is heated in the bulb of the pipe until it vaporizes, and then it is inhaled. When people smoke crystal meth in groups, they often pass it around and then allow it to re-crystallize in between use episodes.

Figure 7.4 Methamphetamine
Source: DEA, 2023
https://www.dea.gov/stories/2021/2021-08/2021-08-24/overdose-crisis-continues

How do people use methamphetamine?

Similar to cocaine, the rush that methamphetamine produces is not very long-lasting. For that reason, people tend to use methamphetamine repeatedly over bursts of time as the effects start to wear off, often referred to as a *binge and crash* pattern.[20] One common binge use pattern involves using methamphetamine every couple of hours for up to a few days, often foregoing eating and sleeping throughout. This is sometimes referred to as a "run." At the other extreme, a person who takes methamphetamine in pill form must patiently wait out a period of delay before they will begin to feel its effects, which sometimes leads to premature, repeated dosing. This can be dangerous because a person can unknowingly place themselves at risk for overdose by taking more and more while waiting for the drug to "work."

Like cocaine, the intensity of the experience people have when they use methamphetamine varies, depending on both the *form* (e.g., crystal meth versus speed, etc.), and the method they use to take it (e.g., swallowing versus smoking or injecting). People who swallow methamphetamine in pill form will experience a "high" within 15 or 20 minutes. This is often referred to as a "euphoric" feeling, meaning intense excitement and/or happiness. Snorting methamphetamine leads to a faster high, within three to five minutes.[21] By contrast, the two methods that produce the most immediate and intense effect on the brain and body, smoking and injecting, lead the person to feel an amplified "rush" or "flash" lasting only a couple of minutes. Although a "rush" may sound similar to a high, they are not the same. The magnitude of the pleasure is much greater when a person experiences a "rush," increasing the risk of developing an addiction to methamphetamine.

One of the most consistent findings from research on methamphetamine use is that *injecting it* leads to a host of medical, psychiatric, and other life problems and makes recovery from this addiction especially difficult. Injecting methamphetamine increases the risk of transmission of HIV and Hepatitis C, as well as fatal overdose. People who inject methamphetamine are also more likely to experience psychological symptoms such as depression, anxiety, and psychosis, or a loss of touch with reality, and they report suicidal thoughts and behaviors more frequently than those who do not inject methamphetamine.[22] A disturbing trend in recent years is emerging, with people who inject methamphetamine *also* smoking the drug, and/or other stimulants such as crack cocaine. Those who use stimulants in both of these ways tend to use methamphetamine more heavily, inject it more often, and have higher rates of violent behavior and criminal activity than those who either inject or smoke it.[23] Complicating the picture even more is the observation of increasing injection use of opioids such as heroin or fentanyl and methamphetamine together,[24] a high-risk practice that is contributing to rising overdose deaths.

How is methamphetamine manufactured?

Methamphetamine is mostly made in "superlabs" in the United States and Mexico. However, ever since the mid 1990s, when individuals who used methamphetamine discovered that they could easily produce it themselves using highly accessible, over-the-counter products like cold medicines, smaller "mom and pop" meth labs were set up in homes, motel rooms, and other small spaces (e.g., trailers), and emerged as a method used by individuals to support their own continuing methamphetamine addiction. Using methods known as "one pot method" and "shake and bake," using ephedrine or pseudoephedrine tablets, typically these smaller scale mom and pop labs, also known as "box labs," produce less than a few ounces of methamphetamine at a time, compared to superlabs which make 80 to 100 pounds of methamphetamine in a single "cook" cycle. Given the small quantities, those who cook meth in these home- or motel-based labs generally use the meth they make or sell it to their friends. Home-based meth lab supplies and equipment can fit into a compact space such as a suitcase, trunk of a car, or bathtub. Word spreads readily about the procedures for manufacturing meth in this way, and some of those who run mom and pop or box labs teach their friends about these production methods.

One of the key over-the-counter ingredients for making meth is pseudoephedrine, which is found in commonly used, over-the-counter decongestants like Sudafed. In 2005, legislative efforts to curb methamphetamine manufacture introduced the Combat Methamphetamine Act, which imposed monitoring requirements and limitations around the quantities of pseudoephedrine-containing products that could be purchased per day. These requirements went into effect in early 2006. With regulations varying by state and local jurisdiction, some states allowed no more than three packages of ephedrine- or pseudoephedrine-containing products at a time, with more restrictive states, such as Oregon and Mississippi, even requiring a prescription for pseudoephedrine-containing products. Restrictions on other chemical ingredients used to manufacture methamphetamine were also imposed in Mexico. Between 2010 and 2017, the results of these collective efforts became increasingly clear: domestic production of methamphetamine decreased dramatically, with 80% fewer domestic methamphetamine laboratory incidents in the United States.[25] By 2017, data on domestic seizures painted a very different picture of domestic methamphetamine production, which had shifted primarily to "mom and pop" type lab settings.[26] Unfortunately, however, where there is a will there's a way. The rise of "smurfing" as a method to acquire ingredients and supplies for making methamphetamine posed new challenges to the intense efforts to curb production of this devastatingly destructive addictive drug.

"Smurfing" is a slang term for driving from one retailer or pharmacy to the next to gather and hoard supplies needed to manufacture methamphetamine; the term is based on the little blue animated "Smurfs," cartoon characters who used similar methods to gather supplies for their village and community. A "smurf" is someone who buys small quantities of ingredients known as *methamphetamine precursor chemicals*, or those chemicals that are needed to produce methamphetamine (including pseudoephedrine-containing products, ice packs, iodine, and lithium) from different locations. Although retailers who sell these products are required to report any suspicious purchasing patterns to the police, and legislation passed after the 2005 ephedrine/pseudoephedrine restrictions made it illegal to hoard these medicines through smurfing operations, smurfing remains problematic. Sometimes people with methamphetamine addiction themselves get involved in smurfing so that they can trade the pills or supplies they gather for methamphetamine to support or maintain their addiction. When hired by drug dealers, smurfs turn over their receipts for the cold medicines that they purchased and are paid as much as triple their "investment" in return.

Some methamphetamine precursor chemical traffickers involve multiple associates in their smurfing operations to acquire large quantities of pseudoephedrine in short periods of time. In 2020, a Pennsylvania man described as a "meth lab mastermind" was arrested, along with his six smurfs, whom he allegedly compensated for gathering supplies and "keeping watch" with steady fixes of the meth he cooked,[27] which totaled around 2000 grams or 4.5 pounds per batch.

Small methamphetamine labs are extremely dangerous for many reasons. First, the chemicals that are used to manufacture methamphetamine are extremely hazardous, including acetone, anhydrous ammonia (fertilizer), ether, red phosphorus, and lithium. Some of these chemicals are especially volatile and can ignite or explode if they are not stored or handled properly. A man inside one home-based methamphetamine lab that exploded in Fresno, California, suffered from burns that affected over 70% of his body. Thankfully, other families and children in neighboring homes were not harmed by the fire. In other cases, innocent bystanders have been less fortunate. Early in 2020, a home-based methamphetamine lab explosion in Lilburn, Georgia, killed three children, ages 3, 4, and 18 months, and the 34-year-old man responsible has been sentenced to 30 years in prison.

Apart from the risk of fires and explosions, the byproducts that emerge from cooking methamphetamine in these labs are toxic to the environment and to people who are exposed to them for extended periods of time. Health risks from exposure to the toxic chemicals that are used to produce methamphetamine include both short- and long-term problems. Well documented health effects include:

- Intoxication
- Dizziness
- Nausea
- Feeling disoriented
- Loss of coordination
- Shortness of breath, cough, and chest pain from inhalation of vapors and gases
- Burns, which are often severe, resulting from chemicals used in methamphetamine production making contact with one's skin
- Pulmonary edema, a condition caused by excess fluid in the lungs, making breathing difficult
- Damage to internal organs

Accidental ingestion of toxic chemicals, for which young children who are in meth laboratory settings are at high risk, is associated with a range of devastating health impacts, including poisoning that can be fatal, internal chemical burns, organ damage, and harm to brain and immune system functioning.

Apart from the risks posed to individuals involved and geographically close to methamphetamine production, the environmental hazards from toxic waste generated in the process can pose health risks long after a laboratory has been shut down. To put this into perspective, for every pound of methamphetamine that is produced in a laboratory, five to seven pounds of toxic waste are produced.[28] People who cook methamphetamine in these labs often dump the waste improperly near or around the lab location, which can cause contamination of the nearby soil and water supply. For these reasons, the US Environmental Protection Agency has provided guidance on the proper cleanup of methamphetamine labs,[29] and for deciding when a former methamphetamine laboratory is clean enough to enable one to live there safely again.

With domestic production of methamphetamine at its lowest point since 2000, the majority of methamphetamine available in America today is manufactured in Mexico and smuggled across the Southwest border. Methamphetamine produced in Mexico has a high level of purity (over 90%), is extremely potent, and is inexpensive, making this drug very appealing.

Is methamphetamine a "designer drug"?

Methamphetamine is an example of a "designer drug," or a drug that is created in an illegal laboratory (sometimes referred to as an "underground" or "clandestine" lab). Typically, designer drugs alter the properties of a substance that comes from a plant (such as cocaine, morphine, or marijuana) to create a new type of experience for those who use it. Apart from methamphetamine, designer drugs include ecstasy or MDMA, ketamine, GHB, Rohypnol, and LSD or acid. Because they are often used in night clubs, these substances are also sometimes known as "club drugs."

How does methamphetamine affect the brain and behavior?

In the short term, methamphetamine has some highly desirable effects, including reducing fatigue and increasing energy, making a person feel very awake, alert, and able to pay attention; an intense rush of pleasure or euphoria; and for those who are trying to lose weight, reduced appetite is also considered a positive. Like cocaine, the highly addictive nature of methamphetamine has to do with its effects on dopamine. But there are some important differences between cocaine and methamphetamine. First, dopamine is increased in more than one way by methamphetamine, leading to larger amounts of it in the brain, and longer periods of time in which dopamine is available when compared to cocaine. The bad news about having a drug that can release so much dopamine and keep it in the brain and body for a long time is that this excessive amount and presence of a powerful brain chemical can change the effects of its actions on the brain and behavior: dopamine can go from producing intense pleasure in the short term, to damaging certain areas of the brain over time, along with the important functions that they control.

Methamphetamine versus Cocaine: What Are the Key Differences?

Both methamphetamine and cocaine are stimulants, but the way they act on the brain and body is different in several important ways:

- Cocaine quickly leaves the body, and is almost completely metabolized.
- Methamphetamine stays in the brain and body for a long time.
- Cocaine prevents dopamine from being recycled into cells, making it available in the brain for longer.
- Methamphetamine not only prevents dopamine from being recycled, but it actually *increases the amount* of dopamine that is released.
- With higher concentrations of dopamine in the brain, there is greater potential for toxic brain effects.

Some of the long-term effects of methamphetamine that likely are related to these toxic effects of prolonged dopamine exposure include the following:

- Problems related to thinking, learning, understanding, and remembering things (also known as *cognitive* difficulties).
- Slowed motor skills.
- Anxiety and/or depression that does not resolve easily.
- Confusion.

- Violent behavior.
- Paranoia, or extreme fear that others are trying to hurt them or give them a hard time. This leads a person to distrust others.
- Hallucinations, or the perception that something is happening even though it is not real. This can include seeing things that aren't really there (*visual hallucinations*), hearing voices that aren't there (*auditory hallucinations*), or feeling sensations in one's body that aren't real (*tactile hallucinations*).
- Increased risk of Parkinson's Disease, a progressive, chronic neurological condition that affects movement, leading to shaking, stiffness, and trouble with walking, balance, and coordination.[30]

What Are the Signs that Someone Uses Methamphetamine?

If you are concerned that a loved one may be using methamphetamine, but are not sure, pay close attention to the following signs:

- Hyperactivity, or talking or moving very fast
- Visible sores on their skin, especially on their face (this is a sign that they have been scratching or digging into their skin, often because they have hallucinations that cause the sensation of bugs or pebbles under their skin)
- Burns on their lips or fingers (from holding hot meth pipes)
- Not eating or sleeping very much
- Mood can change very quickly, from excited to angry and/or violent
- Burns on lips or fingers (from holding a hot pipe used to smoke methamphetamine)
- Feeling afraid that someone is trying to hurt them or "out to get them" (this is paranoia, a sign of methamphetamine psychosis)
- Marks on the person's arms (this is a sign that they are injecting the drug)
- Expressing suicidal thoughts, or desires to end one's life

Can you overdose on methamphetamine?

Like cocaine, a person can overdose on methamphetamine. When this happens, the drug reaches toxic levels in the brain and body, which can lead to a number of physical and mental health complications. Physically, a person who overdoses on methamphetamine is at risk of stroke, heart attack, or other organ problems.

Methamphetamine overdoses are following a concerning upward trend, with nearly 24,000 drug overdose deaths having involved methamphetamine in 2020, increasing to over 32,000 people in 2021.[31] According to the Centers for Disease Control, mixing methamphetamine with opioids, either intentionally or unintentionally, appears to be behind at least half of these overdose deaths, and of those, 50% involved the synthetic opioid fentanyl. Apart from the lethal effects of combining methamphetamine with opioids and other substances, overdosing on methamphetamine can lead to hyperthermia (elevated body temperature) and convulsions, which can be fatal if not treated immediately.

What are prescription stimulants?

Among the 55 countries that adopted the use of medications to treat ADHD in 2003, the United States accounted for more than 92% of the world's spending on these medicines, despite comprising less than 5% of the world population. More recently, prescription stimulant use was found to have more than doubled between 2006 and 2016 even though diagnoses for ADHD increased by very little. And, among commercial insurance plans, the per-patient spending for medication for attention disorders was higher than for asthma, heart disease, or high cholesterol. Misuse of prescription stimulants is common, affecting over 5 million people (nearly one-third of those for whom prescription stimulants were prescribed)[32] and is highly problematic on college campuses in the United States and abroad.[33]

Prescription Stimulants: Why Do People Misuse Them?

Studies show that the most common reasons people misuse prescription stimulants are for the same purposes for which they are prescribed, but as a person loses control over their use of these medications they risk becoming addicted to them, suffering psychiatric and medical complications including death by overdose. Most commonly, people who misuse prescription stimulants access them from one of two sources: (1) friends or relatives, and/or (2) prescriptions or healthcare providers.

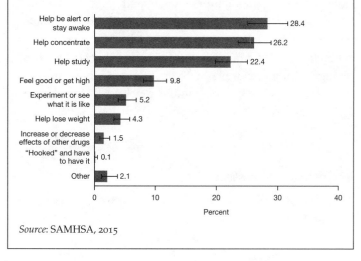

Source: SAMHSA, 2015

Misuse can occur in different ways: some people take these medicines without a prescription; others may take them for a reason other than what the doctor prescribed them for, and many will take them in greater quantities, more often, or over a longer period than they were prescribed. All these forms of misuse are concerning, because adverse effects of excessive stimulant use are not uncommon and can include loss of appetite, anxiety, paranoia, hallucinations, insomnia, increased heart rate, and death. Though these effects are rarely reported among those who are taking prescription stimulants as they are prescribed, misusing them—including long-term use at higher doses than prescribed, and use of these substances intravenously or by crushing up and snorting them (i.e., intranasally)—increases the risk of severe or life-threatening side effects. The most commonly prescribed stimulants include:

- Methylphenidate (trade names, for example, include Ritalin)
- Amphetamine and dextroamphetamine compounds (trade names, for example, include Adderall, Adderall XR, Dexedrine)

Many people wonder why people are misusing prescription stimulants in the first place. Research has shown that the most commonly described reasons that people aged 12 or older misuse prescription stimulants are to help stay awake or alert, concentrate (also known as "cognitive enhancement"), and as a study aid.[32] Less commonly reported reasons, including to get high and help lose weight, are also displayed in the figure above. Young people including teens have described their use of prescription stimulants for the purposes of getting high as something they believe to be a "safer" alternative to taking street drugs. This is a very common misperception that public health officials have been working hard to correct. Another common belief is that misusing prescription stimulants enhances academic performance. Studies actually contradict this notion, demonstrating that stimulant misuse is linked with poorer academic performance.[34] While it is true that, when taken as prescribed, prescription stimulants can be very helpful to people at varying age ranges, when they are taken in doses and/or in ways that they were not prescribed, or by people for whom they were not prescribed, there is often other drug use going on at the same time, which can lead to behaviors (e.g., skipping classes) that can put one's academic performance in jeopardy.

How do stimulants affect the brain?

When a person first uses a stimulant, the acute, short-term effects can be very pleasurable. Stimulants produce euphoria, or an intense rush of positive emotion and sensation. In addition, people who use stimulants can become more talkative, energetic, and self-confident. They often feel more sexual. Other desirable effects include suppressed appetite and feeling less fatigued. Alongside these symptoms, the body undergoes various changes as the central nervous system becomes activated: breathing becomes more rapid, body temperature increases, blood pressure becomes higher, and one's heartbeat becomes faster.

Like other addictive drugs, stimulants produce these short-term effects by changing the brain's reward circuits. Though drugs have different ways of changing these circuits, both cocaine and methamphetamine tamper with the brain's system for releasing dopamine, a naturally occurring brain chemical that is released during pleasurable experiences. Because the use of these drugs overstimulates the brain's nerve cells, causing them to release unusually large quantities of dopamine (far larger than the amount that is released during a healthy, pleasurable activity such as eating a delicious food or connecting with a friend or loved one), powerful connections begin to form in the brain between stimulant use and intense pleasure. Naturally, this leads to a desire to repeat the experience. Over time, this desire can take the form of an intense urge or craving for the drug, and one that is incredibly difficult to resist.

The connections that are formed in the brain between stimulant use and pleasure are even more elaborate than they may sound, because the memory of how incredibly good a person felt when they used stimulants can return and trigger strong cravings under two conditions, either alone or in combination: (1) when a person has access to stimulants and is preparing to or anticipating using them, and (2) in the presence of *cues* that remind them of past experiences when they have used them. After repeated stimulant use, the brain will begin to release dopamine when a person encounters these cues, even if they are not using or under the influence of stimulants at that time. In treatment for stimulant addiction, these cues are referred to as "relapse triggers," because their association with the pleasurable sensations brought on by using stimulants creates a chain reaction. First, dopamine is released: this acts as "teaser," leading to a series of thoughts and emotions that a person with an addiction may or may not be aware of because they happen so quickly and automatically. While releasing dopamine, the addicted part of the brain initiates an inner dialogue to motivate drug use; it says, "Hey, remember how good it felt when you used? You need that right now. Let's go get it." Next, if the person is not able to resist that inner voice, they begin the sequence of actions that are referred to as "drug-seeking," and even that process can trigger more dopamine release, as the events involved in procuring drugs are often described by those with addictions as "exciting," bringing them closer to achieving the goal of repeating that high. Cues that begin this chain reaction can include places where the person has used stimulants, people with whom they have used drugs, or even paraphernalia that were part of their drug use experience (e.g., pipes they used for smoking it, or syringes they used to inject drugs). Cues can also be internal, such as an emotional state that the person has enhanced (e.g., excitement) or alleviated (e.g., sadness/depression or boredom) by using drugs in the past. The powerful memories associated with these cues both support and strengthen repetition of drug use. The more frequently a person uses stimulants, the more places, situations, people, and emotions become linked with that pleasurable experience in their memory. This is how a person's brain begins to "learn" to take stimulants over and over again.

What are the health risks of stimulant use?

When stimulant use becomes prolonged or chronic, a variety of physical and psychiatric health problems can develop, including cardiovascular, pulmonary, and neurological illnesses, dental and skin-related problems, as well as depression and anxiety symptoms, mood instability, paranoia, psychosis, and violence. These risks are explored in further detail below.

What are the physical health risks of using stimulants?

Given the recent rise in fentanyl-adulterated cocaine and methamphetamine, lethal overdose is the most life-threatening risk of stimulant use. Because fentanyl is such a potent opioid, and a person buying stimulants on the street has no way of knowing how much fentanyl has been mixed into them, the risk of overdose resulting from stimulant use is very high, especially among people who inject stimulants.

Cardiovascular effects. Stimulants can have a variety of adverse effects on the cardiovascular system and, in fact, cardiovascular complications following overdose and accidents are the second leading cause of death among people who use methamphetamine.[35] Studies documenting the most common cardiovascular problems bringing those who use stimulants to the emergency room have found chest pain, hypertension (high blood pressure), shortness of breath, and tachycardia (rapid heartbeat) to be some of the most frequent complaints. Although these are transient symptoms that come and go for some people, research has shown that for one-quarter of those who visited the ER with cardiovascular symptoms following methamphetamine use, severe chest pain and discomfort resulted from acute coronary syndrome,[36] a serious medical condition in which sudden, reduced blood flow to the heart either causes or places the person at high risk for a heart attack. Acute coronary syndrome causes severe chest pain or discomfort that begins abruptly, and may be accompanied by other symptoms such as nausea or vomiting, indigestion, shortness of breath, sudden heavy sweating, and lightheadedness, dizziness, or fainting.

The reason that stimulant use, either in the short or long term, can lead to acute coronary syndrome is by causing what is known as acute myocardial ischemia. When a person has ischemia, this means that there is not enough blood flow going to one of the body's organs. When that organ is a person's heart, the ischemia is referred to as *myocardial*. Since the reduced blood flow to an ischemic organ causes it to lack all the nutrients and oxygen it needs, the affected organ begins to malfunction. One of the effects of prolonged or severe malfunctioning of an organ is that its cells can die. When the cells of the heart die, this called an *infarction*, more commonly known as a heart attack. This is a common cardiovascular complication of both methamphetamine and cocaine use. Other cardiovascular problems caused by stimulant use include cardiac arrhythmias (irregular heartbeat), sudden cardiovascular collapse, and cardiogenic shock, a severe form of heart failure in which a person's heart suddenly can't pump enough blood to meet the body's needs. Studies show that *combining stimulants with alcohol or opioids* results in larger amounts of stimulant present in the bloodstream, leading to increased, prolonged cardiovascular risks.[37]

Recent research has shown that there is hope for cardiovascular health among those who are in recovery from stimulant addiction. In 2017, a team of scientists at Johns Hopkins School of Medicine studied changes in cardiovascular health among 700 adults with a history of cocaine use. They examined how reducing or abstaining from cocaine use affected the amount and types of coronary plaques, which are indicators of premature atherosclerosis or "hardening of the arteries." Those who responded well to addiction treatment and cut back or abstained completely from cocaine use experienced a reduction in atherosclerotic plaques, without taking medicines that are usually needed to achieve this such as cholesterol-lowering statin drugs. This suggests that addiction recovery can reverse the process of atherosclerosis for those who use stimulants, preventing coronary artery disease.[38] Abstinence from drugs such as methamphetamine have been described as the "bedrock of reversibility" of cardiovascular disease; even heart muscle damage, known as cardiomyopathy, can heal with successful treatment of metham-phetamine addiction, combined with medications.[39]

Pulmonary Effects. Since many people use stimulant drugs by smoking them, lung illnesses and damage can be chronic and severe. Lung illness frequently affects those who smoke crack cocaine, with symptoms including coughing, wheezing, chest pain, *dyspnea* or shortness of breath, worsening of a pre-existing asthma condition, and bronchitis. *Hemoptysis,* or coughing up blood, and black sputum are also common. Certain respiratory complications of stimulant use are caused by contaminants or additives contained in the drugs; for example, when people in-ject drugs with foreign materials such as talc, they can develop a disease known as *foreign body granulomatosis of the lungs.* This illness is irreversible, develops when these materials become lodged in capillaries (tiny blood vessels) in the lungs, results in worsening lung function over time, and eventually may re-quire a lung transplant.[40] Other potentially serious conditions that can develop from long-term stimulant use are *pulmonary edema,* a condition caused by excess fluid in the lungs, or *pulmonary hypertension,* a type of high blood pressure that affects arteries in the lungs and the heart.

How Do Stimulants Damage the Heart?

Stimulants have been linked to many forms of heart disease. Here are a few types of cardiovascular complications of stimulant use, and why they happen.

Cocaine use restricts blood flow to the heart muscle, limiting the amount of oxygen that can be delivered. This places the cardiovascular system under stress, leading to conditions that include the following:

- *Hypertension* or high blood pressure.
- *Coronary spasm,* which is a tightening of one of the arteries that sends blood to your heart. This can reduce or block blood flow to the heart, causing chest pain, and even a heart attack.
- *Atherosclerosis,* or hardening of arteries and capillaries, which increases the risk of coronary artery disease.

- *Aortic dissection*, which is a sudden tearing of the wall of the aorta.
- *Heart attacks,* resulting either from acute or chronic changes in blood flow to the heart.
- *Coronary artery aneurysms*, dilation of coronary arteries, which can cause a heart attack.
- *Cardiomyopathy*, or damage to the heart muscle.

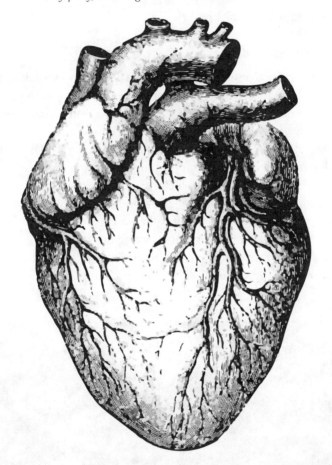

The cardiovascular complications of methamphetamine use share quite a bit of overlap with those from cocaine use, including hypertension, blood vessel spasms, heart attacks and cardiomyopathy. In addition, methamphetamine can cause inflammation of the blood vessels, which can lead to *strokes* and *endocarditis,* an inflammation of the heart valves that can result from injection drug use.

Within 12 hours of stimulant use, acute pulmonary symptoms are experienced in a large proportion of those who use stimulants by smoking them, with nearly half of those who use cocaine reporting coughing of black sputum, and about four in 10 experiencing chest pain;[41] however, these symptoms can resolve among nearly 70% of people who are in recovery from stimulant addiction.[42,43]

Effects on teeth and skin

The use of methamphetamine has been widely known to lead to severe dental problems. Commonly known as "meth mouth," black, rotting, and crumbling teeth with severe tooth decay and gum disease often distinguish those who use methamphetamine in their physical appearance (see Figure 7.5). There are a few reasons that methamphetamine use leads to this condition: first, the addiction itself can lead to poor self-care, which can include long periods of poor oral hygiene. People who use methamphetamine forget to brush their teeth and, at the same time, maintain poor diets, seeking out sodas and sweets, which damages tooth enamel. Sometimes called "buzzing," consuming sugary foods and sodas while high is brought on

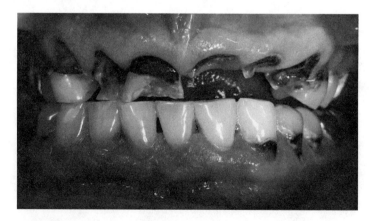

Figure 7.5 Dental effects of methamphetamine use
Source: Shutterstock

by intense and frequent cravings for refined carbohydrates. Second, using methamphetamine can lead to *xerostomia*, or severe dry mouth, which reduces the availability of saliva. The enzymes in our saliva are needed to kill the bacteria that cause cavities and gum disease; without it, people who use methamphetamine suffer from progressive decay along the gumline. Third, methamphetamine use can lead to extensive tooth grinding, also known as *bruxism*, as well as jaw clenching, which, over time, can result in tooth fractures and even tooth loss. Bruxism may arise out of anxiety and restlessness, especially in early recovery from methamphetamine addiction. This can also lead to temporomandibular joint syndrome (TMJ), a painful condition involving the jaw, causing pain in the jaw joint and the surrounding muscles that control jaw movement.

In later stages of oral health decline among those with meth mouth, the cycle of neglectful dental hygiene, chronic dry mouth, gum disease, and a high-sugar diet can lead teeth to decay to the gumline, causing them to fall out. In recent years, studies have shown that the most severely affected individuals who use methamphetamine are those who are over the age of 30. In general, the longer and the more heavily a person uses methamphetamine, the more serious their dental problems are.[44] Cigarette smokers who use methamphetamine appear to be at especially high risk of oral disease, with more cavities and tooth loss than that of nonsmokers. Sadly, nearly half of those with methamphetamine addiction, when surveyed, report that they are embarrassed about their teeth, smile, or their overall appearance as it relates to their dental disease. In recovery, restoring dental health is often an important focus to help someone with a methamphetamine addiction return to a normal life.

In addition to dental disease, use of stimulants can lead to skin damage. People who use methamphetamine can experience what are known as *tactile hallucinations*, which involves feeling like something is touching them when there is nothing really there. This is somewhat like a visual hallucination (i.e., a condition where a person sees imaginary things that aren't actually there)—it involves the false perception that something is there, even though, in reality this is not the case. It is different from a visual hallucination in that it doesn't necessarily involve seeing something; it is based on a physical sensation that leads to some false perceptions that are not grounded in reality. The most common tactile hallucinations people experience when using methamphetamine is the perception that there are bugs crawling under their skin. This leads to excessive scratching and skin-picking, which can cause *excoriations* or scratch marks, and *skin ulcers*, or open sores.

Apart from skin scratches, sores that eventually are likely to scar, and infections that can result from bacteria entering these open sores, there are also skin-related problems that affect people who use stimulants by injecting them. In fact, skin and soft tissue infection are the most common cause for hospital admission of individuals who inject drugs.[45] People who inject stimulants often report *cellulitis*, a common and potentially serious bacterial infection of the skin and tissues that results from injecting bacteria from used or dirty needles, or from not cleaning and disinfecting the skin prior to injecting drugs. Some people lick their skin or use saliva at the injection site rather than using alcohol to kill bacteria, not realizing that rather than removing bacteria, these practices can introduce harmful oral bacteria, increasing the chances of infection. Often a complication of cellulitis, *abscesses* can also result from the introduction of bacteria into the skin and soft tissues. An abscess is an infection of the skin and soft tissue that causes pus to collect under the skin, which, when untreated, can lead to serious health problems.

What Places People Who Use Stimulants At Risk for Skin Infections?

Skin-Popping
Stimulants like cocaine can be injected intradermally (meaning just below the skin's surface), or subcutaneously (meaning it is injected into the tissue layers beneath the skin layers). These methods of delivering

stimulants into the body are also known as "skin-popping." People who use stimulants use these techniques for various reasons. Some who were, at one time, injecting the drug into their veins, become frustrated because they are no longer able to easily access their veins. This can happen when the skin becomes hardened and/or scarred, leading one to "switch" to skin-popping. Some simply miss the vein and inadvertently skin pop. Another reason that people use this method is because the effects of the drug last longer than when it is injected directly into the veins. Though this produces less of a "high," for those who are trying to avoid going into uncomfortable withdrawals, extending the amount of time the drug will last may be preferable to getting a "rush." Studies show that skin-popping is the strongest risk factor for abscesses among those who inject drugs.[a]

Other Injection Practices

The use of unsanitary injection practices, including reusing needles and failing to clean the injection site properly, is a risk factor for skin infections. Research shows that using alcohol to clean the skin prior to injection reduced the likelihood of infection. Another injection practice that is problematic is *booting*, or drawing back blood in the syringe prior to injecting a drug. This has been shown to increase the likelihood of skin infections.

Drug Type

Certain types of drugs can raise the risk of infection, especially those that are adulterated or cut with other substances that can irritate the skin and soft tissues. "Speedballing," or mixing heroin with crack cocaine and injecting it, has been found in studies to increase the risk of abscesses.[a,b]

---

[a] Murphy, E. L., DeVita, D., Liu, H., Vittinghoff, E., Leung, P., Ciccarone, D. H., & Edlin, B. R. (2001). Risk factors for skin and soft-tissue abscesses among injection drug users: A case-control study. *Clinical Infectious Diseases, 33*(1), 35–40.

[b] Khalil, P. N., Huber-Wagner, S., Altheim, S., Bürklein, D., Siebeck, M., Hallfeldt, K., Mutschler, W., & Kanz, G. G. (2008). Diagnostic and treatment options for skin and soft tissue abscesses in injecting drug users with consideration of the natural history and concomitant risk factors. *European Journal of Medical Research, 13*(9), 415–424.

Neurological problems

Stimulant use can lead to a range of neurological symptoms and problems; cocaine use has been linked with headaches, seizures, strokes, and coma. While rare, sudden deaths do occur from cocaine use, sometimes following a person's first time using the drug. Deaths that occur from cocaine use are usually the result of either cardiac arrest or seizures.[46] When a person uses cocaine over a long period of time, neurological effects may include *intracerebral hemorrhage,* which is bleeding within the brain, bulges in the walls of the brain's blood vessels, and movement disorders such as Parkinson's Disease.[47] In relation to a person's intellectual functioning, both cocaine and methamphetamine use can compromise memory and the ability to sustain attention.

Some of the important cognitive functions that are affected by stimulant use propel a person deeper into their addiction, making it more difficult to recover. Chronic use of stimulants causes the part of our brain that enables us to control our impulses to become impaired. Sometimes referred to as *impulse inhibition,* our ability to resist our impulses and exercise sound judgment when making choices is compromised by long-term stimulant use. Let's take Anabelle as an example.

Anabelle is a student in law school who has been taking Adderall that she got from a friend to help her concentrate when studying and doing her assignments. She had started using Adderall in college, and she found it extremely helpful, and though she felt bothered by her increasing dependence on it to ensure high academic performance, she continued to use it anyway because she often worried that her grades would slip if she tried to work without it. She has also been smoking weed for a number of years, usually in the evenings to unwind and to take the edge off, since Adderall sometimes makes her feel overly stimulated and unable to sleep. Over time, the cycle of Adderall and cannabis use begins to have some negative effects.

Lately, Anabelle has noticed not only that she has to take a lot more Adderall than she used to for it to be effective in helping her focus, but when it starts to wear off, she feels really down. And smoking weed doesn't really help her mood as much, as it makes her feel numb and disconnected. To regain control over her use, Anabelle makes a few rules for herself: (1) only use Adderall every other day, and (2) only smoke weed at night when there are no important exams on the following day.

But as she prepares for an upcoming exam, the urge to take Adderall is strong, along with anxiety about how her test performance will be affected if she doesn't take any. She ends up giving in and taking not only her usual dose of Adderall, but just to be sure that she's focused, she takes extra. Later that day, she feels shaky and edgy, and she is internally very upset with herself not only for breaking her rules about Adderall but also for taking more than usual and putting herself into an overly anxious state. The only way she can find to calm herself down is to smoke weed, which makes her feel even more disappointed in herself.

Anabelle clearly shows signs of an addiction to Adderall and perhaps to cannabis as well. She has developed tolerance to Adderall; she is losing control over her use of both Adderall and cannabis, as we can see from the rules that she has made for herself about when and how much to use, only to find that she is unable to keep them. She is also noticing that withdrawal from Adderall is causing her to feel depressed. Yet, in the face of all these troubling consequences, she continues to use both substances anyway. An important observation we can make about her use of Adderall on the day before her exam is that she was clearly having a hard time controlling her impulses and exercising good reasoning and judgment. When faced with the choice to take Adderall or abstain from it that day, a person without an addiction—and with their reasoning, judgment, and impulse control intact—would have thought through the potential consequences of their choices. They might think of alternatives to taking Adderall, like drinking a caffeinated beverage or two to help stay energetic and focused. They might worry that if they took extra Adderall, it could have unwanted effects. But Anabelle's ability to weigh out pros and cons, brainstorm alternative solutions, and select one, has likely become impaired by her chronic use of stimulants.

What are the mental health risks of using stimulants?

It is not uncommon for people who use methamphetamine to experience psychiatric symptoms, including irritability, anxiety, depression, and mood swings. The mood shifts that are brought on by methamphetamine's stimulating effects, followed by withdrawal from it as the drug leaves the brain and body, can at times resemble bipolar disorder, ranging from manic highs to depressive lows. When a person is under the influence of methamphetamine, they can feel and appear *manic*, meaning that their mood is elated, excitable, and at times, irritable. But as the effects of methamphetamine wear off and the brain becomes depleted of dopamine, they can feel depressed and even suicidal. A common related symptom that people experience when withdrawing from stimulants is known as *anhedonia*, or the inability to feel pleasure even when doing things that would ordinarily make them feel good (e.g., spending time with loved ones, eating food that they really like, doing activities that used to bring them joy). This symptom, in combination with anxiety and depression, can make it challenging for people to remain in treatment without relapsing in the early stages of recovery from stimulant addiction.

Psychosis is another psychiatric complication of stimulant use. Although psychotic symptoms are more common, severe, and last longer among those who use methamphetamine, people who use cocaine can also experience episodes of psychosis. Over time, a person who has experienced these symptoms can re-experience them somewhat easily, especially when under stress,[48] and even after using a small amount of methamphetamine or cocaine. The most common symptoms are hearing voices that aren't really there (known as auditory hallucinations) and seeing things that aren't really there (known as visual hallucinations). Methamphetamine use can also lead one to feel sensations that aren't really there, such as bugs crawling under one's skin (known as tactile hallucinations); for this reason, in photos of people with methamphetamine addiction there are often cuts and scabs visible on their face and body, from picking at their skin to relieve those sensations. Voices and thoughts that people experience when they are using stimulants are often accompanied by intense paranoid thoughts, which may be very frightening to the person (for example, seeing threatening strangers or police and believing that someone is after them). A more extreme form of paranoia that can emerge when someone is in a psychotic state is called *persecutory delusions,* or believing that someone is mistreating, spying on, or trying to harm them or someone close to them. These symptoms are linked to increased likelihood of violent behavior and suicidal thoughts.[49] Although these symptoms can resolve in a matter of hours or days and are treatable with psychiatric medications (such as benzodiazepines or antipsychotic medicines), among some more vulnerable individuals who first experience psychosis while under the influence of stimulants the condition can become chronic, persisting even when they are not actively using drugs. Those who develop chronic psychosis can appear very similar to a person with schizophrenia, and to manage the condition they may require the same types of medication and therapy as those with schizophrenia.

What are the available treatments for stimulant use disorders?

Currently, behavioral therapies including cognitive behavioral therapy and contingency management are the only evidence-based treatments to help people overcome stimulant addiction. Although contingency management (in which incentives or prizes are given as rewards for abstinence from stimulants, verified through urine drug test results) is the most effective behavioral treatment approach for stimulant addiction, it is underutilized for reasons you can read more about in in Chapter 11. Other approaches that have been less well studied but have some evidence of being helpful for those with stimulant addiction include exercise, mindfulness meditation-based therapy, and transcranial magnetic stimulation, which is a form of noninvasive brain stimulation.[50] The quest for medications to treat stimulant use disorders has been ongoing for some time, and while we still do not have any FDA-approved medications, recent studies have identified promising pharmaceuticals for the treatment of methamphetamine addiction.[51] These continue to be investigated in the hope of broadening the available treatment options for the pressing stimulant use problem that has complicated the current addiction and overdose crisis.

8

WHAT DO OPIOIDS DO TO THE BRAIN AND BEHAVIOR?

What are the commonly used opioids?

You've probably heard more about the dangerous and widespread impact of opioids in the media than about any other substance. That's because of the dramatic increase in overdoses that has plagued the United States over the past eight years, which we'll discuss in more detail later in this section. But first, let's get a good understanding of what opioids are, which ones are most commonly used, and how they affect the brain and body. Though there are many drugs that are classified as opioids, when we talk about addiction to opioids we are generally referring to three categories of substances:

1. *Prescription opioids*, also known as prescription analgesics, which are pain relievers that can be prescribed by a physician or other healthcare professional who is licensed to prescribe controlled substances (e.g., a nurse practitioner). Examples of commonly used prescription opioids include:
   - Hydrocodone (also known by trade names including Vicodin and Lortab)
   - Oxycodone (also known by trade names including OxyContinand Percocet)
   - Oxymorphone

- Propoxyphene (also known be trade names including Darvocet and Darvon)
- Meperidine (commonly known by the trade name Demerol)
- Codeine
- Fentanyl
- Morphine (also known by trade names including Kadian, Avinza)

2. *Heroin,* an illegal drug made from morphine, which is a natural substance found in the opium poppy plant.
3. *Synthetic opioids,* which are pain-relieving drugs that are manufactured in laboratories with a chemical structure that is very similar to natural opioids. This category of opioids includes fentanyl and tramadol.

How is an opioid different from a narcotic?

You may have heard the term *narcotic* used in reference to substances like heroin or opium, which can be confusing. What you really need to know is that there is nothing especially different between a narcotic and an opioid; the word *narcotic* is a broad term that refers to a range of substances that relieve pain. Originating from the Greek word meaning "stupor," the term *narcotic* has historically been used to describe any substance that dulled the senses and relieved pain. Although some people have used it to refer to all illegal drugs, it technically encompasses only opioids. To avoid confusion, the preferred term is now *opioid.*

How is an opiate different from an opioid?

You have probably heard the terms opioid and opiate used interchangeably—does this mean that they are the same, and if so, why there are two terms to describe the same drug? Though the difference is subtle, they are actually not the same: an *opiate* is a natural opioid that is a product of the poppy plant, which includes morphine and codeine. The term *opioid* is broad and refers to both natural and synthetic or man-made opioids.

How do people misuse opioids?

When opioids are used or taken as prescribed, they can have a range of therapeutic effects, including providing effective treatment for pain and controlling uncomfortable symptoms of other illnesses such as diarrhea and coughing. Taking opioid medications in the short term and as prescribed is both safe and helpful to many people. Opioid use becomes hazardous when people:

1. take more than is prescribed and/or take them more often than they are prescribed;
2. administer them in ways other than the way they are intended to be taken (for example, opening capsules, crushing pills and snorting or sniffing the powder, or dissolving the powdered form or capsule content in water and injecting it into a vein);
3. take illicit forms of opioids, with unknown content (e.g., other substances the drug has been cut with) or potency;
4. take prescription drugs to get high;
5. get and take prescription opioid pills that belong to someone else, such as a friend or family member, possibly prescribed for a medical condition; and
6. take them in combination with other substances, including alcohol, benzodiazepines, and/or other "downers" that could affect their respiratory system and other essential bodily functions.

There are some opioids that aren't available by prescription, such as heroin, and people only use these in efforts to get high.

Why are young people using opioids?

Research studies show that preteens and teens begin taking opioids because of curiosity, peer pressure, and the desire to fit in with their friends.[1] Young people are especially vulnerable to opioid use if they struggle with psychological problems such as depression and anxiety, because some of them may initiate opioid or other drug use as a way of coping with these emotions. One of the toughest challenges to preventing early initiation of substance use among teens and preteens is that, in the face of psychological symptoms that they haven't experienced before, they may not understand why they don't feel quite right (for example, a teen may find that they're having a little trouble catching their breath, or pressing their fingers very tightly around their pencil and pushing their feet intensely into the ground when sitting at their desk, but do not recognize these experiences as indicators of anxiety and tension). If they don't talk about these feelings or experiences, parents may assume that nothing is wrong, especially since many of these symptoms aren't visible to others. And the teen may not realize that something isn't right, instead passing off mental health symptoms as a normal part of the transition from childhood into the teenage years. Yet the discomfort of some of these problems can lead them to want to avoid their feelings and the stressors they face during this challenging transitional time in life. Getting high is one easy way to do that. Research also suggests that a young person's risk for initiating opioid and other drug use early on is strongly affected by their important role models. If a young person has immediate family members (e.g., parents, siblings) whom they observe using alcohol and drugs, this increases the likelihood that they will do the same.[2]

How Can You Tell If a Preteen or Teen is Misusing Opioids?

Changes in behavior can tip you off if a young person you know has been involved with opioids or other drugs. Here are a few to watch for:

- Changes in hygiene habits, such as not brushing their hair or teeth or skipping showers
- Mood swings
- Not getting along with friends and/or family

- Changes in school performance, such as grades and attendance (i.e., skipping classes)
- Changes in eating and sleeping habits (either doing more *or* less of either or both)
- Loss of interest in activities that used to bring the person pleasure
- Getting into trouble at school and/or with law enforcement

How common is opioid use among teens?

Thanks to prevention and outreach efforts from parents and communities over more than a decade, use of Vicodin, one of the most popular prescription opioids among young people, has been declining since 2009—whereas over 10% of 12th-graders reported having misused Vicodin prior to 2009, that rate has decreased to 1.7%.[3] While opioid use has been generally trending downward among teens and adults alike, the rate of opioid misuse begins to increase after the age of 18, with 5.3% of those between ages 18 and 25 reporting past-year opioid misuse.[6] Having early and frequent conversations with teens about drugs is one of the most important things parents can do to prevent the onset of addiction in young people as they transition into adulthood. Experimenting with opioids is very dangerous because of their high potential for addiction and overdose, and educating young people about these risks can make for difficult, but impactful, conversations.

Max's story is an example of a teen who turned to opioids following some traumatic events during his teenage years.

Max's Story

Max was the oldest of two, with a younger brother, Leo. At the young age of 13, Max's mother became very ill with leukemia, and not long after her diagnosis she sadly passed away. This marked a turning point for the entire family. Consumed with grief, Max's father became quite disengaged from Max and Leo, and they both felt alone. They had the freedom to do pretty much whatever they wanted, as their father worked long hours, leaving a lot of idle time for them to fill. Both Max and Leo tried to just move on with life, with no way to process the loss of their mom and the incredible void it left in their family life.

Less than a year after Max lost his mother, an older friend introduced him to marijuana, and he started to smoke with him now and then. Gradually over the years that followed, Max's involvement with drugs expanded. When he reached his junior year, one of his school friends offered him Adderall. They went to the school bathroom, crushed it up, and snorted it. Once he had opened that door, it wasn't such a far stretch for him to experiment with other substances. When one of his friends got hold of Vicodin (a prescription opioid) from his father's medicine cabinet, Max crushed and snorted it, and began using it periodically. Max was struggling with anxiety, grief, and depression throughout high school. Using drugs gave him some respite from these difficult feelings, especially in the absence of support he desperately needed from his family.

When Max entered college, he was surprised to learn that drugs were very readily available, with students all around him selling benzodiazepines, prescription stimulants, marijuana, and prescription opioids. While he was there, he started using "blues," or 30 milligram pills of oxycodone, crushing and snorting them just as he had done with Vicodin when he was in high school. Over the course of a year, he developed such a high degree of tolerance that he was up to using 10 to 15 oxycodone pills per day. At $30 a pill, this became very expensive, and Max began thinking about how unsustainable that felt. Having experienced increasingly frequent withdrawal symptoms that left him no choice but to continue to use prescription opioids daily, he started talking himself into transitioning to heroin. "It's the same chemical, I'm already using it," he found himself saying. "I already know what it does, because it's the life I'm living every day right now." And at $50 a day to support the heroin equivalent to the prescription opioids he had been using, it was almost a no-brainer.

Case Study: What Went Wrong for Max?

Max's experience highlights how many of the risk factors can play out in a young person's life to make them vulnerable to addiction:

- He experienced a traumatic event, the loss of his mother, which increases vulnerability to addiction.

- During his formative teenage years, parental supervision and involvment were absent or minimal.
- Max struggled with mental health difficulties, including anxiety and depression.
- By the time he reached college, which studies identify as a time when initiating problematic opioid use is more common than the earlier teenage years, he had already experimented with various drugs, creating an easy pathway to addiction.

We will come back to Max's story when we talk about the treatment options available for opioid addiction, so that you can learn about how he got into recovery.

What is heroin?

Typically found in white or brown powder form (Figure 8.1), heroin is an opioid made from morphine and extracted from certain poppy plants found in Asia, Mexico, and Columbia.

Figure 8.1 Heroin
Source: DEA

Heroin can also come in a black, sticky form, known as *black tar heroin*. Heroin can be sniffed, snorted, smoked, or injected into a muscle or a vein. Heroin is often cut with other substances including sugar, starch, or powdered milk. It can also be cut with poisons, including strychnine, a white powdered toxin that is found in pesticides, especially those used to kill rodents. Though sugar and powdered milk sound nontoxic and unlikely to cause any serious harm, when snorted or injected into the bloodstream, these substances can clog blood vessels that lead to the lungs, kidneys, liver, or brain, which in turn, can result in permanent damage. Other names for heroin include:

- Smack
- Horse or White Horse
- Hell Dust
- Brown Sugar
- Dope
- H or Big H
- Junk
- Skag
- Negra
- Skunk
- China White

People use heroin in various ways and, at times, in combination with other drugs; studies show that nearly all people who use heroin also use at least one other drug,[45]which is risky given that combining heroin with other drugs or alcohol increases the likelihood of overdose. Some people alternate between snorting lines of heroin and cocaine, which is known as *crisscrossing*. Others combine heroin with crack cocaine and inject it, a practice called *speedballing*. Still, others inject a combination of methamphetamine and heroin, with the resulting substance known as *goofball*.

New Research: Goofball

Goofball, or methamphetamine mixed with heroin, is a drug that people inject, and recent research shows that the use of goofball has *doubled* among people who inject drugs over the past two years. Here are some characteristics of those who use goofball as a main drug:

- Many are under the age of 30.
- Many are female.
- A large percentage have been recently incarcerated.
- Compared to people who inject *either* heroin *or* methamphetamine, more of those who use goofball have witnessed other people experience an opioid overdose.
- Most of those who use goofball would like to change or stop using it altogether.

Source: Glick, S. N., Klein, K. S., Tinsley, J., & Golden, M. R. (2021). Increasing heroin-methamphetamine (Goofball) use and related morbidity among Seattle area people who inject drugs. *The American Journal on Addictions, 30*(2), 183–191. https://doi.org/10.1111/ajad.13115

How do people end up on heroin?

Though it is commonly believed that becoming addicted to heroin is somewhere people "end up" after using other types of opioids such as prescription painkillers like Vicodin or OxyContin, in reality, only 4% of those who started out on prescription opioids went on to "convert" or switch to heroin use within five years, according to a large population-based study,[6] and one-third of those entering treatment for an opioid use disorder report that heroin was the first opioid they used regularly to get high.[7] So, how do we know who is most likely to make that transition from opioid painkillers to heroin? One characteristic that distinguishes those who begin with prescription opioids and end up on heroin versus those who do not make this transition is that they are individuals who frequently use multiple substances, which is known as *polydrug* use.[5] According to one study in which researchers conducted in-depth interviews with 15 young people ages 22 to 31 from Chicago's western suburbs, who either currently or formerly used heroin,[8] three "pathways" describe what led these individuals to begin using heroin:

1. Polydrug Use → Heroin: the most common sequence in over one-third of those interviewed was described as a pattern of using multiple substances prior to being introduced to heroin.
2. Prescription Opioid Pills → Heroin: about one-third of the interviewees had become dependent on prescription opioids such as OxyContin or Vicodin and switched to heroin use when these pills became difficult to obtain.
3. Cocaine Use → Heroin: the remaining third began using heroin as a way to "come down" from cocaine binges. It is not uncommon for people to use some type of depressant, sedative, or "downer" to "take the edge off" from the intensely stimulating effects of cocaine, and/or end a binge so that they can sleep.

Although this study included a small number of individuals, the results are consistent with research findings from many larger studies: although nonmedical use of prescription opioids is a strong risk factor for heroin use (i.e., a high percentage of those who become addicted heroin report having used prescription opioids for nonmedical reasons prior to starting to use heroin), this isn't the whole story. The risk of starting to use heroin is highest among those who

1. use prescription painkillers *frequently* for nonmedical reasons;
2. misuse or are physically and/or psychologically dependent on prescription opioids;
3. are over the age of 25;[9] and
4. have frequently used multiple substances.

Apart from these risk factors, the low cost and high purity of heroin may be driving increased rates of heroin use,[10] making it a cheaper, more easily accessible alternative to prescription painkillers.

Paraphernalia Defined

Paraphernalia refers to any equipment that is used to make, use, or conceal drugs, typically for recreational use. Examples of such equipment include: pipes, water pipes, bongs, rolling papers, roach clips, miniature spoons, and syringes.

Pipes with a bulb on the end are typically used to smoke stimulants such as crack cocaine or methamphetamine.

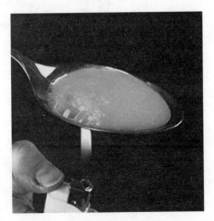

A small spoon is used to dissolve heroin in water so that it can be injected. It is also used to hold small amounts of cocaine that are then snorted directly.

Source, DEA, 2017

Short straws or rolled up paper tubes (dollars), are used to snort drugs in powdered form, such as cocaine or heroin.

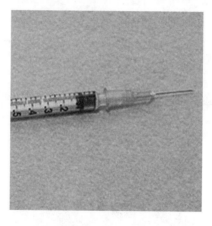

A syringe is used to inject drugs such as heroin or combinations of stimulants and heroin such as "goofball" (heroin and methamphetamine) or "speedball" (heroin and cocaine) directly into the bloodstream.

Tinfoil can be used to smoke heroin or inhale fumes from methamphetamine.

Source: DEA, 2017

How does heroin affect the brain and behavior?

Heroin, like other opioid drugs, changes the way that brain cells communicate with one another. This, of course, affects the way we think, feel emotionally, and act. Normally, our brain cells (which are also called *neurons*) release chemicals (which are called *neurotransmitters*), and the neighboring brain cell or neuron receives the chemicals, bringing them up into the cell by way of a structure that's called a *receptor* (which is like a receiver). In Figure 8.2, you can see two neurons: the top one is called the "presynaptic neuron;" this is the one that is releasing brain chemicals (like dopamine). The bottom one is called the "postsynaptic neuron," which is the neighboring brain cell. This cell has receptors that the chemicals will attach themselves to.

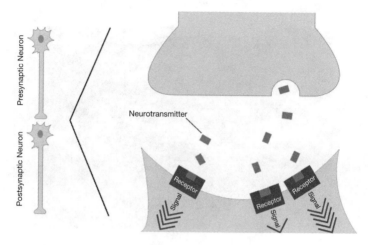

Figure 8.2 How Drugs Activate the Release of Pleasure Chemicals in the Brain

Source: SITN Boston

As we reviewed in Chapter 2, drugs interfere with the way our neurons communicate with each other. In the case of opioids, this class of drugs has a *special* ability to activate the release of chemicals in the brain that make us feel *really* good. The reason for this is because we all have opioid receptors or "receivers" in our brains, a discovery that was made in the 1970s when it was found that drugs like heroin and morphine attach or "bind" to specific areas of the brain that are designed to receive them. In fact, there are three specific types of opioid receptors, known as *mu*, *kappa*, and *delta*. When we are stressed or in pain, our bodies naturally produce opioid-like chemicals or neurotransmitters that attach to these special opioid receptors, and the purpose of these brain chemicals is to block pain from stress or harm. The natural opioid-like substances that we produce include endorphins, enkephalins, and dynorphin. You may have heard of endorphins, which are released during vigorous exercise and are known to lead to a "natural high" that people feel a strong desire to repeat. Enkephalins are the body's naturally produced painkillers.

Finally, dynorphin is involved in many important functions, including learning and memory, controlling one's emotions, and responding to stress and pain. Together, endorphins, enkephalins, and dynorphin are known as *endogenous opioids*, meaning that they are natural.

The highly addictive man-made opioids that have become so problematic over the past few decades were designed to interact with our natural opioid receivers. The structure of heroin, for example, resembles that of the natural endogenous opioids produced in the brain, making it possible for the drug to attach itself to the brain's opioid receptors. The easiest way to understand this is to think of it as though there are certain chemical "keys" that unlock the opioid receptors, allowing the drug to reach the brain cells. People have been able to create a variety of synthetic opioid drugs (such as heroin, OxyContin, and fentanyl) that are similar enough to our natural chemical "keys" to mimic their natural pain-relieving effects. But they also have an added effect, which is the rush or euphoria that they produce—and it is this experience that leads to a strong desire to repeat the use of these drugs, leading to addiction and a variety of other health problems.

In the short term, heroin makes people feel a rush or high, which is intensely pleasurable, followed by a "twilight state" of clouded awareness or disturbed consciousness. In this state, the person feels relaxed and sleepy, and may feel like they are dreaming. Other short-term effects may include:

- Warm flushing of the skin
- Dry mouth
- Heaviness in one's limbs (both arms and legs)
- Nausea and vomiting
- Severe itching, also known as *pruritis*
- Going "on the nod," or alternating between a conscious and semi-conscious state
- Difficulty breathing

In the longer term, people who use heroin can develop a number of health problems, including:

- Addiction
- Insomnia
- Mental health problems, including depression and anti-social personality disorder
- Endocarditis, an infection of the heart's inner lining
- Abscesses, or collections of pus in tissues, causing painful swelling
- Damaged tissue inside the nose for those who sniff or snort heroin
- Constipation and stomach cramping
- Lung complications, including pneumonia
- Sexual dysfunction for men
- Reproductive health problems for women

There are a few other potential adverse effects of long-term heroin use. First, heroin has a high potential for addiction. Second, as a person becomes more severely addicted and develops tolerance to the effects of heroin, they require more and more to achieve the same effects from the drug. For some, this progression leads them to change their method of taking heroin, transitioning from smoking or snorting it to injecting. People who inject heroin become vulnerable to contracting infectious diseases, including Hepatitis C and HIV. The reason for this is that these infectious diseases are transmitted through contact with infected blood or body fluids; people who inject drugs at times share needles and other injection paraphernalia, and when these objects have been used by individuals with infectious diseases, the next person to use them is at risk for contracting the disease. Injecting drugs is not the only way people with addictions can become infected with HIV, Hepatitis C, and/or sexually transmitted infections; a second way is by engaging in risky sexual behaviors, such as having unprotected sex. When a person is under the influence of drugs, their ability to make sound and well-reasoned decisions is compromised, making them more likely to act on impulse and do risky things that they otherwise wouldn't do. For this reason, people who use drugs, whether by injection or not, are more vulnerable to being exposed to others who are infected with transmissible diseases.[11] People who inject heroin are also vulnerable to experiencing a variety of other health problems, including infections of the skin, bones, and joints. When considered all together, the health- and mortality-related risk factors for those with opioid use disorders are numerous, including those related to overdose, suicide, trauma, and infectious diseases. Collectively, the likelihood of early death is a staggering 20 times higher for a person with an opioid use disorder compared to someone without this condition.[12]

New Research: The Body's Natural Opioids Affect the Brain Very Differently from Synthetics

Recent research has uncovered ways that our brain cells react differently to synthetic opioids such as fentanyl and heroin, when compared to the natural opioid chemicals that are created by the body.[a] Researchers created a "biosensor" that attaches to the brain's opioid receptors along with an opioid drug, such as morphine, so that they could see exactly what is happening inside the brain's cells when an opioid is present.

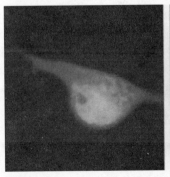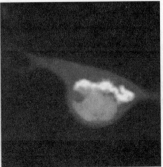

Source: Stoeber et al., 2018

Until very recently, our understanding of the effects of both natural and synthetic opioids on the brain cells was that they both attach themselves to receptors on the *surface* of the neuron or brain cell. New research has shown that in fact, this is not the case; while natural opioids in our bodies attach themselves to the receptors on the brain cells' surface, synthetic opioids do something different. What can be seen in these brain cell images is that when morphine (seenon the left) was applied to a nerve cell, within 20 seconds it left the surface and entered the *inside* of the cell, attaching itself to receptors on the inside (seen in bright white on the right). This may explain why man-made opioid drugs are more intensely rewarding than natural opioids, as they appear to have the ability to affect brain cells in a way that endogenous opioids like endorphins can't.

---

[a] Stoeber, M., Jullié, D., Lobingier, B. T., Laeremans, T., Steyaert, J., Schiller, P. W., Manglik, A., & von Zastrow, M. (2018). A genetically encoded biosensor reveals location bias of opioid drug action. *Neuron, 98*(5), 963–976. https://doi.org/10.1016/j.neuron.2018.04.021

What happens during heroin withdrawal?

As a person becomes more and more physically dependent on heroin, the vicious cycle of withdrawal, followed by more heroin use in efforts to escape or avoid the heroin withdrawal symptoms, can develop rapidly. This is because when heroin or other opioids leave the body, the withdrawal symptoms are probably the most uncomfortable of all the drugs that people can become addicted to. Opioid withdrawal is so incredibly uncomfortable that people will go to great lengths to prevent it from happening, and this is a major driver of addiction to this class of drugs. The withdrawal symptoms from heroin, as with other opioids, can begin within a few hours of the time it was last taken, and include:

- Severe muscle and bone pain
- Restlessness
- Diarrhea
- Vomiting

- Difficulty sleeping
- Cold flashes and goosebumps
- Uncontrollable leg movements
- Strong, intense cravings to use heroin

Studies show that people who use heroin can experience intense *cravings*, which can make it very difficult to cut back or stop using it on their own.[13] Cravings, or an overwhelming desire or need to use a drug, can include physical symptoms, intrusive or unwanted thoughts or obsessions about a substance, and intense emotions. Over time, people, places, or things that were closely linked with using heroin can become *cues* (much like reminders) that come to trigger these urges or cravings. The more a person uses heroin to overcome withdrawal symptoms, the stronger the cravings become when that person experiences withdrawal symptoms or anything that resembles those symptoms (such as stress). This is because the brain forms a connection between heroin use and relief from withdrawal symptoms that strengthens every time it is used as a way of self-medicating the discomfort.

What Are the Signs that Someone Has Become Addicted to Opioids?

If you are concerned that a loved one may be using opioids but are not sure, pay close attention to the following signs:

- Drowsiness or "nodding off" at inappropriate times (for example, during a conversation)
- Weight loss
- Frequent flu-like symptoms (caused by going in and out of opioid withdrawal)
- Opioid prescriptions from various doctors or healthcare providers (from "doctor shopping")
- Isolation from family and friends
- New financial difficulties
- Stealing from family, friends, or other sources
- Pupils appearing small

What is fentanyl?

A powerful synthetic opioid, fentanyl is known for its potency and overwhelming involvement in drug overdose deaths across the nation. In fact, fentanyl-related overdose deaths have quadrupled over the past decade, accounting for over 80% of opioid-related fatalities in America in 2020.[14] Given that it is 50 to 100 times more potent than morphine, for those who suffer from chronic pain and have exhausted other treatment options, fentanyl has been used as an alternative to more commonly used opioid pain relievers.[15] One of its most common uses is for the treatment of severe pain following surgery. In its prescription form, fentanyl is known by various brand names, including Actiq, Abstral, Fentora, Onsolis, and Sublimaze. A slow-release fentanyl patch that is placed on the skin is called Duragesic. The various brands of prescription fentanyl listed above, along with others that have been developed over the years, are distinguished mostly in terms of the way they are taken. These medicines can be taken by injection (i.e., in a shot); in lozenge form, often referred to as fentanyl "lollipops" (Actiq); as an effervescent buccal tablet (i.e., a tablet that dissolves and fizzes when placed in between the check and gum; Fentora); a sublingual tablet (i.e., a tablet that is placed under the tongue to dissolve; Abstral); a sublingual spray (i.e., one that is sprayed under the tongue; Subsys); and a nasal spray (Lazanda).[16]

Fentanyl is also manufactured and used illegally. A large proportion of illicitly produced fentanyl is made in laboratories and imported from China, Mexico, and Canada.[17] Synthetic fentanyl that is made illegally can take on various forms, including powder or pills that look like other prescription opioids. It can be put into nasal sprays or eye droppers, and dropped on blotter paper. Common street names for fentanyl include Apache, China Girl, China Town, Dance Fever, Friend, Goodfellas, Great Bear, He-Man, Jackpot, King Ivory, Murder 8, and Tango & Cash.

How is fentanyl misused?

Depending on the form being used, there are many ways that people misuse fentanyl. When in pill form, fentanyl can be taken orally like any other medicine, but it can also be crushed up and sniffed or snorted, smoked, or injected. Fentanyl patches are misused by emptying their gel contents and ingesting or injecting them. Others freeze the patches, cut them into pieces, and place them under their tongue or in their cheek cavity.[18]

Fentanyl and Other Synthetic Opioids

Fentanyl is available as a prescription, primarily used for anesthesia, treating pain after surgery, or to manage pain among those who are tolerant to the more commonly used opioid pain medicines. The sharp rise in overdose deaths tied to synthetic opioids in recent years is not from prescribed fentanyl, but rather the illicitly manufactured versions of these drugs that have been largely behind this trend. The table below describes the potency, compared to morphine, of fentanyl and many of its analogues, along with other synthetic opioids.

Drug	Potency
Fentanyl	80 times more potent than morphine
Carfentanil	10,000 times more potent than morphine
Acetyl-fentanyl	15 times more potent than morphine
Butyrfentanyl	More than 30 times more potent than morphine
U-47700	12 times more potent than morphine
MT-45	Equivalent to morphine

What is the history of fentanyl misuse?

Fentanyl was first developed in the late 1950s and was introduced in the 1960s as an FDA-approved anesthetic called Sublimaze. Initially delivered only intravenously, the fentanyl market expanded as other formulations that are used today gained FDA approval, including lozenges, skin patches, dissolving tablets, and films. It wasn't until 1980 that illicit fentanyl use and production were discovered; that summer, several individuals who were seeking treatment for heroin addiction in Riverside County, California, reported that they had used a substance they called "China White," a street name for pure Southeast Asian heroin. However, when their urine was tested as part of the standard evaluation procedure to enter treatment, the samples came up negative for heroin, leading to the discovery that what they had actually used was a synthetic substance containing acetyl-fentanyl, a fentanyl analogue drug that is estimated to be 15 times more potent than morphine. Around the same time, the first reports of diversion and misuse of prescription fentanyl among healthcare professionals emerged,[19] particularly among anesthesiologists and nurse anesthesiologists for whom access to fentanyl creates vulnerability to misuse and addiction. This marked the start of an upward and currently continuing trend of fentanyl misuse that expanded from clinicians to individuals who were already misusing or addicted to other prescription opioids.

In the mid-2000s, a surge in fentanyl overdose deaths over a two-year period was traced back to a laboratory in Toluca, Mexico, that was illicitly producing non-pharmaceutical fentanyl. he outbreak ended in 2007 once the laboratory was seized and the DEA placed controls on fentanyl precursors (i.e., chemicals that are used to illicitly manufacture fentanyl).[20] A few years later, non-pharmaceutical fentanyl reemerged, as counterfeit prescription pills containing fentanyl were seized for the first time,[21] and a rise in fentanyl-laced heroin and cocaine led to a doubling in fentanyl-related overdose deaths.[17] Fentanyl analogs have been developed at a rapid pace over the past several decades and have been linked with an increasing number of overdose fatalities. The growing presence of fentanyl in the illicit drug market has been attributed to ease of availability (especially through online vendors), profitability, and restrictions on prescription opioids.[20] Websites are used not only to sell fentanyl and fentanyl analogs, but they also serve as online sources for purchasing tools for pill manufacturing, including pill presses (also known as tableting machines) and pill die molds (which can be used to create a particular shape and stamp or marking on a pill, making a counterfeit pill look like a legitimate prescription medicine). In recent years wholesale prices ranged from $2000 to $4000 per kg of fentanyl or fentanyl analogue.[21] With opioid pill street value ranging from $10 to $20 per pill, 1 kg of fentanyl can translate into $5 to $20 million in retail sales, bringing great appeal to illicit fentanyl sales from a profitability perspective for both individual drug dealers and large-scale drug trafficking organizations. Finally, in addition to fentanyl and fentanyl analogues, novel synthetic opioids (known as AH-7921, U47700, and MT-45) are also making their way into drug markets and are linked with reports of overdoses and fatalities across Europe and the United States.[20]

What are the effects of fentanyl on the brain and body?

Like heroin and other opioids, fentanyl attaches itself to opioid receptors, which are found in areas of the brain that control pain and emotions. As a person repeatedly uses fentanyl, the pain relief and intense pleasure it brings is counteracted by increased pain and less pleasure when it leaves the body. This can bring on an emotional experience that is known as *anhedonia*, which is when a person loses their ability to feel pleasure. As a person's brain becomes dependent on fentanyl or other opioids for pleasure, the loss of pleasure from other natural sources of joy in life can create a vicious cycle: as a person becomes more and more desperate to feel good, they turn to opioids more and more. But as they use opioids more, the brain adapts and changes in ways that make it harder to feel good when doing other pleasurable things, like spending time with family or other loved ones, or having sex, or doing other enjoyable activities. When this takes hold, addiction becomes more serious, so that seeking out, using, and recovering from opioid use becomes central in one's life, and the other parts of life that one once valued fade into the background.

Like other opioids, fentanyl makes a person feel:

- Relaxed
- Euphoric (or extremely happy)
- Temporary relief from physical pain

Its use can also lead to various unpleasant and potentially life-threatening symptoms, including:

- Sedation
- Confusion
- Drowsiness
- Dizziness
- Nausea and/or vomiting
- Constipation
- Difficulty breathing

Myth: Rising Fentanyl Overdoses Are the Result of High User Demand

Some of the media coverage of fentanyl-related overdoses in recent years has characterized this alarming trend as resulting from demand for this drug among people who are addicted to other opioids, like heroin. However, recent research suggests the opposite: people who use heroin prefer to avoid heroin cut with fentanyl whenever possible, and they go to great lengths to try to do this.[a]

Law enforcement and federal agents have been quoted as follows, when discussing surging overdose deaths linked with fentanyl-contaminated heroin,

"The users know that they could die from taking this heroin, but they want the ultimate high."

New Haven Register, 2016[b]

"Heroin cut with fentanyl gives the user a more intense high. In an addict's world they want the ultimate high, taking them right to the edge."

EastbayRI.com, 2016[c]

In contrast to these assumptions, when researchers studied experiences with fentanyl among nearly 150 individuals who were addicted to other opioids (mostly heroin), here's what they learned:

1. *Perceptions about fentanyl's effects were overwhelmingly negative.* Nearly all participants who had used fentanyl or fentanyl-contaminated heroin described a strong dislike for its effects.
2. *Fear of overdose was widespread.* On average, those in the study had witnessed about four overdoses among their friends, and they suspected or confirmed that fentanyl played a role in many of these tragedies. The majority described fentanyl as dangerous and potentially deadly, and preferred to avoid fentanyl-contaminated heroin whenever possible.
3. *Those with heroin addiction used various strategies to avoid exposure to fentanyl.* These included learning to recognize the appearance and smell of fentanyl-laced heroin, taking test hits when they suspected the presence of fentanyl, using trusted dealers whom they have known a long time, and seeking medication treatment for their opioid addiction.

Although some other studies focused on people addicted to prescription pain killers find that fentanyl experiences are more positive and desirable, this study of heroin-addicted individuals was consistent with other research across North America and Canada that has found that a high percentage of those who are exposed to fentanyl encounter it unintentionally (Hempstead & Yildirim, 2014; Amlani et al., 2015).

---

[a] Carroll, J. J., Marshall, B. D. L., Rich, J. D., & Green, T. C. (2017). Exposure to fentanyl-contaminated heroin and overdose risk among illicit opioid users in Rhode Island: A mixed methods study. *The International Journal on Drug Policy, 46*, 136–145. https://doi.org/10.1016/j.drugpo.2017.05.023

[b] Flynn R. (2016). Connecticut, federal law enforcement officials team up to target opioid distributors. Retrieved November 16, 2022, from http://www.nhregister.com/general-news/20160413/connecticut-federal-law-enforcement-officials-team-up-to-target-opioid-distributors.

[c] Rego, M. (2016). East Providence Police intensify heroin interdiction. Retrieved November 16, 2022, from http://www.eastbayri.com/stories/east-providence-police-intensifyheroin-interdiction,17962.

What happens when a person overdoses on fentanyl?

If a person overdoses on fentanyl, their breathing can slow down or even stop. This can lead to *hypoxia*, a condition in which the supply of oxygen to the brain decreases. When this happens, very serious complications can occur, including coma, irreversible brain damage, or death.

Is there treatment available for a fentanyl overdose?

When given immediately, *naloxone* is a medicine that can treat an overdose. It works by quickly attaching itself to the opioid receptors in the brain, and blocking the effects of fentanyl. Studies show that naloxone dosing may not be as straight-forward for fentanyl overdoses as it is for other opioids, since it is such a strong and potent drug. Whereas non-fentanyl overdoses are often treated with a single dose of naloxone, one dose may not be enough to reverse a fentanyl overdose.

What to Do If You Suspect Someone Has Overdosed on Opioids

Since overdosing on certain potent opioids such as fentanyl can require more than one dose of naloxone for treatment to be effective, the most important action to take (apart from administering naloxone, if it is available) is to **call 911** to get the person immediate medical attention.

What treatment is available for opioid use disorders?

Medications, ideally combined with behavioral counseling, are the most effective treatment approach for opioid use disorders. There are several FDA-approved medications available for the treatment of opioid addiction, including buprenorphine (also known as Suboxone or Subutex), methadone, and extended-release naltrexone (also known as Vivitrol). The World Health Organization lists buprenorphine and methadone as "essen-tial medicines," yet they are not as accessible as one would hope given how urgent the need is for effective treatment to make inroads toward reversing the opioid overdose crisis. In fact, *less than half* of privately funded addiction treatment programs offer both medications and behavioral therapy.[22] Chapter 12 goes into depth about how each of the medicines available for opioid addiction treatment work in the brain, and the differences between them, and Chapter 11 reviews effective behavioral therapies for those who are trying to overcome opioid use disorders.

9

HOW DID WE END UP IN AN OVERDOSE CRISIS?

Over the last 15 years, over 500,000 lives have been lost as a result of opioid overdose deaths, leading to a myriad of consequences including a reduction in overall life expectancy in the United States.[1] Over 75,000 such deaths occurred in the 12-month period ending in April 2021. How did we get here? The history of the opioid crisis dates back to the 1990s, when opioid prescribing began surging in response to a number of regulatory guidelines in medicine, coupled with widespread misinformation concerning the safety of long-term use of opioids for chronic pain. Specifically, three major sources fueled the surge in prescriptions.

First, opioid pain medicines became the focus in the medical community as a go-to treatment for all different types of pain.[2] Though scientific research most clearly supported the use of opioid pain medicines for the treatment of acute, short-term, severe pain, and chronic pain for people suffering from advanced or terminal illness (i.e., cancer), doctors began prescribing these medicines for other pain conditions. The use of opioids to treat pain conditions that are chronic and not related to cancer is not clearly supported by medical research, making these prescribing practices controversial—especially given the risk of addiction and the complications, including death, that can result from misusing these medicines.

Second, the American Pain Society released guidelines in 1996 that emphasized the importance of assessing and treating pain at every visit between a patient and a health-care provider. Describing pain as a "5th vital sign," these guidelines marked the launch of a campaign to improve what was regarded as inadequate assessment and treat-ment of pain across the healthcare system. In response to this campaign, agencies that provide accreditation to healthcare facilities, reflecting compliance with national standards for safety and quality of care, began requiring procedures for assessing and managing pain. Soon, asking individuals to rate their pain severity, whether or not pain was the complaint that brought them to see their healthcare provider, became as routine as taking their blood pressure. You might remember having been asked by your nurses or doctors about pain, if you're someone who visits the doctor regularly.

Finally, with pain assessment and treatment planning becoming part of routine medical care, the pharmaceu-tical industry initiated aggressive marketing campaigns to promote the use of opioid pain relievers in the late 1990s. Their marketing initiatives targeted the non–cancer-related pain market, which at the time comprised 86% of the total opioid market.[3] Misinformation about the risks of addic-tion to opioid pain killers spread, leading to a false sense of confidence concerning the safety of using these medicines to treat non–cancer-related pain in the longer term. In 2009, Arthur Van Zee, MD, a primary care physician in Virginia who was troubled by the surge in opioid use disorders in his community, wrote a widely circulated article in the *American Journal of Public Health*, entitled, "The Promotion and Marketing of OxyContin: Commercial Triumph, Public Health Tragedy."[3]

Is Pharmaceutical Industry Marketing of Opioid Products Related to Overdose Fatalities?

Scientists are beginning to evaluate this question, and here is what they've found so far:

- Opioid marketing over a 2-year period reached over 68,000 physicians, with expenditures of $46 million, mostly for meals. That's one in 12 physicians overall who were reached, including one in five who specialize in family medicine.[a]
- As shown in the figure below, for every meal received by a doctor through opioid marketing efforts, the number of opioid prescription claims increased.

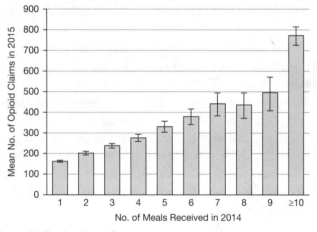

Source: Hadland et al., 2018[b]

- When studying the link between opioid overdose deaths and opioid marketing during the prior year, researchers found that the more physicians there were who received opioid marketing, the higher the opioid overdose death rate in the year that followed. In fact, for each additional physician who received marketing, the overdose fatality rate was *12% higher*.[a]

---

[a] Hadland, S. E., Krieger, M. S., & Marshall, B. D. L. (2017). Industry Payments to Physicians for Opioid Products, 2013-2015. *American journal of public health*, *107*(9), 1493–1495. https://doi.org/10.2105/AJPH.2017.303982

[b] Hadland, S. E., Cerdá, M., Li, Y., Krieger, M. S., & Marshall, B. D. L. (2018). Association of Pharmaceutical Industry Marketing of Opioid Products to Physicians With Subsequent Opioid Prescribing. *JAMA Internal Medicine*, *178*(6), 861–863. https://doi.org/10.1001/jamainternmed.2018.1999

Van Zee highlighted the role of two central sources of the opioid addiction and overdose upsurge: (a) increased availability of opioids in the United States, and (b) marketing and promotion of opioids by the pharmaceutical industry. Although opioid prescribing in America has declined since 2010, current opioid prescribing rates are still three times higher than they were 20 years ago, and they have not readily declined in geographic areas where opioid overdose deaths are occurring with the greatest frequency.[4]

The research findings that link pharmaceutical industry marketing to overdose death rates have focused on the question of whether overdose deaths and marketing activities are related to one another. Despite having found that they are *related*, we cannot conclude with certainty that one *directly caused* the other. One possible explanation for this relationship is that drug companies perhaps targeted their marketing efforts to physicians who were already prescribing opioids to many of their patients. As a marketing strategy, this could lead physicians who already have shown "buy-in" to the opioid products to increase their prescribing further. Studies are ongoing to better understand how such marketing strategies have impacted the opioid crisis.

What is the history of the opioid crisis?

The opioid crisis has been described as dynamic, having evolved in at least three overlapping stages.[5] At the beginning, in 2000, misuse of prescription opioid pain medicines was the dominant cause of surging opioid use and overdoses. The second stage involved rising rates of heroin use, with overdose deaths from heroin escalating in 2007 and surpassing those from prescription opioids by 2015. This was followed by a third stage, in which overdose deaths were accelerated by the emergence of illicitly manufactured fentanyl and its *analogues*, or drugs with a similar structure to fentanyl, resulting in a combination of intentional and unintentional ingestion and fatalities. More recently, a new phase in the crisis, overlapping with the COVID-19 pandemic, has been marked by a sharp rise in overdoses involving stimulants such as cocaine and methamphetamine, which are being used in combination with opioids.

The recent stages of the crisis were met with unprecedented death tolls, with over 107,000 overdose fatalities in 2021 alone, 75% of which involved an opioid.[6] Methamphetamine overdose deaths have increased tenfold over the past decade, reaching 16,500 deaths in 2019.[7] Now roughly equivalent to the number of cocaine overdose deaths annually (16,196), the death toll of overdoses caused by stimulants other than cocaine has increased by 180% over the period from 2015 to 2019, rising from 5,526 to 15,489. Yet, the number of people who used methamphetamine did not increase by nearly as much—which, when combined with studies showing that *riskier ways of using methamphetamine* are becoming more common (e.g., using it very frequently or heavily, injecting it, and/or using it in combination with other drugs) has led experts to conclude that overdose deaths involving methamphetamine may be partially explained by these risky patterns of using it.[8] Both cocaine- and methamphetamine-involved overdose deaths over the past two decades have been increasingly driven by the practice of combining stimulants with synthetic opioids.

Though there are several medications that are quite effective for the treatment of opioid addiction, as you'll learn in Chapter 11, currently there are no FDA-approved medications for stimulant addiction; likewise, while medication is available to reverse the toxic and lethal effects of overdosing on opioids, there are no medicines to save a life when someone is experiencing a stimulant overdose. Helping those with opioid addiction access the highly effective treatments that are available provides the best opportunity for reversing the opioid overdose death crisis.

How common is overdose in teens?

One of the most alarming trends to emerge yet is the rise, for the first time in a decade, in overdose deaths among American teens. According to a recent study, overdose deaths among adolescents nearly doubled from 492 to 954 in the span of a year, from 2019 to 2020. In the year that followed, the death toll increased by another 20%.[9] Public health experts fear that if this trend follows others, it may have yet to peak.[10] What the data show so far is that the culprit behind the rising overdose death rate is fentanyl, which was involved in 77% of fatal overdoses among teens in 2021. How are teens ending up on fentanyl? Studies show that the drugs that teens are most drawn to that could contain fentanyl are prescription opioids (such as Vicodin, OxyContin, hydrocodone) and benzodiazepines (such as Xanax, Ativan)—what most people don't know is that at least one-third of illicitly manufactured pills are contaminated with fentanyl.[11] According to Dr. Nora Volkow, director of the National Institute on Drug Abuse, regarding the emerging threat to young people posed by counterfeit prescription pills, "In the past, you would just get sedated. Now you can take one benzodiazepine, one pill and it can kill you."[10] Putting even those who are experimenting recreationally or occasionally with drugs at risk for fatalities, these counterfeit pills are often sold through social media and e-commerce platforms, making them accessible to anyone with a smartphone.

Fentanyl Contamination in Counterfeit Pills: What Everyone Needs to Know

A dramatic increase has been observed in the number of counterfeit pills that contain a lethal dose of fentanyl, which is only 2 milligrams. Here's what you need to know:[a]

- Drug traffickers are mass producing counterfeit pills and marketing them to the American public as though they were legitimate prescription drugs.

- Counterfeit pills are easy to buy, very accessible, and often contain deadly doses of fentanyl.
- Counterfeit pills look just like commonly used prescription opioids, such as oxycodone and hydrocodone.
- There are also counterfeit pills being sold that look just like prescription benzodiazepines, such as Xanax, and stimulant medications such as Adderall.
- There were over 100,000 overdose deaths in America in both 2021 and 2022, the highest number ever reported.
- Fentanyl has been the primary driver of this unprecedented overdose death trend.
- Four out of every 10 pills with fentanyl contain a potentially lethal dose, according to the DEA.

Young people and adults alike need to know that the ONLY pills that are safe to take are those that are prescribed by a trusted, licensed medical professional and dispensed by a licensed pharmacy. Below are some examples found in DEA investigations of emojis that can help parents identify drug deals in text messages.[b]

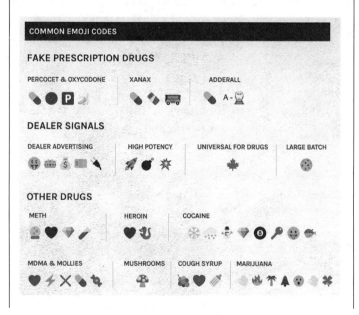

[a] Drug Enforcement Administration. (2021). What every parent and caregiver needs to know about fake pills. Retrieved November 23, 2022 from https://www.getsmartaboutdrugs.gov/sites/default/files/2022-11/DEA-OPCK_Parent%20flyer_V2.pdf

[b] Drug Enforcement Administration. (2022). Emoji drug code decoded. Retrieved September 21, 2022, from https://www.dea.gov/sites/default/files/2021-12/Emoji%20Decoded.pdf

Part 3

THERE IS REAL HOPE

TREATMENTS THAT WORK

10

WHAT ARE
THE GOALS OF TREATMENT
FOR ADDICTION?

Treatment for a substance use disorder has three main goals: (1) to help a person either moderate or discontinue their use of alcohol and/or drugs; (2) to extend their success in controlling or remaining free from alcohol and/or drugs into the long term; and (3) to become fully functional in important areas of life, including work or school, family, and in society. To achieve this, treatment approaches may include:

- Medications
- Behavioral counseling
- Medical devices to treat withdrawal symptoms
- Digital therapeutic tools or apps to provide skills training for relapse prevention
- Evaluation and treatment for mental health conditions that commonly occur simultaneously among those with addiction, such as anxiety, mood disorders, and ADHD
- Long-term follow-up to motivate sustained recovery and prevent relapses

Not all people with addiction will need to make use of all these forms of care. Ideally, the components of treatment are tailored to meet each individual's needs, and sometimes, as the recovery experience unfolds, those needs will change. In the first few months of treatment, closely monitoring a person's physical and mental well-being can help a provider determine what adjustments are needed to the plan of treatment and when. By noticing new needs (e.g., for mental health symptoms to be addressed) as they arise, the likelihood that a person will leave addiction treatment prematurely is reduced, which in turn increases their chances of a successful outcome. Involving at least one family member in the treatment process can help with early recognition of problems or relapse warning signs, as well.

Is total abstinence the only way to recover from a substance use disorder?

Over time, there has been a gradual shift in how practitioners think about the unique aspects of each individual's experience with addiction. This mindset affects how we diagnose a substance use disorder and what we expect recovery to look like for each person. There is an increasing drive away from "cookie cutter" treatment plans, with movement toward understanding the *unique struggles of the individual* and tailoring the plan of care accordingly. This means different things for different people, but ultimately, the common thread is the idea that there are many effective treatment options. Giving a person agency to weigh out the benefits and drawbacks of each, and select an approach that fits in with their health habits, lifestyle, and/or belief systems will make it easier for them to commit to the treatment process.

Not only do the treatment options vary, but so does the definition of "success." Decades of research have shown that the symptoms of addiction can come and go over the course of a person's life, much like other chronic conditions. Although total abstinence has been viewed as the only way to recover from addiction for quite a long time, research and practical experience treating addiction in its many forms are telling us otherwise. While it is true that for some people, abstaining completely from drinking or using drugs is necessary to achieve long-term recovery, others may use treatment as an avenue for drinking or using drugs less often and/or less heavily, and experience sustained benefits to their health and well-being from doing so.[1,2] One good example of this comes from studies of individuals who have reduced their drinking. Though historically, achieving total abstinence from alcohol was viewed as the best indicator of "treatment success" for a person with alcoholism, in recent years the FDA and World Health Organization began exploring different ways of thinking about and measuring outcomes of treatment. According to this newer way of defining success, for those whose goal is to reduce their drinking, the purpose of treatment is to help the person learn to *manage* and *reduce the harms* that are caused by their alcohol use, much like treatments for other chronic diseases like diabetes, obesity, and hypertension (which aim to lower blood sugar, weight, and blood pressure to reduce harms caused by these diseases). This shift was motivated by two observations. First, according to national studies focused on understanding why so few people who need treatment receive it, the majority report that the main reason they haven't pursued professional help is that *they don't want to stop drinking completely,*[3] whereas treatment would be more appealing if a non-abstinence goal was offered.[4] Second, evidence is accumulating that treatments focused on helping people cut back on drinking lead to sustained changes in alcohol use over many years,[5] along with stable improvements in mental and physical health and the ability to fulfill one's responsibilities in various areas of life.

What is harm reduction?

Though controversy continues around the idea that reduced or controlled substance use is a suitable goal for those who struggle with addiction, scientific experts have increasingly emphasized the importance of adopting a harm reduction mindset as part of the societal and public health strategy to overcome the nation's unprecedented addiction crisis.[6] What does that mean, exactly? In his widely cited publication, "Harm Reduction: Come As You Are," the late Dr. Alan Marlatt, a psychologist and pioneer in the field of addiction treatment, described the rationale behind the harm reduction approach to understanding and addressing addictive behaviors.[7] Proponents of this approach, which originated in Europe in the 1980s, sought to move away from the understanding of drug use and addictive behaviors as a moral failing that warrants punishment and/or rehabilitation and instead, shift the focus to the *consequences or effects* of substance use. The goal of this approach is to *reduce the harmful effects of alcohol and drug use*, with the understanding that regardless of whether addictive behaviors are right or wrong, many people drink excessively and use drugs, and transforming our existing society into one that is drug-free is highly unlikely. With a harm reduction mindset, treatment encourages *any movement toward decreased harm* arising from drinking or using drugs rather than focusing exclusively on "total abstinence."

Harm reduction practices started in Amsterdam, where the first needle exchange program for individuals who were injecting drugs was implemented in 1984. The purpose of this program was to reduce the spread of HIV by providing disposable needles and syringes in exchange for used ones, preventing needle sharing as a way of transmitting the virus. Harm reduction strategies are not reserved for the most severe forms of addiction or those who are injecting illicit substances, however; they can be applied to the use of legal substances, and to prevent the progression of a mild problem controlling one's substance use to a full-blown addiction. For tobacco use and addiction, for example, nicotine replacement therapies such as nicotine patches and gum are considered to be less harmful alternatives to smoking, due to the reduced cancer risk associated with their use. Though many people use these therapies to quit smoking, some continue to use them as a means of maintaining a safe level of nicotine use without being subjected to the more severe health risks of smoking. Learning to drink alcohol in moderation is another harm reduction strategy aiming to reduce the physical and psychological health risks and complications associated with chronic, heavy drinking. The use of medications for opioid use disorders such as methadone and buprenorphine is also consistent with the harm reduction model; these medicines stimulate the brain's opioid receptors, which you'll learn about in Chapter 12, and they reduce the risk of opioid overdose, HIV and hepatitis C infection.

For a long time, requiring individuals to be abstinent to participate in addiction treatment has presented a barrier for many people to get started or continue to receive care following a slip or relapse. An important goal of the harm reduction approach is to make it easier for people to initiate and/or continue to receive treatment even when they struggle to become or remain abstinent. Despite the fact that temporary returns to alcohol and drug use are common and expected during treatment and recovery (e.g., a recent study found that for many smokers, it may take 30 or more attempts before they successfully quit),[8] today there are still addiction treatment programs that punish slips and relapses by discharging people from care if they submit a urine drug test that is positive for substances, whether or not they wish to continue treatment. By minimizing requirements for treatment entry and destigmatizing the common experience of setbacks during treatment, advocates of harm reduction aim to remove as many barriers to receiving addiction care as possible. The hope is that by welcoming "anyone who is willing to 'come as they are',"[7] we can narrow the staggering discrepancy between those who need (44 million) and those who receive (3 million) specialty treatment for a substance use disorder.[9] Though there are various explanations for this discrepancy, one of the central reasons is that some individuals with addiction are not ready to give up alcohol or drug use completely.[6] By failing to present different people with different options for how to approach recovery, abstinence-only programs can alienate many individuals who could benefit from treatment.

Harm Reduction: What You Need to Know

- Q: Is harm reduction anti-abstinence?
- A: No. *Harm reduction recognizes abstinence as the safest outcome, while accepting alternatives that reduce harm.* For some people who are not ready or willing to stop drinking or using drugs completely, helping them make gradual changes to reduce the harmful effects

of their behavior is a better first step than delaying treatment until if or when they become ready to abstain completely.

- Q: Do people who "slip up" and drink or use during treatment always return to addictive behavior?
- A: *Not necessarily, although more research is needed to answer this across all addictions.* What we do know from nicotine addiction studies is that when someone has their first cigarette after a period of abstinence, the risk of returning to the same pattern of nicotine use as they did prior to treatment increases, especially for vulnerable people with psychological symptoms. But not all people follow this pattern, and some can recover from the slip and remain abstinent afterward.[a] Presently there is little evidence to support the idea that any time someone slips, their treatment gains are completely undermined.

---

[a] Muench, C., Malloy, E. J., & Juliano, L. M. (2020). Lower self-efficacy and greater depressive symptoms predict greater failure to recover from a single lapse cigarette. *Journal of Consulting and Clinical Psychology, 88*(10), 965–970. https://doi.org/10.1037/ccp0000605

Is there a single "best" treatment approach to addiction?

Many people find that the different terms that are used for "treatment" are confusing—you may have heard some people refer to "rehab," "residential treatment," "outpatient," or "intensive outpatient treatment"—which one is the right approach for addiction? And what are the differences between them? One thing that we have learned over time about the science of addiction treatment is that there is no one-size-fits-all approach. While we have various types of medications, therapies, and treatments available that differ in terms of the setting in which they are received (e.g., an inpatient program housed in a hospital, versus outpatient therapy in an office), as well as the specific techniques that they draw on (e.g., some focus on strengthening motivation to change behavior, while others focus on managing temptations and establishing social support), people who are in recovery from addiction often need to try different medicines, therapy approaches, and may shift over time between high-intensity and lower intensity treatments to meet their unique needs.

11

WHAT PSYCHOTHERAPIES ARE EFFECTIVE FOR ADDICTION?

Getting sober was the single bravest thing I've ever done and will ever do in my life. Not [running] a 5K—facing an addiction. Being courageous enough to acknowledge it privately with my family and friends. Working really hard at solidifying it, getting support around it and being healthy. And then talking about it publicly. That is the single greatest accomplishment of my life.

–Jamie Lee Curtis

How can psychotherapy help someone seeking addiction recovery?

It is very common for addiction specialists to recommend psychotherapy as a central part of the treatment plan to help change addictive behaviors. And there is strong evidence to support this practice: studies show that 58% to 79% of those who receive therapy to overcome their addictions achieve treatment outcomes that are better than those who do not receive therapy as part of their treatment.[1,2] This is true for those who struggle with addictions to a range of substances, including alcohol, cannabis, opioids, and stimulants.

You may remember the story of Max, who became addicted to heroin after years of experimenting with other substances including marijuana, cocaine, and prescription pain relievers. Max was nearing his mid-20s when he realized that his future was looking dark and uncertain. The cycle of using heroin, withdrawing from it, and seeking more had taken over his life. He felt like he didn't care if he lived or died, and as he witnessed some of his friends who started using opioids around the same time he did, going to prison and treatment, and, in some sad situations, overdosing, he began taking a serious look at his life. He had lost an aunt to a heroin overdose in recent years, so he knew firsthand how this story could end. Max started to talk to a therapist. He didn't want medication initially, but he felt like he needed some tools to help him through the discomfort of coming off heroin, and some guidance to figure out how to build a life without using drugs. Over time, and as he developed a trusting relationship with his therapist over the course of many failed attempts to come off heroin, he decided to at least give medication a try. And although taking buprenorphine helped him establish a period of abstinence from opioids without the discomfort of intense cravings, there were other problems that bubbled to the surface a few months into his recovery. He was depressed and socially anxious, and he had never received treatment for either. With the help and support of his therapist, he was able to learn about some of the underlying problems that may have led him to self-medicate with substances, and he began to address them in treatment.

Psychotherapy is not reserved for those like Max who are on the fence about medications. In fact, as you'll learn later in this chapter, there are several types of addictions (including stimulant and cannabis use disorders) for which there are no FDA-approved medications, and the scientific evidence to date shows that psychotherapy is not only the most accessible type of treatment but is highly effective in helping change addictive behaviors. Medications for addictions have an important role to play in stabilizing the brain, managing withdrawal symptoms, and reducing cravings. One of the most important things that psychotherapy can do is to help a person with addiction become a "self-expert,"[3] or someone who understands their own cycle and patterns of addictive behaviors inside and out. They come to learn what triggers their cravings, what coping skills usually don't work, and which types of coping skills can help them get through a difficult day or hour. They come to understand the buildup of a relapse mindset and how it starts (not necessarily at the moment they relapse, but sometimes days or weeks beforehand), and they learn how to catch it early on, before it leads them to drink or use substances again. They also become knowledgeable about buffers that help them prevent a relapse. For example, an obvious buffer is having support in place from a therapist and/or a friend or family member to whom they can turn when they're having a difficult time. But not getting behind on "business" such as paying bills, getting enough sleep to prevent mood shifts, and exercising regularly may be equally important as means of avoiding a relapse mindset. In therapy, those with addictions learn how to recognize the subtle and not-so-subtle behavior patterns that could lead them to relapse, and respond to them in a way that preserves their recovery. If it's affordable, and/or if insurance can cover some (or all) of the costs of it, and you or your loved one can identify a skilled therapist with expertise in addiction, then pursuing and remaining in therapy for as long as it is useful is highly recommended. In general, weekly hour-long psychotherapy visits to an individual therapist (and when helpful, a couples or family therapist) are beneficial. Some people find it helpful to supplement therapy with a self-help group, and we will review the various types of groups that are available below. Since there are ups and downs in addiction recovery, like any illness, sometimes more frequent sessions of psychotherapy and/or self-help groups are needed to stay or get back on track and to keep motivation strong.

What can psychotherapy do for someone with addiction?

The central reason to seek psychotherapy is to learn how to manage one's addiction and the problems in one's personal and professional life that are related to it. Once a person successfully reduces or stops using alcohol or drugs, psychotherapy provides additional steps to help make those changes stick, including gaining a thorough understanding of the illness, an opportunity to work through some of the problems it has caused in their life, and a plan for preventing a relapse to addictive behaviors.

Another reason to seek therapy is to address personal issues that perhaps were troubling prior to developing the addiction and that don't necessarily "go away" when a person changes their use of alcohol or drugs. For example, the risk of developing an addiction is higher in people who suffer from trauma or losses early in life. Going back to Max's situation, he lost his mother in his early teens, and his father, absorbed in his own grief, became emotionally disconnected from Max and his brother after that happened, so Max never really had the chance to make sense of his feelings of abandonment at that time. By the time Max sought out therapy for his addiction, over a decade later, he had not yet experienced a successful romantic relationship, an issue that he was able to address with his therapist. He learned in therapy that because of the abandonment he experienced from the loss of his mother, it was hard for him to trust and feel close to people, especially women. With this understanding, he was able to work through his anxiety and fear of loss when forming new romantic relationships. Max's situation is not unusual. Many people with addiction also struggle with relationship issues, whether or not these difficulties stem from trauma. Some also have unfulfilling jobs or careers, which may or may not have anything to do with how their addiction developed. Addressing these life areas with support from a skillful therapist can provide inspiration for a person to remain in stable recovery from their addiction. The more motivated a person is to keep a job they are passionate about, or a rewarding relationship, the more deeply committed they become to their goals related to changing or eliminating their use of alcohol and drugs.

Seven Ways Psychotherapy Can Help
to Overcome Addiction

- By helping a person identify relapse triggers and learn a different or healthy way to respond to them
- By helping to identify relapse warning signs and creating a relapse prevention plan to address them
- By providing a forum for discussion of medication as a potential option
- By teaching a person healthy coping tools to address stressful or difficult experiences without drinking or using substances
- By exploring ways to deal with the social stigma around addiction
- By helping a person identify and cope with comorbid conditions such as mood, anxiety, or medical illnesses that complicate their recovery from addiction
- By addressing family or relationship problems that have been caused or worsened by addictive behaviors

How does one find the right therapy—and the right therapist?

Just as we reviewed various types of medication treatments for addictions to different substances, there are many different types of psychotherapy approaches. Depending on the size of your community, you may be able to identify therapists who practice using a range of different approaches. This can be a little overwhelming when you're not sure exactly what you're looking for. In the sections that follow, we will review the most effective forms of psychotherapy or behavioral therapy for addictions.

One key piece of information to keep in mind when looking for a therapist is that research studies on how and why therapy works have consistently come to one conclusion: when researchers examine all of the different possible aspects of therapy that could help people to feel better and change their behavior, one key finding emerges: it's the "therapeutic relationship" that carries the most weight in driving success.[4] In other words, the feeling of connectedness in that relationship drives a person's ability to make meaningful life changes as a result of therapy. So, what does that mean for someone who is seeking treatment for an addiction? It means that finding a therapist that a person respects, trusts, and connects with will enable them to get the most they can out of the process. Spending some time talking on the phone with a potential therapist, and even meeting with them once or twice before deciding whether to continue, are very reasonable ways to figure out whether they're the right fit for one's needs and personality. It is also important to find a therapist who thoroughly understands the illness of addiction. If you find that you need to explain the illness to a therapist in the same way that you would to a friend or family member who doesn't know anything about it, then that is likely not the best therapist for this problem. One way to find a competent therapist is to ask people you know and trust whether they could recommend someone; that might include a primary care doctor that you see, or anyone in your family or friendship network who is a healthcare provider or works in an environment where they might know other healthcare providers. If you don't have a primary care doctor, you have a few alternative options: (1) you can call your health insurance company to ask about therapists who are covered in your network; (2) you can consult the resources section of this book to find several web-based sources of information about addiction-specialized healthcare providers, including the American Society of Addiction Medicine, the American Psychological Association, and the SAMHSA Treatment Locator; and (3) if you don't have health insurance, you can search the SAMHSA Treatment Locator for community-based treatment programs that receive state or local government funding.

What questions should one ask a potential therapist?

In addition to seeking a referral source whom you know and trust, some questions you can ask a therapist to help decide if they have the right qualifications to provide treatment for a substance use disorder are:

1. *Do you work regularly with clients who have addictions?* Look for a professional who is experienced in treating addiction and is doing ongoing work with clients who are suffering from this problem.

2. *In what ways will you address my addiction? What skills will you teach me? Are there studies of this approach (and if so, what are the results of the studies)?* The goal is to find a therapist who will explore and help strengthen motivation to change alcohol or drug use, teach skills to manage temptations and cravings, help the individual understand their unique triggers for addictive behaviors, develop a plan for relapse prevention, and address lifestyle issues that need adjustment to promote success in recovery. These approaches, which typically involve the use of motivational interviewing, cognitive behavioral therapy, and mindfulness-based relapse prevention, are among the most well-studied treatment methods, and a skilled therapist who is using them should have awareness of the research supporting their use.

3. *Will we talk about what's happening right now in my life, in addition to my past experiences?* Effective therapies for addiction devote most of the time to understanding and changing current behavior patterns. Though discussing how the past led to problems in the here and now can be helpful, it is important to focus on the present to successfully change drinking or drug use.

4. *Will you help me understand and work through the effects that addiction has had on my ability to work and my important relationships?* Ultimately, the goal of addiction treatment is not only to change one's use of alcohol or drugs, but to regain the ability to function well both in personal and professional areas of life. For therapy to be successful, once alcohol and substance use behaviors are under control, then resolving personal and/or professional

problems that have been caused or worsened by the addiction should be the focus of treatment.

5. *Will you work in collaboration with the physician who is providing medication to me?* If medication is prescribed for the addiction or a related psychological condition, then communication between the therapist and the prescribing provider can help make treatment a success.

What therapies are effective for addiction?

When a person first seeks therapy for addiction, they are usually in a vulnerable place. Withdrawal symptoms are common and create physical and emotional discomfort in the early stages of treatment, making it more difficult to stay the course of changing or abstaining from alcohol and drug use. Depending on the substance, these symptoms can take from weeks to months to fully resolve. There is also the issue of ambivalence—a lot of questions during those first days and weeks without alcohol and drugs can occupy a person's mind. Will I always feel this way? Can I truly live without drinking or using drugs? Do I even want to? Will life be enjoyable in recovery?

Thankfully, there are a few well-studied therapeutic techniques that can help a person work their way through these doubts and fears about their ability to recover, and what life will look like in recovery. Let's learn about Tracy's story, and what techniques her therapist used to help her.

Tracy is a 43-year-old woman who had been drinking since her teenage years. A mother of two daughters, she had been in treatment for bipolar disorder since her 20s and was seeing her psychiatrist every few months to check in. She had a healthy relationship with her husband, and a very rewarding career as a journalist. Though there were many parts of her life that were going well, her relationship with alcohol caused her a lot of stress, inner conflict, and shame. She was drinking increasing amounts of alcohol, becoming intoxicated at social events, and often blacking out. Though she attempted to control her drinking, she had a hard time following the rules she had made for herself and inevitably fell into the same patterns. The next day after a heavy drinking night, when she would wake up with fuzzy memories of how and when she left the party she had been at with her husband—and at times, her children as well—she felt overcome with shame. But somehow, she found herself continuing to drink anyway. She asked her psychiatrist for a referral to a therapist who was specialized in addiction.

When Tracy first met with her therapist, they started talking about her goals, and Tracy set a goal to quit drinking at the beginning of her daughters' summer break. This was about five weeks away at the time. But as she neared the date, she began to feel overcome with anxiety. Would she have to give up her social life to avoid the temptation to drink? Would her life become boring and lonely? Was this the end of her ever having a drop of alcohol again? But if she didn't stop drinking, what would happen to her? When she shared these concerns with her therapist, they started doing some motivational exercises.

What are motivational therapies?

Just as it sounds, motivational therapies (which are sometimes referred to as motivational interviewing, or motivational enhancement therapy) are intended to help a person develop and sustain the motivation to change important health behaviors, including drinking and other substance use. This approach has been used in psychotherapy for decades, not only to help people change their alcohol and drug use, but also to change other behaviors that are important to maintaining good health, including healthy eating, exercising, taking prescribed medications regularly, and participating in behavioral treatment. The theory behind motivational therapies is that people progress through different psychological stages of readiness to make changes, as you can see from Figure 11.1.

There are five stages of change:

- **Precontemplation.** In this stage, a person is not yet thinking about changing their behavior. When someone in this stage seeks treatment or help with substance use, it is usually motivated by either a loved one or another concerned party in their life (such as an employer). But even if they take the action of seeking help, the individual with the problematic alcohol or drug use who is in the precontemplation stage has not yet come to believe that something needs changing.
- **Contemplation.** A person who has entered this stage is beginning to think about changing their use of alcohol and/or other drugs. They may be starting to

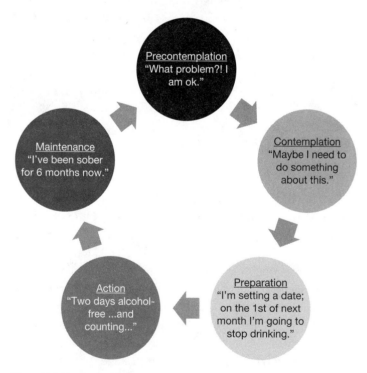

Figure 11.1 The Stages of Change

notice that there are ways that their drinking or drug use is affecting them and their life that they are not happy with. A person at this stage can be somewhat conflicted about whether there is a way to continue to drink or use while minimizing the negative impacts of it, while at the same time they may also be wondering whether change is necessary. They may be thinking about how they would go about making changes to their habits.

- **Preparation.** When a person enters preparation, they are starting to look more closely at their options for making a successful change to their behavior, whether that involves self-help or professionally led treatment. They may set a target date for initiating these changes: for example, a smoker would set a "quit date," or a person who is trying to change their alcohol use may make a plan for when and by how much they will begin to reduce their drinking.

- **Action.** An individual who is in the action stage has now started to make meaningful changes. They may begin receiving treatment, or start taking steps toward their goals: for example, they may have removed all of the alcohol from their house and started to cut back on their drinking.

- **Maintenance.** Once a person has initiated action and changed their behavior successfully, then they enter the maintenance stage. Typically, a change in drinking or drug use that has continued for six months or longer indicates that a person has transitioned from action into maintenance. However, even when a person is in this stage, they may still be vulnerable to slip or relapse. Vigilance at this stage remains important as far as maintaining a stable support system, continuing to engage in treatment (even if less frequently than in earlier stages of addiction recovery), and having a plan in place to address a slip or relapse if it does occur.

How does motivational therapy work?

In motivational enhancement therapy, a clinician or healthcare professional uses an empathic, nonjudgmental style to guide a person to build the motivation to change their use of alcohol or drugs. This approach is neither "pushy" nor prescriptive. Rather than "telling" a person why they should change their alcohol or drug use, the clinician helps the individual engage in a series of self-reflective therapy exercises to help them understand what stage of change they are in, and to *come to their own conclusions* about changes they need to make. The theory behind this technique is that when you help a person recognize the disconnect between their unhealthy behaviors (e.g., heavy drinking or use of drugs, such as cocaine) and their healthy goals (e.g., to succeed professionally, or to live a long life), they become more likely to begin contemplating and talking about change in positive ways. This is referred to as *change talk,* and that process of hearing oneself argue for change can be highly *motivating.* By encouraging a person to think about changing their behavior in positive terms, the focus of this short-term therapy approach is to:

1. help a person explore the benefits and drawbacks of continuing to drink or use drugs as they are presently;
2. envision how life could change if they were to successfully reduce or stop drinking or using drugs;
3. develop a plan to begin making behavioral changes that are consistent with a recovery-oriented life; and
4. build confidence in their ability to change.

Let's turn back to Tracy's story to see how her therapist used this approach to help her.

Tracy and her therapist began exploring her motivation to change her drinking. One of the first themes that came up in this conversation was her *ambivalence* about stopping. This is a central concept in motivational therapy—having mixed feelings about changing a behavior (especially when it's something that's very hard to change) is perfectly normal and doesn't mean that a person is unlikely to change successfully. Recognizing the ambivalence, acknowledging that it is a normal feeling, and exploring how to work through it and make lifestyle changes for the better are some of the most important themes a psychologist or other qualified counseling professional can help bring to the surface.

Even though Tracy knew that drinking was causing a lot of problems in her life, both psychologically and in terms of her ability to function, a *part of her* was afraid to try to stop—afraid that she would fail, that she would have to give up her social life to be successful, that she would struggle emotionally without the ability numb difficult feelings with alcohol. Over a series of therapy sessions, Tracy first identified her current stage of change and rated her motivation to stop her drinking. She realized that she was in the *preparation stage* because she was mentally preparing to change her drinking but was struggling to decide when and how to move into the *action stage*. Next, she and her therapist did a *decisional balance* exercise, in which she listed all the pros and cons of continuing to drink, and the pros and cons of stopping, and weighed them out to help inform her decision about what to do next. The benefits of continuing to drink were that:

- She wouldn't have to face her fears about stopping.
- She could continue to see her friends without having to confront the possibility that she would be the one person not drinking in the crowd.
- She wouldn't have to feel compelled to explain why she wasn't drinking to people in her social circles who might judge her.

These were pretty meaningful benefits for Tracy. When she started to think about the drawbacks of continuing to drink, she realized that she was very worried about her future and the future of her family if things were to continue as they were. She was worried about how her children, who were entering their teenage years, might be impacted by observing her drinking behavior. She was also worried about her own mental health. Her depression had been worsening for the last couple of months, and she was concerned that if she couldn't get those symptoms under control relatively soon, then her family would become impacted and she wouldn't be able to manage all of her responsibilities.

Once she and her therapist discussed these potential pros and cons of continuing to drink, as well as the benefits and drawbacks of quitting, Tracy decided that she needed to see how her life would change if she tried to stop drinking. Tracy's therapist encouraged her to create a goal that felt attainable, and to then re-evaluate closer to the end of that period whether she wanted to keep it going. Tracy felt much more comfortable with this idea, and set the goal of being abstinent from alcohol for 30 days. She started preparing to stop drinking when her children finished school for the summer.

Do motivational therapies work?

Meta-analyses have shown that motivational therapies are more effective than no treatment, and at least as effective as other treatments for a variety of behaviors that promote recovery from addiction.[5,6] Though motivational therapies are usually brief, the health benefits can be quite impactful, and include reducing alcohol and drug use, motivating participation in addiction treatment, and reducing risky behaviors (such as injecting drugs) that can lead to more complex health problems among people with substance use disorders. Usually, this type of treatment is ideal as a "first stage" of psychotherapy for addiction, and the outcomes are best when it is followed by other evidence-based therapies (such as cognitive behavioral therapy, or CBT). After helping a person solidify their commitment to changing their substance use, the next stage of treatment focuses on teaching skills that will help a person manage their addiction in daily life, using a set of techniques that we review next.

What is cognitive behavioral therapy?

Cognitive behavioral therapy (CBT) is a form of talk therapy that can be used to teach, encourage, and support individuals who are working toward the goal of reducing or stopping alcohol or drug use. CBT is used in all stages of recovery, including the early phases, when a person is first trying to make changes to their patterns of drinking or drug use, and in the later phases, when they are trying to maintain those changes. The "cognitive" component of CBT refers to the *thoughts* that people experience. When addiction develops, the mind can become preoccupied with the desire to drink or use drugs, and this desire or craving can occupy a lot of one's thoughts. These thoughts can be irrational (for example, telling oneself that there's no harm in having *just one drink*, even though it's been a long time since the person has been able to control themselves and stop after one). The "behavioral" part of CBT refers to the *actions* or *behaviors* that are connected to these thoughts. For example, if a person with addiction has *thoughts* about having a single drink, and convinces themselves, in that moment, that this is possible (even though evidence from their past year's drinking patterns suggests otherwise), the resulting *behavior* might be binge drinking and blacking out. A variety of techniques are used in CBT to encourage a person to recognize the relationship between their thoughts, feelings, and behaviors. Once a person becomes more familiar with their typical addiction-related thought and behavioral patterns, then they can focus on changing the way they think, their actions, and their lifestyle choices to help prevent relapse. Two of the essential strategies a counselor or therapist will use in CBT to help a person achieve these changes are (1) helping the person to identify relapse triggers, and (2) teaching strategies to cope with these triggers without falling back into old behavior patterns of drinking or using drugs.

How does CBT work?

Since CBT has proven highly effective as a treatment for addictions to various substances,[7,8] there has been a lot of interest among scientists and clinicians in understanding how it works. Studies show that CBT works in several ways to help people change their behavior: first, it increases *self-efficacy*, or one's confidence in one's ability to handle temptations to drink or use drugs. Second, it works by teaching healthy *coping skills*, such as ways to manage cravings without giving into them, strategies for dealing with feelings that are uncomfortable (such as anxiety, anger, or sadness) without drinking or using drugs, and how to respond when someone offers alcohol or drugs.[9,10] Let's turn back to Tracy's situation and see how her therapist used CBT to help her begin changing her drinking.

Once Tracy decided that she really needed to stop drinking, and she planned the date she would begin abstaining from alcohol, her therapist asked her to give some thought to a few important questions. First, how could she change her thinking so that she could cope with some of the stressors in her life without turning to drinking? Second, what could she do to prevent returning to drinking (or relapsing)? The next week, when she returned to therapy, she hung her head down, lifting her gaze upwards toward her therapist with a shameful expression. "I was doing so well the first three days after our last session," she said, "but then I messed it all up. I slipped up and drank."

Tracy's therapist began the process of "relapse analysis," which is a way to understand the circumstances that led up to the decision to drink, as well as what happened afterwards. In CBT, relapsing does not get people "kicked out" of treatment. Because relapse is understood as part of the expected ups and downs of the illness of addiction, evidence-based treatments *do not penalize relapses* by withholding help and support for recovery. Instead, a CBT therapist will help a person with addiction to make sense of how and why a relapse happened and learn how to prevent it in the future. This might mean making different types of decisions (such as avoiding certain people or places), or some needed life adjustments (such as a career shift) that will increase the likelihood of success in managing temptations or urges to drink or use drugs.

Tracy's therapist asked her lots of questions to help her "unpack" and understand the sequence of events and experiences that led her to slip up and drink. They talked about what time of the day she drank, how much she drank, what her mood was like prior to drinking, and how she felt afterwards. Tracy shared that the day she ended up drinking, she received some negative feedback from her boss at work, which she took pretty hard. Later that day, she was invited to happy hour by a co-worker and felt self-conscious about being the only one who wasn't drinking.

Tracy's therapist talked with her about some of the most common relapse triggers. She was surprised and a little bit relieved to learn that two of her experiences on that day have been found in studies to be powerful and common relapse triggers: (1) negative emotions (which can account for at least 35% of relapses), and (2) social pressure to drink (which can play a role in at least 20% of relapses).[11] This helped her to make sense of the fact that the combination of a trying day, feeling down on herself, and going out for happy hour could have set her up to slip up and drink.

Tracy's therapist helped her to work on learning how to cope with pressures that come about in social situations. In therapy, she explored how much information she wanted to share with people in her life about her reasons for stopping drinking. She learned some assertive communication skills that she could use to say "no" politely, but firmly when friends or co-workers offered her alcohol. She practiced what she would say when people who knew her as a drinker who was the life of the party noticed that she was ordering seltzer water. Over time, as she developed and practiced these CBT skills, Tracy became more confident and less nervous about navigating the social aspects of her decision to stop drinking. She also realized that as someone who was early on in her recovery process, she needed to find a balance between talking candidly about her decision to abstain from alcohol use in certain social situations where it naturally came up, and avoiding certain types of social events entirely. These were key steps to help her maintain the profound lifestyle change she was trying to make: transitioning from a frequent and often heavy drinker to a non-drinker.

Does CBT work?

Over the past several decades, at least three studies have been published on the use of CBT for alcohol and drug use disorders,[12,13,14] summarizing the results of more than 30 randomized clinical trials that included over 2,300 study participants. These studies have consistently shown that, when compared to control groups such as those receiving general drug counseling or usual care, people who receive CBT use drugs and/or alcohol less often and in lesser quantities, as well as having higher rates of abstinence from alcohol and drugs.

When summarizing the outcomes of a group of clinical trials, one of the key metrics that is often used in meta-analyses is known as the *effect size*. The effect size is a statistic that can range from small to large, and it tells us a few things: (1) whether a therapy approach like CBT is effective (or provides a greater benefit than either no treatment or another treatment it is being compared to), and (2) how effective it is (or how *large* the difference is between the outcomes of treatment for those who received CBT and the other study group it is being compared to). Essentially, an effect size tells us how much difference a treatment makes. The most recent meta-analyses have found that CBT is linked with sustainable changes in alcohol and drug use, and when compared to not receiving any treatment, receiving CBT makes a moderate to large difference.[15] To put this into context, antidepressants and psychotherapy[16] have been found to make a small to moderate difference in depression outcomes, and the effect sizes of medications for common medical conditions (e.g., cardiovascular disease, diabetes) range from small to large.[17] Based on the current scientific evidence, CBT for addiction performs much like medication and behavioral treatments that are reasonably effective for other chronic physical and mental health conditions.

What is mindfulness-based relapse prevention?

Mindfulness meditation is a technique that emerged through research over the past two decades as a promising practice for individuals who are in addiction recovery.[18] Rooted in Buddhist traditions, this approach involves meditation exercises to enable a person to pay attention to various aspects of their experience, in the present moment, without judgment, and with self-compassion. Why would this be an important skill set for someone with addiction? To put this into context, for most people, paying attention, with focus on what is happening in the here and now, doesn't come so naturally. The mind naturally either fast-forwards (e.g., to what is going to happen in an hour, or at the end of the day, or what is planned in the days or weeks to come), or rewinds backward (e.g., thinking about things that happened in the recent or remote past). It can be challenging to stay in the "now," especially when a person's experience is unpleasant. For example, if a person is feeling sad or lonely, their natural inclination may be to want to "get rid of" that feeling. So, rather than paying a lot of attention to it, they may look for a quick remedy—maybe a conversation with someone who makes them feel better, perhaps another distracting activity, or, maybe, for someone with an addiction, drinking or using a substance will "kill" that feeling. Over time, those responses that are aimed at escaping from uncomfortable feelings can become like habits—drinking, for example, becomes a "reaction" to unwanted experiences or feelings. Being "reactive" means taking actions like smoking, drinking, or finding other ways to distract ourselves from the present moment, without thinking about it or even realizing it at times. When practicing mindfulness as part of addiction treatment, the focus is on being present in the moment, even if it is unpleasant, and building the skills to be able to tolerate being purposefully aware of those unpleasant moments *without drinking or using substances.*

How does mindfulness-based relapse prevention work?

According to Buddhist principles, "craving for things to be otherwise" leads to suffering.[19] Feeling intoxicated or high may lead a person to want to amplify or continue that feeling, and when this craving or desire leads to repeated substance use, suffering may emerge in the form of addiction. Another way in which alcohol or drug use can be related to suffering is as follows: trying to escape or avoid pain or discomfort through substance use can lead to increasing unhappiness with the way things are. One of the central ideas behind mindfulness is that liberating oneself from patterns of negative thoughts (e.g., "I can't handle feeling anxious, I need to drink") and self-destructive actions (e.g., drinking or using drugs) will alleviate suffering. How does meditation liberate a person from negative thoughts? The answer lies in the acceptance component of mindfulness practice—when using mindfulness meditation during a craving, for example, the person learns to purposely focus their attention on the negative thoughts or feelings that are fueling their desire to drink or use drugs in that moment, with the goal of experiencing them, learning more about them, and accepting the discomfort of that desire as it is without attempting to change it. Going back to Tracy's experience, let's see how her therapist used mindfulness to help her solidify her recovery.

Tracy noticed something important about herself in relation to her recovery from alcoholism. She felt very uneasy in social situations, and for many years, she had been using alcohol to numb those feelings at parties, dinners out, and other social functions. In general, she struggled with a tendency to compare herself with others and criticize herself harshly for her flaws in the process. Rather than suffering through the negative self-talk, it was much easier when she went out somewhere to just start drinking as soon as she felt that uneasiness start to creep in. Tracy had been invited to a luncheon with some of her girlfriends, one of whom was always very competitive, and she was really conflicted about how to best handle herself there. "I never go into these situations without a drink in my hand. I don't know how I'll get through it without drinking," she told her therapist. Tracy's therapist talked with her about how she could use mindfulness skills while she was at the luncheon, and in other social situations. She taught her a brief meditation exercise, known as SOBER,[20] an acronym which she could use as follows:

- **Stop**: Tracy's therapist encouraged her to *pause*, to give herself the opportunity to *observe* and reflect on her emotional, physical, and cognitive experience when she felt uneasy in a social situation.
- **Observe:** She could start by observing how her body was feeling (e.g., was she tense or anxious at the luncheon? Where in her body did she experience that?). Next, she could observe the thoughts that were going through her mind (e.g., "I really need a drink"). Finally, she could observe how she was feeling emotionally (e.g., was she feeling anxious or depressed? Or overwhelmed by a strong desire to drink?).
- **Breathe:** Having made some observations about her experience, Tracy could now turn her attention to her breath, and focus on the movement of air through her

nose as she inhaled, and exhaled. She could do this for a matter of seconds or minutes. This would give her a way to focus her attention on something purposefully and practice meditation.

- **Expand** awareness: Once she spent some time focusing her attention on her breathing, the next step in the meditation was to expand her awareness to her surroundings and the rest of her body.

- **Respond mindfully:** Finally, having carefully observed her negative thoughts, feelings, and physical sensations, rather than *"reacting"* to them in an impulsive, perhaps self-destructive way (for example, by drinking alcohol), she could *"respond mindfully"* instead. Responding mindfully means deliberately choosing to do something to take care of oneself. For Tracy, rather than "reacting" to her social discomfort and craving for alcohol by drinking to eliminate or get rid of it, she could choose to leave the luncheon early, or say something positive to herself, like, "Just because I'm feeling a strong desire for alcohol doesn't mean that I have to do anything. I can feel this way without acting on it in this moment." She could also make positive statements to herself to help her feel less self-critical, like, "I'm proud of myself for coming, I don't have to be perfect to feel good about myself."

Coming back to the idea of accepting discomfort, you may have noticed that Tracy's therapist was not trying to get her to get rid of her urge to drink alcohol in social situations, but rather, to *tune into the discomfort* of the craving, *explore,* and *understand* it. The SOBER exercise was intended to help her recognize that even in the face of a compelling desire, she could choose what is probably the most challenging—but entirely achievable—response: *not to react.* By learning this skill, Tracy can practice alternatives to *drinking as a reaction* when other things are challenging in life.

Does mindfulness-based relapse prevention work?

The use of meditation techniques has been studied in recent years in combination with CBT skills to help people recognize and cope with common triggers for relapse such as depression, anxiety, or cues in their environment that lead to temptation or cravings to return to drinking or substance use. Mindfulness-Based Relapse Prevention,[21] is relatively new to the field of addiction treatment, and because of this, experts have only a small pool of studies from which to draw conclusions about effectiveness. While the most recent studies could not draw conclusions with certainty about the effectiveness of mindfulness-based treatments for addictions,[22,23] there is strong evidence for the benefits of mindfulness-based therapy for people who suffer from depression, anxiety, and stress.[24,25] It may be the case that those who struggle with these same types of symptoms would get the most out of using mindfulness to overcome their addictions.

At least one study of mindfulness as part of addiction treatment found that those who benefited most from this approach had not only addiction, but also struggled with diagnosable depression and anxiety.[26] More research is needed to confirm whether people with certain types of addictions and/or overlapping psychological symptoms would be most likely to benefit from incorporating mindfulness into their treatment. That said, there is enough evidence to support including mindfulness meditation training as part of the addiction therapy "toolbox," along with other well-studied approaches.

What is contingency management?

Contingency management is an evidence-based therapy technique that involves providing rewards, or incentives, for positive health-related behaviors, such as abstaining from drug use. The "target behavior" (i.e., the behavior that a person is trying to change in therapy, such as drinking or drug use) is measured, and then, if there is evidence that the person has achieved it, a reward is provided to them immediately. For example, if the "target" is abstinence from cocaine, then the individual would be asked to provide a urine sample that tests for the presence of cocaine a few times a week. Each time the sample tests negative for cocaine, the person is immediately rewarded. Rewards are also referred to as *reinforcers*, because they "reinforce" positive behaviors (such as abstaining from drug use), making them more likely to be repeated and as a result, set a person with addiction on a path toward longer-term recovery. The reinforcers that are used in this therapy are chances to win prizes or vouchers of varying monetary value. The vouchers can be exchanged for goods or services. Contingency management is based on the theory and principles of *behavioral economics*, which combines elements of economics and psychology to understand how people make decisions (such as the decision to pursue a non-drug reward when given the choice between that reward and using drugs).

How does contingency management work?

Given the focus of contingency management on behaviors and rewards without a talk-therapy component, it might be a little hard to imagine how it is done. The "fishbowl" method of providing contingency management is a good example, as it has been widely studied and used to treat addictions to various substances. Using this method, a person comes to a clinic two or three times a week to submit a urine sample, and if the sample tests as drug-free, then the person gets to draw a slip of paper out of a fishbowl. Half of the messages contain motivational, encouraging messages, such as "Great job!" whereas the other half are vouchers for goods and services, ranging from $1 to $100. As the individual continues to remain sober, the number of slips they get to draw increases. If they skip clinic visits, or test positive, then they go back to drawing one slip, but can build it up to more again. Though it might seem as though the unpredictable size of the rewards may not be enough of an incentive to inspire behavior change, the research and lived experiences described by those who have received contingency management suggest otherwise; the success of this approach may be more about the process of looking forward to earning an incentive and having one's achievements recognized than it is about the reward itself. As one individual who accessed contingency management when he was in recovery from stimulant addiction described, "I've been to a lot of rehabs, and there were no incentives except for the idea of being clean after you finished," said Mr. Kelty, 61, of Winfield, Pennsylvania. "Some of us need something to motivate us—even if it's a small thing—to live a better life."[27]

Does contingency management work?

There is no question about the effectiveness of contingency management; studies have consistently found that this method reduces drug use among populations with various types of addictions,[28] and these treatments have been used not only in the United States but in many countries around the world. Meta-analyses and reviews evaluating several different types of behavioral treatments for substance use disorders have found that contingency management often results in larger effect sizes than other approaches, meaning that the size of its impact on drug use is greater than that of some of the other highly effective, evidence-based therapies.[29,30] Contingency management is known for its effectiveness in treating addiction to stimulants, including both cocaine and methamphetamine,[31,32] and given the resurgence of stimulant use disorders among individuals with opioid addiction, there is increasing urgency to make this approach more widely available.

Why isn't contingency management more widely available?

If you're a healthcare consumer who likes to do your research, you might find that you've come across many of the therapy approaches that we've reviewed here, but contingency management has less of a presence than other treatments you've been reading about. This is not an incorrect observation. In fact, the underutilization of this highly effective treatment method gained national attention in recent years, and the *New York Times* published an article to explore this issue: "This Addiction Treatment Works. Why Is It So Underused?" Despite 30 years' worth of strong scientific evidence, emotionally driven criticisms have been expressed both by treatment providers and society more broadly, namely that this approach is much like "bribery," calling into question the ethics of compensating people for "doing what they're supposed to."[33] As one of the world's leading experts on contingency management argued, however, these objections seem to be tied specifically to those who are trying to overcome addictions, because monetary rewards and incentives are widely used to reward behaviors such as good job performance and are often given to other vulnerable individuals to help them learn prosocial behaviors, such as those with autism or mental retardation.[34] These arguments against rewarding therapeutic behavior changes related to substance use likely reflect stigmatized views of people who struggle with addiction, or a limited understanding of addiction as a chronic illness.

Another concern that has been raised about contingency management is that the behavioral changes it produces may reverse once the rewards are no longer being provided. From the perspective of scientific and clinical experts in addiction treatment, including Dr. Richard Rawson, who has led many of the most influential clinical trials out of UCLA evaluating contingency management, solving the problem of addiction requires a realistic, pragmatic approach to discovering and making use of the treatments that work. Rawson suggests that contingency management should be used for an indefinite period, just as medications for opioid addiction, for many are a long-term or lifelong treatment. In other words, since addiction is a chronic brain disease, "treatments need to be designed to accommodate this reality."[35]

At the policy level, other barriers pose challenges to the use of contingency management. Providers are hesitant about giving monetary rewards to their patients out of fear that they will violate anti-kickback laws and lose their federal funding support. Because of concerns about potential fraud, there is reluctance to allow Medicaid to reimburse clinics for the costs of contingency management. Rawson and others are advocating to shift regulations that limit the use of incentives in addiction treatment, and add contingency management to the list of reimbursable, evidence-based treatments offered through Medicaid.[36] The most successful system to have made use of contingency management is the Department of Veterans Affairs, where the treatment has been provided to 5,600 veterans since 2011, with positive outcomes.[37,38]

What is family therapy?

If you or someone you know suffers from addiction, you probably know that this illness does not just affect the person who is living with it; addiction can take a toll on family, friends, and even others who rely on that person, such as their co-workers. While seeing a loved one start treatment is usually a great relief to the friends and family of an addicted person, that is just the beginning of the healing process. The feelings a family is left with once addiction takes hold can be complicated—on the one hand, they may feel compassion for their loved one's suffering and have a desire to help. On the other hand, they may feel angry, hurt, and resentful about some of the behaviors that they were affected by over the course of months, or even years. Those feelings don't vanish when a person stops drinking or using drugs. In fact, sometimes they intensify. Some family members may be burned out from having taken too much responsibility for their loved one's substance use, while others may just shut down or even act out. You may recall the story of Alisa from Chapter 1. When she stopped drinking, her family had a difficult time moving past all the pain, suffering, and worry that her alcoholism had caused them. The family dynamics shifted, leading her to fear that her family wouldn't trust her again—how could her life have meaning if she no longer felt like a trusted member of her family?

These worries and conflicts are, in fact, pretty normal for a family that has been impacted by a loved one's addiction. Based on the idea that a family is a system with different parts, and changes in one part (e.g., a family member being affected by an addiction) will trigger changes in all the other parts, *family therapy* is a form of treatment that is used to help the whole family heal as their loved one with addiction goes through their own healing process. Without help and support, a family can remain stuck in unhealthy patterns even after the family member with addiction begins to recover. Without some attention devoted to recovery as a family unit, it can be hard for the family to adjust to a member's changes in behavior and provide the support a loved one now needs to sustain their recovery.

How does family therapy work?

Anyone the individual in treatment for addiction considers to be family can be included in the family therapy process, regardless of whether they are immediate family or blood-related.[39] Below are examples of those who may participate in family treatment, if the individual who is recovering from addiction designates them as an important part of their healing:

√ parents	√ godparents
√ spouses or partners	√ godchildren
√ in-laws	√ blended family members
√ siblings	√ extended family members
√ children	√ friends
√ elected, chosen, or honorary family members	√ fellow veterans
√ other relatives	√ colleagues who care

√ stepparents   √ mutual-help group members
√ stepchildren   √ sponsors
√ foster parents
√ foster children

The timing of when to start family therapy is important and is usually after the person who is in treatment for addiction has made some progress in recovery, which can range from a few months to years into the process. The danger of starting too early is that without the right skills onboard to manage difficult feelings such as guilt or anger that can come up when exploring family problems, a person in recovery can find themselves rationalizing drinking or using over these feelings, and the family work can become a trigger for relapse. If instead the person has the opportunity to get really invested in their own recovery from addiction and is learning and practicing skills to resist triggers and cravings, adhere to medication regimens, and avoid temptations to rationalize drinking or drug use, then they will be in a better place to begin the challenging family work that will help their loved ones heal along with them.

There are two main goals of family therapy. First, keeping in mind that the family will be healthier as long as the addicted family member is stable and healthy, an important goal of this treatment is to help the family learn how to support their loved one's recovery and help them to avoid a relapse. The second goal is to strengthen the whole family's emotional health, so that everyone can thrive. Although the specific areas of focus in treatment to achieve these goals are going to be different for each family, the overarching goals are the same, and the family should collaborate with the therapist to identify and prioritize the topics and themes to work on.

In family therapy, family members work with a therapist to try to understand how they act with one another and whether their relationship dynamics are helpful or hurtful. They learn to adapt their behavior to meet the needs of the family member who is in recovery, and at the same time support the needs of the entire family. To achieve this, they often have to learn new and better ways of communicating with each other, and practice new ways of talking, relating, and acting toward one another. The therapist helps the family make changes so that members support each other and treat each other with respect, stop enabling behaviors, and learn to trust each other. Coming back to the family relationships in Alisa's story in Chapter 1: Alisa's husband Jay didn't trust her, and his constant suspicions about her having relapsed were triggering for her. In family therapy he learned that it was normal to feel this way, and to be patient with the process of rebuilding trust. Alisa and Jay learned new ways of checking in about her drinking that didn't feel intrusive or come across as being fraught with suspicion and a lack of confidence in her. By learning healthier ways to have direct conversations about this theme, the family began to repair their relationships.

Does family therapy work?

Studies suggest that behavioral treatment for addiction that includes family therapy works better than treatment that does not. Family therapy can be especially helpful to those who have mental health issues overlapping with addiction, and research shows that these individuals, when offered family therapy in combination with individual therapy, are more likely to take their prescribed medications and experience improvements in mental health symptoms, and less likely to relapse to alcohol or drug use and/or to be hospitalized.

Family Therapy: Frequently Asked Questions

- Who conducts the sessions?
  Family therapy requires specialty training and may be facilitated by a licensed family therapist, social worker, psychologist, psychiatrist, counselor, clergy member, or other qualified professional.
- Who attends the sessions?

Family therapy involves the entire family meeting together. Sometimes part of the family meets, and in some situations the therapist may work one-on-one with a family member in addition to the whole family.

- What is the focus of the sessions?

This will change over the course of therapy depending on the specific problems that need to be addressed. Sessions may focus on the person in treatment for addiction, or on another family member, or on the family as a whole. Some sessions may feel low-key, while others are intense, depending on the topic or theme that is discussed. Sessions are typically one hour long, once a week.

- Who does most of the talking—the therapist or the family?

The therapist may use different techniques to help the family. Sometimes, the family therapist may ask questions, or listen and observe while the family members talk to one another. This helps the therapist learn how the family members behave and communicate with each other, what their strengths are, and what they need help with to improve their relationships with one another. At other times, the therapist may do more talking, to educate the family about their loved one's addiction and recovery process and/or to teach communication skills and ways of handling some of the ups and downs in the cycle of addiction.

- Is there really enough time for the therapist to address the problems each family member has with the member who is in recovery?

Everyone in the family brings their own personality, history, and personal challenges that affect the way that they cope with their loved one's addiction. Some family members may have their own mental health or even addiction issues, life stressors, and negative experiences with their addicted loved one that they need time and space to process. When there is much more going on with some of the individual family members than the family therapist can adequately address in a weekly one-hour meeting, then the therapist may refer the individual members to extra sources of help. This may be in the form of individual counseling, self-help groups, or classes they can take on topics such as parenting or anger management.

- What will the individual members of the family learn to do differently?

The therapist will teach the family coping skills, such as how to deal with anger, resentment, or sadness. Ideally, being in treatment will give some of the family members the opportunity to let out their feelings and talk about them, which is part of the process of gaining understanding and healing. Some of the sessions may involve taking a problem the family isn't sure how to talk about or solve, and coaching the individual members about how to discuss and come to a solution about it in a healthy, productive way. The therapist may teach the family members listening skills and assertive communication skills to achieve this. Finally, to practice new, positive, and healthy ways of interacting with each other, the therapist will assign homework in between sessions, such as eating a meal together, acknowledging positive things that their loved one is doing (rather than focusing all of their interactions only on the addictive behaviors), or doing something fun together.

As we discussed in the section on motivational psychotherapy techniques, it is not uncommon for a person with addiction to have mixed feelings about entering or remaining in treatment. Family therapy has been shown to help individuals to decide to start treatment, and it can reduce their risk of dropping out of treatment prematurely.[40] Family therapy has also been shown to reduce stress, and the risk of alcohol or drug use, among the addicted individual's family members. Research also shows that family therapy can improve how couples treat each other, how children behave, and how the whole family gets along.[41]

The following excerpt from Stephen D'Antonio's stories of "lessons learned from the perspective of a dad dealing with his son's addiction" offers some reflections on the role of the family in a person's recovery.

"An addiction counselor once told me: "You didn't cause it, you can't control it, you can't cure it". As I listened to those unsettling words I thought to myself: "Then what the hell can I do?"

It turns out, a lot.

Almost every addiction counselor will advise parents and caregivers that they are critical to the recovery process and that there are four primary things that they can and should do to help their loved one:

Get educated about the disease. This is a complicated and vexing disease, particularly in the way that the symptoms manifest themselves within relationships and within the family. Without a doubt, the more that you know the higher the likelihood that you will be helpful to the recovery process. Early on, I was detrimental to my son's recovery. I didn't know that. Then I learned and made the necessary adjustments.

Get professional help for your child. We know that addiction is a brain disease. And we know that active addiction is a life-altering and many times a life-threatening health issue. The science shows that professional treatment increases the chances for recovery. Given all that, seeking professional help seems like a no-brainer, just like for any other health issue. The recovery roadmap is also fraught with twists and turns, difficult messages to deliver, and complicated situations. Professionals are able to deliver much needed wisdom, judgement, and tactics. In my view, professionals saved my son's life. I will be forever grateful.

The #1 recommendation that I hear from experienced parents, and my #1 recommendation, is to work with professional clinicians.

Get support. The idea that I would need to join a parent support group as part of the process for my son's recovery was a ridiculous concept to me. No way! Yet, today, after spending years attending these groups for myself and years attending groups as a Parent Peer Volunteer, I am convinced that these groups are life-changing assets for parents.

Nearly all of us that attend these meetings attended our first meeting completely skeptical about the value of the meeting and most of us were certain that our situation was unique. We all felt alone and isolated. Within two or three meetings, almost everyone remarks that they no longer feel alone, that they feel supported, that their situation is far less unique than they thought, and that they are learning critical things about how to handle their loved one within the household. Invaluable! The secret sauce is that under the guidance from a clinical moderator, participants share stories, information and strategies that resonate. A clinician might talk about a concept, but there is something exceptionally powerful that happens when a parent talks about their experiences with their addicted child. The impact is extraordinary.

Attending parent group meetings moderated by a professional is my #2 recommendation.

Take Care of Yourself. I didn't do it. I could not justify focusing on myself when my son's life was on the line. I lost weight, and not in a good way, and I was on edge constantly. At one point, I was so frustrated and strung out that I threw my Blackberry and it literally stuck in our den wall, half in half out. We had a Blackberry sized slice in our wall for years—I am not proud of that at all. But, it came to symbolize something important: this process is a marathon and not a sprint and that if you do not take care of yourself then you will not be at your best when called upon to handle tough circumstances.

Dealing with a child's addiction is a massive ask. It is a powerful and complicated health issue. As a Parent Peer Volunteer, I often tell parents, when they are strung out and frustrated, that their kids are the lucky ones. Many parents turn a blind eye to the problem. The parents that dig in are heroes to their kids, whether their kids appreciate it or not.

The bottom line is that to best help your child, it is important to access resources and get involved in the process."[42] Source: D'Antonio, 2022.

Where do self-help groups for addiction fit in?

As you can see from our review of behavioral therapy approaches to addiction, there are many pathways to addiction recovery. One pathway that has been traveled by as many as 1.8 million people in the United States over the course of a year is involvement in 12-step and mutual/self-help groups.[43] These groups, which include Alcoholics Anonymous (AA), Cocaine Anonymous (CA), and Narcotics Anonymous (NA), are different from *treatment*—whereas treatment involves assessment, diagnosis, and therapeutic services that are led by healthcare professionals with formal training or credentials in addiction care, 12-step and mutual/self-help groups are peer-led support groups structured around a particular philosophy about what addiction is and how it can be overcome. Self-help programs can support a person's recovery process in several ways. For some who do not wish to or aren't able to seek formal treatment, self-help may be their only source of support for changing their alcohol or drug use. Research shows that around a third of those who are involved in self-help groups are also receiving formal treatment services at the same time[44] and are using the groups as an added source of support. For others who have completed formal or professionally led treatment, these groups can be a source of continuing care and community support. Self-help groups are highly accessible and are available at no cost in communities throughout the world, serving as important resources in addiction recovery.

12-Step Mutual Self-Help Groups: How it Works

- What is required for membership in 12-Step groups?
  The only requirement is a desire to stop drinking and/or using drugs. Service and helping other members become and remain sober is also emphasized.
- What is the 12-Step philosophy?
  The 12-Step philosophy focuses on the importance of accepting addiction as a disease that can be arrested but never cured, enhancing maturity and spiritual growth, and helping others with addiction.

- What do the 12 steps involve?

  The 12 consecutive "steps" refer to activities the new member completes, usually with guidance from a more experienced 12-step member (i.e., a "sponsor") who is stable in their recovery. These steps include accepting one's powerlessness over alcohol and drugs, taking a moral inventory of oneself, admitting the nature of one's wrongs, making a list of individuals whom they have harmed, and making amends to those people.

- What is the purpose of the groups, if much of the 12-step work is done individually?

  The groups provide support for remaining alcohol- and/or drug-free, a social network to lean on in the process, and a set of guiding principles ("12 steps and 12 traditions") to follow during their recovery process.

Do self-help groups work?

According to scientific reviews, participation in AA and NA is linked with greater likelihood of achieving abstinence from alcohol and drugs, often for prolonged periods. Treatment outcomes for individuals who are in professionally led programs and participating in 12-step groups at the same time are better, particularly if people begin attending early in their course of treatment and attend frequently (3 or more meetings per week) and consistently.[45] It is also important to know that meeting attendance alone is not necessarily the driver of success in becoming or remaining sober. Studies show that *involvement in 12-step group activities* is more likely to lead to abstinence from alcohol or drugs; these activities can include doing service at meetings (such as setting up coffee or speaking at a meeting), doing "step work," getting a sponsor, calling other 12-step group members, and taking others to meetings. It may be that these activities lead to a stronger sense of affiliation and connectedness to the 12-step community, deepening a person's commitment to the process of recovery. Or it could be that a person feels a greater sense of accountability to others who are part of the recovery community by being involved in more 12-step activities, and that helps them keep their recovery on track. Studies show that the aspects of 12-step participation that are most strongly tied to changes in substance use are the social or "fellowship" aspects of the experience, which lead to rewarding social relationships and more time spent with people who are supportive of recovery rather than those who might trigger temptations to use substances,[46] along with the development of skills to cope with urges to use substances. To get the most benefit out of 12-step group participation, it is helpful to keep in mind the importance of getting involved with the 12-step community in ways that supplement attending meetings.

Given the scientific support for the benefits of participating in 12-step groups, it probably sounds like a no-brainer—shouldn't everyone who is trying to change their alcohol or drug use be involved in 12-step groups? Although it seems like this would be ideal, one of the challenges with these groups is that many people with substance use disorders are reluctant to attend them, which leads to low or inconsistent participation rates and dropouts.[47] Some of the things that interfere with participation include the natural ups and downs in motivation and readiness to commit to changing one's alcohol or drug use, social anxiety or other psychological problems that can make group participation difficult, and for some, a lack of compatibility between their personal or treatment belief systems and philosophies and those that are core to the 12-step program. For example, some individuals feel that they are not a match for a philosophy that emphasizes spirituality and/or the concept of a higher power. Others struggle with the idea of being powerless over their use of alcohol or drugs, which is central to the first of the 12 steps. Studies have shown that people with addictions typically fall into one of 3 groups regarding their involvement with 12-step programs: some never connect with 12-step groups or programs, some connect briefly but then drop out, and a third group develops a strong affiliation and maintains consistent rates of attendance.[48]

Fortunately, self-help groups have expanded tremendously over the years. In 1975, 40 years after AA was founded, the first secular alternative to the 12-step approach emerged: Women for Sobriety (WFS)[49] was the first of many alternative self-help approaches. Since then, many other secular alternatives have arisen, including the American Atheists Alcohol Recovery Group, in 1980; Secular Organization for Sobriety (SOS), in 1985; Rational Recovery, in 1986; Smart Recovery (SMART) and Moderation Management, both of which emerged in 1994; and LifeRing Secular Recovery (LifeRing), in 1999. These alternatives provide additional options for those who have a hard time connecting with the philosophy and other aspects of AA. The table below describes various self-help groups one can choose from.

Types of Self-Help Groups

Group	How to access it	Guiding principles
12-Step Programs Including: Alcoholics Anonymous Narcotics Anonymous Marijuana Anonymous Cocaine Anonymous Dual Recovery Anonymous . . . and many more	https://alcoholicsanonymous.com/find-a-meeting/ Local and online meetings are available http://www.draonline.org/	Disease concept of addiction Reliance on a higher power Recovery is linked to working the 12 steps Working the steps with the support of a sponsor is recommended
IntheRooms	https://www.intherooms.com/home	Global online community; both 12-step and non-step live online meetings
SMART Recovery	https://www.smartrecovery.org/ Local and online meetings are available	CBT based alternative to the spiritual focus of 12-step groups

Group	How to access it	Guiding principles
Al Anon	https://al-anon.org	Mutual support for those who have been affected by someone else's addiction
Women for Sobriety	https://womenforsobriety.org/ Local and online meetings are available	Secular addiction recovery group for women "Release the past – plan for tomorrow – live for today"
Moderation Management	https://moderation.org Local and online meetings, active online support community available	Support for learning to control alcohol use, harm-reduction oriented
LifeRing	https://lifering.org/ Local and online meetings are available	Secular abstinence-based addiction recovery group
Secular Organization for Sobriety	https://www.sossobriety.org/ Local and online meetings are available	Anonymous, secular path to sobriety

12

WHAT MEDICATIONS ARE EFFECTIVE FOR ADDICTION?

Is medication an option for treating an addiction?

Many people are surprised to learn that medications are available to treat addictions to various substances, including alcohol, tobacco, and opioids. And this is not to say that everyone with a substance use disorder would benefit from taking medication. Since the severity of substance use disorders can range from one person to another, from just a few problems related to alcohol or drug use (i.e., a mild disorder) to six or more symptoms (i.e., an addiction), there are many factors to take into consideration when deciding whether medication is the right treatment for yourself or a loved one. For someone with a mild substance use disorder, learning strategies to control one's alcohol or drug use through behavioral counseling, coupled with recognizing the signs of a progressing or worsening substance use disorder may, be sufficient to enable a person to make impactful changes to their behavior. For someone with a moderate to severe substance use disorder—depending on individual circumstances, symptoms, responses to prior treatment efforts, and the presence of any other physical or psychological health conditions that can be affected by worsening problems with alcohol or drug use—combining medications with behavioral or psychological treatment can be a potentially effective approach. Medications are not only used to help someone reduce or stop their use of alcohol or drugs; they can also be used to treat withdrawal symptoms and enable them to enter longer-term addiction recovery.

In addition to considering how serious the problems caused by substance use have become, and how any attempts to change one's drinking or drug use without medications have gone thus far, it can also be helpful to become knowledgeable about the current state of the science concerning the effectiveness of treatments for addiction to different substances. Specifically, familiarizing yourself with studies on how addictions to different substances respond to treatments that include medications, versus those that do not, can help inform some of these important decisions. In this chapter, we consider scientific evidence for the use of behavioral treatment with or without medication for addictions to different substances. For example, as you'll see later in this chapter, the evidence concerning treatment of opioid addiction indicates overwhelmingly that people who take medication as part of their treatment for opioid use disorder do better than those who receive counseling and other services without medications;[1] we will review these studies below.

How do healthcare providers decide what medicines to prescribe for addiction?

When medications are used to treat substance use disorders, there are two different sets of circumstances that inform a prescriber's decision: the first is when a medication has received approval from the US Food and Drug Administration (FDA) for use in treating symptoms of a particular substance use disorder. To gain FDA approval, medications have to be shown to be safe and effective through *randomized clinical trials* (RCTs). Most RCTs involve the comparison of the medication to a *placebo*, or a pill that is made of sugar or another substance that doesn't have any therapeutic effects on the health condition it's being studied for. People who participate in RCTs are assigned by the flip of a coin to receive either the medication or a placebo. The reason that placebos are used as a comparison to the medication is because sometimes the expectation of getting well, and the time and attention that a person receives from being prescribed a medicine by a medical provider, can lead to some changes in symptoms. In most clinical trials, the goal is to see whether the medication influences a person's symptoms and recovery from addiction *beyond* what would be expected from interacting with a medical provider and becoming hopeful about getting better (i.e., the potential benefits of a placebo). To acquire approval from the FDA, the medication must work better than a placebo in reducing symptoms of a substance use disorder. It is also important that studies show that the benefits of the medication outweigh the discomfort and/or health risks associated with its side effects.

A second set of circumstances that can inform a healthcare practitioner's decision to prescribe a medicine is when they give a drug that the FDA has approved to treat a condition that is different from a substance use disorder. This is referred to as *off-label* prescribing. This practice is legal and common, with one in five prescriptions written today for off-label use. However, this practice should always be informed by scientific evidence that supports the use of a medicine for a condition other than the one it is FDA-approved for.[2] As a patient, it is important to ask questions about the evidence supporting the use of any medicine to understand whether or not it is FDA approved, and if not, the risks and benefits of off-label use.

In the sections that follow, we'll review various RCTs, focusing mostly on FDA-approved medications for addiction treatment. Considering recent developments in studies of potentially promising medication treatments for addictions to different substances, we will also review some off-label uses of medications. Though the details about the methods and statistics that were used won't be discussed here, one way of summarizing where the science stands on the effectiveness of these treatments is to focus on *meta-analyses*, which will be described here whenever possible. A meta-analysis is a method of combining data from many RCTs to draw conclusions about the therapeutic benefits of a medication, or whether it is more effective than a placebo for outcomes such as changing one's drinking or drug use and the negative impacts of substance use on a person's ability to function.

Behavioral therapies can also be studied in RCTs. Often, these clinical trials help us understand whether there's an advantage to combining behavioral therapy with medication, versus receiving treatment with either method on its own. This is achieved by designing a research study in which people are assigned by a coin flip to receive either medication alone, or the combination of medication with behavioral therapy. Though the FDA does not evaluate or approve behavioral treatments the way that it does medications, this is beginning to shift as psychotherapies are being delivered more and more using digital health platforms such as apps that can be downloaded on to a smartphone. The FDA has a process in place to evaluate and approve what are referred to as *digital therapeutics*, so in the coming years, some of the emerging digital addiction treatment programs that include behavioral therapy may become FDA approved.

How can medications help?

Medically supervised withdrawal management ("detoxification")

Medications can be useful in different stages of addiction recovery and can be included as part of various types of treatment. For example, a person who is severely physically dependent on or addicted to alcohol may need to undergo medically supervised withdrawal management (also known as *detoxification*, a term that has changed to destigmatize the process). This involves the use of medications to safely achieve an alcohol-free state, relieve the acute, very uncomfortable, and at times life-threatening symptoms of alcohol withdrawal, and treat any co-occurring medical or psychiatric conditions that can be affected by chronic alcohol use. Detoxification is often done in an inpatient treatment setting (e.g., a hospital), but can sometimes be managed on an outpatient basis depending on addiction severity. Medications are often used for opioid detoxification as well.

An important consideration regarding the use of medications for detoxification is that the relapse rates after this form of treatment are extremely high *if detoxification isn't immediately followed by another form of care.* For example, rates of relapse to opioid use following detoxification have been found to exceed 90%,[3] with the majority of those who relapse quickly (i.e., within a week of leaving detoxification treatment) failing to access another form of care. This is not surprising, given that medically supervised withdrawal management is not meant to be a "cure" for addiction, but rather a steppingstone on the path to long-term recovery. The best addiction treatment outcomes are linked to the length of time a person spends in some form of treatment; the longer a person remains in treatment, the better their long-term outcomes.[4] This is not to say that *intensive* treatment is needed long term—but rather that some form of treatment that meets the dynamically changing needs of individuals with addiction at different stages of recovery can play an important role in achieving and maintaining success. For some, this will involve weekly therapy after a period of intensive treatment; for others, this can be achieved through a monthly or even quarterly visit with a primary care or addiction-specialized provider who is prescribing medication. For others, the combination of ongoing social support via self-help meetings and professionally guided individual or group therapy is needed, especially when one suffers from other co-occurring mental health conditions that can make recovery more challenging. When completing an intensive treatment episode, discussing the options for ongoing or "continuing care" with one's treatment provider can help prevent gaps in care that increase the risk of relapse.

How do medications change a person's desire to drink or use drugs?

Either when a person has completed detoxification treatment, or when they enter behavioral treatment directly to begin their recovery, one of the primary ways that medication helps with addiction recovery is by reducing cravings for alcohol or drugs. The powerful cravings that people experience, particularly in early recovery, can be very difficult to manage, making it challenging to establish lasting periods of abstinence or reductions in alcohol or drug use. Because of the profound effects of craving on addictive behaviors, reducing the intensity and frequency of cravings with anti-craving medications can effectively prevent relapse to compulsive alcohol and drug use.

Three Things Medications Can Do to Aid Addiction Recovery

1. Control uncomfortable withdrawal symptoms during early recovery, enabling a person to safely and successfully enter the next phase of addiction care.
2. Reduce urges or cravings to drink or use substances, making a person more successful in efforts to abstain from substance use.
3. Block the brain's pleasure response when a substance is used, so that when a person drinks or uses substances, they don't feel its effects. This leads a person to drink or use drugs less than before.

Sometimes referred to as "replacement therapy" or "substitution therapy" that can be very helpful to those with either nicotine or opioid addiction, these medicines were developed to help people with addictions who have very strong physical withdrawals. With nicotine addiction, for example, the powerful cravings that make it so difficult for people to cut back on or quit smoking are signs of nicotine withdrawal. For daily smokers, those withdrawal symptoms are experienced throughout the day, prompting the mind to become preoccupied with the idea of smoking that next cigarette, an obsession that just won't stop nagging. The only way to get rid of it is to replenish the brain with nicotine or wait long enough in discomfort for it to subside. For hours and days, it will keep on coming back again, making the "cold turkey" quit attempt very challenging and uncomfortable. It is largely for this reason that only 5% of those who attempt to stop in this way are successful. Replacement therapy for tobacco addiction is a way of preventing the ups and downs of going into nicotine withdrawal repeatedly throughout the day, prompting cravings and relapse for those who are trying to cut back or stop. Instead, by keeping a low but steady level of nicotine in the bloodstream, nicotine replacement medication provides relief from withdrawal, which enables focus on staying motivated to quit, and learning new ways of coping with situations and emotions that previously triggered addictive behavior. The rationale for opioid replacement therapy is similar—preventing the rollercoaster of highs followed by intensely unpleasant withdrawals from opioids, these medications stabilize the brain with a steady dose that enables the person to feel normal and able to function. Since the psychological and behavioral consequences of the highs and lows people with opioid addiction experience are far more complex than those related to nicotine addiction, the "opioid use disorder" section below includes a thorough discussion of the rationale for medication treatment.

What medications are available to treat tobacco use disorder?

Nicotine replacement therapy

Nicotine replacement therapy (NRT) includes nicotine gum, patches, lozenges, nasal spray, and inhalers, and is considered the *first-line treatment* for tobacco addiction. First-line treatment is the first treatment that is standardly given for a particular disease because it is considered, based on scientific evidence, to be the best treatment for that condition. Indeed, studies show that using medications increases success rates for quitting smoking; according to a review of 150 clinical trials, the use of NRT increases the rate of quitting by 60%.[5] Because of the intense cravings that they experience, most smokers who are unable to stop successfully relapse within the first two weeks of attempting to quit. However, there are a range of options for medication treatment, and because it's such a difficult addiction to quit, people typically require many attempts to stop smoking before the behavior change sticks for good. With that in mind, it's important to keep on trying no matter what, knowing that there are many different forms of nicotine replacement to try both individually and in combination if the first one or two aren't helpful. In fact, research shows that combining the nicotine patch with another replacement therapy such as the gum or lozenges is more effective than using a single form of NRT.[6,7] Sometimes, when people struggle within the first few weeks of attempting to quit smoking, part of the reason is that they're not using enough nicotine replacement or not using it for long enough, so working with a behavioral therapist and/or physician with experience helping people stop smoking can be helpful to ensure that they're getting the greatest possible benefit from medication. In addition, becoming knowledgeable about the benefits and potential side effects of nicotine replacement, as well as the correct dosing and length of treatment, can increase the likelihood of the next quit attempt being successful.

How does the nicotine patch work?

The nicotine patch slowly releases nicotine into the body, providing a steady low level of nicotine throughout the day. This prevents the cycle of tobacco use followed by periods of withdrawal that can be uncomfortable and distracting until one repeats smoking or other forms of nicotine use. By using the patch, a smoker can quit without experiencing withdrawal symptoms in the process, which are quite uncomfortable and include symptoms like depressed mood, insomnia, irritability, frustration, anxiety, and restlessness. The nicotine patch is an over-the-counter medication that is available in three different strengths: 7mg, 14mg, and 21mg. Usually, people will start this form of replacement therapy at the highest strength and gradually reduce or taper the dose after the first two to four weeks on the medication, eventually reaching the lowest dose before discontinuing the medication altogether. The patch is worn continuously for 16 to 24 hours, and can even be worn while showering or bathing. For those who struggle with intense cravings, the addition of other forms of NRT as needed, including nicotine gum, lozenges, inhaler, or spray can be very helpful.

What are the side effects of the nicotine patch?

Although uncommon, side effects from the nicotine patch can occur. The most typical side effects are skin irritation where the patch has been placed, and vivid dreams that require removal of the patch before going to sleep.

For how long should NRT be used?

The recommended length of treatment with the nicotine patch is 8 to 12 weeks. Although some people may use the patch for shorter or longer periods than that, research shows that using NRT (including the patch and other formulations such as gum and/or lozenges) for a relatively short period of time (i.e., for less than 4 weeks) makes a person even less likely to quit successfully than someone who didn't use NRT at all.[8] However, using it for 8 to 12 weeks more than triples the likelihood of quitting. Because the health risks associated with tobacco use greatly outweigh those of longer-term use of nicotine replacement therapy, the Centers for Disease Control recommends extending the use of NRT for up to five months if it is helpful in preventing relapse to tobacco use. Generally, studies have found that use of NRT beyond 12 weeks is helpful, but not as effective as treatment ranging between 8 and 12 weeks, with at least two studies reporting no difference in quit rates between those who used NRT for the recommended 8-to-12-week timeframe versus those who continued to use it for 24 or 28 weeks.[5] Thus, while the added benefit of longer use of NRT beyond 12 weeks is questionable, the usefulness of extended treatment may depend on the individual.

What are nicotine lozenges?

Nicotine lozenges are available in standard and "mini" sizes, each of which are offered in 2mg and 4mg strengths. The lozenge dissolves slowly after being placed in the mouth, and cannot be chewed or swallowed. This method leads nicotine to be absorbed over 20 to 30 minutes, or a briefer 10-minute period if the mini-lozenge is used. The most frequently reported side effects include headaches and hiccups.

What is nicotine gum?

Like the lozenge, nicotine gum is available in 2mg and 4mg strengths. When using this form of NRT, alternating between chewing and "parking" the gum between the gum and cheek, nicotine is absorbed across the lining of the mouth. Side effects may include nausea and hiccups.

What is nicotine nasal spray?

As the fastest acting NRT method, the nasal spray can come in handy as an immediate behavioral and biochemical "antidote" for an urge or craving. Due to its quick delivery of nicotine to the brain, the spray is recommended for use among those who struggle with intense cravings, and can be used as an add-on "as needed" treatment for those who are using the nicotine patch. Side effects typically improve with regular use, and commonly include nasal irritation, sinus irritation, and/ or watery eyes.

Types of Nicotine Replacement Therapy

Type	How to Get It	How It Works	Pros and Cons
Nicotine Patch	Over the counter	Placed on the skin for 16 to 24 hours at a time. Releases nicotine into the bloodstream.	**Pros**: Easy to use, applied only once daily, few side effects. **Cons**: Dosing isn't flexible, mild skin rashes.
Nicotine Lozenge	Over the counter	As it dissolves, nicotine is delivered through the lining of the mouth. 8 to 9 lozenges are used daily.	**Pros**: Easy to use, nicotine doses are 25% higher than nicotine gum. **Cons**: Can't eat/drink 15 min before use, no chewing the lozenges, can cause nausea.
Nicotine Gum	Over the counter	Gum is "parked" in between the cheek and gum (not chewed). Nicotine is delivered through the lining of the mouth while gum is "parked." Initial dosing is 10 to 12 pieces per day.	**Pros**: Nicotine is delivered faster than patches, flexible dosing. **Cons**: Not a fit for those with dental problems, can't eat/drink 15 minutes before use, requires frequent dosing to be effective.
Nicotine Nasal Spray	Prescription	Nicotine is delivered through the lining of the nose when spray is used. Used 1 to 2 times per hour initially, then tapered down.	**Pros**: Fastest delivery of nicotine compared to other forms of NRT, can be used in response to smoking urges/cravings. **Cons**: Requires frequent dosing to be effective, may cause nose and throat irritation.

Type	How to Get It	How It Works	Pros and Cons
Nicotine Inhaler	Prescription	Nicotine is delivered through the lining of the mouth (not to the lung) when a nicotine vapor is puffed thorough a cylinder containing a cartridge.	**Pros**: Good substitute for the hand-to-mouth behavior of smoking, **Cons**: Requires frequent dosing to be effective, throat irritation.

What is a nicotine inhaler?

Many smokers describe the hand-to-mouth activity involved in their smoking habit as an important factor to consider and replace in a healthy way when they quit. This is partly where the concern about weight gain comes in. The nicotine inhaler can provide a satisfying replacement for this aspect of the smoking cessation process, as the device resembles a cigarette, which the person puffs into their mouth and throat, where the nicotine is absorbed. This method is often combined with a nicotine patch. Side effects include couth and sore throat.

What is combination NRT?

The various forms of NRT reviewed here can be combined and used together (e.g., the nicotine patch combined with nicotine gum), a treatment approach that is known to increase quit rates by 34% to 54% when compared to using the nicotine patch alone.[9,10] Below, we'll review how this combination approach compares to other medication treatments for smoking cessation.

Combination NRT involves the use of a long-acting nicotine replacement medication (such as the patch) together with a short-acting form of nicotine replacement (such as the gum, lozenge, inhaler, or nasal spray). Combining two or more forms of nicotine replacement provides relief from multiple sources of cravings and potential relapse to smoking behavior in the following ways: (1) by providing constant levels of nicotine replacement, the patch prevents severe uncomfortable nicotine withdrawal symptoms from developing as a person discontinues smoking; and (2) by delivering nicotine at a faster rate than the patch, the short-acting forms can help control cravings that are so powerful that they "break through" even when the patch is being used. These cravings can come along when a person is triggered by common situations or experiences that have been linked with nicotine use repeatedly in the past (for example, finishing a meal or when drinking coffee). A recent review of 63 clinical trials concluded that there is strong evidence supporting the use of combination NRT over a single form of NRT.[6]

What non-nicotine medications are effective for tobacco cessation?

When describing medications, you'll notice that they have at least two names: a generic name (which will be described first) that reflects the chemical makeup of the drug, and a brand name (which will be denoted in parentheses) created by the pharmaceutical company for commercial purposes. The two most commonly used medicines for smoking cessation that are not NRT are an antidepressant, *buproprion* (Zyban, Wellbutrin), and a drug that was developed specifically as a smoking cessation aid, *varenicline* (Chantix).

Bupropion (Brand names: Zyban, Wellbutrin)

Wellbutrin is an antidepressant that increases the availability of two natural chemicals in the brain that are involved in regulating mood and motivation: norepinephrine and dopamine. Initially FDA approved to treat depression in 1985, an exciting observation among people with depression who were taking Wellbutrin was that it was also helpful in reducing cravings for tobacco and helping them quit smoking without gaining weight. This led researchers to begin studying its effectiveness for smoking cessation in the 1990s, and by 1997 it was FDA approved as a smoking cessation treatment. There are several reasons why antidepressants are thought to be potentially helpful as an aid for smoking cessation:

- Smokers are more likely to have a history of diagnosable depression than non-smokers.
- In some smokers, nicotine can have antidepressant effects, making it harder to stop.
- Depressed mood is one of the symptoms of nicotine withdrawal; since smoking can improve mood, this withdrawal symptom leads some to be more vulnerable to relapse.

How well does bupropion work? In a meta-analysis of antidepressant clinical trials specifically for their effects on smoking cessation, which included 115 studies across various medications, researchers concluded that bupropion was 64% more effective than placebo in increasing long-term quit rates, up to six months after treatment.[11] The same meta-analysis indicated that bupropion is as effective as NRT, and that combining it with NRT does not improve smoking cessation further than using either approach alone. One drawback of bupropion that emerged from this study was that nearly 10% of those who took bupropion reported unwanted side effects (mostly related to mental health), and that these effects may increase the chances that people will stop taking the medicine prematurely. On balance, bupropion is a highly effective option for smoking cessation and works as well as NRT, with effects lasting through six months post-quit.

How does bupropion work? Although the exact way that bupropion works in the brain to help people to stop smoking is not well understood, there is some evidence suggesting that this medication acts on some of the brain's "receivers" for nicotine, which are known as *nicotinic receptors*. By blocking certain nicotinic receptors, to which nicotine usually attaches itself, bupropion blocks the brain's ability to feel the stimulating effects of nicotine. This way, it is not so pleasurable or rewarding to smoke. Consistent with these known brain effects of bupropion, studies show that bupropion may help individuals quit smoking successfully by doing one or a combination of three things:

1. blocking the effects of nicotine;
2. relieving nicotine withdrawal symptoms;[12,13] and/or
3. reducing feelings of depression.[14]

Are there any side effects when using bupropion? All medications have some side effects, and when taking any medication, it is important to be aware of possible side effects so that if or when the body experiences these changes, they are not alarming or unexpected. The most common side effects of bupropion are headache, insomnia, and dry mouth. Although rare, the risk of seizure is a known potential side effect of bupropion, so those who have a history of seizure disorder would not be prescribed this medication. In general, side effects can be controlled or managed in various ways, and some side effects go away after the body adapts to the medication over a period of time. Recording side effects and discussing them with the prescribing provider can be very useful, both to ensure that the medication is the right fit for a given individual and to prevent early discontinuation of a medicine that could be very helpful.

Varenicline (Chantix)

Varenicline was initially developed as a smoking cessation medication by Pfizer in 1997, and after six randomized clinical trials were conducted in over 3,600 participants in the

United States, it was approved by the FDA in 2006. By 2008, about 5 million people worldwide were taking varenicline, the majority of whom were in the United States.[15] When pooled together, studies comparing the effects of varenicline across many clinical trials found that urges to smoke are reduced in response to either varenicline or bupropion treatment when compared to placebo. In addition, both varenicline and bupropion improve nicotine withdrawal symptoms such as depression, anxiety, difficulty paying attention or concentrating, irritability, and insomnia. Like bupropion, varenicline works on the nicotine receptors in the brain (see Figure 12.1).

How effective is varenicline when compared to some of the other treatments we've discussed? When evaluating several clinical trials that examined abstinence from tobacco lasting more than a few months, researchers found that 44% of those who took varenicline were able to maintain abstinence compared to 30% of individuals who took bupropion and only 18% of those who received placebo.[16] Varenicline's short-term effectiveness has also come through in meta-analyses, the largest of which combined the effects of 101 smoking cessation trials involving over 40,000 participants and found that taking varenicline more than tripled the likelihood of achieving short-term abstinence from smoking, whereas bupropion and NRT roughly doubled the odds of abstinence.[17,18] Although results from individual trials and meta-analyses comparing the different medication options for smoking cessation tend to follow the same pattern, with varenicline leading to higher rates of success, followed by bupropion and NRT,[19] one sometimes overlooked treatment option that performs similarly to varenicline is *combination NRT*. According to a review of 267 clinical trials on smoking cessation, combination NRT and varenicline were equally effective.[20]

How does varenicline work? Varenicline works in some similar ways to bupropion. Like bupropion, varenicline acts on the nicotine receptors, which we have also referred to as nicotine "receivers" in the brain. By blocking those receptors,

How Varenicline Can Help You Quit Smoking

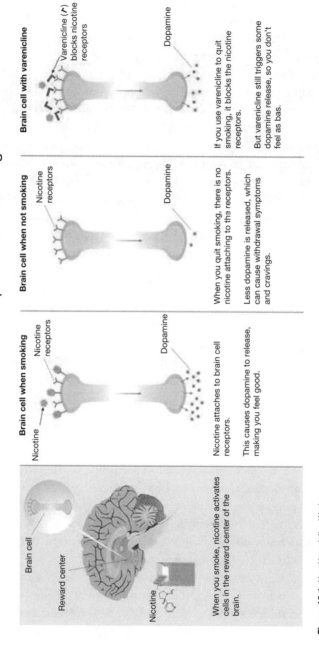

Figure 12.1 How Varenicline Works

Source: CDC (2021)

when a person smokes, the nicotine cannot attach itself to them, making it chemically impossible for the person to experience the psychological, rewarding effect of tobacco use in that moment. This makes smoking less enjoyable. Not only does varenicline block those pleasurable effects of nicotine, but at the same time it does something else that is different from bupropion: it stimulates the brain to release dopamine—not as much as it would release if the person was smoking, but enough to satisfy the urge for that chemical effect of smoking, so that there is a lot less motivation to seek out a source of nicotine.

Are there any side effects when using varenicline? The most commonly experienced side effects of varenicline, according to research studies, include nausea, which can occur in nearly one-third of those who take it; difficulties with sleep (including both insomnia and bad or unusual dreams); and other forms of gastrointestinal discomfort, including constipation, gassiness, and/or vomiting. One of the major concerns that arose about varenicline relatively early on was reflected by the FDA's placement of a black box warning in 2009 for "serious neuropsychiatric events," including depressed mood, suicidal thoughts and attempts, hostility, agitation, psychosis, and severe injuries. Though for the most part these symptoms seemed to resolve once varenicline was discontinued, some cases required continued monitoring and support. About six years later, the warning was updated based on the effects of drinking alcohol while taking varenicline. The *Warnings and Precautions* section of the drug label was modified to include some of the reported effects of mixing alcohol with varenicline, such as lower tolerance to the effects of alcohol, becoming intoxicated more easily than usual, aggression and memory loss after drinking while taking varenicline, and increased risk of seizures.[21] Around the same time, a large clinical trial comparing varenicline, bupropion, NRT, and placebo among over 8,000 participants found that, among those without any history of psychiatric illness, "neuropsychiatric events" among those who were taking varenicline were not any more likely than any of the other treatments or placebo.[22] Even among those who had suffered in their lifetime from psychiatric illness, the neuropsychiatric risks of varenicline were low, which led the FDA to remove the black box warning.

Three Things to Know About Varenicline

1. The black box warning about neuropsychiatric effects was removed in 2016, after a large clinical trial showed that the risk of psychiatric adverse events is pretty low, especially for those without a history of psychiatric illness.
2. Varenicline is not recommended for people operating vehicles (such as aircraft, train, bus, and other vehicle operators) and heavy machinery.
3. Though some studies found adverse cardiovascular effects related to use of varenicline, subsequent research found that the likelihood of these effects is low among those without a preexisting condition, and concerns about these effects should be weighed against the risk of cardiovascular disease due to smoking itself.

Generally, the research on varenicline points to several important considerations for someone contemplating taking this medication: first, while it has emerged across many clinical trials as the most effective treatment, compared to other widely used therapies (e.g., bupropion, NRT), scientists have noted that nearly all of the clinical trials supporting varenicline over other approaches have been sponsored by its manufacturer, Pfizer. Although the study teams involved in these trials have taken steps to remove bias and to increase confidence in the findings from these Pfizer-sponsored studies (such as assigning study participants to different treatments at random, and keeping both the research staff and the participants unaware of which medication each person was taking, a scientific method known as "blinding"), additional studies by scientists who are independent from Pfizer would be helpful. Second, if well tolerated, varenicline is a highly effective medication option for smoking cessation. Third, those with a past or current psychiatric or cardiovascular illness should speak with a prescribing provider about the risk associated with their use of this medication, and ideally, if they take it, be closely monitored for any adverse neuropsychiatric or cardiovascular effects.

Alcohol use disorder

What medications are available for alcohol use disorder?

Decades of research on the way that heavy and chronic alcohol use affects the brain has led to the development of effective medication treatments for alcoholism. Currently there are four FDA-approved medications for the treatment of alcohol use disorders (disulfiram, naltrexone in both pill and injectable form, and acamprosate). These medicines have been shown in randomized clinical trials to be effective in helping people to either reduce or stop drinking. Importantly, despite the fact that the 88,000 alcohol-related deaths between 2006 and 2010 accounted for nearly 10% of all deaths in the United States,[23] studies show that medications are prescribed to less than 9% of individuals with moderate to severe alcohol use disorders who are likely to benefit from them. With this in mind, although medications are just one component of effective treatment and they do not necessarily work for everyone, if you or someone you know is struggling to control their drinking, becoming well versed in the types of medications that are available, how they work, and the benefits and risks of taking them can help inform the important decision of whether and how to incorporate medicine into one's recovery plan.

What's the Goal of Treatment for Alcohol Use Disorder?

In recent years, there has been a shift toward forming treatment goals for those with alcohol use disorders more flexibly. Traditionally, the goal of treatment has been to quit or abstain completely from alcohol use. However, studies have shown that for many, the goal of giving up drinking completely and permanently is overwhelming and can make it hard to initiate or engage in treatment. When a more flexible mindset is adopted, many (though not all) people with alcohol use disorders can reduce their alcohol consumption, which can have a sizable impact on a person's ability to function and live a healthy life.[a] In the largest clinical trial of medications for alcohol use disorders, researchers found that the more days a person drank in a heavy binge pattern, the more problems alcohol caused in their life.[b] This led the FDA to conclude that the goal of *eliminating binge drinking* (versus stopping drinking altogether) is an acceptable alternative.[c] Though the best outcomes of treatment are observed among those who abstain completely, those who can successfully cut back on drinking experience fewer life problems and better health over the long term, even if they don't quit.

---

[a] Ambrogne J. A. (2002). Reduced-risk drinking as a treatment goal: What clinicians need to know. *Journal of Substance Abuse Treatment, 22*(1), 45–53. https://doi.org/10.1016/s0740-5472(01)00210-0
[b] Anton, R. F., O'Malley, S. S., Ciraulo, D. A., Cisler, R. A., Couper, D., Donovan, D. M., Gastfriend, D. R., Hosking, J. D., Johnson, B. A., LoCastro, J. S., Longabaugh, R., Mason, B. J., Mattson, M. E., Miller, W. R., Pettinati, H. M., Randall, C. L., Swift, R., Weiss, R. D., Williams, L. D., Zweben, A., . . . COMBINE Study Research Group. (2006). Combined pharmacotherapies and behavioral interventions for alcohol dependence: the COMBINE study: A randomized controlled trial. *JAMA, 295*(17), 2003–2017. https://doi.org/10.1001/jama.295.17.2003
[c] U.S. Department of Health and Human Services, Center for Drug Evaluation Research (CDER). (2015). Alcoholism: Developing drugs for treatment, guidance for industry. Retrieved October 19, 2022 from https://www.fda.gov/files/drugs/published/Alcoholism---Developing-Drugs-for-Treatment.pdf

Disulfuram (Antabuse)

Disulfiram was the first medicine developed for the treatment of alcoholism, having been discovered in the 1920s and approved for this purpose in 1949. It is the only medicine that is designed to change drinking behavior by triggering a very unpleasant physiological reaction to drinking. This reaction, occurring only when a person consumes or is exposed to products or medicines containing alcohol (more on this below) while taking disulfiram, includes nausea, flushing, vomiting, sweating, low blood pressure, and palpitations. Rarely, this reaction can become life threatening, leading to cardiovascular collapse or a severe drop in blood pressure that leads to loss of consciousness and can result in cardiac arrest. For 40 years, disulfiram was the only medicine that doctors could offer to their patients who were struggling with alcoholism.

How does it work? Disulfiram creates an intense fear in the person who is taking it, of experiencing the discomfort that drinking will bring on. The reason that they become so sick if they drink while taking this medicine is because disulfiram makes the body unable to break down or metabolize alcohol properly. Normally, when alcohol enters the body, it is converted into a compound called *acetaldehyde,* and then into acetic acid. When a person takes disulfiram, the acetaldehyde can't break down any further, and it builds up in the bloodstream. This toxic buildup of acetaldehyde leads a person to feel quite sick.

Disulfiram can't be taken too soon after a person has consumed alcohol, because if it interacts with alcohol that is still in the body it will cause the person to feel ill. For this reason, a person should wait until at least 12 hours have passed since their last drink before they take this medication. In addition, the risk of a disulfiram–alcohol interaction leading to illness is not only present when a person drinks alcohol but can also occur if a person takes certain medications or eats certain foods that contain even small amounts of alcohol. For example, certain over-the-counter cold and cough medications contain small amounts of alcohol that can trigger a reaction in a person who is taking disulfiram, as can food products such as vinegars, kombucha, and some sauces. Exposure to alcohol-containing products should also be avoided, including rubbing alcohol, aftershave, certain mouthwashes, perfumes, hand sanitizers, and certain hair sprays.

Does it work? A meta-analysis summarizing the results of 22 studies that included over 2,400 participants found that taking disulfiram produced a higher alcohol abstinence success rate when compared to taking a placebo (i.e., a sugar pill).[24] Importantly, disulfiram was superior to other treatments *only* in studies in which the participants knew that they had been given disulfiram, but not in studies that used a procedure called *blinding*, which is when participants are not told what type of treatment they received (whether it was disulfiram, or a sugar pill or other medicine). This confirmed what many studies had been pointing to as the key to this medication working: knowing that one is taking disulfiram is an important part of its effectiveness. In other words, for this treatment approach to help someone resist the urge to drink, the person must both *anticipate* and become *fearful* of getting sick from drinking while they are taking disulfiram. Another enlightening observation was that disulfiram produced better drinking outcomes than other treatments when compliance with the medication regimen was supervised by a healthcare provider, but not when it was unsupervised. Experts have concluded that because the key to disulfiram's effectiveness is the psychological effect of knowing what the medicine does, a person has to have strong motivation to take it to benefit from it. Research has consistently supported this idea, that those who will have the best outcomes from taking disulfiram are individuals who are highly motivated to use this form of treatment and likely to take it consistently, or are supervised to ensure that they take it as prescribed, whereas an individual who is less motivated and would like to continue to drink will just stop taking it. Involving a supportive spouse or partner in disulfiram treatment has been found to improve outcomes.[25,26]

The side effects of disulfiram can be found in the table entitled "FDA Approved Medications for Alcohol Use Disorder." The most common side effect reported in large clinical trials, other than the effects of drinking alcohol while taking disulfiram (i.e., primarily flushing, rapid heart rate, nausea, and vomiting) was drowsiness, reported in 8% of those who were treated with a standard daily dosage.

Naltrexone

In 1994, the FDA approved naltrexone for the treatment of alcohol use disorders, after two randomized clinical trials provided evidence that individuals with alcoholism who were recently abstinent were less likely to relapse to alcohol use over a three-month course of treatment.[27,28] Naltrexone was originally used to treat opioid use disorders by blocking the effects of these drugs in the brain, making a person unable to feel the intense rush or euphoria that they seek from repeated opioid use. Studies show that naltrexone also blocks the pleasurable effects of drinking. It can be given either in pill form, which is taken daily, or by injection, which acts as an extended-release formulation that is given every four weeks, or monthly. Clinical trials have mostly studied the use of naltrexone over a period of three to four months, though experts recommend that medications for the treatment of alcohol use disorders be provided for a period of six months, at which time the usefulness can be reevaluated to inform decisions about whether or not to prolong their use.[29] Any healthcare practitioner who is licensed to prescribe medications can prescribe naltrexone.

How does naltrexone work? Naltrexone is not addictive, it does not lead to psychological dependence, and it does not cause withdrawal symptoms upon cessation. Therefore, there is no concern about misuse or diversion of this medicine. Although the precise brain mechanism that explains naltrexone's effect on drinking behavior is not known, there are three known impacts of this medicine that are helpful in the treatment of alcohol use disorders:

1. Naltrexone can reduce urges or cravings for alcohol.
2. Naltrexone can help individuals remain abstinent from alcohol.
3. If a person slips or lapses after a period of abstinence and consumes one or more drinks, naltrexone can interfere with the person's desire to continue drinking.

Does it work? The majority of clinical trials show that naltrexone is an effective treatment for alcohol use disorders. According to a recent meta-analysis that summarized 16 studies including over 2,300 individuals with alcohol use disorders, naltrexone effectively reduced the risk of alcohol relapse and binge drinking.[29] Those who tend to benefit the most from naltrexone are people with alcohol use disorders who (1) experience strong cravings for alcohol; and (2) have a family history of alcoholism.[30,31]

The side effects of naltrexone are typically mild and not very long-lasting. People who are taking naltrexone usually report that they're mostly unaware that they're on a medicine, which is consistent with what is known about its effects—those who take it do not feel high, nor down. Naltrexone can be discontinued at any time without producing any withdrawal symptoms, since taking it does not cause physical dependence. The one drug interaction of naltrexone that it is important to be aware of is that it makes opioid pain medications ineffective. So, if a person is having surgery, for example, and will need pain medications afterward, they should consult their doctor about discontinuing naltrexone in advance of the surgery so that any opioid pain medications they take will be effective. Some experts have recommended that individuals who take naltrexone carry a card explaining that they are taking this medication, with instructions to medical staff about pain management. Naltrexone will also block the effects of certain opioid-containing prescription cough medicines. Apart from these effects, naltrexone does not interfere with the actions of other commonly used medicines, such as antibiotics, non-opioid painkillers (such as Tylenol or Ibuprofen), and allergy medicines.

What happens if you drink while taking naltrexone? Unlike disulfiram, drinking while taking naltrexone does not lead a person to feel sick. However, it may reduce the pleasurable effects that one typically experiences when they drink, which in turn can curb the desire to drink more. It is important to know that even though naltrexone can interfere with the positive emotions that are tied to enjoying drinking, it does not reduce the effects of alcohol use that impair driving and coordination, so it does not make drinking any "safer." When oral naltrexone is used, engaging family members or other individuals to support adherence to the regimen can be very helpful.

Extended-release naltrexone (Vivitrol)

In addition to the oral form of naltrexone (Revia), an extended-release injectable form (Vivitrol) is also an option. The injection is given once per month as an intramuscular gluteal injection, meaning that it is injected into the gluteal muscle (i.e., the buttocks). As a more practical consideration, the cost of injectable naltrexone is greater than that of the oral form.

How does extended-release naltrexone work? The extended-release form of naltrexone works the same way in the brain as the oral form, with three potential advantages as an alternative to the daily dosing pill regimen: (1) those who take oral naltrexone may have unpleasant side effects such as nausea because of the rapid rise in blood levels of the medicine after it is initially taken. An injectable form, by providing a slow release of naltrexone, may make these unpleasant effects less likely, which would help maintain compliance with monthly dosing; (2) since it doesn't require a person to remember to take a tablet daily, an injectable form boosts adherence to the regimen; and (3) because the blood level of the medicine remains steady throughout the month following injection, the most effective therapeutic dose is present in the body consistently, optimizing the outcomes of treatment.

Does it work? To date, one study evaluated the effect of extended-release naltrexone compared to a placebo and found that extended-release naltrexone was effective in over 600 participants, with those who took the optimal dose (380 mg per month) reducing their binge drinking from 19 days per month to three days per month on average.[32] A follow-up study found that those who were able to remain abstinent from alcohol for a minimum of four days prior to receiving the injection had a great treatment response, with prolonged abstinence, fewer days drinking, and fewer days drinking heavily.[33] Consistent with these observations, injectable naltrexone was FDA approved for treating individuals with alcohol use disorders who can abstain from drinking prior to initiating the injection regimen. Some considerations when considering taking injectable naltrexone are as follows:

- Once injected, naltrexone cannot be removed from the body, so any potential discomfort may last for up to 30 days.
- Though the effects of naltrexone may occur within hours of the injection, full effectiveness may not occur for two to three days following the injection.
- Pain treatment can be complicated when someone is taking injectable naltrexone, since it will block the effects of opioid painkillers for up to 30 days.
- For those with a history of opioid use, the use of injectable naltrexone can reduce tolerance for opioids, leading to opioid overdose risk.
- Injectable naltrexone is more likely to be effective when it's combined with counseling.
- Research concerning the ideal length of treatment with injectable naltrexone is ongoing, but current recommendations based on clinical trial outcomes are to take monthly injections for six months.
- For those who struggle with co-occurring psychiatric illness, combining treatment with naltrexone and an antidepressant may be beneficial, according to studies of those with depression[34] and post-traumatic stress disorder.[35]

Do You Still Need Therapy If You Take Naltrexone for an Alcohol Use Disorder?

The short answer is yes; research has shown that naltrexone, as well as other medications for alcohol use disorders, are most effective when combined with behavioral therapy.[a] While medication can help with cravings and block the desire to drink heavily, behavioral therapy can help people to understand their addictive behavior patterns, learn skills to manage temptations, and change their lifestyle in important ways that support their longer-term recovery from alcoholism.

Studies have found behavioral therapy to be effective both for heavy alcohol use and diagnosable alcohol use disorders,[b,c] and the majority of clinical trials showing successful outcomes of alcoholism treatment medications (such as naltrexone) provided the medicine together with behavioral therapy. In one large clinical trial, medication was combined with either brief or high-intensity behavioral therapy, to try to understand which form of therapy was the most helpful to pair with the medication. When combined with medication for treating alcohol use disorders, both brief therapy and intensive therapy were effective in helping individuals reduce the number of days on which they drank and their risk of heavy drinking. This led experts to conclude that, at a minimum, brief counseling should be delivered in conjunction with medications like naltrexone, and higher intensity counseling can also be helpful either in the early phases of treatment if desired, or, for those who prefer not to do intensive counseling, this can be reserved as an option if initial treatment with the medicine is not successful.[d]

---

[a] Ray, L. A., Meredith, L. R., Kiluk, B. D., Walthers, J., Carroll, K. M., & Magill, M. (2020). Combined Pharmacotherapy and Cognitive Behavioral Therapy for Adults With Alcohol or Substance Use Disorders: A Systematic Review and Meta-analysis. *JAMA network open, 3*(6), e208279. https://doi.org/10.1001/jamanetworkopen.2020.8279

[b] Kaner, E. F., Beyer, F. R., Muirhead, C., Campbell, F., Pienaar, E. D., Bertholet, N., Daeppen, J. B., Saunders, J. B., & Burnand, B. (2018). Effectiveness of brief alcohol interventions in primary care populations. *The Cochrane Database of Systematic Reviews, 2*(2), CD004148. https://doi.org/10.1002/14651858.CD004148.pub4

[c] Garbutt, J. C., Kampov-Polevoy, A. B., Pedersen, C., Stansbury, M., Jordan, R., Willing, L., & Gallop, R. J. (2021). Efficacy and tolerability of baclofen in a U.S. community population with alcohol use disorder: A dose-response, randomized, controlled trial. *Neuropsychopharmacology: Official Publication of the American College of Neuropsychopharmacology, 46*(13), 2250–2256. https://doi.org/10.1038/s41386-021-01055-w

[d] Anton, R. F., O'Malley, S. S., Ciraulo, D. A., et al. (2006). Combined pharmacotherapies and behavioral interventions for alcohol dependence—the COMBINE study: A randomized controlled trial. *JAMA, 295,* 2003–2017.

Acamprosate (Campral)

Acamprosate gained FDA approval for the treatment of alcohol use disorders in 2004, based on positive findings from clinical trials that were conducted in Europe, where it was approved as a treatment for alcohol dependence in 1989. Since that time, acamprosate has been approved for use not only in the United States, but also in Canada and Japan. Around the time of its FDA approval, meta-analyses summarizing published studies including over 4,000 individuals with alcohol use disorders found that a larger percentage of those who received acamprosate were able to maintain abstinence from alcohol use for six months, compared to those who received an inactive (i.e., placebo) medicine,[36,37] and acamprosate was effective in reducing heavy drinking. Since then, several large US- and Germany-based clinical trials failed to find any benefit of acamprosate on drinking behavior; this discrepancy between European and US- based study findings led to more targeted scientific efforts to understand which types of individuals are likely to benefit the most from acamprosate. As a result, both individual studies[38] and a more recent meta-analysis[39] concluded that treatment with acamprosate reduces the risk of returning to drinking among those who have already achieved abstinence. This is different from the effects of naltrexone, which can help those who are actively drinking to drink less heavily. Because the data point clearly to the benefit of acamprosate to those who have had early success in abstaining from alcohol use, the medication is now FDA approved to *sustain abstinence* among individuals with alcohol use disorders who have successfully stopped drinking.

How does acamprosate work? While both oral and injectable naltrexone act to affect the release of dopamine, acamprosate works on a different set of brain chemicals known as gamma-aminobutyric acid (GABA) and glutamate. GABA is an inhibitory brain chemical that acts to slow down or block certain impulses or signals in the central nervous system (the brain and spinal cord). GABA is known for producing a calming effect, and is also involved in controlling anxiety, stress, and fear, by preventing excitation of nerve cells. On the other hand, glutamate is what is known as an excitatory brain chemical, which does the opposite of GABA, stimulating the transmission of electrical messages between nerve cells. Glutamate is associated with arousal, fight or flight responses, and focus.

For the brain to function normally, a balance between excitation and inhibition is essential (see Figure 12.2). In the short term, alcohol use disrupts this balance by *increasing inhibitory brain chemicals like GABA,* causing some of the sedating effects of drinking as well as the relaxing, calming, or anti-anxiety effects. At the same time it inhibits or *descreases the activity of the glutamate system,* so that there is less excitation in the brain, which also contributes to the sedating effects of alcohol use. These effects can range from slight drowsiness to blackouts.

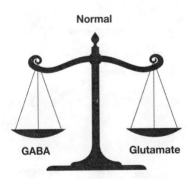

Figure 12.2 The balance between brain chemicals GABA and Glutamate when in a normal state.

Over the long term, however, drinking has the opposite effect on the GABA/glutamate balance. To compensate for the chronic depressant effects of alcohol and restore the balance between GABA and glutamate, the brain *decreases GABA activity* and *increases glutamate*.

The effect of putting the brain into a more excitatory state with increased activity of the glutamate system is to make it more difficult for alcohol to produce sedation and relaxation, which a person experiences as tolerance to alcohol. Tolerance can then lead to escalating drinking behavior. But now that the brain is in a hyperexcitable state, with the GABA-glutamate balance tilted toward glutamate, a person who discontinues their use of alcohol can be more vulnerable to experiencing *alcohol withdrawal* symptoms (Figure 12.3). These symptoms, which occur when the central nervous system is hyperexcited, can include anxiety, tremors, seizures, hallucinations, irritability, insomnia, and confusion.

Even after the most immediate effects of alcohol withdrawal have passed, the glutamate system can continue to be hyperactive, so these symptoms can persist, making a person vulnerable to relapse.

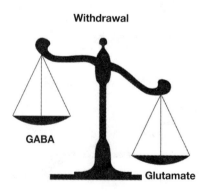

Withdrawal

GABA

Glutamate

Figure 12.3 The imbalance between brain chemicals GABA and Glutamate when in a state of alcohol withdrawal.

Acamprosate acts on the glutamate system and, by reducing some of the brain's hyperexcitability, reduces what are known as post-acute alcohol withdrawal symptoms. Post-acute withdrawal symptoms can affect a person's mood, sleep patterns, and responses to stress, and typically last for several months among those who are in recovery from alcoholism, though they can, in some, resolve over a period of weeks. These symptoms can include insomnia, anxiety, restlessness, and depressed mood.

How long will treatment be needed? Decisions about treatment length will depend on many factors, including: (1) the person's preference, (2) how severe their alcohol use disorder is, (3) their history of relapses, (4) how serious the potential consequences of a relapse would be for the individual, (5) how they have responded to acamprosate, and (6) how well they tolerate the medicine. Experts suggest that treatment be started as soon as a person becomes abstinent and continue even if the individual relapses to alcohol use.[40]

The most common side effect of acamprosate is diarrhea. Other less common side effects may include nausea, vomiting, stomachache, headache, and dizziness, although the extent to which acamprosate directly causes these side effects is not well understood. One of the distinctive aspects of acamprosate is that, unlike naltrexone, it is not metabolized through the liver, which can be important given that those with alcoholism are vulnerable to liver disease. While other medications for alcohol use disorders such as naltrexone may adversely affect liver function, especially among those with acute hepatitis or liver failure, acamprosate does not carry this risk. On the other hand, acamprosate is excreted through the kidneys, so this medicine is not recommended for individuals with severe kidney disease or malfunction.

FDA-Approved Medications for Alcohol Use Disorder

Medicine	Who Can Benefit	Dosage	Most Common Side Effects	Special Considerations
Disulfiram	Those with alcohol use disorder who seek enforced sobriety.	250 mg–500 mg/day	Drowsiness, metallic aftertaste. More severe adverse effects (such as hepatitis, neuropathy, psychosis, optic neuritis, and confusion) are rare.	Since drinking while taking this medicine can result in a medical emergency, disulfiram is best for those with an abstinence (rather than controlled drinking) goal.
Naltrexone	Those with alcohol use disorder.	Starting dose from 25 mg–50 mg/day Target:50 mg/day	Drowsiness, nausea, vomiting, decreased appetite, abdominal pain, insomnia, dizziness.	For people who are physically dependent on opioids, naltrexone can trigger opioid withdrawal symptoms.
Extended-Release Naltrexone (Vivitrol)	Those with alcohol use disorder who can abstain from drinking while in outpatient treatment.	380 mg in the form of a monthly injection	Same as the oral form of naltrexone, as well as reactions at the injection site.	For people who are physically dependent on opioids, naltrexone can trigger opioid withdrawal symptoms.

Medicine	Who Can Benefit	Dosage	Most Common Side Effects	Special Considerations
Acamprosate	Those who have already stopped drinking and are looking to maintain abstinence from alcohol use.	1998 mg/day	Diarrhea.	Because it isn't metabolized, this medicine is safe for use among people who have liver disease.

Note: This chart summarizes some of the most common effects for each of the above medications. It is not intended to be a complete source of information or to replace package inserts. Any decisions about medicines should be made in consultation with a physician.

What off-label (non-FDA approved) medications for alcohol use disorders have been studied?

Though not approved by the FDA, there are several medications that are currently being evaluated for the treatment of alcohol use disorders, and prescribers sometimes use these options off-label (meaning that FDA-approved medications are being used for a purpose *not* approved by the FDA). Shown in the table below, the most well-studied and widely used off-labels include topiramate, gabapentin, baclofen, and nalmefene. Below, we briefly review what is known about these treatments thus far.

Topiramate

Topiramate is an oral medication that is FDA approved to treat epilepsy, to prevent migraine headaches, and for weight loss. Now considered one of the most promising medications for the treatment of alcohol use disorders,[41] one of its major advantages is the possibility of starting treatment while a person is still actively drinking. This way, the medicine can help support an individual who is trying to initiate abstinence, rather than requiring them to achieve abstinence before being prescribed medication. Despite not having FDA approval for alcohol-related problems, topiramate is a recommended treatment for alcohol use disorder in the US Department of Veterans Affairs.[42] Though topiramate has been generic for many years now and may never be FDA approved for the treatment of alcohol use disorders, prescribers have relied on it increasingly as an off-label treatment option, especially since it has shown therapeutic effects on alcohol use and is included in the American Psychiatric Association's practice guidelines for medication treatment of alcohol use disorders.[43]

How does topiramate work? Though the precise action of topiramate in the brain is not understood, like acamprosate it is thought to work by increasing GABA and reducing glutamate in the brain, which in effect reduces the release of dopamine. Since dopamine is involved in the experience of reward and pleasure, these neurochemical effects are thought to make drinking less pleasurable. At the same time, it probably helps to restore balance in the brain circuits that control responses to rewards, which are impaired among people who drink and/ or use other substances heavily or chronically.[44] Another way that topiramate may affect drinking behavior is by reducing cravings for alcohol, which is thought to result from its effect on glutamate.[45]

Does it work? Meta-analyses and reviews of the existing trials of topiramate have found that, among those with alcohol use disorders and heavy drinking, it substantially reduced heavy alcohol use and increased abstinence.[46,47] In addition, studies show that topiramate reduces alcohol craving, improves overall well being, and improves physical health functions that are affected by chronic alcohol use, such as blood pressure, body mass index, and cholesterol.[44] Although some of the studies required participants to be abstinent for days prior to starting treatment with topiramate, even when participants continued drinking as they initiated the medicine they were able to successfully reduce their alcohol consumption. Since many individuals who seek treatment to change their relationship with alcohol are either not willing or not able to make it through a week or a few days shy of that timeframe without drinking prior to starting medication, topiramate has potential appeal for those who can benefit from medication treatment to address their alcohol use, including those for whom (1) the transition from actively drinking to becoming abstinent is difficult, and/or (2) the option of going to residential or inpatient treatment is either not desirable or not feasible. Additionally, because weight loss is observed in between 4% and 21% of those who take topiramate, it may be worth considering for individuals with alcohol use disorders who struggle with obesity.[48] Importantly, in randomized clinical trials to date, topiramate was effective in changing drinking behavior when it was given together with behavioral therapy, either on a weekly basis or more frequently, over a period of three to four months.

The greatest barrier to treatment with topiramate is its potential for side effects, especially those affecting cognitive abilities and memory. The likelihood and severity of these effects increase in relation to dosage and, accordingly, it is recommended that the dosage be increased gradually with close monitoring of the response.[49] Those who are considering taking topiramate should have a thorough discussion with the prescriber of the risks and benefits as well as the potential side effects and adverse reactions (particularly cognitive side effects) prior to deciding whether to take it. Cognitive side effects such as mental slowing and difficulty with producing words comfortably when speaking are often temporary problems in early stages of treatment with topiramate while the dosage is being adjusted, but nonetheless, these symptoms can be disruptive.[50] Other more common side effects are listed in the table below.

Gabapentin

Gabapentin is FDA-approved for the treatment of epilepsy and neuropathic pain, or pain that results from the nervous system not working correctly. Nearly one-third of neuropathic pain happens because of diabetes, but other diseases including alcoholism can cause this form of pain. Gabapentin was suggested as a medication that could be helpful in the treatment of alcohol and drug addiction because it has a mild side-effect profile, does not produce cognitive side effects, and was initially thought not to have any potential to be misused or abused,[51] though more recent studies indicate some shifts in our understanding of how and by whom it can be misused.

How does gabapentin work? Like acamprosate and topiramate, the precise actions of gabapentin in the brain are still not fully understood. What we do know is that it works on the GABA and glutamate systems, increasing GABA and regulating the GABA/glutamate balance.

Does it work? So far, results from randomized clinical trials of gabapentin for alcohol use disorders are mixed. Though several trials showed positive results, with gabapentin producing reductions in heavy drinking,[52] at least one large study with an extended-release formulation of the medication did not show any difference between gabapentin and a placebo.[53] The first meta-analysis summarizing the seven trials to date of gabapentin for alcohol use disorders found a benefit of the medicine over placebo, but its success was limited to one outcome: the percentage of days on which a person engaged in heavy drinking.[54]

The most commonly reported side effects of gabapentin include dizziness, drowsiness, impaired muscle coordination, and swelling in the lower legs or hands. In recent years, some concerns have been raised about the potential for abuse of gabapentin, and a systematic review showed that about 1% of the general population has misused it, for three categories of reasons: recreation (e.g., to experience a rush or high or substitute for more expensive drugs), self-harm, and self-medication (e.g., to alleviate pain or withdrawal symptoms from alcohol or other drugs).[55] Most of the misuse of gabapentin is among people who have a prescription for it but use more than is prescribed, and often in combination with use of other substances such as alcohol. Though more studies are needed to better understand who is at greatest risk for misusing gabapentin, studies have found that the majority of those who take more of it than prescribed have a history of addiction to other substances, particularly individuals with a history of or current opioid misuse.

Baclofen

Baclofen is a type of muscle relaxant that is FDA-approved for the treatment of spasms, cramping, and tightness of muscles caused by certain medical problems such as multiple sclerosis or certain injuries to the spine. In 2014, in France it was formally approved in 2018 for treatment of alcohol dependence. In addition, it has been used off label to treat alcohol use disorders for over a decade in other European countries and in Australia.[56]

How does baclofen work? Baclofen is a GABA receptor agonist, which means that it increases the presence of GABA. By enhancing the natural effect of GABA, which may be calming, especially when our brain cells are overexcited (e.g., when a person is experiencing alcohol withdrawal or another source of anxiety), baclofen is thought to suppress alcohol cravings, especially among individuals who are dependent on alcohol. Studies show that when a person is addicted to alcohol, that first drink (or even the first sip) of alcohol can "prime" the brain to crave more, which can trigger continued heavy drinking.

This is known as the "priming effect." In a recent study, baclofen was found to block that priming effect,[57] suggesting that eliminating the craving after that first drink may be an important part of how it works to help people change their drinking behavior.

Does it work? Meta-analyses and reviews of baclofen's effects on alcohol use have found mixed results. According to a review of 13 randomized clinical trials that included nearly 1,500 participants, while taking baclofen, abstinence rates were higher and individuals who achieved abstinence could sustain it for longer, when compared to those who received a placebo. However, among those who were not abstinent, the frequency of drinking was no different between those who took baclofen versus placebo,[58] and baclofen does not have a clear benefit for those who are trying to change binge drinking behavior.[294] There is also some debate about the most effective dosage of baclofen for the treatment of alcohol use disorders, with some evidence suggesting that lower doses between 30 mg and 60 mg are more effective in delaying relapses to drinking than high doses above 60 mg.[58] The consensus currently is that the dosage should be tailored to the individual, depending on how heavily they drink when starting treatment and how well they tolerate the medicine.[56] In summary, what we know from research to date about the effectiveness of baclofen is the following:

- It is especially effective for people who drink heavily.
- Its most pronounced effects are on delaying a return to alcohol use and/or helping to prolong abstinence.
- Increasing the dosage beyond 60 mg per day doesn't appear to improve its benefit.
- It may be helpful in treating alcoholism among individuals with liver disease.

When prescribed in lower doses (30 mg daily), the most common side effects were drowsiness, dizziness, headache, and confusion; other observed effects are listed in the medications summary table. In higher doses, sedation is the most concerning side effect, reported by nearly half of those taking it.[59]

Nalmefene (Selincro)

Originally developed in the 1990s as an antidote for opioid overdose, a series of studies conducted in Europe found that nalmefene was also helpful in reducing cravings and drinking among those with alcohol use disorders. It was approved in the European Union in 2012, and is now also approved in Japan and several other countries, for reducing alcohol use among individuals with alcohol dependence who drink heavily. In the United States, nalmefene was FDA approved in 2023 as a medication to reverse opioid overdose. When used to treat alcohol-related problems in the United States it is prescribed off label.

How does nalmefene work? Nalmefene, like naltrexone, is an opioid antagonist. Though there are some differences in the way that nalmefene acts on the opioid receptors in the brain, studies show that nalmefene reduces cravings for alcohol to an extent that is comparable to naltrexone.[60]

Does it work? In the three trials in Europe that led to approval of nalmefene for the treatment of alcohol use disorders, individuals who were actively drinking were instructed to take it "as needed." In other words, they could take it only when they were feeling tempted to drink alcohol. In these studies, which included men who consumed at least four drinks per day and women who consumed at least three drinks per day, nalmefene effectively reduced heavy drinking (both the number of days during which the participants drank heavily, and the total amount of alcohol they drank on those days).[61] The ability to take nalmefene only when needed is desirable for many people.

Studies have used different dosages of nalmefene (ranging from 5 mg to 40 mg) and have found that the 20 mg tablet is as effective as higher dosages but has fewer side effects. At higher doses, the most uncomfortable reported symptom is nausea, which has been observed in nearly one-quarter of those who took nalmefene (compared to nearly 6% of those who took a placebo).[62] Other side effects include dizziness, insomnia, headache, vomiting, fatigue, and drowsiness.

Off-Label (Non-FDA Approved) Medications for Alcohol Use Disorder

Medicine	Who Can Benefit	Dosage	Most Common Side Effects	Special Considerations
Nalmefene	Those with alcohol use disorder who consume an average of at least 3 (for women) or 4 (for men) drinks per day.	18 mg per day	Nausea, dizziness, difficulty sleeping, headache, vomiting, fatigue, drowsiness.	Though used in Europe in the treatment of alcohol use disorders, nalmefene is not approved in the United States for this purpose; it is FDA approved as a treatment to reverse opioid overdose.
Baclofen	Those with alcohol use disorder.	30 mg–80 mg/day in 3 divided doses	Drowsiness, dizziness, headache, confusion, muscle stiffness, sweating, itching, abnormal muscle movements, numbness, slurred speech.	Recommended for management of alcohol use disorder in France at a dose of up to 80 mg/day.

Medicine	Who Can Benefit	Dosage	Most Common Side Effects	Special Considerations
Gabapentin	Those with alcohol use disorder.	900 to 1800 mg per day	Dizziness, drowsiness, difficulty coordinating movement, leg swelling.	There is a small body of research on this medicine as a treatment for alcohol use disorder; more is needed.
Topirimate	Those with alcohol use disorder.	75 mg–300 mg/day in 2 divided doses	Tingling sensations, altered sense of taste, loss of appetite, trouble concentrating, nervousness, dizziness, itching.	Dosing should be adjusted gradually to reduce risk of adverse effects, and people with certain medical conditions cannot take topiramate.

Note: This chart summarizes some of the most common effects for each of the above medications. It is not intended to be a complete source of information or to replace package inserts. Any decisions about medicines s hould be made in consultation with a physician.

Are there medication treatment options for stimulant use disorders?

As of this time, the FDA has not approved any medications for the treatment of individuals with stimulant use disorders. The primary recommended treatment for stimulant addiction is psychotherapy (including cognitive behavioral therapy, motivational interviewing, and relapse prevention), and contingency management has also been found to be highly effective in promoting engagement in treatment and reducing dropout.[63] Effective behavioral treatments can usually be delivered in the context of outpatient addiction care settings. Though more than 50 clinical trials investigating potential medication treatments for stimulant addiction have been published, systematic reviews and meta-analyses have not found strong evidence for the effectiveness of the medications that have been studied. However, a few candidate treatments are promising, and may be used off label on the basis of the current evidence.[64] These include:

- **Bupropion**, which may be effective in conjunction with contingency management and is particularly well suited for individuals who struggle with depression;
- **Topiramate**, which may be helpful to promote abstinence from stimulant use; and
- **Psychostimulants**, a class of medications that might act as a form of "replacement therapy" in a similar manner to some of the medications that are widely used to treat opioid addiction.

Finally, given that 30% to 80% of individuals who use heroin have overlapping issues with stimulant use,[65] coupled with the rising overdose death rates among those who use stimulants and opioids in combination, treating opioid use disorders among those who also have stimulant addiction may have the added benefit of improving stimulant use. Research to inform recommendations about this approach is ongoing.

Opioid use disorder

What medications are available for opioid use disorder?

Through all of the darkness, despair, and loss of life that has stemmed from the opioid overdose crisis, there is still a ray of light. Science has established very clearly over decades of research that opioid addiction is a *treatable* disease. It is indeed a very serious illness, as we know that repeated use of opioids leads the brain to change in ways that affect behavior negatively and profoundly. Fortunately, with medication that reduces cravings and opioid withdrawal symptoms, the effects of these brain changes can be effectively treated, lives can be saved, and "living" can be restored to those who sustain their recovery. In the section that follows, you will gain a better understanding of medications for opioid use disorders in two ways: (1) you'll become familiarized with the different available medication treatments, and (2) myths about medications that prevent people from making use of them will be outlined and clarified with scientifically based information. The reality is, we have very effective lifesaving treatments available, but very few people use them. Part of the reason for this is because of the stigma that not only surrounds addiction, but also the idea of taking medication for an addiction.

There are currently four FDA-approved medications for opioid use disorders and opioid withdrawal: methadone, buprenorphine, extended-release naltrexone, and lofexidine. Although we have emphasized the importance of medications in treating opioid addiction, they are not the entire picture. Pairing medication with counseling, social support from peers and/or community-based recovery support groups, primary care, and other needed services increases the chances that an individual will remain engaged in treatment and make meaningful life changes in recovery.

Effective Treatment: Three Reasons to Seek Medication Treatment for Opioid Addiction

- According to large studies and clinical trials, those who receive medication treatment for opioid addiction are less likely to die from overdose or other causes related to their addiction.
- The likelihood of injecting drugs is lower among those who receive medication for opioid addiction, when compared to those who don't.
- People who take medication for opioid addiction are more successful in maintaining their recovery for the long term, and their functioning and quality of life in many important areas of life (in terms of work/career, social, family, and overall well being) can become as satisfying as someone who has never struggled with addiction.

What is agonist treatment?

You may recall that in Chapter 8 we discussed the presence of natural opioids in the brain and body, including the receptors in our brain that "receive" opioids. These receptors are designed to receive natural opioid-like chemicals (or endogenous opioids) the body releases to block pain from stress or harm. Synthetic opioids like heroin and fentanyl mimic the chemical structure of our body's natural opioid-like chemicals, acting as chemical "keys" that can unlock our body's opioid receptors. This produces pain relief, combined with euphoria, or a rush of pleasure. Two of the FDA-approved medications for opioid addiction are what we call *agonist* medications. This means that they are similar enough to our natural chemical "keys" that they can unlock our body's opioid receptors, but they do this in a *controlled, systematic way*. This differs in an important way from the cycle that maintains a person's addiction to opioids, namely the highs and lows of taking opioids, feeling their effects, and then going into withdrawal, which creates both a physical and psychological desperation to take more.

The physical withdrawal is intensely uncomfortable, and the psychological mindset that accompanies it fuels the addiction cycle; feeling trapped and controlled by an intense fear of entering withdrawal, people who become addicted to opioids often find themselves frantically and obsessively seeking ways to either avoid or relieve the discomfort of withdrawal. The alternating highs and lows of euphoria and opioid withdrawal (see Figure 12.4) puts the body and mind on a constant rollercoaster, one that can lead a person to do things that are completely out of character, such as lying and stealing. You may recall from Chapter 8 that there are three different types of opioid receptors, one of which is the *mu receptor*. Agonist medications, including methadone and buprenorphine, both act on the mu opioid receptor, delivering a consistent, steady dose to activate it in a *stable* way. Though methadone and buprenorphine act on the mu

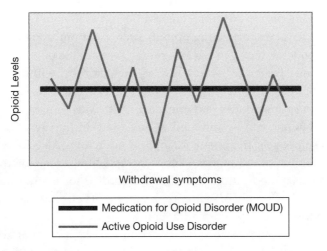

Figure 12.4 Opioid addiction: the cycle of opioid use and withdrawal in the brain.

receptor in different ways, their intended effects of stabilizing the amount of opioid-like chemicals in the brain are the same. Even sustained-release naltrexone works on the mu receptor, but it is not an agonist medicine; naltrexone is known as a different type of treatment called an *antagonist*. Below you will learn more about how each of these medicines affect the mu receptor.

What is methadone?

How does methadone work? Methadone is an agonist medication that fully activates the mu opioid receptors in the brain, in a way that is similar to the action of prescription or illicit opioids. Since it fully activates the mu opioid receptors, it is known as a *full agonist*. Methadone, which has been used to treat opioid addiction for over 60 years, is both synthetic and long-acting, meaning that its effects last as long as 24 to 36 hours after a dose is taken. For this reason, it only needs to be taken once a day for the treatment of opioid addiction. By attaching to the mu opioid receptors and "occupying" them for long periods of time, when a person who is in recovery tries to take short-acting opioids such as heroin, codeine, or oxycodone, they can't get as good a pleasurable or euphoric feeling. They also won't feel as impacted by withdrawal symptoms. Unlike buprenorphine, which must be started when a person is experiencing withdrawal symptoms, methadone can be initiated at any time during the course of someone's treatment for opioid addiction. Also known under the brand names Dolophine and Methadose, methadone is a medication that has been studied for many years, with a large body of evidence in favor of its effectiveness for the treatment of opioid addiction.

Some things to consider concerning risks, potential side effects, and other limitations related to methadone treatment are as follows: first, those who take methadone continue to be physically dependent on opioids; in other words, skipping one or more doses can lead to opioid withdrawal symptoms. Second, there is a risk of opioid overdose, which can be fatal. This risk is highest within the first two weeks of treatment with methadone.[66] However, once that two-week period is over, the risk is dramatically reduced, and opioid overdose becomes less likely for those who are in ongoing methadone treatment than it is for those with untreated addiction.[67,68] Some people who are at especially high risk of overdose from methadone, such as those who are taking other medicines that slow down or "depress" the central nervous system (e.g., benzodiazepines or other sedatives), could overdose by combining high doses of these medicines with methadone. Despite these risks, the FDA advises that access to methadone treatment be provided even to those who are taking these types of medications, because the likelihood of overdose death is higher if they continue to struggle with an untreated opioid addiction.[69] Another potential adverse effect of taking methadone is hypogonadism, or low testosterone, a common condition related to long-term use of opioid medications across the spectrum.[70]

Methadone: What Does the Research Tell Us?

As the medicine that has been around the longest as a treatment for opioid use disorder (since 1947), many studies have been published on the effectiveness of methadone. What's the bottom line? As is shown in the figure below, which summarizes some of the key studies, methadone treatment is consistently effective in reducing opioid use. You can see this by looking closely at the grey shaded bars, which show a lower percentage of patients taking methadone who are actively using opioids when compared to those who received a placebo (i.e., a pill that doesn't contain an active ingredient to help with symptoms, such as a sugar pill), represented by the solid black bars. Here are some of the other findings from research into methadone:

- Methadone in combination with counseling results in reduced opioid use, along with lower rates of transmission of infectious diseases that are linked with injection opioid use (e.g., HIV, Hepatitis C) and crime.[a]
- Though many studies show that methadone in combination with counseling is effective, it can also be a highly effective treatment without counseling.[b,c]

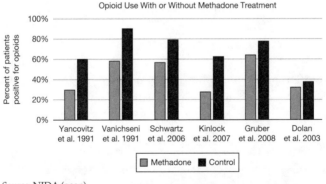

Opioid Use With or Without Methadone Treatment

Source: NIDA (2021)

---

[a] Mattick, R. P., Breen, C., Kimber, J., & Davoli, M. (2009). Methadone maintenance therapy versus no opioid replacement therapy for opioid dependence. *Cochrane Database of Systematic Reviews*, (3). https://doi.org/10.1002/14651858.CD002209.pub2

[b] Schwartz, R. P., Kelly, S. M., O'Grady, K. E., Gandhi, D., & Jaffe, J. H. (2012). Randomized trial of standard methadone treatment compared to initiating methadone without counseling: 12-month findings. *Addiction*, 107(5), 943–952. https://doi:10.1111/j.1360-0443.2011.03700.x.

c Schwartz, R. P., Highfield, D. A., Jaffe, J. H., Brady, J. V., Butler, C. B., Rouse, C. O., Callaman, J. M., O'Grady, K. E., Koudstaal, P. J., & Breteler, M. M. (2006). A randomized controlled trial of interim methadone maintenance. *Archives of General Psychiatry, 63*(1), 102–109. https://doi:10.1001/archpsyc.63.1.102

What is buprenorphine?

How does buprenorphine work? Buprenorphine, like methadone, acts on the opioid mu receptor, and it has several similar effects to methadone. It can relieve symptoms of opioid withdrawal, and by occupying the receptor it also blocks the pleasurable effects a person experiences if they try to take other opioids while they're actively taking buprenorphine. But it is different from methadone in some important ways. First, unlike methadone, which is a full agonist and activates the opioid mu receptor in the same way that other opioids do, buprenorphine is a *partial agonist*, meaning that it only activates the receptor partially. There are a few advantages to this: first, unlike full-agonist opioids, which can have risky or life-threatening adverse effects when a person takes excessive amounts, by only *partially* activating the opioid mu receptor, buprenorphine has less of an effect on the respiratory system. Since opioid overdose deaths are generally caused by depression of the respiratory system (which is what leads a person to stop breathing), the risk of overdose is much less a concern with buprenorphine than it is with a full-agonist opioid. Second, as a partial agonist, there is something called a "ceiling effect" of buprenorphine. This means that the opioid effects that a person can feel from buprenorphine can reach a maximum, and once that limit is reached, taking more does not increase the physical and psychological effect of the medicine. This "ceiling" is typically reached between the 12mg and 16mg dose. This makes it less likely that people will try to use it in efforts to get high. In fact, the most commonly used forms of buprenorphine (tablets or films that are dissolved under the tongue) have a special chemical structure that is designed to prevent people from crushing, attempting to inject it, or otherwise misusing it. There is a second medication contained in the buprenorphine which is activated if the person attempts to misuse it, and when this medication gets activated, it leads to unpleasant withdrawal symptoms. This second medication is naloxone (discussed further later in this chapter), and it is typically given as a lifesaving medication to someone who has overdosed on opioids. Known as an opioid *antagonist,* when naloxone is "activated" or released into the bloodstream, it has the effect of "kicking the opioids off" of the receptors, which triggers opioid withdrawal symptoms. So, if someone tried to crush and inject their buprenorphine, the naloxone would get activated, causing the person to enter opioid withdrawal. While not harmful, this is highly unpleasant, discouraging those who take buprenorphine from misusing it as a means of getting high.

What are long-acting forms of buprenorphine?

When the possible misuse or diversion of buprenorphine is a concern, there are a few long-acting formulations of this medicine that are more difficult to misuse and could be worth considering.

Sublocade. Also known as RBP-6000, or extended-release buprenorphine, Sublocade is an injectable form of buprenorphine that was approved by the FDA in late 2017 and has been marketed in the United States since 2018. Since evidence shows that taking buprenorphine for six months or longer prevents future relapse and lowers the risk of opioid overdose, taking a longer-lasting form of buprenorphine can help prevent early treatment dropout and poor outcomes, especially for those who have a difficult time staying in treatment or sticking with their medication regimen. Sublocade injections are dosed on a monthly basis. Studies to date have spanned up to a 12-month course of treatment.[71] When compared to placebo injections, Sublocade produces substantially higher opioid abstinence rates,[72] and reduced rates of hospital admissions.[73] In terms of adverse effects, extended-release buprenorphine is considered to be relatively safe, though irritation at the site of injection, reported in approximately 13% of those who receive it, can discourage some people from using this form of treatment.[71]

Buvidal. Buvidal, also known as Brixadi, or CAM 2038, is another relatively new form of buprenorphine injection that is approved in Europe and was FDA approved in 2023 for use in the United States. Like Sublocade, it is injected subcutaneously (under the skin), but unlike Sublocade the dosing is flexible and can be administered either on a weekly or monthly basis, and refrigeration is not a storage requirement. Studies of Buvidal have shown that, when given weekly over the first 12 weeks of treatment followed by monthly over the next 12 weeks, it was at least as effective as oral buprenorphine in reducing opioid use.[74] Like Sublocade, the most commonly reported side effect was mild irritation where the injection was placed, occurring in 18%–22% of those who participated in the study.[75] As a relatively new treatment, studies are ongoing to fully evaluate the safety and outcomes of taking this medicine.

What are the key differences between buprenorphine and methadone?

Unlike methadone, buprenorphine does not have to be given in a special licensed clinic, and those who take it do not have to return regularly in person to receive their daily dose. Buprenorphine is often given as a prescription either by a primary care doctor or an addiction medicine specialist; the patient can fill the prescription at a pharmacy, and take their prescribed dose independently. Though close monitoring and frequent visits to the prescribing provider are common during the early phases of treatment, as the buprenorphine dosage is adjusted and stabilized, those whose treatment is going well are usually able to start spreading out their visits to the provider—first to monthly, and eventually for some, to a quarterly basis.

Because buprenorphine acts as an opioid substitute, some of the side effects to be aware of with buprenorphine, as with methadone, include the possibility of entering withdrawal if the medicine is discontinued, though the withdrawal symptoms are likely to be more severe and uncomfortable from skipped doses of methadone than buprenorphine. However, even though it is not life threatening, the first dose of buprenorphine can, in some people, trigger a very unpleasant withdrawal syndrome known as *precipitated withdrawal.* This is because, when buprenorphine is taken, it displaces other opioids, "kicking them off" of the brain's opioid receptors and replacing them with an opioid that is only a partial agonist. This means that for people who were taking full agonist opioids like heroin, buprenorphine activates the receptor only a portion of how fully it was activated before. The body and brain experience this as a form of opioid withdrawal, in which the person rapidly develops symptoms within one or two hours of taking buprenorphine (e.g., aches, nausea and vomiting, diarrhea and abdominal cramps, dilated pupils, running nose, yawning). These symptoms usually resolve within six to 24 hours, but understandably when a person's initiation of buprenorphine leads them to experience this intense discomfort, they are often reluctant to continue the treatment.

One way to avoid this happening, which is guided by a buprenorphine prescriber, is to wait until the person is in moderate withdrawal from opioids before initiating buprenorphine treatment—this way, the opioids they are taking have already left the receptors, and the buprenorphine will not "kick off" any other opioids. There are certain factors that can place a person at risk for precipitated withdrawal when they start buprenorphine, an adverse effect that has been observed in as many as 9% of those who are taking it for the first time: (1)

transferring from a full-agonist medication (such as metha-done) to buprenorphine; (2) recent use of benzodiazepines (such as Xanax or Ativan); (3) heavy alcohol use; (4) being "buprenorphine naïve," meaning that this is the first time the person has ever taken this drug; and (5) being prescribed a low dose of buprenorphine. Prescribers of buprenorphine have access to guidelines concerning ways to avoid triggering precipitated withdrawal. When starting this medication, concerns about the potential for precipitated withdrawal can be discussed openly with the prescribing provider to under-stand their approach to reducing this risk.

Summary: Four types of medications for opioid use disorders

- Full-agonist (methadone) attaches itself to the opioid receptors; the higher the dose, the stronger the effects on the brain and body.
- Partial agonist (buprenorphine) only partially activates the opioid receptors; those who have used opioids chron-ically *do not experience stronger effects* on the brain and body as the dose of this medicine gets higher, making overdose much less likely.
- Antagonist (naltrexone, naloxone) attaches to the opioid receptors but does not activate them. This blocks the re-ceptor and therefore blocks the effects of taking any opioids.
- A fourth type of medication, not depicted in Figure 12.5, is an adrenergic receptor agonist (lofexidine), which attaches to and activates the adrenergic receptors in the brain and alleviates withdrawal symptoms.

What is extended-release naltrexone (Vivitrol)?

How does naltrexone work? Naltrexone is the only non-agonist medication treatment option currently approved for opioid addiction. This medicine is known as a *full antagonist* of the mu opioid receptor, which means that it blocks the pain-relieving and pleasurable effects of all opioids. In other words,

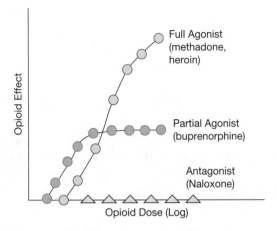

Figure 12.5 Three FDA Approved Medicines for Opioid Addiction
Source: SAMHSA (2021)

this medicine does not replace or substitute for opioids; rather, it removes all motivation to use them because they no longer do anything that feels good. You might wonder, then, why would anyone take this medicine? And that's a great question. People who have certain types of circumstances or needs may get the most out of this form of treatment, such as those who (1) need to avoid agonist treatments (such as methadone and buprenorphine), (2) have established a few weeks or longer of abstinence from opioids but are at risk of relapse, (3) have not responded well to other treatments, and (4) use small quantities of opioids and/or use them sporadically (for example, someone who is not severely addicted and is able to maintain a few days at a time opioid free, but is beginning to lose control over their use of opioids). It is also used in some treatment settings for individuals who struggle with overlapping opioid and alcohol use disorders.

Since it is relatively common for someone in recovery from opioid addiction to try using opioids while they're on extended-release naltrexone, ideally this learning experience, in which they find that opioids don't have any rewarding effects, makes them less likely to feel interested in using while they're on this medication. Then, after remaining on naltrexone for some time, their cravings diminish.[76,77]

The pill form of naltrexone was found not to be an effective medication for those with opioid use disorders in research studies, as it was no better than a placebo (i.e., a sugar pill) in helping people stop using opioids.[63] People treated with the pill form of naltrexone also have a higher risk of overdose if they return to opioid use, compared to methadone.[78] Currently, the only FDA-approved form of naltrexone for the treatment of opioid addiction is the extended-release (Vivitrol) formulation.

Does it work? Though more extensively studied for alcoholism, according to a systematic review, the research on extended-release injectable naltrexone as a medication for opioid use disorder has consistently shown that taking it helps people remain in treatment for longer and reduce their cravings and use of opioids.[79] However, there are some limitations to consider. Since naltrexone can trigger severe withdrawal symptoms, it is recommended that for someone who undergoes medically supervised opioid withdrawal, waiting an additional four to seven days while opioid free (including being free from any opioids used in medication treatment such as methadone and buprenorphine) is necessary before the medication can be given.[80] Since someone with severe opioid addiction will find it very difficult to remain opioid free for that long, especially without access to opioid replacement therapies, people can relapse before they even have the opportunity to initiate treatment with extended-release injectable naltrexone. This begins the cycle of two weeks of required abstinence over again, delaying access to much-needed care for opioid addiction.

What is lofexidine?

How does lofexidine work? Lofexidine, a non-opioid drug that was originally developed as a medication for high blood pressure, was approved by the FDA in 2018 as the first medication targeted specifically to treat the physical symptoms of opioid withdrawal. These symptoms, which include stomach cramps, aches and pains, coldness, muscle spasms or tension, pounding heart, runny eyes, feeling sick, and insomnia, along with other uncomfortable symptoms, are the primary reason why people with opioid addiction find it intolerable to stick to their withdrawal treatments and relapse early on in the recovery process. Unlike buprenorphine and methadone, which are typically given while a person is actively experiencing withdrawal symptoms, and extended-release naltrexone, which can only be initiated after a person has been fully withdrawn physically from opioids, lofexidine can be given during those initial uncomfortable stages of opioid discontinuation. Lofexidine is an oral tablet that is taken as needed. In a randomized clinical trial comparing this medicine to a placebo among over 600 individuals with opioid addiction who were entering medically managed opioid withdrawal, those who received lofexidine were 71% to 85% more likely to complete opioid discontinuation treatment without dropping out, compared to those who received placebo.[81] Though studies of lofexidine are ongoing, this large trial provided support for the use of this medication for treatment of opioid withdrawal when (1) a non-opioid medication is either preferred or necessary; (2) an agonist medication for withdrawal is not available; (3) agonist medication triggered precipitated withdrawal, and (4) as a first step in the process of medically supervised withdrawal, prior to transitioning an individual into treatment with methadone, buprenorphine, or extended-release naltrexone.

What considerations will lead a healthcare provider to recommend a particular medicine for an opioid use disorder?

Although all three of the FDA-approved medications for ongoing management of an opioid use disorder work on the same part of the brain (the opioid mu receptor), they each do this in very different ways, and there is no single "best medication" that is the most effective for most people. In fact, according to clinical trials research, methadone, extended-release naltrexone, and buprenorphine have each been found to be more effective than no medication in reducing opioid use.[82] In addition, treatment with either methadone or buprenorphine effectively reduced the risk of overdose death.[83,84] The optimal dosage of each of these medicines can also vary, not only being different from one person to another but also, over the course of a person's recovery, the dosage that helps them maintain abstinence from opioids can change over time. Research suggests that there are four important considerations that can guide selection of a medication for opioid addiction:

1. the person's response to prior treatment using medications for opioid addiction,
2. how severe the person's physical dependence is (i.e., whether they are taking high doses of opioids),
3. the presence of any overlapping conditions such as other addictions or mental health problems, and
4. the person's individual preference.[85]

For example, for a person who has both an opioid use disorder and an alcohol use disorder, naltrexone might be especially helpful since it is known to be effective as a treatment for alcoholism. For someone with an opioid use disorder who is also struggling with depression, buprenorphine may be a preferable option since it has some antidepressant effects. For pregnant women, because of the limited information available concerning the safety of naltrexone, methadone or buprenorphine is recommended at this time.

Selecting a Medication for Opioid Use Disorder

Medicine	Who Could Benefit	Reasons
Methadone	Someone with severe opioid tolerance.	Buprenorphine could trigger withdrawal.
	Those who tend to drop out of treatment.	Retention in treatment is generally better with methadone than other medicines.
Buprenorphine	Someone with clinical depression.	People with depression symptoms tend to respond well to this medicine.
Extended-Release Naltrexone (Vivitrol)	Someone with co-existing opioid addiction and alcoholism.	Naltrexone has proven effectiveness for the treatment of alcoholism.
	Someone with mild addiction symptoms.	Able to stay opioid free for the required 7-day period before starting Vivitrol.

What are some common myths about opioid addiction and medication treatment?

Myth #1: Taking opioid maintenance medications like buprenorphine and/or methadone is just replacing one addiction with another.

Reality: Addiction, by definition, is loss of control over use of a drug, leading to compulsive use despite the devastating consequences it brings. Taking opioid maintenance medication, on the other hand, is the use of a prescribed medication to manage a chronic illness. These are very different health-related sets of behaviors. To illustrate the meaning of this distinction, let's examine this further.

Though the fact that maintenance medications are opioids themselves makes it hard to view their use as being different from addictive behavior, there are several key differences. *First,* those who are addicted to opioids respond differently to maintenance medications than people who are not. Someone who is what we would call "opioid naïve," meaning their brain and body is not accustomed to opioids, would feel euphoric or high if they took methadone or buprenorphine. But someone who has used opioids repeatedly and has become addicted to them will have a very different response; they become sick and very uncomfortable when opioids leave their body, leading them to intensely crave opioids despite the pain and suffering that repeated opioid use is causing them in their life. If that person takes methadone or buprenorphine, they will not feel high or euphoric. They will simply have a different reaction to discontinuing their use of the opioid drugs that they used to take to get high: they will not experience intense sickness and discomfort, nor the cravings that were once linked to those feelings. Once the opioid withdrawal sickness and cravings are no longer present, the person can begin to function in important areas of life like they once did, before they felt trapped in the cycle of using opioids, coming off opioids and entering withdrawal sickness, and seeking more opioids to relieve the discomfort. In short, taking maintenance medications keeps withdrawal symptoms and cravings at bay while the individual works on rebuilding their life in recovery.

A *second* and related key difference between taking maintenance medications and addictive behavior is that, without the highs and lows of using and feeling sick that a person with opioid addiction typically experiences, the erratic and dysfunctional types of behaviors that are often linked with opioid addiction are very unlikely to occur. For example, unlike the compulsive drug-seeking and obsessive thinking that is common among those who are addicted to heroin, people who are taking buprenorphine are not preoccupied constantly with cravings for buprenorphine and worries about how to acquire more of it, and the effects of taking or trying to avoid withdrawal from it do not lead them to neglect important life responsibilities or do things that may be out of character, such as lying or stealing. The physiological and psychological *stability* that regularly taking a maintenance medication restores is not something that can be achieved through daily use of heroin or other opioid drugs such as fentanyl. It is this key difference that can enable an understanding of why taking agonist medications such as methadone or buprenorphine is not replacing one addiction with another. The chart below, titled "Effects of Maintenance Medication versus Addiction to Opiods," highlights effects of opioid use that are unique to addiction compared to the effects of taking maintenance or agonist medication. Though a person who takes maintenance medication will be *physically dependent* on the medicine, the other 10 signs and symptoms of a severe opioid use disorder or addiction are not typically observed among people who are receiving treatment with an agonist medication.

Effects of Maintenance Medication versus Addiction to Opioids

Effect	Addiction to Opioids	Maintenance Medication
Physical Tolerance	X	X
Withdrawal if discontinued or doses skipped	X	X
Taking more than intended	X	
Excessive time spent using/ recovering from using	X	
Repeated unsuccessful attempts to cut back or stop	X	P*
Important activities missed or neglected due to use	X	
Use in hazardous situations	X	
Physical or psychological problems caused/worsened by use	X	
Cravings	X	

Effect	Addiction to Opioids	Maintenance Medication
Social/interpersonal relationship problems caused by use	X	
Continued use despite problems caused by it	X	

*P: indicates that this is not a known typical effect, but a possible one, since some people whose goal is to taper off of maintenance medications have a difficult time discontinuing completely due to recurrence of symptoms.

Myth #2: Opioid replacement medications are only for people with heroin addiction.

Reality: Opioid replacement medications are used for the treatment of addiction to any opioid drug, such as morphine, opium, and commonly used prescription painkillers such as oxycodone, Vicodin, and codeine. Addiction to fentanyl can also be treated effectively with methadone or suboxone.

Myth #3: To truly be in recovery, a person must be completely abstinent from all opioids (including medicines that contain them).

Reality: Experts in the field define recovery as *a voluntarily maintained lifestyle . , . characterized by sobriety, personal health, and citizenship.*[86]

Sobriety, according to this definition, refers to "abstinence from alcohol, and all other nonprescribed drugs." Though medications for the treatment of opioid use disorders are opioid-containing drugs, as *prescribed* medicines for the management of opioid addiction their use is not only part of a plan of *recovery* but also for the purpose of making sobriety possible.

The fundamental misconception that leads some people to believe that those who take opioid-containing medications are not truly "in recovery" is that abstinence from all opioid use is the ultimate goal of treatment for opioid addiction. If opioid addiction were a short-term, acute condition like a broken bone or a stomach virus, a short-term treatment would be perfectly appropriate. But, as we've reviewed in Chapter 2, decades of research on the effects on the brain of opioid and other substance use have shaped our understanding of addiction as a chronic illness, much like diabetes or hypertension. We know that diabetes and hypertension affect major organs such as the pancreas and the heart, and that removing ongoing treatment for these chronic conditions will cause their core symptoms (such as high blood sugar or high blood pressure) to return. The goal of treatments for these conditions is to effectively *manage* rather than to cure them, and the same is true of opioid addiction—having been altered by chronic opioid use, it may not be possible to completely cure or restore the brain to its original, pre-addiction state. However, by managing the withdrawal symptoms and cravings, and blocking the euphoria that would be produced by a return to addictive behavior (such as using opioids), treatment with an agonist medication such as buprenorphine or methadone can prevent the return of opioid use disorder symptoms.

Does science support the idea that total abstinence (including abstinence from opioid-containing medicines) is an effective pathway to sustained recovery from opioid addiction? Here's what we know: One of the most widely used abstinence-oriented approaches to initiating opioid addiction treatment is what was previously known as *inpatient detoxification,* now termed *medically supervised discontinuation* (to reduce stigmatizing language), in which a person is supervised in a medical setting over days or weeks while they discontinue their use of opioids. Studies have shown that short-term, abstinence-oriented treatments for opioid addiction, such as inpatient medically supervised discontinuation, are associated with relapse rates as high as 90% within six months.[87] Of greatest concern in relation to this elevated relapse rate after detoxification is the well-known danger that within the first days and weeks of total abstinence from opioids, there is an increased risk of overdose death among individuals who relapse. Not only has this been observed among people who leave treatment after a very brief period of time (such as those who receive short-term detoxification treatments),[88] but those who leave incarceration after an enforced period of abstinence are 5 to 10 times more likely to die of an opioid overdose in the first few weeks after they are released than at any other time in their lives.[89] With the use of medication viewed by some people as a sign that that a person is not "truly in recovery," there is a risk that evidence-based treatments are undervalued, leading those who can benefit the most from them skeptical, ashamed, and hesitant to engage in lifesaving care. Based on these findings, inpatient detoxification followed by abstinence is considered not only unsafe but ineffective.[87] On the other hand, meta-analyses summarizing studies that included over 15,000 individuals with opioid addiction have concluded that opioid agonist treatments such as buprenorphine and methadone reduce the risk of overdose deaths by 70% to 79%, when compared to the risk for those who are not receiving this treatment.[68] Despite this and many other well-documented health benefits of medications for opioid use disorders, only 36% of the opioid addiction treatment programs in America offer at least one of these medications and 6% offer all three,[90] a shortfall that experts and leaders in the addiction science field attribute largely to stigma. The stigma surrounding not only drug addiction but the use of medications to treat the illness has reinforced the view that total abstinence, even from medications containing opioids, is paramount to recovery.

Although the decision to take medication as part of treatment for opioid addiction is a very personal one, and some people are able to recover successfully without medication, the idea that total abstinence from opioids, including opioid-containing medicines, is the best pathway to recovery is not supported by scientific evidence.

Myth #4: Mostly, opioid medications are misused and diverted to get people high.

Reality: Any opioid or opioid-containing medication carries a risk of diversion and misuse. That said, studies show that the majority of those who acquire buprenorphine and methadone without a prescription are using it as a means of trying to come off heroin or other opioids to which they are addicted, and/or to reduce withdrawal symptoms in the process, rather than to get high. In fact, in a series of surveys of people with opioid addiction who were using buprenorphine that they bought on the street, 97% reported that the reason they were taking it was to prevent cravings, 90% to prevent withdrawal, and 29% to save money.[91] Although some of those surveyed reported that they were using it to get high, this group was in the minority, ranging from 8% to 25%. Since buprenorphine doesn't fully activate the opioid receptor, its rewarding effects are not as intense as some other opioids (e.g., full agonists), so it's not surprising that the rate at which people use it to get high has decreased over time. This has been interpreted as suggesting that once people experience the effects of buprenorphine and realize that it is not as rewarding as they expected, they are more likely to lose interest in using it to get high.[92] What's more, buprenorphine is rarely mentioned as a substance that people in addiction treatment are struggling to control using.[93]

Medications for Opioid Use Disorder		
Medicine	Dosage	Side Effects
Methadone	Starts at 10 mg–30 mg/day Long-term dose: 60 mg–120 mg/day	Physical tolerance, dependence Risk of overdose (especially in the first 2 weeks) Opioid withdrawal if discontinued or doses skipped Hypogonadism (low testosterone)

Medicine	Dosage	Side Effects
Buprenorphine	Dose ranges from 8 mg–24 mg/day	Physical tolerance and dependence
	Optimal target dose: 16 mg/day	Opioid withdrawal if discontinued or doses skipped
		First buprenorphine dose can trigger withdrawal
		Hypogonadism (low testosterone)
Extended-Release Naltrexone (Vivitrol)	380 mg delivered via intramuscular injection into the buttocks every 4 weeks	Headache, nausea, insomnia Pain at injection site Liver enzyme abnormalities

Note: This chart summarizes some of the most common effects for each of the above medications. It is not intended to be a complete source of information or to replace package inserts. Any decisions about medicines s hould be made in consultation with a physician.

Kratom: What do we know so far?

Kratom is an herbal extract from the leaves of an evergreen tree in the coffee family (*Mitragyna speciosa*), found in Thailand and other tropical countries (see Figure 12.6)In Southeast Asia, traditionally, its leaves have been either chewed or placed into a tea that is used to counteract fatigue and improve work productivity. Kratom has also been used as a substitute for opium in the treatment of medical conditions including pain and diarrhea. In addition, it has been used traditionally during religious ceremonies. In recent years, Kratom has been the focus of increasing interest in Western countries as a potential herbal remedy for opioid withdrawal symptoms. People take kratom to ease withdrawal because it produces feelings of euphoria, and some people believe it is helpful in reducing anxiety and depression. In addition, because it is sold as a dietary supplement and is not regulated in the United States, it can be obtained more easily than other medications for the treatment of opioid

Figure 12.6 Kratom.
Source: NCCIH (2021)

withdrawal. That said, Kratom is illegal to buy, use, or sell in several states, and is a controlled substance in 16 countries.[94]

There are two compounds in kratom leaves, mitragynine and 7-hydroxymitragynine, that interact with opioid receptors in the brain. These compounds act as partial agonists at the mu opioid receptor, sharing some properties in common with certain opioid substitution medications. In low doses, kratom makes a person feel alert. In high doses, like commonly used opioids, the effect of kratom on the opioid receptors produces feelings of sedation, pleasure, and decreased pain. With effects that are similar to those of opioids that people become addicted to, then would addiction be a possible outcome of taking kratom? That is one of the questions that researchers have been working to understand, given the growing interest in kratom for opioid withdrawal.

What does the research say? Although there is enthusiasm about the idea of using an herbal remedy for managing opioid withdrawal and/or treating opioid addiction, several case studies detailing the experiences of people who were using kratom for this purpose have reported that individuals can form addiction to kratom itself.[95] Over time, like other opioids, people can develop tolerance to kratom, requiring higher doses to achieve the same effect, and over the long term, people who use kratom may experience withdrawal symptoms if they stop using it. In fact, in many documented cases of addiction to kratom, recovery has necessitated treatment with the same medications that are used to treat heroin and prescription opioid addiction (such as buprenorphine), and evidence suggests that this approach is effective in the management of kratom withdrawal and addiction.[96]

Research concerning the safety of taking kratom has produced mixed results. Though animal studies have found that high doses of kratom may be less likely to be fatal than high doses of opioids, deaths related to kratom use have been reported. Between 2010 and 2015 there was a 10-fold increase in calls to poison centers related to kratom exposure, with 152 overdose deaths between 2016 and 2017 involving kratom. In the majority of these cases, ingestion of at least one other substance was detected.[97] So, while it is difficult to know whether kratom toxicity was the primary cause of these deaths or if it was due to the mixture of kratom with other substances, there is a growing list of reports of severe toxicity with kratom use. The documented health complications that can arise from kratom toxicity include overdose, bacterial infection from use of contaminated products, withdrawal symptoms in babies born to mothers who had been using kratom (also known as "neonatal abstinence syndrome"), thyroid problems, liver damage, respiratory failure, seizures, and psychiatric problems such as psychosis.[98,99]

In 2016, the US Drug Enforcement Administration (DEA) announced its intent to temporarily classify the two main active ingredients in kratom as drugs with no currently accepted medical use and a high potential for abuse (a classification known as Schedule I; other substances classified in this category include heroin and LSD). However, strong public opposition led to the withdrawal by the DEA of this proposed action.[100] At this time, the consensus concerning the use of kratom is that there is little definitive evidence concerning its safety or effectiveness as a treatment for opioid addiction, and there are currently no FDA-approved therapeutic uses of kratom. That said, despite the ongoing debate about regulating kratom and its potential role in the treatment of pain and opioid addiction, kratom is becoming increasingly popular due to its low addiction potential compared to other opioids, the need for alternatives to opioids for pain, and its potential usefulness for managing opioid withdrawal and reducing use of prescription and other opioids.[101] For the healthcare consumer to arrive at an informed decision about using it, it is important to weigh these benefits against concerns about the lack of scientific evidence supporting kratom use for these purposes, coupled with the unknown purity and absence of uniform dosing or dosing guidelines.

Why do people overdose on opioids and how can they be saved?

What places me or someone I care for at risk for an opioid overdose?

Although we know quite a bit about the conditions and characteristics that make a person vulnerable to overdose on opioids, those who take opioids may not be aware of these risk factors. And even if they are aware, many people have a tendency to view themselves as an exception, which of course, makes it easier for them psychologically to continue their addictive behavior. This well-studied phenomenon, known as *optimistic bias,* is when a person believes that his or her personal risk for a particular outcome is lower than that of others who are in the same or a similar risk group. Research studies have found that people who misuse and/or are addicted to opioids tend to perceive themselves as being safe from overdose risk, even if they have overdosed in the past.[102,103]Raising awareness of these risks, as well as being aware of the natural human tendency to discount them, is an important part of the response necessary to reverse the escalating drug overdose crisis.

Who Is At Risk for an Opioid Overdose?

Studies have shown that there are certain conditions that create increased risk for opioid overdose. These include:

- Having an opioid addiction
- Taking opioids by injecting them
- Relapsing to opioid use after a period of abstinence (e.g., after receiving detoxification treatment or after a period of incarceration)
- Using prescription opioid medications without medical supervision
- Using opioids in combination with alcohol and/or other substances that slow down or suppress the respiratory system (including benzodiazepines and sedatives)
- Using opioids in combination with stimulants, such as cocaine
- Taking high doses of prescribed opioids (more than 100 mg of morphine or an equivalent drug daily)

Research has also shown that certain individual characteristics are linked with overdose risk. Men, people who have a history of prior overdoses, and people with a history of arrest or incarceration, have elevated risk of opioid overdose.[a]

---

[a] Wilder, C. M., Miller, S. C., Tiffany, E., Winhusen, T., Winstanley, E. L., & Stein, M. D. (2016). Risk factors for opioid overdose and awareness of overdose risk among veterans prescribed chronic opioids for addiction or pain. *Journal of Addictive Diseases*, 35(1), 42–51. https://doi.org/10.1080/10550887.2016.1107264

How can an opioid overdose be reversed?

In 1961, scientists developed a lifesaving medication called *naloxone*, which at the time it was patented was intended to treat constipation caused by chronic opioid use. Researchers quickly realized that this drug acted to block the receptors in the brain that opioids attach themselves to, creating the capability to reverse an opioid overdose. Ten years later, naloxone was approved by the FDA in injectable form as a treatment for opioid overdose. At that time, naloxone was used only by hospital personnel. But finding and getting someone to the hospital who has overdosed on opioids may not afford enough time to save a life; in fact, nearly 80% of opioid overdose deaths occur outside of a medical setting.[104] As the use of opioids began to increase in the 1990s, scientists began to explore ways for laypersons to give naloxone safely and quickly in emergency situations involving an opioid overdose. By the late 1990s, over 30% of US states began making take-home naloxone kits available to non-medical personnel, and studying the results of these efforts. According to the Centers for Disease Control, over 26,000 opioid overdoses were reversed by laypersons over the span of the first 18 years these kits were available, ending in 2014. Shortly thereafter, the first naloxone nasal spray, Narcan was approved by the FDA. In 2019, the first generic naloxone nasal spray was approved, and in 2023, Narcan nasal spray was FDA approved for over-the-counter nonprescription use.

Naloxone is also available as an autoinjector, Evzio, which is given through an EpiPen-like delivery system. The autoinjector not only has written instructions for use, but it contains a speaker that provides voice instructions to guide the person using it through each step of the injection. The autoinjector also has a generic equivalent. Finally, naloxone is available in an injectable form, which involves first filling a syringe with the drug from a small vial and then injecting that into the muscle of the thigh or shoulder.

Is one delivery system better than another? There are three FDA-approved forms of naloxone: (1) a nasal spray, (2) an autoinjector, and (3) injectable form. All three of these delivery systems have been found to be very effective in reducing opioid overdose. However, many first responders, police, family, and friends of individuals who suffer overdoses are not formally trained or comfortable with giving an injection to someone in an emergency situation. Historically, many first responders have used an adaptor to convert the liquid naloxone product into a nasal spray. This has been referred to as an "improvised" method of giving naloxone.[105] In 2019, researchers evaluated how well this method worked compared to the FDA-approved nasal spray and autoinjector forms of naloxone. Their study found that the amount of naloxone that reached the bloodstream was much lower when the "improvised" method of creating a nasal spray was used, compared to the amount of naloxone in the systems of those for whom the FDA-approved, prepackaged nasal spray or the autoinjector were used. In fact, of all the products tested, the one that resulted in the greatest quantity of naloxone reaching the bloodstream was the FDA-approved nasal spray.[106] Because people are overdosing on stronger, more potent opioids like fentanyl with increasing frequency, which may require higher doses of naloxone to reverse than would be needed for other opioids, it has become especially important to use a form of naloxone that can quickly reach the bloodstream in high concentrations. It is therefore highly recommended that FDA-approved forms of naloxone are used rather than improvised forms.

Is a naloxone prescription needed? Although one way to get naloxone is by prescription, because of the steep rise in opioid overdoses, state governments have taken steps to make naloxone more easily accessible to caregivers, concerned loved ones, and first responders. In efforts to break down barriers to accessing this lifesaving treatment, in 2023, Narcan nasal spray was FDA approved for over-the-counter, nonprescription use.

How much does it cost? The cost of naloxone varies widely; for those with health insurance, some of the cost may be covered, and for those without insurance, some but not all pharmacies provide naloxone free of charge. Now that naloxone is available over the counter, a set of two doses is being sold at around $45. When acquired by prescription, according to one study, the average out-of-pocket cost of naloxone among those with health insurance averaged around $31.[107] Because the cost of naloxone can be a barrier to using this lifesaving drug, various initiatives have been rolled out to help people access affordable naloxone. For example in New York, the Department of Health and Mental Hygiene has made naloxone kits available free of charge at partner pharmacies, which includes both small local pharmacies and larger chains like Walgreens and Rite Aid. Addressing the cost barriers to naloxone access and use remains a work in progress across the United States.

How does it work? Naloxone belongs to a class of medications known as *opioid antagonists*, meaning that it opposes or blocks the effects of opioid drugs on brain cells. If a person has overdosed on opioids, when they take naloxone it attaches itself to the opioid receptors, knocking the opioids off and blocking their effects (Figure 12.7). Since the most dangerous effect of opioids on the brain in an overdose situation is slowing down a person's breathing to the point where breathing can stop altogether, giving the person naloxone to reverse the opioid's effects means that their breathing can be rapidly restored to normal.

Are there side effects? Naloxone is known to be a very safe medication. When someone overdoses, giving them naloxone reverses the effects of opioids that they have taken by "kicking them off" of the opioid receptors; hence the side effect this can lead to is opioid withdrawal symptoms. This makes sense if you think about it, because in opioid withdrawal, a person is experiencing the effects of the opioid leaving the brain and body, and naloxone in essence "fast tracks" that process—it "kicks the opioid out" of the brain. Not everyone will experience uncomfortable or intense withdrawal symptoms as side effects, but if they do, these symptoms can include headache, nausea, vomiting, rapid heart rate (also known as *tachycardia*), blood pressure changes, tremors, and sweating. When weighing the pros and cons of giving someone naloxone, the lifesaving impact of giving it to them will clearly outweigh the uncomfortable but relatively harmless withdrawal side effects.[108]

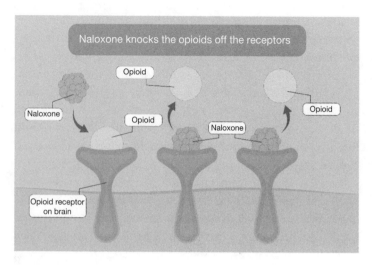

Figure 12.7 How naloxone works to reverse an opioid overdose
Source: Shutterstock

Who can give a person naloxone? Naloxone kits are designed to enable friends, family, caregivers, and bystanders to save the life of a person who is at risk of an opioid overdose death. Studies demonstrate that broadening access to naloxone to include laypersons resulted in a decrease in opioid overdose deaths.[109,110] To protect those who take this lifesaving measure without professional medical training from any legal repercussions for doing so, as of 2018 Good Samaritan Laws have been in place in 46 states and the District of Columbia.[111]

Terminology Check: Why Are Medicines for Opioid Addiction Called Different Things?

If you've been doing research on medications for opioid addiction, you might have come across two different terms: *Medication Assisted Treatment* (MAT), and *Medication-based treatment for Opioid Use Disorders* (MOUD). What's the difference? The answer is, they are not different: they both refer to the same set of medications that are used to treat opioid use disorders, which you'll learn more about in the section that follows. But there has been a gradual shift toward using the term MOUD, and here's why:

- Leading experts in addiction science and treatment emphasize that medications are *central* to the treatment of opioid addiction.
- Medications are understood to be part of a longer-term treatment plan for opioid addiction for many people.
- The term Medication-*Assisted* Treatment (MAT) has been interpreted to mean that medications are either an "add-on" to opioid addiction care or a very temporary phase of treatment. Currently, accumulating research has found a link between *longer term* use of medications and *success* in opioid addiction recovery.
- The term Medication-*based* treatment for Opioid Use Disorders (MOUD) highlights the key role that science has shown medication to play in recovery from opioid addiction.
- The decision to take medication to treat an opioid addiction is a very personal one and there is no "one size fits all" regimen for whether or for how long medicine should be taken. Many studies highlight the lifesaving potential of these medicines, which is an important consideration for you or your loved one who may be struggling with this addiction.

How can you learn more about how to access and/or give someone naloxone? There are a number of training videos and even an online certificate that can be earned for those who would like to get more comfortable with giving naloxone in an opioid overdose emergency.

- For training on giving naloxone, look here: https://www.getnaloxonenow.org/#home
- If you're looking for naloxone free of charge in your community, you can Google your county + naloxone, or you can check the website for your state department of health.
- You can also check with Next DISTRO: https://nextdistro.org/. Depending on the state where you reside, they may be able to mail naloxone to you free of charge.

Keep in mind that naloxone is now available over the counter at many drug stores, convenience stores, and grocery stores, including Walmart, CVS, Target, and Rite Aid.

Helping Someone Who Has Overdosed On Opioids

You might wonder why it is so important to **call 911** immediately if you suspect that someone has overdosed on opioids and have given that person naloxone. This is partly because naloxone doesn't stay active in the body for very long. After 30 to 90 minutes, the effects of naloxone can wear off, putting the body back into a state of shallow breathing or leading the person to stop breathing altogether again.

What are some of the reasons people don't access treatment for opioid addiction?

Even though there are highly effective treatment options for opioid use disorder, for various reasons access to these treatments remains problematic. Methadone treatment is highly regulated, restricted only to state and federally certified opioid treatment programs, or OTPs, which historically were referred to as "methadone clinics." Often, to receive ongoing treatment with methadone a patient is required to visit the clinic in person daily, where their dose will be given to them. In addition, there are other requirements to fulfill to be eligible for continued treatment, such as attending counseling sessions on a regular basis. Take-home doses are eventually allowed for some patients if they meet certain criteria that demonstrate good treatment progress. These conditions often create obstacles to long-term treatment participation. Similarly, since buprenorphine was initially FDA approved for the treatment of opioid addiction in 2002, a number of rules have governed its use, including extensive training and certification requirements to enable medical practitioners to prescribe it, coupled with limits to the quantity of patients who can be treated with buprenorphine by an individual practitioner.

Because of these restrictions, many patients have struggled to find someone who can act as their buprenorphine provider, which poses a frustrating and dangerous challenge to accessing the medicine, as studies show that delaying the initiation of medication for opioid addiction increases a person's mortality risk.[112] Despite these known risks, only 6% of specialty addiction treatment facilities offered all three FDA-approved medications for opioid addiction in 2016.[90]

After drug overdose deaths soared in the wake of COVID-19, increasing by an unprecedented 29.4%,[113] the federal government removed one of the biggest hurdles for prescribers to make buprenorphine available to those who desperately need effective treatment for opioid addiction. As of January 2023, the extensive training and certification requirements to enable clinicians to prescribe buprenorphine were eliminated. This is great progress toward making highly effective, lifesaving treatment with buprenorphine more accessible, and in changing common misperceptions about treatments for opioid addiction and the role that a variety of prescribing providers could play in providing this care. That said, more changes will need to occur to make a meaningful impact on the millions of Americans who have not yet accessed the treatment they need for this devastating condition. For example, because medical training for addiction is lacking across many disciplines within the healthcare system, progress has been slow in breaking through the misinformed ideas that buprenorphine is a more dangerous medication than other opioids, and that only addiction specialists can provide treatment to address problematic substance use.[114] By removing extensive training and regulatory requirements to enable practitioners to prescribe buprenorphine, it is hoped that some of these perceptions will begin to shift, so that a broader group of healthcare professionals with prescribing capabilities will incorporate medications for opioid use disorders into their practice.

Stigma. Accumulating research suggests that the strikingly small numbers of people who seek out treatment for addiction can be partially explained by the impact of stigma. In fact, a recent "secret shopper" study conducted across the United States in over 450 primary care clinics found that people who take opioid medications for chronic pain may be less likely to be accepted as new patients in a primary care clinic if they indicate that they are seeking treatment with opioids.[115] Individuals who struggle with opioid addiction report that they avoid seeking needed healthcare services to treat their addiction because they have encountered stigmatizing attitudes from healthcare professionals and fear repetition of this experience. Spreading knowledge about the disease of addiction, challenging myths about addictive behavior (e.g., the inaccurate yet commonly held belief that addiction is a choice) and judgments about the implications of addiction in regard to a person's character (e.g., the idea that "giving in" to the compulsion to drink or use drugs in an addictive behavior pattern reflects a moral failing), making treatment more widely accessible, and modeling open conversations about addiction are a few ways to begin to break through the effects of stigma.

What medicines are available for treating common co-occurring psychiatric conditions?

Many people with substance use disorders also struggle with mental health difficulties. Also referred to as *comorbidity* (which means having two or more conditions at the same time, or occurring one after the other), the most common co-occurring mental health problems that affect those with addictions include mood disorders (such as major depression and bipolar disorder), anxiety disorders (e.g., post-traumatic stress disorder or PTSD, generalized anxiety disorder, and social anxiety disorder), attention-deficit hyperactivity disorder (also known as ADHD), and for some people, psychotic disorders such as schizophrenia. Comorbidity is common: nearly 40% of those with a substance use disorder also have a mental health diagnosis. Yet more than half of those with these co-occurring conditions don't receive treatment for either, and less than 10% receive treatment for both problems. People describe many reasons for this, including difficulties affording treatment, not feeling a need or readiness for treatment, not knowing where to go to access care, and worries about treatment either not working or leading people to stereotype them.[116] That said, it is important for anyone struggling with addiction and a second condition like depression or anxiety to know that treating both disorders simultaneously is the gold standard. Because those with comorbidity tend to have more difficulty functioning across the board, finding ways around barriers to treating *both conditions* can impact one's prognosis. For example, treating co-occurring PTSD along with a substance use disorder increases the likelihood that a person will remain stable in their recovery give years after treatment,[117] and successfully treating depression along with addiction reduces substance use, at least in the short term.[118] Medications can play an important role in this process. Below we review some of the most common mental health symptoms and diagnoses that could warrant treatment with medicine while a person is receiving treatment for addiction.

Depression

Clinical depression is a common but serious mood disorder that affects how a person feels, thinks, and manages daily activities and responsibilities, such as eating, paying attention, or working. Those who have a diagnosable depressive syndrome experience some of the following signs and symptoms most of the day, or nearly every day, for a period of two weeks or longer:

- Feeling sad, nervous, or "empty"
- Loss of pleasure or interest in things that used to bring joy (e.g., hobbies or other activities)
- Feeling irritable, frustrated, or restless

- Feeling guilty, worthless, or hopeless
- Decreased energy, fatigue, or feeling "slowed down"
- Having trouble concentrating, remembering, or making decisions
- Difficulty falling or staying asleep, or oversleeping
- Changes in appetite and/or weight
- Thoughts of death or suicide, or suicide attempts
- Aches or pains, headaches, or digestive problems without a clear physical cause and that don't respond well to treatment(s)

Some people experience only a few symptoms while others suffer from many. Antidepressant medications can improve the way that the brain uses certain chemicals to control one's mood or stress response. Finding the right medication that improves one's symptoms with manageable side effects can involve some trial and error with more than one medicine. It also takes some patience to determine whether a medicine is working, since antidepressants can take four to eight weeks to take effect, and while symptoms such as insomnia can be the first to improve, the sadness can take longer to lift.

According to meta-analyses, among those who have both depression and a substance use disorder, antidepressant medication can be successful in alleviating depressive symptoms and in some cases can help reduce alcohol or drug use. The minimum length of time that medication treatment is necessary to produce these changes is six weeks.[119] The most commonly prescribed antidepressants are a class of medicines known as selective serotonin reuptake inhibitors (SSRIs), which stop or delay the body from reabsorbing a naturally produced brain chemical, serotonin. This leaves more serotonin available for the body to use. Raising the amount of serotonin the brain and body has available can help improve mood, appetite, digestion, sleep, and many other body functions that are affected by depression. SSRIs including sertraline (sold under the brand name Zoloft) and fluoxetine (sold under the brand name Prozac) are recommended as the first-choice treatment for individuals with depression and substance use disorders because they have fewer side effects than older types of antidepressants, and the risks associated with the use of alcohol or other drugs when a person is taking them are relatively low compared to other medications.

Even though older antidepressant medications known as tricyclic antidepressants can have more side effects, they can be very helpful for some people whose depression does not improve in response to the use of SSRIs. In fact, of all the alternatives to SSRIs that have been studied in clinical trials for those with depression and substance use disorders, tricyclic antidepressants including imipramine and nortriptyline have accumulated the most evidence of effectiveness. The primary problem that has limited the use of these types of medicines is that many people don't tolerate their side effects very well and discontinue treatment prematurely. Apart from the tricyclic antidepressants, bupropion, venlafaxine, and mirtazapine are alternative medicines that have been studied and have evidence supporting their use.[119]

Combining antidepressants with psychotherapy can lead to greater and more sustained improvements in depression and substance use than what can be achieved with either treatment on its own. This has been shown consistently in studies of SSRIs in combination with cognitive behavioral therapy (CBT) for individuals with alcohol use disorders and depression, where neither CBT nor antidepressant medication alone were as effective as their combination in reducing depression and alcohol use.[120,121]

Anxiety

Though anxiety, like depression, is among the most common psychological struggles reported by people with substance use disorders, one of the challenges in determining the best course of treatment is that it can be hard to know whether the symptoms were caused by the effects of alcohol or drug use. Anxiety, like depression, can be caused by the effects on the brain of intoxication or withdrawal from alcohol or drugs. If this is the case, then discontinuing one's use of alcohol or drugs might reverse the symptoms. However, some people—whether because they were vulnerable to anxiety in the first place, or the anxiety was already there before they started drinking or using drugs—experience persistent and disabling anxiety that overlaps with addiction. Since psychological symptoms can lead some people to use substances to self-medicate, experiencing severe anxiety in combination with a substance use disorder can fuel the cycle of psychological discomfort and addictive behavior. There are several diagnosable psychiatric conditions involving anxiety, including PTSD, social anxiety disorder, panic disorder, and generalized anxiety disorder. The anxiety disorder that co-occurs most frequently with substance use disorders is generalized anxiety disorder (GAD), which is diagnosed when a person feels a persistent feeling of anxiety or dread that interferes with how they live their daily life. Those with GAD feel extremely worried or nervous about various important areas of life, such as health, money, or family problems, even when there is little or no reason for concern about them. Symptoms of GAD include:

- Worrying excessively about everyday things
- Difficulty controlling the worry, despite recognizing that the worry is excessive
- Feeling restless and having a hard time relaxing
- Difficulty concentrating
- Irritability, or feeling "on edge"
- Feeling easily startled
- Insomnia
- Often tired or becoming tired easily
- Having headaches, muscle aches, stomach aches, or unexplained pains
- Difficulty swallowing

- Frequently sweating, feeling lightheaded, or out of breath
- Trembling or twitching

Among those with GAD and substance use disorders, buspirone, an anti-anxiety medication, has been studied in several randomized clinical trials with positive results indicating improvements in anxiety and alcohol consumption.[122] Benzodiazepines (such as Xanax, Ativan, or Valium) are also effective in treating GAD, but because they have addictive potential and act on some of the same brain chemicals as alcohol, their use in the treatment of individuals with addictions is controversial. Unlike benzodiazepines, which can be taken "as needed" to manage acute symptoms of anxiety, buspirone must be taken daily.

Social anxiety disorder also overlaps frequently with substance use disorders, and studies show that individuals who experience this form of anxiety report self-medicating their symptoms with alcohol or drugs, especially as a go-to strategy to enable them to socialize.[123] SSRIs such as paroxetine (which is sold under the brand name Paxil) have been found to be effective for those with social anxiety and alcohol use disorders. The main disadvantage is sexual side effects from the medication, which led to high rates of premature treatment discontinuation.[124]

Post-traumatic stress disorder (PTSD) and/or a history of trauma can make people vulnerable to developing addictions, and the symptoms, if not addressed, can complicate addiction treatment, making it more challenging to successfully change one's use of alcohol or drugs. A few of the medications reviewed earlier in this chapter have been found to be helpful for individuals with overlapping alcohol use disorders and PTSD in reducing drinking, cravings, and PTSD symptoms, including topiramate, naltrexone, and disulfiram.[125,126]

Similar to the research on combination treatments to address depression among those with substance use disorders, the use of CBT together with medications has been found to improve both anxiety symptoms and substance relapse risk among those with anxiety and opioid, alcohol, and other substance use disorders.[127] In fact, there are several CBT-based therapies designed specifically to help people manage anxiety while in addiction recovery that have evidence of effectiveness, including:

- Seeking Safety, a treatment approach that is used to help those with PTSD and addiction learn "safe coping skills," focused on changing alcohol or drug use, letting go of unhealthy relationships, and gaining control over anxiety symptoms.[128]
- Concurrent Treatment of PTSD and Substance Use Disorders using Prolonged Exposure (COPE), a structured 12-session program that combines CBT for changing alcohol and/or drug use with evidence-based techniques (prolonged exposure) for addressing trauma. The prolonged exposure approach involves reviewing traumatic experiences in detail while practicing coping skills to reduce anxiety.[129]
- Mindfulness-based relapse prevention, a therapy approach that combines mindfulness meditation with CBT techniques for relapse prevention.[130,131]

Recently, CBT approaches to anxiety and substance use have been transported to digital formats to make them more accessible, and initial studies found evidence that delivering CBT through a computerized format, with some therapist direction, can be highly effective.[132]

Attention-deficit hyperactivity disorder (ADHD)

ADHD affects between 8% and 46% of people who seek treatment for a substance use disorder,[133,134] and involves three main symptoms: inattention (e.g., difficulty focusing and/or staying organized), hyperactivity (e.g., a need to move about constantly), and impulsive behavior (e.g., acting without thinking or having a hard time with self-control). ADHD can easily go unrecognized among those with substance use disorders if treatment providers don't ask relevant questions to evaluate for it. On the other hand, it can also be over-diagnosed when the symptoms are confused with intoxication and withdrawal symptoms from drugs and/or alcohol. Some of the key aspects to think about to gain an understanding of how substance use relates to the symptoms are: (1) when the symptoms started (ADHD starts by or before age 12), and (2) whether the symptoms started before the substance use disorder developed. An ADHD diagnosis can be made with greater confidence when the symptoms start in childhood or adolescence and were observed during periods when the person was not using any substances.

ADHD is typically treated using medication, although combining some behavioral and family psychotherapy techniques with medication can also be beneficial.[119] Medications that are most commonly prescribed fall into two categories: stimulant and non-stimulant. The use of stimulant medications has been somewhat controversial since they have the potential for misuse, and this raises concerns about dependency and worsening of addiction. Nevertheless, this has not been shown in clinical trials; when ADHD is treated using modest dosages of stimulant medications, some studies have shown that the treatment reduces substance use as well.[135,136] Stimulant medications include methylphenidate (sold under the brand name Ritalin), Concerta, and longer lasting, slow-release medications such as Vyvanse and Adderall XR. Research has shown that slow-release medications are less likely to be misused, making them a good option when there is a concern about misuse or diversion (e.g., for someone who is addicted to prescription stimulants and/or someone who has misused or diverted their medication in the past).[137] The first non-stimulant medication that was FDA approved for the treatment of adult ADHD is atomoxetine (sold under the brand name Strattera).

Though clinical trials have shown mixed results in the treatment of substance use disorder with overlapping ADHD, the first-choice treatment according to the existing evidence is stimulant medication, which has been shown to be relatively safe, with a low risk of misuse when closely monitored by the treatment provider.

Other mental health conditions

There are a few other mental health conditions that overlap with substance use disorders, though they are less common than mood and anxiety disorders and ADHD. These include psychosis (e.g., schizophrenia), and personality disorders, including borderline personality disorder and antisocial personality disorder. Psychosis can be caused or worsened by the use of certain types of drugs, such as stimulants and cannabis, and is treated using both (1) antipsychotic medications, and (2) psychotherapy or medications to address the substance use disorder. Borderline personality disorder is a pattern of unstable moods, behavior, and relationships. At the core, people with this mental illness have a very difficult time regulating their emotions. Effective psychotherapies for borderline personality disorder include CBT and dialectical behavior therapy (DBT), which uses mindfulness and acceptance along with other skills to help people control intense emotions, reduce self-destructive behaviors, and improve relationships. Medications can also be helpful to control some of the psychological symptoms of borderline personality disorder.

13

WHY IS ADDICTION STIGMATIZED?

What is the impact of stigma on individuals with addiction?

If we are to help bring people with addictions "out of the shadows," we need to begin by understanding what makes it so hard to face the world openly with this problem. Unlike other chronic diseases such as diabetes, cardiovascular illness, and even depression, which is more widely accepted by society today as a medical illness, the stigma and shame surrounding addiction is palpable. This is largely because many people continue to feel skeptical about the idea that addiction is a disease. People with addictions can engage in behaviors that are potentially harmful to others, socially unacceptable, and disruptive. As a person with addiction progressively loses control over their use of alcohol or drugs, they may lie about the extent of their substance involvement. They may steal or engage in other illegal and seemingly desperate behaviors to procure drugs and avoid the discomfort of withdrawal. They may become aggressive verbally or even physically, especially when they are intoxicated or experiencing withdrawal symptoms. Addiction experts readily recognize these behaviors as a reflection of the illness taking hold of a person's life. But this is a distinctive feature of addiction; other chronic illnesses, with the exceptions of certain forms of serious mental illness, dementia, or traumatic brain injury, do not alter a person's personality and behavior in these socially unacceptable ways. Anyone who has had experience with someone close to them struggling with an addiction has likely experienced a range of emotions toward that person, from compassion to worry to frustration, anger, and disappointment. It is hard to separate the person from the addictive behaviors they exhibit—in other words, when a loved one is caught lying to conceal their addictive behaviors, it is easy to view the person as a liar. It is harder to view the person as unwell because chronic substance use has altered their brain chemistry in damaging ways. For those who are close to someone with addiction, it can be difficult to separate one's feelings about a person from their feelings about the person's addiction.

One of the core drivers of stigma surrounding addiction is the lack of awareness and acceptance of addiction as a chronic illness. We have known for decades in the addiction science community that, like other chronic illnesses:

1. *some people are especially vulnerable* to brain changes from substance use that can lead them to lose control over their alcohol or drug use and develop a substance use disorder; and
2. *chronic alcohol or drug use leads to brain pathology* that affects one's ability to control their impulses, exercise good judgment, and make healthy decisions.

Despite extensive scientific literature demonstrating similarities between addiction and other chronic diseases, this knowledge has not yet translated into a major shift in stigmatizing attitudes and behaviors toward people with addictions. To bring many with this illness out of isolation, it is crucial that we move away from the unfounded idea that "all you need is willpower to recover from addiction." It is because of widely held views such as these that people who desperately need help to overcome this illness are often treated very poorly and dismissively, even by healthcare professionals. Sometimes they are turned away from receiving medical care, with complications of substance use considered to be "self-inflicted" and therefore lower in priority than the healthcare needs of someone whose illness is thought to be beyond their control. Following experiences of being rejected by healthcare providers, who refuse to treat them to begin with or discharge them from their clinical practice when addictive behaviors become apparent, it is not uncommon for people with addictions to come away feeling ashamed, hopeless, and avoidant of future interactions with the healthcare system. This can lead to what is known as *internalized stigma*, which is when a person with a stigmatized condition "internalizes" the negative beliefs and feelings others have expressed about their illness. A person with internalized stigma may come to believe that they don't deserve treatment, or even that they don't deserve a good life because they "screwed up their own life and future by choosing to drink and use drugs." These beliefs may have started or been fueled by the reactions of other people to their addictive behaviors, ranging from their own family members or friends to healthcare professionals.

Worrying about being labeled as an "addict" or "alcoholic" has other negative impacts. For one, people may be hesitant to seek help because of the stigma attached to the treatments themselves, or even the ways that they may be judged by others after they enter recovery. For example, even though lifesaving medical treatments are available for opioid addiction, when interviewed, many people describe a profound shame attached to taking these medicines.[1] One person we spoke to as part of a research study described hiding his medicine in his backpack by concealing it in multiple bags with tape around them, tucked into a small compartment. He expressed feeling very nervous about his peers in recovery judging him for taking medicine as part of his treatment for opioid addiction. Another individual said that her friends and family viewed the medication that was prescribed to help her stop injecting opioids as "pharmaceutical heroin." A third person who enrolled in a research-based treatment program to receive a combination of medication for his opioid addiction and psychotherapy dropped out after a week, when his significant other expressed her disapproval, insisting that the medication was just "substituting one drug for another."

Apart from the negative judgments and opinions that are frequently linked with medications for opioid use, people with alcohol use disorders often struggle with their fears about how others will perceive them if they become non-drinkers. They worry that other people will notice they are not drinking when they're out at social functions and will draw the conclusion that they must be an "alcoholic." Recent studies have confirmed these perceptions, showing that abstaining from alcohol can lead to negative social consequences and can even be viewed as "deviant" or unusual behavior, especially in situations where most people are drinking.[2] In the same way that people who are taking medications for their opioid addiction may feel the need to justify those choices to people who are judgmental about them, individuals who refrain from drinking alcohol in social situations often feel compelled to "legitimize" abstinence, providing reasons that others will accept as "valid," such as religious or health-related restrictions.[3] Some cope with the stigma attached to being a nondrinker by hiding the fact that they aren't drinking, for example by ordering "mocktails." Still others avoid or withdraw from situations where there will be social pressure to drink, which can make addiction recovery a lonely or isolating experience. For this, among other reasons, having a strong social support system is an important part of the recovery process, and studies have shown that people with support have increased chances of long-term success.[4]

Part 4

ADDICTION AND RECOVERY LONG TERM

THE PROGNOSIS CAN BE GREAT

14

WHAT IS LIFE LIKE BEYOND ADDICTION?

We can talk ourselves into death or we can talk ourselves into the best life we've ever lived.

—Anthony Hopkins, 45 years sober

Is addiction for life?

In my practice, one of the most frequently asked questions from those who are new to treatment, and even from those not so new but struggling to make behavioral changes stick, is whether addiction is going to be a lifelong battle. Families of those who struggle with addiction have similar thoughts and worries. Will they always be waiting for the next "crisis"? Will they be able to take what their loved one says at face value and trust them ever again, or are those relationships forever changed? Does anyone truly "recover fully" from addiction? Addiction is frightening and frustrating, and for many people, both those directly and indirectly affected, the impacts of the illness can be traumatic and devastating. When we experience something traumatic, the fear of it happening over and over can be consuming. The core struggle then becomes the feeling of being trapped. *Will I ever be free from this?*

The answer is not so simple, but as Anthony Hopkins conveyed so succinctly and eloquently, those with addiction *can* and *do* get to the other side of the illness, and live rewarding and fulfilling lives with meaning and purpose. In this chapter, we will review some recent scientific learnings about the likelihood of recovery, examine some real-world examples of individuals and families who have recovered, and consider answers to common questions about how to envision the future while coming to terms with addiction as a chronic illness.

Do people recover?

If there's one takeaway from this book that is important, it's the fact that scientific evidence suggests that *most people with addiction recover*. With the widespread media coverage of overdose deaths in recent years, many people come away believing that addiction is either a condition from which people rarely get better, or even worse that it is a death sentence. Despite the unprecedented rise in drug-related deaths over the past several years, several recent studies have shed light on the prevalence of recovery and remission from substance use disorders, and the findings paint an uplifting picture. The first, a national study led by Dr. John Kelly of Harvard Medical School, sought to understand (1) what proportion of the American population has resolved, or achieved remission from a substance use disorder, and (2) the various pathways that led them to recover (e.g., formal treatment versus self-help or other avenues that led them to get better). This groundbreaking study revealed that 22.3 million Americans, which constitutes over 9% of the population, report living in recovery or having a resolved a significant problem with alcohol or drug use.[1] A second large study led by the CDC and the National Institute on Drug Abuse found that out of the 27.5 million individuals who have experienced a substance use disorder in their lifetimes, nearly 75%, or 20.5 million reported that they were currently in recovery or had recovered from their substance use problem.[2]

That means that three out of every four people who have had a substance use disorder recover eventually. Collectively, these studies, conducted by leading scientific experts in addiction treatment and recovery, affirm that people who suffer from this illness *do recover*. In the reflective words of Stephen D'Antonio, whose stories of "lessons learned from the perspective of a dad dealing with his son's addiction" have helped many parents and families, there are things he wished he had known prior to embarking on the long, difficult, and often seemingly endless journey to his son's eventual recovery. With this knowledge, you, as someone who may be struggling with an addiction or who cares about someone who is going through the ups and downs of an addiction, can hold awareness of the reasons to find and hold on to hope for the future.

> "I wish I knew that there was hope, a lot of hope, and that recovery was likely to happen for my son. I wish I knew that my son could live an amazing life, drug and alcohol free." —Stephen D'Antonio, 2022

Stephen's son Stevie suffered from a severe addiction to alcohol beginning in his teenage years. He also had clinical depression and came close to taking his own life. The stress, unpredictability, and constant worry about Stevie became a dominant and overwhelming source of conflict and tension, affecting Stephen's marriage and their entire family for years. Despite the profoundly low lows that Stevie and his family experienced throughout that time, Stevie pulled through and is living a fulfilling life in recovery.

> "We almost lost Stevie four times by the time he was seventeen. I felt defeated as a father. I had zero hope for my son.
> I was wrong.

Today, Stevie is twenty-five years old, and he is six years in recovery. He spent nearly four of those years living on a college campus and graduated on time with a degree in Psychology. He currently works in the addiction treatment industry, giving back, and sharing his story to help adolescents and young adults find their way to beautiful new lives. He is happy, he is healthy, he is hilarious, he has a ton of friends and he is a loving brother, son and uncle. He has a beautiful soul. I could not be more-proud!"

Stephen D'Antonio, 2022
https://addictionlessons.com

How do people recover?

Recovery success can be achieved through different methods. Treatment is an important pathway to success, with those who report having received formal treatment nearly twice as likely to be in recovery.[2] That being said, between 46% and 60% of individuals who report resolution of their substance use problem used methods other than professionally led treatment to support their recovery. Different pathways to success include professionally led services such as inpatient or outpatient treatment, medications to control cravings and prevent relapse to alcohol and/or opioid use, the use of self-help groups (such as AA or NA), and recovery support services such as sober living environments and recovery community centers. It is important to keep in mind that there are many ways to recover, and some people succeed by combining approaches such as therapy, medication, and self-help group support, while others rely solely on one form of support which may or may not involve professional help.

Historically, one of the barriers to individuals receiving formal treatment has been limited access to evidence-based care. Now, the rapid expansion of telemedicine approaches to addiction treatment, which was accelerated by both policy changes and increased consumer acceptance and utilization of remote healthcare services during the COVID-19 pandemic, has been and will continue to be a game changer. As just one example, a large study comparing those who received treatment for opioid use disorders before versus during the COVID-19 pandemic found that those in the pandemic group were not only far more likely to receive telehealth services to treat their addiction, but receiving these services reduced the risk of drug overdose.[3] Still, there are some ethnic minority groups who are less likely to receive telehealth services for addiction, highlighting the need for continued efforts to reduce inequities in care access and eliminate the digital divide.

Treated versus Untreated Individuals: Do They Recover Differently?

Research suggests that many people recover from substance use disorders naturally, or on their own, without professional help. That raises a few questions: first, who is most likely to seek or require treatment in order to recover? Second, does treatment make a difference? Here's what we know:

First, those who recover by entering treatment are different from those whose alcohol or drug-related problems resolve without treatment in the following ways:

- They tend to be more vulnerable to developing addiction (based on personal and environmental risk factors).
- Their substance-related problems are more severe and intense (e.g., involving multiple substances and heavier, riskier substance involvement).
- They experience more psychiatric and medical overlapping conditions.
- They face greater obstacles to recovery (personally, environmentally, and psychologically).

Second, as far as what treatment does, studies that followed individuals with substance use disorders over 16 or more years have shown that those who recover *after having received help*, either via professionally led treatment or self-help groups such as 12-step programs, are at lower risk of short-term (3 years later) and long-term relapses (16 years later) than individuals who remitted without any help, and the difference in relapse rates is substantial. Whereas nearly 60% of those who were in remission from their addiction three years after receiving help remained in stable remission 16 years after treatment, less than 40% of those who remitted without any remained in stable remission 16 years afterward.[a]. This highlights the potentially impactful role that treatment can play in one's ability to achieve stable, long-term recovery.

[a] Moos, R. H., & Moos, B. S. (2006). Participation in treatment and Alcoholics Anonymous: A 16-year follow-up of initially untreated individuals. *Journal of Clinical Psychology*, 62(6), 735–750. https://doi.org/10.1002/jclp.20259

Is there freedom from addiction?

More than two decades ago, leading experts in addiction science began to spread the knowledge that addiction is a chronic illness that shares many commonalities with other chronic diseases, such as heart disease and diabetes.[4] This realization—which scientific and clinical thought leaders in addiction continue to communicate to healthcare professionals, lay people, and policymakers—has provided a framework for understanding the illness, yet at the same time has raised many questions. If I'm someone with addiction and I'm told that I have a chronic illness that is like diabetes, except that it affects my brain and behavior, then what does that mean about how I should go about treatment and how long I'm going to need it? Does it mean that I will never be free from it, just as a person with diabetes will always require insulin to survive? The question of whether there is such a thing as *freedom from addiction*, once a person has it, really comes down to how freedom is defined. Here are a few common questions and answers that can help shape some scientifically informed ways to think about it:

Q: Can one become free from symptoms of a severe substance use disorder?

A: Yes. According to our diagnostic system for substance use disorders, it is possible to achieve remission, and many people do. When we talk about someone in remission it means that they once met the criteria for a diagnosis of substance use disorder, but they no longer meet the criteria; once it has been at least three months since they last had a diagnosable substance use disorder, the individual is in "early remission." After a year or longer, this is reclassified as "sustained remission." However, it's important to know that remission doesn't mean the same thing for everyone—some people become completely abstinent while others will reduce their use of alcohol or drugs to the point where it no longer causes the problems that it used to. Studies show that reducing alcohol or other substance use can lead to meaningful changes in a person's physical and mental health, quality of life, and ability to function, highlighting that remission not only means different things for different people, but there are health benefits to both reducing and abstaining completely from substance use.[5]

Q: Is controlled drinking or drug use achievable?

A: Controlled drinking is one possible pathway to remission from an alcohol use disorder, so for some individuals it is indeed achievable. In general, the prognosis for achieving remission by reducing or controlling one's alcohol use is best for people who (1) are younger; (2) have a drinking problem that is relatively mild or, at most, moderate in severity; and (3) have fewer overall problems related to their alcohol or drug use. For example in one study, nearly 60% of those who had three symptoms of an alcohol use disorder were able to reduce their drinking and sustain the reduction for a year; on the other hand, none of the participants with six or more symptoms of an alcohol use disorder had been able to sustain a healthy reduced drinking pattern over that same timeframe.[6] In other words, the more severe the problem, the more challenging it may be to control one's substance use and maintain control over time.

Studies of long-term substance use behavior patterns suggest that starting the journey to recovery by becoming abstinent is a worthwhile strategy to promote future success. For example, research shows that when people with an alcohol use disorder can control their drinking over a period of a couple of months, it *doesn't necessarily predict stability of controlled drinking* over a longer period of time (i.e., 1 year or longer). However, when they can abstain from drinking for two or three months, this *early success with abstinence does predict better long-term outcomes* (whether those outcomes are continued abstinence or successfully controlling one's drinking over a one-year timeframe).[7] Similarly, when adults with alcohol use disorders were followed over three years, drinking in moderation one year after treatment did not increase the likelihood of continued success drinking moderately by year three.[8] A seminal study in the field of alcoholism, in which men with alcohol use disorders were followed over a period of 60 years, found that the most common pattern over many years was cycling between controlled drinking and problematic drinking. In fact, only 20% of the men drinking in a controlled manner at age 50 were able to sustain controlled drinking at follow-up, two decades later.[9] Evidence from this and other studies indicate that abstinence is more stable over time than controlled drinking. Abstinence is a safe strategy. But not all people in recovery choose that pathway, and for a subset of individuals, controlled drinking is achievable.

Q: Is there a particular point in one's recovery when long-term remission from addiction is more certain or more likely?

A: We know from decades of research that the longer a person is in recovery, the more stable their remission becomes and the lower the likelihood of relapse.[10] This is true whether the person achieved recovery with or without formal treatment. Studies have followed those with alcohol and drug use disorders for up to 60 years to try and find out when a person reaches true stability (i.e., at what point does the likelihood of relapse drop low enough to where one can be confident that recovery will be sustained in the long term?), and found that this comes about four to five years into continuous recovery (i.e., uninterrupted by one or more slips or relapses). In fact, in a long-term study in which Harvard undergraduates and inner-city adolescents were followed over several decades, only 9% of those who achieved five years of abstinence from alcohol returned to drinking, and none did after six years of abstinence.[11] This has led to the recommendation that, like remission from cancer, remission from addiction should be monitored for the first 5 years following the start of one's recovery.[12] The length of time a person spends in treatment is closely tied to their recovery prognosis as well; those who are in remission spend longer in treatment than those who continue to be addicted.[13]

Q: Do you have to attempt recovery repeatedly throughout your life to be successful?

A: Despite the widely held belief that most people who try to beat their addiction face an endless battle,[1] recent studies have found that many people achieve stable, lasting recovery after a relatively low number of dedicated attempts. In fact, one study of nearly 900 people in recovery found that after their first serious attempt to recover from addiction, two-thirds of the participants successfully changed their alcohol or drug use and were able to maintain these changes with either minimal or no setbacks.[14] Along similar lines, results of a large national study of Americans who resolved their alcohol or drug addiction found that for most people, two recovery attempts were made before they found success.[15] Though estimates may vary between studies depending on the population and the methods used to measure "stable recovery," the studies described here represent the few that have evaluated how many times recovery was attempted before changes in substance use were sustained over time.

You might wonder how you would know whether you or someone you care about is likely to fall into the group that recovers after their first or second attempt, versus the third of individuals who struggle more to change their alcohol or drug use and make it stick. Studies have shown that there are indeed some people who need to try five or more times before they can overcome an alcohol or drug use disorder. Those who experience more setbacks in the process tend to have more complicated and severe symptoms and fewer buffers to protect them psychologically from stress.[16] Some of the characteristics that might signal the possibility that recovery could be more challenging for someone include:

- Being addicted to more than one substance
- Having used one or more substances in unhealthy ways for many years
- Having experienced many negative consequences, including high levels of psychological distress, legal difficulties, and/or problems functioning in daily life in relation to alcohol or drug use
- Having one or more psychiatric conditions in addition to a substance use disorder

Although those who experience this higher level of addiction severity and complexity may need treatment services of greater intensity over longer periods of time to achieve sustained recovery, it is important to keep in mind that not all people with addiction experience it in the same way. The stereotyped notion of addiction as an illness for which successful outcomes are rare and require repeated episodes in "rehab" is not, in fact, the story that the majority of those in recovery would tell. Some people certainly benefit from the most intensive forms of professionally led treatment (such as inpatient care), but these severe cases are not the norm. Because the way people experience and recover from addiction varies so widely, there isn't a one-size-fits-all approach to overcoming a problem with alcohol or drug use.

Q: Can you ever stop worrying about slipping or relapsing once you've struggled with an addiction?

A: First, let's make an important distinction: *worrying* is one thing, and *remaining mindful and vigilant* to preserve one's recovery is another. As far as the worrying goes, it may be helpful to keep in mind that worry is a form of anxiety, and not all anxiety is bad. Anxiety is what keeps us aware of potential dangers so that we can mobilize and protect ourselves when we need to. For someone with an addiction, the potential to relapse is a form of danger (i.e., a threat to their safety and well-being), so feeling worried about that can lead one to take actions that help guard against it.

Over time, as a person gets further into their recovery and feels more stable in their remission from a substance use disorder, the worry should naturally diminish. What's important is that this doesn't lead to self-neglect. After successfully changing their substance use for a while, some people will stop doing many of the things that preserve their well-being in recovery (e.g., attending therapy or self-help groups, maintaining ties with people who supported their recovery, exercising, practicing healthy coping skills, avoiding triggers for substance use, etc.). Doing very little of the healthy behaviors that formed the pillars of one's recovery may become an unintentional "setup" for a slip or relapse. It is not necessary to worry endlessly about returning to alcohol or drug use, but it is

322 ADDICTION AND RECOVERY LONG TERM

prudent to (1) identify and continue the self-care practices that preserve one's recovery, and (2) create a "relapse prevention plan," a common practice in cognitive behavioral therapy that outlines specific actions a person can take to help them stay on track with their recovery when they're especially vulnerable to relapse. This plan is designed so that it can be easily enacted when, inevitably, a person reaches a tough or challenging moment or phase of life during which it is hard to resist drinking or using drugs. A therapist, counselor, or other healthcare professional with specialty training in addiction care can help with both (1) and (2).

What does a relapse prevention plan look like?

Jesse, a 36-year-old man working as a financial analyst, was in recovery from opioid addiction. His opioid use began when he was in his twenties and injured his back while playing college football. After several back surgeries, he became increasingly dependent on opioid pain killers, with his use escalating progressively until he was trapped in a cycle of using high doses of prescription opioids, withdrawing from them, and seeking more. Overcome by his addiction, he sought out many ways to maintain his supply, ensuring that he wouldn't get very far into the dreaded state of opioid withdrawal—to this end, he had found multiple doctors to issue him prescriptions, and he was buying pills from dealers. His relationship with his girlfriend started to suffer, and he was painfully aware of how little control he had over his opioid use. When he was in his late twenties, he checked himself into an inpatient program to undergo medically supervised withdrawal or "detox." This failed the first time, as he relapsed very soon after he discharged from care. Months later, he tried for a second time, but this time he started on opioid replacement therapy before he left the inpatient detoxification program, and he transitioned to outpatient treatment for four months. After that, he remained stable on his medication (suboxone) and opioid-free for seven years, got married to the woman who was with him through all the ups and downs, and had two children.

By the time he reached seven years opioid-free, apart from his quarterly visits with his addiction medicine physician, Jesse had been in therapy for three years. He found therapy tremendously helpful for relapse prevention, as well as addressing his anxiety and ADHD. When Jesse was given added responsibilities at work, he started canceling his weekly therapy sessions to give him extra time to get caught up. Feeling constantly overscheduled, he stopped exercising, which previously was a therapeutic outlet for his anxiety. He had never been much of a drinker, but he found himself drinking wine in increasing amounts during the evenings to relax and take the edge off. His wife Sherry became upset about his drinking, and they began to argue more frequently. The heavy drinking led him to put on weight, and between the weight gain and being out of shape, he ended up slipping a disc in his lower back. Feeling upset with himself, suffering in pain, and overwhelmed by the stressors in his life, Jesse decided to request a prescription for Vicodin (an opioid painkiller) from his new primary care doctor, who was not aware of his addiction history. A few weeks later his wife called his therapist, noting that she was seeing some familiar and concerning patterns of addictive behavior. Though it took some time, Jesse eventually agreed he needed help and called his therapist; she started meeting with him weekly, reconnected him with his psychiatrist, and helped him to restart his opioid replacement therapy (suboxone) and get his drinking under control.

A relapse episode can impact a person's life profoundly. For Jesse, his work productivity, physical health, and marital relationship suffered. If an episode of recurring substance use can be contained at the early stages when a person first "slips," this can prevent a whole host of negative effects that follow that first setback. The longer a person who has recently relapsed is "in it" (i.e., stuck in relapse mode both mentally and in the way they are acting), the harder it can become to return to a recovery mindset. The difference between catching and responding to a slip early and letting it go on can make months, years, and even a life-or-death outcome of a difference. To make life in recovery as stable as it can be, it is important to know that temptations are going to present themselves repeatedly and to anticipate that they may lead to temporary setbacks or recurrences of substance use. That being said, *with a solid relapse prevention plan in place, people with addictions can reduce their risk of returning to alcohol or drug use.* And even in the event of a setback, they can learn to recognize when they are beginning to enter a danger zone and put plans into motion to prevent things from worsening. In Jesse's case there were several early warning signs, and more could have been done at those stages to prevent the relapse to opioid use that he experienced. You'll learn more about how Jesse and his wife learned to anticipate and act on signs of a relapse before it's too late.

It is best to make relapse prevention plans when a person is doing well, because it's difficult to think rationally once a person's mindset starts shifting and bringing them closer to drinking or using drugs. The three key elements of developing a relapse prevention plan are as follows:[17]

- Identifying personal relapse triggers
- Generating a list of preventive behaviors
- Creating a written plan to guide how to respond to warning signs or triggers

The first component of the plan, *identifying personal relapse triggers*, involves making alist of early relapse warning signs, which is usually done with help from an addiction-specialized counselor or therapist. Family or loved ones can also be very helpful in generating the list. The second element, *generating a list of preventive behaviors*, involves thinking through various categories of behaviors that can help prevent a slip or relapse, including ways of thinking or actions that can be taken if a person feels tempted or triggered as well as lifestyle changes the individual has already made in their recovery that are important to remaining stable (e.g., avoiding places where they may be tempted, continuing wellness activities such as exercising, seeing their addiction medicine doctor regularly). The third phase, *creating a written plan to guide how to respond to warning signs,* is something that is often done in collaboration with family and members of the person's treatment team (e.g., a counselor and/or a doctor providing addiction care services).

Step 1: Identifying triggers and early warning signs

Research conducted by Alan Marlatt, a psychologist who pioneered the cognitive behavioral therapy approach to relapse prevention, found that the situations and circumstances that can trigger a relapse generally fall into two categories: *immediate* (or happening right before a person slips back into drinking or using drugs) or *covert* (or circumstances that play an important role but are less obviously linked to the relapse).[18] Examples of immediate triggers include:

- *High-risk situations,* or situations that make a person more vulnerable to relapse (e.g., being around other people they used to drink or use drugs with, being in situations where alcohol or other substances are available and/or are being offered to them, being exposed to people or situations that evoke difficult emotions).
- *Poor coping skills.* Those who do not cope well with being in high-risk situations may be more likely to "give in" when they are tempted. In addition, some people will turn to alcohol or other substances to cope with difficult things that are happening in their lives.
- *Abstinence violation effect.* A very common, but irrational mindset among people in recovery is that once they've slipped and experienced a return to drinking or using

drugs, they've "ruined everything." This black-or-white way of thinking can set a person up to continue a relapse episode over a longer period than they would have if they had adopted a different frame of mind about it. For example, a person who thinks, "Ok, well, I had one bad night; that doesn't erase all of the progress I've made over the past two months" will be more likely to talk with their counselor or another supportive person about the slip, put it into a healthy perspective, acknowledge it as an imperfection, and return to the continued pursuit of their recovery goals. On the other hand, someone who has fallen into the abstinence violation effect mindset would tell themselves a very different story, like, "I've messed it all up now, and I may never get it right; I might as well keep on drinking."

Covert relapse triggers can be happening over a longer period prior to the relapse, including:

- *Persistent urges or cravings.* These can be experienced as thoughts (e.g., "I need it"), physical sensations (e.g., heart racing, a pit in one's stomach), or emotions (e.g., excitement, anxiety).
- *Lifestyle imbalance*, which can take on many forms. For example, imbalance can mean having more sources of stress than pleasure, or excessive work, family, or other pressures without much time to practice self-care.

In Jesse's case, lifestyle imbalance was a covert trigger that was building up over time. He was so stressed with work and the emerging conflict in his marital relationship that he stopped doing some of the important self-care activities that were protecting him from a relapse, such as attending therapy and exercising. This imbalance also increased his risk of re-injuring his back, since he was out of shape and gained weight as he became more sedentary and developed heavy drinking habits.

Poor coping was one of the more immediate triggers, as Jesse turned to alcohol to cope with the stress he was experiencing on multiple fronts, and that pattern was part of what made him vulnerable to returning to opioid use.

Step 2: Generating a list of preventive behaviors

What should a person do when they are feeling triggered and either on the verge of slipping or starting to drink or use drugs again? First, it's important to note that it really helps people who are trying to recover from a substance use disorder when they have someone in their life who is supportive of their recovery and to whom they feel comfortable being accountable. Recovery is still possible even without that support structure, but it's harder. Whether a family member, a close friend, or a sponsor from a self-help program, having someone to check in with when things are going well, or when they're not going so well, can be a "protective factor" or a buffer, reducing the risk of falling into a relapse. Though sometimes the relapse triggers that a person encounters while they're reducing or eliminating substance use are unavoidable, here are some steps that can be taken when a person is confronted with temptations or other circumstances that make a return to substance use more likely:

First, immediate responses to feeling triggered or tempted to return to drinking or drug use can include:

- Meditating
- Distracting oneself
- Calling someone who is supportive of their recovery
- Leaving a risky situation
- Getting away from the risky environment (e.g., going out for a walk or other activity)
- Exercising
- Praying
- Attending a mutual self-help meeting

- Calling one's counselor or doctor to make an appointment (if they have one)
- Reflecting on successes in recovery up until this point
- Thinking about something or someone who is an inspiration for continued recovery

Second, broader lifestyle changes that can be made to help keep the individual on track include:

- Increasing time spent with people who are supportive of recovery
- Avoiding people who are stressful or difficult to be around (and especially those who trigger urges to drink or use drugs)
- Staying away from people with whom the individual used to drink or use drugs
- Making sure that drinking or drugs are not easily accessible (e.g., remove alcohol, drugs, and paraphernalia from the home, car, or other immediate environment; delete dealers' phone numbers from one's cell phone/block them as callers, etc.)
- Increasing activities that are incompatible with drinking or drug use (e.g., exercise)
- Making money less accessible, if having money is a trigger for buying drugs (e.g., have someone else hold on to credit cards, manage paychecks, etc.)

Though there are many more techniques and skills that can be helpful, identifying the most practical ways of protecting oneself from a relapse is an essential step when creating a relapse prevention plan.

Step 3: Creating a written relapse prevention plan

One way of thinking about the relapse prevention plan is to imagine you are creating a tailor-made handbook for keeping yourself healthy. For someone with addiction, this handbook emphasizes ways of steering clear of a relapse to alcohol or drug use. Ideally the relapse prevention plan will include typical triggers, thoughts, and behaviors that a person with a substance use disorder and their loved ones should be tuned into; the steps that the individual and those who are close to them can take to prevent a full-blown relapse; and the supportive people (including healthcare providers) who can be contacted if and when concerns arise. The person who is in recovery should ideally speak with each person who is part of the plan, discussing their role ahead of time *when things are going well*.

Sometimes, discussing this with family or other loved ones can bring up unpleasant memories of prior relapse and different opinions about what should have been done differently. This is completely expected. People who are close to someone with addiction go through a rollercoaster of emotions themselves, but ultimately if they are willing to be part of the solution, then it is worth weathering the discomfort of these conversations to develop a future strategy.

Adjusting the relapse prevention plan

Things got better for Jesse after he got back on his medication and started seeing his therapist again. He met with his psychiatrist several times over the first two months after his relapse to ensure that he reached a stable dose of his opioid replacement medication, and revisited and made some adjustments to his medication regimen for his anxiety and ADHD symptoms. Jesse and Sherry met together with his psychologist to go over his relapse prevention plan. They came up with a list of his typical pre-relapse thoughts and behaviors, which included de-prioritizing self-care, and distancing himself from those who offer their help and/or support (such as his treatment team and his wife). They identified the environmental conditions that served as the "setup" for his relapse: marital conflict, circumstances that impeded his work productivity (e.g., family dynamics when working from home), and inadequate support.

Jesse and Sherry discussed several relapse prevention steps. They came up with some ways she could help him to manage some of the stressors that were triggering for him (for example, they identified consistent, scheduled blocks of time when she could take the kids out of the house to enable Jesse to work uninterrupted). They agreed, as a couple, to make time to talk without any distractions each night after the kids went to sleep, to be sure that they were connecting and supporting one another. They also agreed to remove all the alcohol from their home to minimize temptations for Jesse to turn to drinking as a coping strategy for stress. Finally, Jesse agreed that if he was neglecting himself or skipping treatment visits, Sherry could call his therapist or psychiatrist and schedule a session for them to attend together, and he promised in advance that he would go.

A relapse prevention plan is an evolving guidebook to a person's health. Coming up with a plan collaboratively with a family member or other loved one is the first step, but the effectiveness of the plan needs to be tested out in "real life" before one can be confident that the right steps to prevent a relapse are in place. If a relapse still occurs after putting this together and following it, then it's time to go back and retrace the circumstance that led to it and fill in the gaps. It could be, for example, that medication adjustments for managing anxiety or other symptoms needed to have been made right away (i.e., without having to wait for an appointment). One potential improvement to the relapse prevention could be for Jesse to discuss a plan in advance with his psychiatrist, with instructions as to the types of medication adjustments he can try when his anxiety worsens in the face of stress. He could write the instructions into the plan, with the understanding that he will follow it when his early relapse warning signs emerge (e.g., "increase my gabapentin when I feel more anxious about work and I'm not able to control it on my own") and schedule an appointment as soon as possible in the interim. Other problems that could make the plan ineffective include some of the recommendations causing more conflict in the marital relationship—for example, if it was too stressful to keep the children out of the house for as many hours as Jesse needed to get his work done, that could cause even more tension between him and Sherry. If that were to happen, then they could do a little bit of brainstorming to renegotiate how to achieve the quiet time that Jesse needed for his work. In other words, troubleshooting the plan over time as a family, Jesse and Sherry can find alternatives to the parts that don't work and ultimately come up with an effective set of strategies to minimize the likelihood that a relapse will occur and/or progress into an extended episode of using alcohol or drugs.

Looking forward

Substance use disorders have a profound impact on the lives not only of those who suffer from the illness but also the people who love, befriend, work with, know, and count on them. It is sometimes hard for those without lived experience with a substance use disorder to understand what it really means to lose control over drinking or using drugs, some of the challenges that are posed by this illness, and what it takes to return to a normal life once that loss of control has set in. Now that you have reached the end of this book, you have a breadth of knowledge about how addiction develops, what that experience can be like for an individual and other people who are close to them, and what makes certain people more vulnerable to this illness.

You now know how to recognize the signs and symptoms of a substance use disorder, the ways that each of the most commonly used addictive substances affect the brain and behavior, the evidence-based psychotherapy and medication options that are effective in helping people overcome addictions to various types of substances, and the ways that family members and healthcare providers can support sustained recovery as part of a relapse prevention plan. You not only know that recovery from a substance use disorder is possible and experienced by millions of Americans, but you can also distinguish between very commonly believed myths and the true facts about substance use disorders and their treatment. Breaking through the myths and the stigma that is attached to them with knowledge of the truth is at the heart of resolving our global addiction problem. Having read this book, you are now part of the solution.

RESOURCES FOR PEOPLE WITH ADDICTION

* Finding Treatment for Substance Use Disorders
  - FindTreatment.gov [https://findtreatment.gov]
    • Substance Abuse and Mental Health Services Administration (SAMHSA)—Find a treatment facility
    • Information on what to expect (treatment options, understanding addiction, paying for treatment, understanding mental health)
  - SAMHSA's National Helpline: https://www.samhsa.gov/find-help/national-helpline
    • Treatment referral and information services in English and Spanish
    • Other suggested resources
  - Find a Physician: https://www.asam.org/publications-resources/patient-resources/fad
    • ASAM database for physician addiction specialists
  - National Institute on Alcohol Abuse and Alcoholism: Treatment Navigator: https://alcoholtreatment.niaaa.nih.gov
    • Find a treatment center for alcohol use disorder
    • Additional resources
* Finding medication treatment for substance use disorders
  - Buprenorphine Treatment Practitioner Locator | SAMHSA: https://www.samhsa.gov/medication-assisted-treatment/find-treatment/treatment-practitioner-locator

- Find practitioners authorized to treat opioid use disorder with buprenorphine by state
- Opioid Treatment Program Directory: https://dpt2.samhsa.gov/treatment/directory.aspx
  - Find opioid treatment programs by state
- VIVITROL.com | Find a Provider: https://www.vivitrol.com/alcohol-dependence/find-a-provider
  - Find providers by state or zip code who prescribe Vivitrol for alcohol use disorders
* Substance Use Disorder Educational Resources
  - Medications for Substance Use Disorders | SAMHSA: https://www.samhsa.gov/medications-substance-use-disorders
  - Take Action to Prevent Addiction | CDC: https://www.cdc.gov/drugoverdose/pdf/Prevent-Addiction-Fact-Sheet.pdf
  - Drugs, Brains, and Behavior: The Science of Addiction: Preface | NIDA: https://nida.nih.gov/research-topics/addiction-science/drugs-brain-behavior-science-of-addiction
  - Stop Overdose: https://www.cdc.gov/stopoverdose/index.html
  - Partnership to End Addiction: https://drugfree.org/recovery-resource-center
* Crisis, harm reduction, and other resources
  - 988 Suicide & Crisis Lifeline: https://988lifeline.org/
    - 24/7 free and confidential support
    - Additional resources
  - Crisis Text Line: https://www.crisistextline.org/
    - Text HOME to 741741 to connect with a crisis counselor
  - Veterans Crisis Line/Chat: https://www.veteranscrisisline.net/
    - Confidential crisis support for veterans via phone or text
    - It is not necessary to be enrolled in VA benefits or healthcare to use

➤ FindHelp: https://www.findhelp.org/
  - Find support for financial assistance, food pantries, medical care, and other free or reduced-cost help
➤ Staying connected is important: virtual recovery resources, SAMHSA: https://www.samhsa.gov/sites/default/files/virtual-recovery-resources.pdf
  - List of (virtual) social support options
➤ North American Syringe Exchange Network: https://nasen.org/
  - Find a local syringe exchange
➤ NAMI HelpLine | NAMI: National Alliance on Mental Illness: https://www.nami.org/help
  - Find mental health support/resources

NOTES

Chapter 1

1 Substance Abuse and Mental Health Services Administration. (2021). *Key substance use and mental health indicators in the United States: Results from the 2020 National Survey on Drug Use and Health* (HHS Publication No. PEP21-07-01-003, NSDUH Series H-56). Rockville, MD: Center for Behavioral Health Statistics and Quality, Substance Abuse and Mental Health Services Administration. Retrieved from: https://www.samhsa.gov/data/.

Chapter 2

1 Brewer, E. C. (1894). Brewer's dictionary of phrases and fables. https://doi.org/10.1093/acref/9780199990009.001.0001

2 Hasin, D. S., O'brien, C. P., Auriacombe, M., Borges, G., Bucholz, K., Budney, A., . . . & Grant, B. F. (2013). DSM-5 criteria for substance use disorders: recommendations and rationale. *American Journal of Psychiatry, 170*(8), 834–851.

3 Lin, L. A., Casteel, D., Shigekawa, E., Weyrich, M. S., Roby, D. H., & McMenamin, S. B. (2019). Telemedicine-delivered treatment interventions for substance use disorders: A systematic review. *Journal of Substance Abuse Treatment, 101*, 38–49. https://doi.org/10.1016/j.jsat.2019.03.007

4 Fiacco, L., Pearson, B. L., & Jordan, R. (2021). Telemedicine works for treating substance use disorder: The STAR clinic experience during COVID-19. *Journal of Substance Abuse Treatment, 125*, 108312. https://doi.org/10.1016/j.jsat.2021.108312

5   Substance Abuse and Mental Health Services Administration. (2022). *Key substance use and mental health indicators in the United States: Results from the 2021 National Survey on Drug Use and Health* (HHS Publication No. PEP22-07-01-005, NSDUH Series H-57). Center for Behavioral Health Statistics and Quality, Substance Abuse and Mental Health Services Administration. https://www.samhsa.gov/data/report/2021-nsduh-annual-national-report

6   Substance Abuse and Mental Health Services Administration. (2022). *Key substance use and mental health indicators in the United States: Results from the 2021 National Survey on Drug Use and Health* (HHS Publication No. PEP22-07-01-005, NSDUH Series H-57). Center for Behavioral Health Statistics and Quality, Substance Abuse and Mental Health Services Administration. Retrieved from: https://www.samhsa.gov/data/report/2021-nsduh-annual-national-report

7   Substance Abuse and Mental Health Services Administration. (2020). *Key substance use and mental health indicators in the United States: Results from the 2019 National Survey on Drug Use and Health* (HHS Publication No. PEP20-07-01-001, NSDUH Series H-55). Rockville, MD: Center for Behavioral Health Statistics and Quality, Substance Abuse and Mental Health Services Administration. Retrieved from https://www.samhsa.gov/data/

8   McLellan A. T. (2017). Substance misuse and substance use disorders: Why do they matter in healthcare? *Transactions of the American Clinical and Climatological Association, 128*, 112–130.

9   Warner, L. A., Kessler, R. C., Hughes, M., Anthony, J. C., & Nelson, C. B. (1995). Prevalence and correlates of drug use and dependence in the United States. Results from the National Comorbidity Survey. *Archives of General Psychiatry, 52*(3), 219–229. https://doi.org/10.1001/archpsyc.1995.03950150051010

10   Kessler, R. C., Berglund, P., Demler, O., Jin, R., Merikangas, K. R., & Walters, E. E. (2005). Lifetime prevalence and age-of-onset distributions of DSM-IV disorders in the National Comorbidity Survey Replication. *Archives of General Psychiatry, 62*(6), 593–602.

11   Hanson, K. L., Medina, K. L., Padula, C. B., Tapert, S. F., & Brown, S. A. (2011). Impact of adolescent alcohol and drug use on neuropsychological functioning in young adulthood: 10-year outcomes. *Journal of Child & Adolescent Substance Abuse, 20*(2), 135–154.

12   Magnan, S. (2017). Social determinants of health 101 for health
      care: Five plus five. *NAM Perspectives*. Discussion Paper, National
      Academy of Medicine, Washington, DC. https://doi.org/
      10.31478/201710c
13   Hood, C. M., Gennuso, K. P., Swain, G. R., & Catlin, B. B. (2016).
      County health rankings: Relationships between determinant
      factors and health outcomes. *American Journal of Preventive
      Medicine, 50*(2), 129–135.
14   Karriker-Jaffe, K. J. (2011). Areas of disadvantage: A systematic
      review of effects of area-level socioeconomic status on substance
      use outcomes. *Drug and Alcohol Review, 30*(1), 84–95. https://doi.
      org/10.1111/j.1465-3362.2010.00191.x
15   Weerakoon, S. M., Jetelina, K. K., Knell, G., & Messiah, S. E.
      (2021). COVID-19 related employment change is associated with
      increased alcohol consumption during the pandemic. *American
      Journal of Drug and Alcohol Abuse, 47*(6), 730–736. https://doi.org/
      10.1080/00952990.2021.1912063
16   Gratz, K. L., Scamaldo, K. M., Vidaña, A. G., Richmond, J. R., &
      Tull, M. T. (2021). Prospective interactive influence of financial
      strain and emotional nonacceptance on problematic alcohol use
      during the COVID-19 pandemic. *American Journal of Drug and
      Alcohol Abuse, 47*(1), 107–116. https://doi.org/10.1080/00952
      990.2020.1849248
17   Substance Abuse and Mental Health Services Administration.
      (2019). *Key substance use and mental health indicators in the United
      States: Results from the 2018 National Survey on Drug Use and
      Health* (HHS Publication No. PEP19-5068, NSDUH Series H-
      54). Rockville, MD: Center for Behavioral Health Statistics
      and Quality, Substance Abuse and Mental Health Services
      Administration. Retrieved from: https://www.samhsa.gov/
      data/.
18   Galea, S., Ahern, J., Tracy, M., Rudenstine, S., & Vlahov, D.
      (2007). Education inequality and use of cigarettes, alcohol, and
      marijuana. *Drug and Alcohol Dependence, 90*, S4–S15. https://doi.
      org/10.1016/j.drugalcdep.2006.11.008
19   Opara, I., Leonard, N. R., Thorpe, D., & Kershaw, T. (2021).
      Understanding neighborhoods' impact on youth substance use
      and mental health outcomes in Paterson, New Jersey: Protocol
      for a community-based participatory research study. *JMIR
      Research Protocols, 10*(5), e29427. https://doi.org/10.2196/29427

Chapter 3

1   National Institute on Alcohol Abuse and Alcoholism. (2023).
Understanding the dangers of alcohol overdose. Retrieved from:
https://www.niaaa.nih.gov/publications/brochures-and-fact-
sheets/understanding-dangers-of-alcohol-overdose.

2   Oscar-Berman, M., & Marinković, K. (2007). Alcohol: Effects on
neurobehavioral functions and the brain. *Neuropsychology Review,*
17(3), 239–257. https://doi.org/10.1007/s11065-007-9038-6

3   Grant, B. F., & Dawson, D. A. (1997). Age at onset of alcohol use
and its association with DSM-IV alcohol abuse and dependence:
Results from the national longitudinal alcohol epidemiologic
survey. *Journal of Substance Abuse, 9,* 103–110. https://doi.org/
10.1016/S0899-3289(97)90009-2

4   Sullivan, E. V., Zahr, N. M., Sassoon, S. A., Thompson, W.
K., Kwon, D., Pohl, K. M., & Pfefferbaum, A. (2018). The role
of aging, drug dependence, and hepatitis C comorbidity in
alcoholism cortical compromise. *JAMA Psychiatry, 75*(5), 474–483.
doi.org/10.1001/jamapsychiatry.2018.0021

5   National Institute on Alcohol Abuse and Alcoholism. (2023).
Women and alcohol. Retrieved from: https://www.niaaa.nih.gov/
publications/brochures-and-fact-sheets/women-and-alcohol.

6   Shield, K. D., Soerjomataram, I., & Rehm, J. (2016). Alcohol
use and breast cancer: A critical review. *Alcoholism: Clinical and*
Experimental Research, 40(6), 1166–1181. https://doi.org/10.1111/
acer.13071

7   Kendler, K. S., Edwards, A., Myers, J., Cho, S. B., Adkins, A., &
Dick, D. (2015). The predictive power of family history measures
of alcohol and drug problems and internalizing disorders in
a college population. *American Journal of Medical Genetics Part*
B: Neuropsychiatric Genetics, 168(5), 337–346. https://doi.org/
10.1002/ajmg.b.32320

8   Erol, A., & Karpyak, V. M. (2015). Sex and gender-related
differences in alcohol use and its consequences: Contemporary
knowledge and future research considerations. *Drug and Alcohol*
Dependence, 156, 1–13. https://doi.org/10.1016/j.drugalc
dep.2015.08.023

9   Annis, H. M., Sklar, S. M., & Moser, A. E. (1998). Gender in
relation to relapse crisis situations, coping, and outcome among
treated alcoholics. *Addictive Behaviors, 23*(1), 127–131. https://doi.
org/10.1016/s0306-4603(97)00024-5

10 Zywiak, W. H., Stout, R. L., Trefry, W. B., Glasser, I., Connors, G. J., Maisto, S. A., & Westerberg, V. S. (2006). Alcohol relapse repetition, gender, and predictive validity. *Journal of Substance Abuse Treatment, 30*(4), 349–353. https://doi.org/ 10.1016/ j.jsat.2006.03.004..

11 National Institutes of Health. (2020, July 16). Why alcohol-use research is more important than ever | NIH MedlinePlus Magazine. *NIH MedlinePlus*. Retrieved from: https://magazine. medlineplus.gov/article/why-alcohol-use-research-is-more-important-than-ever.

12 Acuff, S. F., Strickland, J. C., Tucker, J. A., & Murphy, J. G. (2022). Changes in alcohol use during COVID-19 and associations with contextual and individual difference variables: A systematic review and meta-analysis. *Psychology of Addictive Behaviors, 36*(1), 1. https://psycnet.apa.org/doi/10.1037/adb0000796

13 Rodriguez, L. M., Litt, D. M., & Stewart, S. H. (2020). Drinking to cope with the pandemic: The unique associations of COVID-19-related perceived threat and psychological distress to drinking behaviors in American men and women. *Addictive Behaviors, 110*, 106532. https://doi.org/10.1016/j.addbeh.2020.106532

14 Martinez, P., Karriker-Jaffe, K. J., Ye, Y., Patterson, D., Greenfield, T. K., Mulia, N., & Kerr, W. C. (2022). Mental health and drinking to cope in the early COVID period: Data from the 2019–2020 US National Alcohol Survey. *Addictive Behaviors, 128*, 107247. https://doi.org/10.1016/j.addbeh.2022.107247

15 Canadian Centre on Substance Use and Addiction. (2020). Mental health and substance use during COVID-19: Summary report. Retrieved from: https://mentalhealthcommission.ca/resource/ mental-health-and-substance-use-during-covid-19-summary-rep ort/.

16 National Institute on Alcohol Abuse and Alcoholism. (2022). Rethinking drinking. NIH Publication No. 21-AA-3770. Retrieved from: https://www.rethinkingdrinking.niaaa.nih.gov/How-much-is-too-much/What-counts-as-a-drink/Whats-A-Standard-Drink.aspx?.

17 US Department of Agriculture and US Department of Health and Human Services. (2010). *Dietary guidelines for Americans, 2010*, 7th ed. US Government Printing Office, Washington, DC.

18 GBD 2020 Alcohol Collaborators. (2022). Population-level risks of alcohol consumption by amount, geography, age, sex, and year:

A systematic analysis for the Global Burden of Disease Study 2020. *Lancet*, *400*(10347), 185–235. https://doi.org/10.1016/S0140-6736(22)00847-9

19 NIAAA (2023). Alcohol's effects on health: Binge drinking. Retrieved from: https://www.niaaa.nih.gov/alcohols-effects-health/alcohol-topics/health-topics-binge-drinking.

20 Esser, M. B., Hedden, S. L., Kanny, D., Brewer, R. D., Gfroerer, J. C., & Naimi, T. S. (2014). Peer reviewed: Prevalence of alcohol dependence among US adult drinkers, 2009–2011. *Preventing Chronic Disease*, *11*. https://doi.org/10.5888/pcd11.140329

21 National Highway Traffic Safety Administration (NHTSA). (2022). *Traffic Safety Facts 2020 Data: Alcohol-Impaired Driving* (Report No DOT HS 813 294). Washington, DC.

22 Centers for Disease Control and Prevention. (2015). Alcohol poisoning deaths. Centers for Disease Control and Prevention. Retrieved from: https://www.cdc.gov/vitalsigns/alcohol-poisoning-deaths/index.html.

23 Schulenberg, J. E., Patrick, M. E., Kloska, D. D., Maslowsky, J., Maggs, J. L., & O'Malley, P. M. (2016). Substance use disorder in early midlife: A national prospective study on health and well-being correlates and long-term predictors. *Substance Abuse*, *9*(Suppl 1), 41–57. https://doi.org/10.4137/SART.S31437

24 Graham, K., Bernards, S., Wilsnack, S. C., & Gmel, G. (2011). Alcohol may not cause partner violence but it seems to make it worse: A cross national comparison of the relationship between alcohol and severity of partner violence. *Journal of Interpersonal Violence*, *26*(8), 1503–1523. https://doi.org/10.1177/088626051037059

25 Naimi, T. S., Brewer, R. D., Mokdad, A., Denny, C., Serdula, M. K., & Marks, J. S. (2003). Binge drinking among US adults. *JAMA*, *289*(1), 70–75. https://doi.org/10.1001/jama.289.1.70

26 World Health Organization. (2018). *Global Status Report on Alcohol and Health—2018*. Geneva, Switzerland: World Health Organization.

Chapter 4

1 Substance Abuse and Mental Health Services Administration. (2022). Key substance use and mental health indicators in the United States: Results from the 2021 National Survey on Drug Use and Health (HHS Publication No. PEP22-07-01-005, NSDUH

Series H-57). Center for Behavioral Health Statistics and Quality, Substance Abuse and Mental Health Services Administration. https://www.samhsa.gov/data/report/2021-nsduh-annual-national-report

2 Schulenberg, J. E., Patrick, M. E., Johnston, L. D., O'Malley, P. M., Bachman, J. G., & Miech, R. A. (2021). Monitoring the Future National Survey Results on Drug Use, 1975-2020. Volume II, College Students & Adults Ages 19–60. Ann Arbor: Institute for Social Research, The University of Michigan. Available at: http://monitoringthefuture.org/pubs.html#monographs

3 Loflin, M., & Earleywine, M. (2014). A new method of cannabis ingestion: the dangers of dabs? *Addictive Behaviors*, 39(10), 1430–1433. https://doi.org/10.1016/j.addbeh.2014.05.013

4 Mehmedic, Z., Chandra, S., Slade, D., Denham, H., Foster, S., Patel, A. S., Ross, S. A., Khan, I.A., & ElSohly, M. A. (2010). Potency trends of Δ9-THC and other cannabinoids in confiscated cannabis preparations from 1993 to 2008. *Journal of Forensic Sciences*, 55(5), 1209–1217. https://doi.org/10.1111/j.1556-4029.2010.01441.x

5 Mackie, K. (2008). Cannabinoid receptors: Where they are and what they do. *Journal of Neuroendocrinology*, 20, 10–14. https://doi.org/10.1111/j.1365-2826.2008.01671.x

6 Volkow, N. D., Swanson, J. M., Evins, A. E., DeLisi, L. E., Meier, M. H., Gonzalez, R., Bloomfield, M. A., Curran, H. V., & Baler, R. (2016). Effects of cannabis use on human behavior, including cognition, motivation, and psychosis: A review. *JAMA Psychiatry*, 73(3), 292–297. https://doi.org/10.1001/jamapsychiatry.2015.3278

7 Meier, M. H., Caspi, A., Ambler, A., Harrington, H., Houts, R., Keefe, R. S., McDonald, K., Ward, A., Poulton, R., & Moffitt, T. E. (2012). Persistent cannabis users show neuropsychological decline from childhood to midlife. *Proceedings of the National Academy of Sciences of the United States of America*, 109(40), E2657–E2664. https://doi.org/10.1073/pnas.1206820109

8 Pope, H. G., Gruber, A. J., Hudson, J. I., Huestis, M. A., & Yurgelun-Todd, D. (2001). Neuropsychological performance in long-term cannabis users. *Archives of General Psychiatry*, 58(10), 909–915. https://doi.org/10.1001/archpsyc.58.10.909

9 Solowij, N., & Battisti, R. (2008). The chronic effects of cannabis on memory in humans: a review. *Current Drug Abuse Reviews*, 1(1), 81–98. https://doi.org/10.2174/1874473710801010081

10   National Academies of Science, Engineering, and Medicine. (2017). Health effects of marijuana and cannabis-derived products presented in new report. Retrieved from: https://www. nationalacademies.org/news/2017/01/health-effects-of-mariju ana-and-cannabis-derived-products-presented-in-new-report.

11   Volkow N. D. (2020). Collision of the COVID-19 and addiction epidemics. *Annals of Internal Medicine, 173*(1), 61–62. https://doi. org/10.7326/M20-1212

12   Guan, W. J., Liang, W. H., Zhao, Y., Liang, H. R., Chen, Z. S., Li, Y. M., Liu, X. Q., Chen, R. C., Tang, C. L., Wang, T., Ou, C. Q., Li, L., Chen, P. Y., Sang, L., Wang, W., Li, J. F., Li, C. C., Ou, L. M., Cheng, B., Xiong, S;China Medical Treatment Expert Group for COVID-19 (2020). Comorbidity and its impact on 1590 patients with COVID-19 in China: A nationwide analysis. *The European Respiratory Journal, 55*(5), 2000547. https://doi.org/10.1183/13993 003.00547-2020

13   Radhakrishnan, R., Wilkinson, S. T., & D'Souza, D. C. (2014). Gone to pot—a review of the association between cannabis and psychosis. *Frontiers in Psychiatry, 5*, 54. https://doi.org/10.3389/ fpsyt.2014.00054

14   Joseph, C., Ojo, O., Popoola, O., Azizi, H., Khan, T., Pramanik, O., et al. (2018). A case of brief psychosis upon cannabis withdrawal. *MOJ Addiction Medicine & Therapy, 5*(6), 258–260.

15   Di Forti, M., Quattrone, D., Freeman, T. P., Tripoli, G., Gayer-Anderson, C., Quigley, H., Rodriguez, V., Jongsma, H. E., Ferraro, L., La Cascia, C., La Barbera, D., Tarricone, I., Berardi, D., Szöke, A., Arango, C., Tortelli, A., Velthorst, E., Bernardo, M., Del-Ben, C. M., Menezes, P. R.;EU-GEI WP2 Group. (2019). The contribution of cannabis use to variation in the incidence of psychotic disorder across Europe (EU-GEI): A multicentre case-control study. *Lancet Psychiatry, 6*(5), 427–436. https://doi.org/ 10.1016/S2215-0366(19)30048-3

16   Hall, W. (1998). Cannabis use and psychosis. *Drug and Alcohol Review, 17*(4),433–444. https:// doi.org/10.1080/ 09595239800187271

17   Thomas, H. (1996). A community survey of adverse effects of cannabis use. *Drug and Alcohol Dependence, 42*(3), 201–207. https://doi.org/10.1016/s0376-8716(96)01277-x

18   Arseneault, L., Cannon, M., Witton, J., & Murray, R. M. (2004). Causal association between cannabis and psychosis: Examination

of the evidence. *British Journal of Psychiatry, 184,* 110–117. https://doi.org/10.1192/bjp.184.2.110

19 Weiss, S. R. B., Blanco, C., & Wargo, E. M. (2017). Clarifying the link between cannabis use and risk for psychosis. *Acta Psychiatrica Scandinavica, 136*(1), 3–4. https://doi.org/10.1111/acps.12764

20 Kraan, T., Velthorst, E., Koenders, L., Zwaart, K., Ising, H. K., van den Berg, D., de Haan, L., & van der Gaag, M. (2016). Cannabis use and transition to psychosis in individuals at ultra-high risk: Review and meta-analysis. *Psychological Medicine, 46*(4), 673–681. https://doi.org/10.1017/S0033291715002329

21 ElSohly, M. A., Mehmedic, Z., Foster, S., Gon, C., Chandra, S., & Church, J. C. (2016). Changes in cannabis potency over the last 2 decades (1995-2014): Analysis of current data in the United States. *Biological Psychiatry, 79*(7), 613–619. https://doi.org/10.1016/j.biopsych.2016.01.004

22 Budney, A. J., Sofis, M. J., & Borodovsky, J. T. (2019). An update on cannabis use disorder with comment on the impact of policy related to therapeutic and recreational cannabis use. *European archives of psychiatry and clinical neuroscience, 269*(1), 73–86. https://doi.org/10.1007/s00406-018-0976-1.

23 Englund, A., Freeman, T. P., Murray, R. M., & McGuire, P. (2017). Can we make cannabis safer? *Lancet Psychiatry, 4*(8), 643–648. https://doi.org/10.1016/S2215-0366(17)30075-5

24 Zhu, H., & Wu, L. T. (2016). Trends and correlates of cannabis-involved emergency department visits: 2004 to 2011. *Journal of Addiction Medicine, 10*(6), 429–436. https://doi.org/10.1097/ADM.0000000000000256

25 Park-Lee, E., Lipari, R. N., Hedden, S. L., Kroutil, L. A., & Porter, J. D. (2017). Receipt of services for substance use and mental health issues among adults: Results from the 2016 National Survey on Drug Use and Health. In *CBHSQ Data Review.* (pp. 1–35). Substance Abuse and Mental Health Services Administration (US).

26 Piomelli, D., Haney, M., Budney, A. J., & Piazza, P. V. (2016). Legal or illegal, cannabis is still addictive. *Cannabis and Cannabinoid Research, 1*(1), 47–53. https://doi.org/10.1089/can.2015.29004.rtd

27 Budney A. J. (2006). Are specific dependence criteria necessary for different substances: How can research on cannabis inform this issue? *Addiction, 101 Suppl 1,* 125–133. https://doi.org/10.1111/j.1360-0443.2006.01582.x

28 Anthony, J. C., Warner, L. A., & Kessler, R. C. (1994). Comparative epidemiology of dependence on tobacco, alcohol, controlled substances, and inhalants: Basic findings from the National Comorbidity Survey. *Experimental and Clinical Psychopharmacology, 2*(3), 244–268. https://doi.org/10.1037/1064-1297.2.3.244

29 Joy, J. E., Watson, S. J., & Benson, J. A. (2017). *Marijuana and medicine: Assessing the science base.* Washington, DC: National Academies Press..

30 Hasin, D. S., Saha, T. D., Kerridge, B. T., Goldstein, R. B., Chou, S. P., Zhang, H., Jung, J., Pickering, R. P., Ruan, W. J., Smith, S. M., Huang, B., & Grant, B. F. (2015). Prevalence of marijuana use disorders in the United States between 2001-2002 and 2012-2013. *JAMA Psychiatry, 72*(12), 1235–1242. https://doi.org/10.1001/jamapsychiatry.2015.1858

31 Hasin, D. S., Kerridge, B. T., Saha, T. D., Huang, B., Pickering, R., Smith, S. M., Jung, J., Zhang, H., & Grant, B. F. (2016). Prevalence and correlates of DSM-5 cannabis use disorder, 2012-2013: Findings from the National Epidemiologic Survey on Alcohol and Related Conditions-III. *American Journal of Psychiatry, 173*(6), 588–599. https://doi.org/10.1176/appi.ajp.2015.15070907

32 Hasin D. S. (2018). US epidemiology of cannabis use and associated problems. *Neuropsychopharmacology, 43*(1), 195–212. https://doi.org/10.1038/npp.2017.198

33 Winters, K. C., & Lee, C. Y. (2008). Likelihood of developing an alcohol and cannabis use disorder during youth: Association with recent use and age. *Drug and Alcohol Dependence, 92*(1-3), 239–247. https://doi.org/10.1016/j.drugalcdep.2007.08.005

34 Bahji, A., Stephenson, C., Tyo, R., Hawken, E. R., & Seitz, D. P. (2020). Prevalence of cannabis withdrawal symptoms among people with regular or dependent use of cannabinoids: A systematic review and meta-analysis. *JAMA Network Open, 3*(4), e202370. https://doi.org/10.1001/jamanetworkopen.2020.2370

35 Budney, A. J., & Hughes, J. R. (2006). The cannabis withdrawal syndrome. *Current Opinion in Psychiatry, 19*(3), 233–238. https://doi.org/10.1097/01.yco.0000218592.00689.e5

36 Elkashef, A., Vocci, F., Huestis, M., Haney, M., Budney, A., Gruber, A., & el-Guebaly, N. (2008). Marijuana neurobiology and treatment. *Substance Abuse, 29*(3), 17–29. https://doi.org/10.1080/08897070802218166

37 Huestis M. A. (2005). Pharmacokinetics and metabolism of the plant cannabinoids, delta9-tetrahydrocannabinol, cannabidiol and cannabinol. *Handbook of Experimental Pharmacology, 168*, 657–690. https://doi.org/10.1007/3-540-26573-2_23

38 Allsop, D. J., Copeland, J., Norberg, M. M., Fu, S., Molnar, A., Lewis, J., & Budney, A. J. (2012). Quantifying the clinical significance of cannabis withdrawal. *PloS One, 7*(9), e44864. https://doi.org/10.1371/journal.pone.0044864

39 Cornelius, J. R., Chung, T., Martin, C., Wood, D. S., & Clark, D. B. (2008). Cannabis withdrawal is common among treatment-seeking adolescents with cannabis dependence and major depression, and is associated with rapid relapse to dependence. *Addictive Behaviors, 33*(11), 1500–1505. https://doi.org/10.1016/j.addbeh.2008.02.001

40 Greene, M. C., & Kelly, J. F. (2014). The prevalence of cannabis withdrawal and its influence on adolescents' treatment response and outcomes: A 12-month prospective investigation. *Journal of Addiction Medicine, 8*(5), 359–367. https://doi.org/10.1097/ADM.0000000000000064

41 Gruber, A. J., Pope, H. G., Hudson, J. I., & Yurgelun-Todd, D. (2003). Attributes of long-term heavy cannabis users: a case-control study. *Psychological Medicine, 33*(8), 1415–1422. https://doi.org/10.1017/s0033291703008560

42 Stephens, R. S., Babor, T. F., Kadden, R., Miller, M., & Marijuana Treatment Project Research Group (2002). The Marijuana Treatment Project: Rationale, design and participant characteristics. *Addiction, 97 Suppl 1*, 109–124. https://doi.org/10.1046/j.1360-0443.97.s01.6.x

43 Budney, A. J., Roffman, R., Stephens, R. S., & Walker, D. (2007). Marijuana dependence and its treatment. *Addiction Science & Clinical Practice, 4*(1), 4.

44 Hughes, J. R., Naud, S., Budney, A. J., Fingar, J. R., & Callas, P. W. (2016). Attempts to stop or reduce daily cannabis use: An intensive natural history study. *Psychology of Addictive Behaviors, 30*(3), 389.

45 Gates, P. J., Sabioni, P., Copeland, J., Le Foll, B., & Gowing, L. (2016). Psychosocial interventions for cannabis use disorder. *Cochrane Database of Systematic Reviews, 5*. https://doi.org/10.1002/14651858.CD005336.pub4

46 Sherman, B. J., & McRae-Clark, A. L. (2016). Treatment of cannabis use disorder: Current science and future outlook.

Pharmacotherapy: The Journal of Human Pharmacology and Drug Therapy, 36(5), 511–535.

47   Secades-Villa, R., Garcia-Rodríguez, O., Jin, C. J., Wang, S., & Blanco, C. (2015). Probability and predictors of the cannabis gateway effect: a national study. *International Journal on Drug Policy, 26*(2), 135–142. https://doi.org/10.1016/j.drugpo.2014.07.011

48   Weinberger, A. H., Platt, J., & Goodwin, R. D. (2016). Is cannabis use associated with an increased risk of onset and persistence of alcohol use disorders? A three-year prospective study among adults in the United States. *Drug and Alcohol Dependence, 161*, 363–367. https://doi.org/10.1016/j.drugalcdep.2016.01.014

49   Agrawal, A., Neale, M. C., Prescott, C. A., & Kendler, K. S. (2004). A twin study of early cannabis use and subsequent use and abuse/dependence of other illicit drugs. *Psychological Medicine, 34*(7), 1227–1237. https://doi.org/10.1017/s0033291704002545

50   Lynskey, M. T., Heath, A. C., Bucholz, K. K., Slutske, W. S., Madden, P. A., Nelson, E. C., Statham, D. J., & Martin, N. G. (2003). Escalation of drug use in early-onset cannabis users vs co-twin controls. *JAMA, 289*(4), 427–433. https://doi.org/10.1001/jama.289.4.427

51   Kandel, D., & Kandel, E. (2015). The gateway hypothesis of substance abuse: Developmental, biological and societal perspectives. *Acta Paediatrica, 104*(2), 130–137. https://doi.org/10.1111/apa.12851

52   Kandel, E. R., & Kandel, D. B. (2014). A molecular basis for nicotine as a gateway drug. *New England Journal of Medicine, 371*, 931–942.

53   National Institute on Drug Abuse; National Institutes of Health; U.S. Department of Health and Human Services. (2020). *Cannabis (Marijuana) Research Report.* Retrieved from: https://nida.nih.gov/publications/research-reports/cannabis-marijuana.

54   Carliner, H., Brown, Q. L., Sarvet, A. L., & Hasin, D. S. (2017). Cannabis use, attitudes, and legal status in the U.S.: A review. *Preventive Medicine, 104*, 13–23. https://doi.org/10.1016/j.ypmed.2017.07.008

55   Allem, J. P., Escobedo, P., & Dharmapuri, L. (2020). Cannabis surveillance with Twitter data: Emerging topics and social bots. *American Journal of Public Health, 110*(3), 357–362. https://doi.org/10.2105/AJPH.2019.305461

56   Gorelick, D. A., Levin, K. H., Copersino, M. L., Heishman,
     S. J., Liu, F., Boggs, D. L., & Kelly, D. L. (2012). Diagnostic
     criteria for cannabis withdrawal syndrome. *Drug and Alcohol
     Dependence, 123*(1-3), 141–147. https://doi.org/10.1016/j.drugalc
     dep.2011.11.007
57   Katz, G., Lobel, T., Tetelbaum, A., & Raskin, S. (2014). Cannabis
     withdrawal – a new diagnostic category in DSM-5. *Israel Journal
     of Psychiatry and Related Sciences, 51*(4), 270–275.
58   Walsh, Z., Gonzalez, R., Crosby, K., S Thiessen, M., Carroll, C., &
     Bonn-Miller, M. O. (2017). Medical cannabis and mental health:
     A guided systematic review. *Clinical Psychology Review, 51*, 15–29.
     https://doi.org/10.1016/j.cpr.2016.10.002
59   Whiting, P. F., Wolff, R. F., Deshpande, S., Di Nisio, M., Duffy,
     S., Hernandez, A. V., Keurentjes, J. C., Lang, S., Misso, K.,
     Ryder, S., Schmidlkofer, S., Westwood, M., & Kleijnen, J. (2015).
     Cannabinoids for medical use: A systematic review and meta-
     analysis. *JAMA, 313*(24), 2456–2473. https://doi.org/10.1001/
     jama.2015.6358
60   Gorfinkel, L. R., Stohl, M., & Hasin, D. (2020). Association of
     depression with past-month cannabis use among US adults aged
     20 to 59 years, 2005 to 2016. *JAMA Network Open, 3*(8), e2013802.
     https://doi.org/10.1001/jamanetworkopen.2020.13802
61   Bahorik, A. L., Leibowitz, A., Sterling, S. A., Travis, A., Weisner,
     C., & Satre, D. D. (2017). Patterns of marijuana use among
     psychiatry patients with depression and its impact on recovery.
     Journal of Affective Disorders, 213, 168–171. https://doi.org/
     10.1016/j.jad.2017.02.016
62   Wilkinson, S. T., Stefanovics, E., & Rosenheck, R. A. (2015).
     Marijuana use is associated with worse outcomes in symptom
     severity and violent behavior in patients with posttraumatic
     stress disorder. *Journal of Clinical Psychiatry, 76*(9), 1174–1180.
     https://doi.org/10.4088/JCP.14m09475
63   Bonn-Miller, M. O., Boden, M. T., Bucossi, M. M., & Babson, K.
     A. (2014). Self-reported cannabis use characteristics, patterns and
     helpfulness among medical cannabis users. *American Journal of
     Drug and Alcohol Abuse, 40*(1), 23–30. https://doi.org/10.3109/
     00952990.2013.821477
64   Swift, W., Gates, P., & Dillon, P. (2005). Survey of Australians
     using cannabis for medical purposes. *Harm Reduction Journal, 2*,
     18. https://doi.org/10.1186/1477-7517-2-18

65   Davis, M. L., Powers, M. B., Handelsman, P., Medina, J. L., Zvolensky, M., & Smits, J. A. (2015). Behavioral therapies for treatment-seeking cannabis users: A meta-analysis of randomized controlled trials. *Evaluation & the Health Professions, 38*(1), 94–114. https://doi.org/10.1177/0163278714529970

66   Sherman, B. J., & McRae-Clark, A. L. (2016). Treatment of cannabis use disorder: Current science and future outlook. *Pharmacotherapy: The Journal of Human Pharmacology and Drug Therapy, 36*(5), 511–535.

67   Budney, A. J., Stanger, C., Tilford, J. M., Scherer, E. B., Brown, P. C., Li, Z., Li, Z., & Walker, D. D. (2015). Computer-assisted behavioral therapy and contingency management for cannabis use disorder. *Psychology of Addictive Behaviors, 29*(3), 501–511. https://doi.org/10.1037/adb0000078

Chapter 5

1   NIDA. (2023, December 14). What is the scope of tobacco, nicotine, and e-cigarette use in the United States?. Retrieved from https://nida.nih.gov/publications/research-reports/tobacco-nicotine-e-cigarettes/what-scope-tobacco-use-its-cost-to-society on 2024, January 28.

2   National Institute on Drug Abuse. (2018). Nicotine, tobacco, and e-cigarettes. Retrieved from: https://nida.nih.gov/sites/default/files/1344-tobacco-nicotine-and-e-cigarettes_0.pdf.

3   McLaughlin, I., Dani, J. A., & De Biasi, M. (2015). Nicotine withdrawal. *Current Topics in Behavioral Neurosciences, 24*, 99–123.

4   Hatsukami, D. K., Stead, L. F., & Gupta, P. C. (2008). Tobacco addiction. *Lancet, 371*(9629), 2027–2038

5   NIDA. (2024, January 5). What are the physical health consequences of tobacco use?. Retrieved from https://nida.nih.gov/publications/research-reports/tobacco-nicotine-e-cigarettes/what-are-physical-health-consequences-tobacco-use on 2024, January 28.

Chapter 6

1   Cooper, M., Park-Lee, E., Ren, C., Cornelius, M., Jamal, A., & Cullen, K. A. (2022). Notes from the field: E-cigarette use among

middle and high school students — United States, 2022. *Morbidity and Mortality Weekly Report*, *71*, 1283–1285. http://dx.doi.org/10.15585/mmwr.mm7140a3

2 American Heart Association. (2020). Talking with your teen resources help parents have conversations about ending teen e-cigarette use. Retrieved from: https://newsroom.heart.org/news/talk-vaping-with-your-teen-resources-help-parents-have-conversations-about-ending-teen-e-cigarette-use.

3 National Institute on Drug Abuse. (2020). Vaping devices (electronic cigarettes) DrugFacts. Retrieved from: https://nida.nih.gov/publications/drugfacts/vaping-devices-electronic-cigarettes.

4 Center for Disease Control and Prevention. E-Cigarette, or Vaping, Products Visual Dictionary. Available at: https://www.cdc.gov/tobacco/basic_information/e-cigarettes/pdfs/ecigarette-or-vaping-products-visual-dictionary-508.pdf.

5 Raber, J. C., Elzinga, S., & Kaplan, C. (2015). Understanding dabs: Contamination concerns of cannabis concentrates and cannabinoid transfer during the act of dabbing. *Journal of Toxicological Sciences*, *40*(6), 797–803. https://doi.org/10.2131/jts.40.797

6 Arterberry, B. J., Treloar Padovano, H., Foster, K. T., Zucker, R. A., & Hicks, B. M. (2019). Higher average potency across the United States is associated with progression to first cannabis use disorder symptom. *Drug and Alcohol Dependence*, *195*, 186–192. https://doi.org/10.1016/j.drugalcdep.2018.11.012

7 Loflin, M., & Earleywine, M. (2014). A new method of cannabis ingestion: The dangers of dabs? *Addictive Behaviors*, *39*(10), 1430–1433. https://doi.org/10.1016/j.addbeh.2014.05.013

8 Krishnan-Sarin, S., Morean, M., Kong, G., Bold, K. W., Camenga, D. R., Cavallo, D. A., Simon, P., & Wu, R. (2017). E-cigarettes and "dripping" among high-school youth. *Pediatrics*, *139*(3), e20163224. https://doi.org/10.1542/peds.2016-3224

9 Talih, S., Balhas, Z., Salman, R., Karaoghlanian, N., & Shihadeh, A. (2016). "Direct dripping": A high-temperature, high-formaldehyde emission electronic cigarette use method. *Nicotine & Tobacco Research*, *18*(4), 453–459. https://doi.org/10.1093/ntr/ntv080

10 Kosmider, L., Sobczak, A., Fik, M., Knysak, J., Zaciera, M., Kurek, J., & Goniewicz, M. L. (2014). Carbonyl compounds in electronic

cigarette vapors: Effects of nicotine solvent and battery output voltage. *Nicotine & Tobacco Research, 16*(10), 1319–1326. https://doi.org/10.1093/ntr/ntu078

11 National Academies of Sciences, Engineering, and Medicine. (2018). *Public health consequences of e-cigarettes*. Washington, DC: The National Academies Press. https://doi.org/10.17226/24952.

12 Madison, M. C., Landers, C. T., Gu, B. H., Chang, C. Y., Tung, H. Y., You, R., Hong, M. J., Baghaei, N., Song, L. Z., Porter, P., Putluri, N., Salas, R., Gilbert, B. E., Levental, I., Campen, M. J., Corry, D. B., & Kheradmand, F. (2019). Electronic cigarettes disrupt lung lipid homeostasis and innate immunity independent of nicotine. *Journal of Clinical Investigation, 129*(10), 4290–4304. https://doi.org/10.1172/JCI128531

13 Centers for Disease Control (2020). Outbreak of lung injury associated with the use of e-cigarettes, or vaping products. Retrieved from: https://www.cdc.gov/tobacco/basic_information/e-cigarettes/severe-lung-disease.html

14 Leventhal, A. M., Strong, D. R., Kirkpatrick, M. G., Unger, J. B., Sussman, S., Riggs, N. R., Stone, M. D., Khoddam, R., Samet, J. M., & Audrain-McGovern, J. (2015). Association of electronic cigarette use with initiation of combustible tobacco product smoking in early adolescence. *JAMA, 314*(7):700–707. https://doi.org/10.1001/jama.2015.8950

15 Bold, K. W., Kong, G., Cavallo, D. A., Camenga, D. R., & Krishnan-Sarin, S. (2017). E-cigarette susceptibility as a predictor of youth initiation of e-cigarettes. *Nicotine & Tobacco Research, 20*(1), 140–144. https://doi.org/10.1093/ntr/ntw393

16 US Department of Health and Human Services. (2016). *E-cigarette use among youth and young adults: a report of the surgeon general—executive summary*. Atlanta, GA: US Department of Health and Human Services, Centers for Disease Control and Prevention, National Center for Chronic Disease Prevention and Health Promotion, Office on Smoking and Health.

17 Weaver, S. R., Huang, J., Pechacek, T. F., Heath, J. W., Ashley, D. L., & Eriksen, M. P. (2018). Are electronic nicotine delivery systems helping cigarette smokers quit? Evidence from a prospective cohort study of U.S. adult smokers, 2015-2016. *PloS One, 13*(7), e0198047. https://doi.org/10.1371/journal.pone.0198047

18 Kulik, M. C., Lisha, N. E., & Glantz, S. A. (2018). E-cigarettes associated with depressed smoking cessation: A cross-sectional study of 28 European Union countries. *American Journal of Preventive Medicine, 54*(4), 603–609. https://doi.org/10.1016/j.amepre.2017.12.017

19 Hartmann-Boyce, J., Lindson, N., Butler, A. R., McRobbie, H., Bullen, C., Begh, R., Theodoulou, A., Notley, C., Rigotti, N. A., Turner, T., Fanshawe, T. R., & Hajek, P. (2022). Electronic cigarettes for smoking cessation. *Cochrane Database of Systematic Reviews, 11*(11), CD010216. https://doi.org/10.1002/14651858.CD010216.pub7

20 NIDA. (2024, January 5). What are the physical health consequences of tobacco use?. Retrieved from https://nida.nih.gov/publications/research-reports/tobacco-nicotine-e-cigarettes/what-are-physical-health-consequences-tobacco-use on 2024, January 28.

Chapter 7

1 Rawson, R. A., Erath, T. G., & Clark, H. W. (2023). The fourth wave of the overdose crisis: Examining the prominent role of psychomotor stimulants with and without fentanyl. *Preventive Medicine, 176*, https://doi.org/10.1016/j.ypmed.2023.107625.

2 National Institute on Drug Abuse. (2021). Fentanyl. Retrieved from: https://nida.nih.gov/research-topics/fentanyl.

3 Cole, C., Jones, L., McVeigh, J., Kicman, A., Syed, Q., & Bellis, M. A. (2010). *CUT: A guide to adulterants, bulking agents and other contaminants found in illicit drugs.* Liverpool: John Moores University.

4 Tallarida, C. S., Egan, E., Alejo, G. D., Raffa, R., Tallarida, R. J., & Rawls, S. M. (2014). Levamisole and cocaine synergism: A prevalent adulterant enhances cocaine's action in vivo. *Neuropharmacology, 79*, 590–595.

5 Solomon, N., & Hayes, J. (2017). Levamisole: A high performance cutting agent. *Academic Forensic Pathology, 73*(1), 469-476.

6 Ahmad, F. B., Anderson, R. N., Cisewski, J. A., Rossen, L. M., Warner, M., Sutton, P. (2023). County-level provisional drug overdose death counts. Centers for Disease Control, National Center for Health Statistics. Retrieved from: https://www.cdc.gov/nchs/nvss/vsrr/prov-county-drug-overdose.htm.

7 Drug Enforcement Administration (2020). Alarming spike in fentanyl-related overdose deaths leads officials to issue public warning. Retrieved from: https://www.dea.gov/press-releases/2020/08/06/alarming-spike-fentanyl-related-overdose-deaths-leads-officials-issue.

8 Goldstein, R. A., DesLauriers, C., Burda, A., & Johnson-Arbor, K. (2009). Cocaine: history, social implications, and toxicity: A review. *Seminars in Diagnostic Pathology, 26*(1), 10–17. https://doi:10.1016/j.disamonth.2008.10.002

9 National Institute on Drug Abuse. (2021). What are the short-term effects of cocaine use? Retrieved from: https://nida.nih.gov/publications/research-reports/cocaine/what-are-short-term-effects-cocaine-use.

10 Gawin, F. H., & Kleber, H. D. (1986). Abstinence symptomatology and psychiatric diagnosis in cocaine abusers: Clinical observations. *Archives of General Psychiatry, 43*(2), 107–113. https://doi.org/10.1001/archpsyc.1986.01800020013003

11 Helmus, T. C., Downey, K. K., Wang, L. M., Rhodes, G. L., & Schuster, C. R. (2001). The relationship between self-reported cocaine withdrawal symptoms and history of depression. *Addictive Behaviours, 26*(3), 461–467.

12 Schmitz, J. M., Stotts, A. L., Averill, P. M., Rothfleisch, J. M., Bailley, S. E., Sayre, S. L., & Grabowski, J. (2000). Cocaine dependence with and without comorbid depression: A comparison of patient characteristics. *Drug and Alcohol Dependence, 60*(2), 189–198.

13 Carroll, K. M., Nich, C., Ball, S. A., McCance, E., Frankforter, T. L., & Rounsaville, B. J. (2000). One-year follow-up of disulfiram and psychotherapy for cocaine-alcohol users: Sustained effects of treatment. *Addiction, 95*(9), 1335–1349.

14 Kampman, K. M., Pettinati, H., Volpicelli, J. R., Kaempf, G., Turk, E., Insua, A., Lipkin, C., Sparkman, T., & O'Brien, C. P. (2002). Concurrent cocaine withdrawal alters alcohol withdrawal symptoms. *Journal of Addictive Diseases, 21*(4), 13–26.

15 Centers for Disease Control (2022). Stimulant overdose. Retrieved from: https://www.cdc.gov/drugoverdose/deaths/stimulant-overdose.html.

16 Substance Abuse and Mental Health Services Administration. (2015). Results from the 2014 National Survey on Drug Use and Health: Detailed tables. Retrieved from: http://www.samhsa.

gov/data/sites/default/files/NSDUH-DetTabs2014/NSDUH-DetTabs2014.htm#tab7-3b.

17 McCall Jones, C., Baldwin, G. T., & Compton, W. M. (2017). Recent increases in cocaine-related overdose deaths and the role of opioids. *American Journal of Public Health*, *107*(3), 430–432. https://doi.org/10.2105/AJPH.2016.303627

18 Jones, C. M., Logan, J., Gladden, R. M., & Bohm, M. K. (2015). Vital signs: Demographic and substance use trends among heroin users—United States, 2002–2013. *Morbidity and Mortality Weekly*, *64*(26), 719–725.

19 State Library of New South Wales (2023). What is the difference between ice and speed? Retrieved from: https://druginfo.sl.nsw.gov.au/news/what-difference-between-ice-and-speed.

20 National Institute on Drug Abuse. (2019). Methamphetamine DrugFacts. Retrieved from: https://www.drugabuse.gov/publications/drugfacts/methamphetamine.

21 National Institute on Drug Abuse. (2021). How is methamphetamine misused? Retrieved from: https://nida.nih.gov/publications/research-reports/methamphetamine/how-methamphetamine-misused.

22 Han, B., Compton, W. M., Jones, C. M., Einstein, E. B., & Volkow, N. D. (2021). Methamphetamine use, methamphetamine use disorder, and associated overdose deaths among US adults. *JAMA Psychiatry*, *78*(12), 1329–1342.

23 McKetin, R., Sutherland, R., Peacock, A., Farrell, M., & Degenhardt, L. (2021). Patterns of smoking and injecting methamphetamine and their association with health and social outcomes. *Drug and Alcohol Review*, *40*(7), 1256–1265. https://doi.org/10.1111/dar.13364

24 Daniulaityte, R., Silverstein, S. M., Crawford, T. N., Martins, S. S., Zule, W., Zaragoza, A. J., & Carlson, R. G. (2020). Methamphetamine use and its correlates among individuals with opioid use disorder in a Midwestern US city. *Substance Use & Misuse*, *55*(11), 1781–1789. https://doi.org/10.1080/10826084.2020.1765805

25 Drug Enforcement Agency. (2018). 2017 National drug threat assessment. Retrieved from: https://www.dea.gov/sites/default/files/2018-07/DIR-040-17_2017-NDTA.pdf.

26 National Institute on Drug Abuse, (2020). How is methamphetamine manufactured? Retrieved from: https://nida.

nih.gov/publications/research-reports/methamphetamine/
how-methamphetamine-manufactured.

27 Luciew, J. (2020, June 22). Accused meth-cooking ringleader, age
70, busted in PA., along with 6 'smurfs.' *Penn Live*. Retrieved
from: https://www.pennlive.com/crime/2020/06/accused-
meth-cooking-ringleader-age-70-busted-in-pa-along-with-6-smu
rfs.html.

28 US Department of Justice. (ND). Methamphetamine laboratory
identification and hazards. Retrieved from: https://www.justice.
gov/archive/ndic/pubs7/7341/7341p.pdf

29 National Institute on Drug Abuse. (2013). Research report series.
Methamphetamine. Retrieved from: https://nida.nih.gov/sites/
default/files/methrrs.pdf.

30 Curtin, K., Fleckenstein, A. E., Robison, R. J., Crookston, M.
J., Smith, K. R., & Hanson, G. R. (2015). Methamphetamine/
amphetamine abuse and risk of Parkinson's disease in Utah: A
population-based assessment. *Drug and Alcohol Dependence, 146*,
30–38. https://doi.org/10.1016/j.drugalcdep.2014.10.027

31 National Institute on Drug Abuse. (2023). National Drug
Involved Overdose Deaths, 1999–2021. Accessed at https://nida.
nih.gov/research-topics/trends-statistics/overdose-death-rates.

32 Compton, W. M., Han, B., Blanco, C., Johnson, K., & Jones, C. M.
(2018). Prevalence and correlates of prescription stimulant use,
misuse, use disorders, and motivations for misuse among adults
in the United States. *American Journal of Psychiatry, 175*(8), 741–
755. https://doi.org/10.1176/appi.ajp.2018.17091048

33 Weyandt, L. L., Oster, D. R., Marraccini, M. E., Gudmundsdottir,
B. G., Munro, B. A., Rathkey, E. S., & McCallum, A. (2016).
Prescription stimulant medication misuse: Where are we
and where do we go from here? *Experimental and Clinical
Psychopharmacology, 24*(5), 400–414. https://doi.org/10.1037/pha
0000093

34 Volkow, N. D., Fowler, J. S., Wang, G. J., Telang, F., Logan, J.,
Wong, C., Ma, J., Pradhan, K., Benveniste, H., & Swanson, J.
M. (2008). Methylphenidate decreased glucose the amount of
needed by the brain to perform a cognitive task. *PloS One, 3*(4),
e2017. https://doi.org/10.1371/journal.pone.0002017

35 Kevil, C. G., Goeders, N. E., Woolard, M. D., Bhuiyan, M. S.,
Dominic, P., Kolluru, G. K., Arnold, C. L., Traylor, J. G., & Orr,
A. W. (2019). Methamphetamine use and cardiovascular disease.

Arteriosclerosis, Thrombosis, and Vascular Biology, 39(9), 1739–1746. https://doi.org/10.1161/ATVBAHA.119.312461

36 Turnipseed, S. D., Richards, J. R., Kirk, J. D., Diercks, D. B., & Amsterdam, E. A. (2003). Frequency of acute coronary syndrome in patients presenting to the emergency department with chest pain after methamphetamine use. *Journal of Emergency Medicine, 24*(4), 369–373. https://doi.org/10.1016/s0736-4679(03)00031-3

37 Reddy, P. K. V., Ng, T. M. H., Oh, E. E., Moady, G., & Elkayam, U. (2020). Clinical characteristics and management of methamphetamine-associated cardiomyopathy: State-of-the-art review. *Journal of the American Heart Association, 9*(11), e016704. https://doi.org/10.1161/JAHA.120.016704

38 Sandfort, V., Bluemke, D. A., Vargas, J., Brinker, J. A., Gerstenblith, G., Kickler, T., Zheng, G., Li, J., Chen, S., Lai, H., Fishman, E. K., & Lai, S. (2017). Coronary plaque progression and regression in asymptomatic African American chronic cocaine users with obstructive coronary stenoses: A preliminary study. *Journal of Addiction Medicine, 11*(2), 126–137. https://doi.org/10.1097/ADM.0000000000000282

39 Paratz, E. D., Cunningham, N. J., & MacIsaac, A. I. (2016). The cardiac complications of methamphetamines. *Heart, Lung & Circulation, 25*(4), 325–332. https://doi.org/10.1016/j.hlc.2015.10.019

40 Naik, P., Cashin, L., Huitron, S. (2016). A case of pulmonary foreign body granulomatosis secondary to intravenous injection of acetaminophen/oxycodone. *Military Medicine, 181*(10), e1404–e1406. https://doi.org/10.7205/MILMED-D-15-00486

41 Tashkin D. P. (2001). Airway effects of marijuana, cocaine, and other inhaled illicit agents. *Current Opinion in Pulmonary Medicine, 7*(2), 43–61. https://doi.org/10.1097/00063198-200103000-00001

42 Tseng, W., Sutter, M. E., & Albertson, T. E. (2014). Stimulants and the lung: Review of literature. *Clinical Reviews in Allergy & Immunology, 46*(1), 82–100. https://doi.org/10.1007/s12016-013-8376-9

43 Leece, P., Rajaram, N., Woolhouse, S., & Millson, M. (2012). Acute and chronic respiratory symptoms among primary care patients who smoke crack cocaine. *Journal of Urban Health, 90*, 542–551.

44 Shetty, V., Harrell, L., Murphy, D. A., Vitero, S., Gutierrez, A., Belin, T. R., Dye, B. A., & Spolsky, V. W. (2015). Dental disease

patterns in methamphetamine users: Findings in a large urban sample. *Journal of the American Dental Association (1939)*, *146*(12), 875–885. https://doi.org/10.1016/j.adaj.2015.09.012

45 Binswanger, I. A., Kral, A. H., Bluthenthal, R. N., Rybold, D. J., & Edlin, B. R. (2000). High prevalence of abscesses and cellulitis among community-recruited injection drug users in San Francisco. *Clinical Infectious Diseases*, *30*(3), 579–581. https://doi.org/10.1086/313703

46 Goldstein, R. A., DesLauriers, C., Burda, A., & Johnson-Arbor, K. (2009). Cocaine: history, social implications, and toxicity: a review. *Seminars in Diagnostic Pathology*, *26*(1), 10–17. https://doi.org/10.1053/j.semdp.2008.12.001

47 Riezzo, I., Fiore, C., De Carlo, D., Pascale, N., Neri, M., Turillazzi, E. & Fineschi, V. (2012). Side effects of cocaine abuse: Multiorgan toxicity and pathological consequences. *Current Medicinal Chemistry*, 19(33), 5624–5646.

48 Glasner-Edwards, S., & Mooney, L. J. (2014). Methamphetamine psychosis: Epidemiology and management. *CNS Drugs*, *28*(12), 1115–1126. https://doi.org/10.1007/s40263-014-0209-8

49 Diaconescu, A. O., Hauke, D. J., & Borgwardt, S. (2019). Models of persecutory delusions: A mechanistic insight into the early stages of psychosis. *Molecular Psychiatry*, *24*(9), 1258–1267. https://doi.org/10.1038/s41380-019-0427-z

50 Yuan J, Liu W, Liang Q, Cao X, Lucas MV, Yuan T. (2020). Effect of low-frequency repetitive transcranial magnetic stimulation on impulse inhibition in abstinent patients with methamphetamine addiction: A randomized clinical trial. *JAMA Network Open*,*3*(3), e200910. https://doi.org/10.1001/jamanetworkopen.2020.0910

51 Trivedi, M. H., Walker, R., Ling, W., Dela Cruz, A., Sharma, G., Carmody, T., et. al. (2021). Bupropion and naltrexone in methamphetamine use disorder. *New England Journal of Medicine*, *384*(2), 140–153.

Chapter 8

1 Abraham, O., Szela, L., Thakur, T., Brasel, K., & Brown, R. (2021). Adolescents' perspectives on prescription opioid misuse and medication safety. *Journal of Pediatric Pharmacology and Therapeutics*, *26*(2), 133–143. https://doi.org/10.5863/1551-6776-26.2.133

2   National Institute on Drug Abuse. (2014). Prevention. Retrieved
    from: https://nida.nih.gov/research-topics/prevention.
3   Johnston, L. D., Miech, R. A., O'Malley, P. M., Bachman, J. G.,
    Schulenberg, J. E., & Patrick, M. E. (2020). *Monitoring the Future
    National Survey Results on Drug Use 1975-2019: Overview, key
    findings on adolescent drug use*. Ann Arbor: Institute for Social
    Research, University of Michigan.
4   Cicero, T. J., Ellis, M. S., & Kasper, Z. A. (2020). Polysubstance
    use: A broader understanding of substance use during the opioid
    crisis. *American Journal of Public Health, 110*(2), 244–250. https://
    doi.org/10.2105/AJPH.2019.305412
5   Jones, C. M., Logan, J., Gladden, R. M., & Bohm, M. K. (2015).
    Vital signs: Demographic and substance use trends among heroin
    users—United States, 2002–2013. *Morbidity and Mortality Weekly,
    64*(26), 719–725.
6   Muhuri, P. K., Gfroerer, J. C., & Davies, M. C. (2013). CBHSQ data
    review. *Center for Behavioral Health Statistics and Quality, Substance
    Abuse and Mental Health Services Administration, 1*, 17. Retrieved
    from: https://img3.reoveme.com/m/25e062e91894208c.pdf.
7   National Institute on Drug Abuse. (2019). Heroin DrugFacts.
    Retrieved from: https://www.drugabuse.gov/publications/
    drugfacts/fentanyl..
8   Kane-Willis, K., Schmitz, S. J., Bazan, M., Narloch, V. F., &
    Wallace, C. B. (2011). *Understanding suburban heroin use*. Roosevelt
    University. Retrieved from: https://candorhealthed.org/files/
    Understanding_suburban_heroin_use.pdf.
9   Substance Abuse and Mental Health Services Administration.
    (2021). *Key substance use and mental health indicators in the United
    States: Results from the 2020 National Survey on Drug Use and
    Health* (HHS Publication No. PEP21-07-01-003, NSDUH Series
    H-56). Rockville, MD: Center for Behavioral Health Statistics
    and Quality, Substance Abuse and Mental Health Services
    Administration. Retrieved from: https://www.samhsa.gov/
    data/,
10 Compton, W. M., Jones, C. M., & Baldwin, G. T. (2016).
    Relationship between nonmedical prescription-opioid use and
    heroin use. *New England Journal of Medicine, 374*(2), 154–163.
    https://doi.org/10.1056/NEJMra1508490
11 National Institute on Drug Abuse. (2021). Why does heroin use
    create special risk for contracting HIV/AIDS and hepatitis B and

C? Retrieved from: https://nida.nih.gov/publications/resea
rch-reports/heroin/why-are-heroin-users-special-risk-contract
ing-hivaids-hepatitis-b-c..

12 Schuckit, M. A. (2016). Treatment of opioid-use disorders. *New England Journal of Medicine, 375*(4), 357–368. https://doi.org/10.1056/NEJMra1604339

13 McHugh, R. K., Park, S., & Weiss, R. D. (2014). Cue-induced craving in dependence upon prescription opioids and heroin. *American Journal on Addictions, 23*(5), 453–458. https://doi.org/10.1111/j.1521-0391.2014.12129.x

14 Centers for Disease Control and Prevention (2023). Overdose deaths and the involvement of illicit drugs. Retrieved from: https://www.cdc.gov/drugoverdose/featured-topics/VS-overd ose-deaths-illicit-drugs.html.

15 Garnock-Jones, K. P. (2016). Fentanyl buccal soluble film: A review in breakthrough cancer pain. *Clinical Drug Investigation, 36*(5), 413–419. https://doi.org/10.1007/s40261-016-0394-y

16 Department of Justice, Drug Enforcement Administration. (2022). Fentanyl. Retrieved from: https://www.dea.gov/sites/default/files/2023-03/Fentanyl%202022%20Drug%20Fact%20Sheet.pdf.

17 Gladden, R. M., Martinez, P., & Seth, P. (2016). Fentanyl law enforcement submissions and increases in synthetic opioid-involved overdose deaths—27 states, 2013–2014. *Morbidity and Mortality Weekly Report, 65*(33), 837–843.

18 Drug Enforcement Administration. (2020). Fentanyl. Accessed at: https://www.dea.gov/sites/default/files/2020-06/Fenta nyl-2020_0.pdf

19 Silsby, H. D., Kruzich, D. J., & Hawkins, M. R. (1984). Fentanyl citrate abuse among health care professionals. *Military Medicine, 149*(4), 227–228.

20 Armenian, P., Vo, K. T., Barr-Walker, J., & Lynch, K. L. (2018). Fentanyl, fentanyl analogs and novel synthetic opioids: A comprehensive review. *Neuropharmacology, 134*, 121–132. https://doi.org/10.1016/j.neuropharm.2017.10.016

21 Drug Enforcement Administration (2016). Counterfeit prescription pills containing fentanyls: a global threat. DEA-DCT-DIB-021-16. Retrieved from: https://www.dea.gov/sites/default/files/docs/Counterfeit%2520Prescription%2520Pills.pdf.

22 Jones, C. M., Campopiano, M., Baldwin, G., & McCance-Katz, E. (2015). National and state treatment need and capacity for

opioid agonist medication-assisted treatment. *American Journal of Public Health, 105*(8), e55–e63. https://doi.org/10.2105/AJPH.2015.302664

Chapter 9

1 Hedegaard, H., Miniño, A.M., & Warner, M. (2020). Drug overdose deaths in the United States, 1999–2018. NCHS Data Brief, National Center for Health Statistics, *356*.

2 Rosenblum, A., Marsch, L. A., Joseph, H., & Portenoy, R. K. (2008). Opioids and the treatment of chronic pain: controversies, current status, and future directions. *Experimental and Clinical Psychopharmacology, 16*(5), 405–416. doi:10.1037/a0013628

3 Van Zee, A. (2009). The promotion and marketing of oxycontin: Commercial triumph, public health tragedy. *American Journal of Public Health, 99*(2), 221–227. https://doi:10.2105/AJPH.2007

4 Guy Jr, G. P., Zhang, K., Bohm, M. K., Losby, J., Lewis, B., Young, R., Murphy, L. B., & Dowell, D. (2017). Vital signs: Changes in opioid prescribing in the United States, 2006–2015. *Morbidity and Mortality Weekly Report, 66*(26), 697–704. https://doi.org/10.15585%2Fmmwr.mm6626a4

5 Volkow, N. D., & Blanco, C. (2021). The changing opioid crisis: Development, challenges and opportunities. *Molecular Psychiatry, 26*(1), 218–233. https://doi.org/10.1038/s41380-020-0661-4

6 Centers for Disease Control and Prevention. (2023). Overdose deaths and the involvement of illicit drugs. Accessed on February 4, 2023 at https://www.cdc.gov/drugoverdose/featured-topics/VS-overdose-deaths-illicit-drugs.html

7 Ahmad, F. B., Anderson, R. N., Cisewski, J. A., Rossen, L. M., Warner, M., & Sutton, P. (2023). County-level provisional drug overdose death counts. *National Center for Health Statistics*. Retrieved from: https://www.cdc.gov/nchs/nvss/vsrr/prov-county-drug-overdose.htm.

8 National Institute on Drug Abuse. (2021). Methamphetamine overdose deaths rise sharply nationwide. Retrieved from: https://nida.nih.gov/news-events/news-releases/2021/01/methamphetamine-overdose-deaths-rise-sharply-nationwide.

9 Friedman, J., Godvin, M., Shover, C. L., Gone, J. P., Hansen, H., & Schriger, D. L. (2022). Trends in drug overdose deaths among US

adolescents, January 2010 to June 2021. *JAMA, 327*(14), 1398–1400. https://doi.org/10.1001/jama.2022.2847

10 National Public Radio. (2022). Teen and overdose deaths rose sharply in 2020, driven by fentanyl-laced pills. Retrieved from: https://www.npr.org/sections/health-shots/2022/04/12/109 2309418/teen-drug-overdose-deaths-rose-sharply-in-2020-dri ven-by-fentanyl-laced-pills.

11 Palamar, J. J., Ciccarone, D., Rutherford, C., Keyes, K. M., Carr, T. H., & Cottler, L. B. (2022). Trends in seizures of powders and pills containing illicit fentanyl in the United States, 2018 through 2021. *Drug and Alcohol Dependence, 234*, 109398. https://doi.org/10.1016/j.drugalcdep.2022.109398

Chapter 10

1 Hasin, D. S., Wall, M., Witkiewitz, K., Kranzler, H. R., Falk, D., Litten, R., et al. (2017). Change in non-abstinent WHO drinking risk levels and alcohol dependence: A 3 year follow-up study in the US general population. *Lancet Psychiatry, 4*(6), 469–476. https://doi.org/10.1176/appi.ajp.2013.12060782

2 McCann, D. J., Ramey, T., & Skolnick, P. (2015). Outcome measures in medication trials for substance use disorders. *Current Treatment Options in Psychiatry, 2*(2), 113–121.

3 US Food and Drug Administration. (2018). A reduction in the WHO risk drinking levels of alcohol consumption as an efficacy outcome in AUD clinical trials. Accessed at: https://www.fda. gov/media/131766/download

4 Probst, C., Manthey, J., Martinez, A., & Rehm, J. (2015). Alcohol use disorder severity and reported reasons not to seek treatment: A cross-sectional study in European primary care practices. *Substance Abuse Treatment and Prevention Policy, 10*, 32. https://doi.org/10.1186/s13011-015-0028-z.

5 Witkiewitz, K., Kranzler, H. R., Hallgren, K. A. et al. (2021). Stability of drinking reductions and long-term functioning among patients with alcohol use disorder. *Journal of General Internal Medicine* 36, 404–412. https://doi.org/10.1007/s11 606-020-06331-x

6 National Institute on Drug Abuse. (2022). Making addiction treatment more realistic and pragmatic: The perfect should not be the enemy of the good. Retrieved from https://nida.nih.gov/

about-nida/noras-blog/2022/01/making-addiction-treatment-more-realistic-pragmatic-perfect-should-not-be-enemy-good..

7   Marlatt G. A. (1996). Harm reduction: Come as you are. *Addictive Behaviors*, *21*(6), 779–788. https://doi.org/10.1016/0306-4603(96)00042-1

8   Chaiton, M., Diemert, L., Cohen, J. E., Bondy, S. J., Selby, P., Philipneri, A., & Schwartz, R (2016). Estimating the number of quit attempts it takes to quit smoking successfully in a longitudinal cohort of smokers. *BMJ Open*, *6*(6), e011045. https://doi.org/10.1136/bmjopen-2016-011045

9   Substance Abuse and Mental Health Services Administration. (2022). Key substance use and mental health indicators in the United States: Results from the 2021 National Survey on Drug Use and Health (HHS Publication No. PEP22-07-01-005, NSDUH Series H-57). Center for Behavioral Health Statistics and Quality, Substance Abuse and Mental Health Services Administration. https://www.samhsa.gov/data/report/2021-nsduh-annual-national-report

Chapter 11

1   Dutra, L., Stathopoulou, G., Basden, S. L., Leyro, T. M., Powers, M. B., & Otto, M. W. (2008). A meta-analytic review of psychosocial interventions for substance use disorders. *American Journal of Psychiatry*, *165*(2), 179–187. https://doi.org/10.1176/appi.ajp.2007.06111851

2   Magill, M., & Ray, L. A. (2009). Cognitive-behavioral treatment with adult alcohol and illicit drug users: A meta-analysis of randomized controlled trials. *Journal of Studies on Alcohol and Drugs*, *70*(4), 516–527. https://doi.org/10.15288/jsad.2009.70.516

3   Glasner-Edwards, S. (2015). *The addiction recovery skills workbook.* San Francisco:New Harbinger.

4   Wampold, B. E. (2001). *The great psychotherapy debate: Models, methods, and findings.* Mahwah, NJ: Lawrence Erlbaum Associates.

5   Lundahl, B., & Burke, B. L. (2009). The effectiveness and applicability of motivational interviewing: A practice-friendly review of four meta-analyses. *Journal of Clinical Psychology*, *65*(11), 1232–1245. https://doi.org/10.1002/jclp.20638

6   Frost, H., Campbell, P., Maxwell, M., O'Carroll, R. E., Dombrowski, S. U., Williams, B., Cheyne, H., Coles, E., & Pollock,

A. (2018). Effectiveness of motivational interviewing on adult behaviour change in health and social care settings: A systematic review of reviews. *PloS One, 13*(10), e0204890. https://doi.org/10.1371/journal.pone.0204890

7 Magill, M., Ray, L., Kiluk, B., Hoadley, A., Bernstein, M., Tonigan, J. S., & Carroll, K. (2019). A meta-analysis of cognitive-behavioral therapy for alcohol or other drug use disorders: Treatment efficacy by contrast condition. *Journal of Consulting and Clinical Psychology, 87*(12), 1093. Retrieved from: https://psycnet.apa.org/doi/10.1037/ccp0000447.

8 Magill, M., Kiluk, B. D., & Ray, L. A. (2023). Efficacy of cognitive behavioral therapy for alcohol and other drug use disorders: Is a one-size-fits-all approach appropriate? *Substance Abuse and Rehabilitation, 14*, 1–11. https://doi.org/10.2147/SAR.S362864

9 Magill, M., Tonigan, J. S., Kiluk, B., Ray, L., Walthers, J., & Carroll, K. (2020). The search for mechanisms of cognitive behavioral therapy for alcohol or other drug use disorders: A systematic review. *Behaviour Research and Therapy, 131*, 103648. https://doi.org/10.1016/j.brat.2020.103648

10 Mastroleo, N. R., & Monti, P. M. (2013). Cognitive-behavioral treatment for addictions. In B. S. McCrady & E. E. Epstein (Eds.), *Addictions: A comprehensive guidebook* (pp. 391–410). New York: Oxford University Press.

11 Marlatt, G. A., & George, W. H. (1984). Relapse prevention: Introduction and overview of the model. *British Journal of Addiction, 79*(4), 261–273.

12 Dutra, L., Stathopoulou, G., Basden, S. L., Leyro, T. M., Powers, M. B., & Otto, M. W. (2008). A meta-analytic review of psychosocial interventions for substance use disorders. *The American Journal of Psychiatry, 165*(2), 179–187. https://doi.org/10.1176/appi.ajp.2007.06111851

13 Magill, M., & Ray, L. A. (2009). Cognitive-behavioral treatment with adult alcohol and illicit drug users: a meta-analysis of randomized controlled trials. *Journal of Studies on Alcohol and Drugs, 70*(4), 516–527. https://doi.org/10.15288/jsad.2009.70.516

14 Magill, M., Ray, L., Kiluk, B., Hoadley, A., Bernstein, M., Tonigan, J. S., & Carroll, K. (2019). A meta-analysis of cognitive-behavioral therapy for alcohol or other drug use disorders: Treatment efficacy by contrast condition. *Journal of Consulting and Clinical*

Psychology, 87(12), 1093. https://psycnet.apa.org/doi/10.1037/ccp0000447

15   Magill, M., Ray, L., Kiluk, B., Hoadley, A., Bernstein, M., Tonigan, J. S., & Carroll, K. (2019). A meta-analysis of cognitive-behavioral therapy for alcohol or other drug use disorders: Treatment efficacy by contrast condition. *Journal of Consulting and Clinical Psychology, 87*(12), 1093. https://psycnet.apa.org/doi/10.1037/ccp0000447

16   Cuijpers, P., Sijbrandij, M., Koole, S. L., Andersson, G., Beekman, A. T., & Reynolds, C. F., 3rd (2013). The efficacy of psychotherapy and pharmacotherapy in treating depressive and anxiety disorders: a meta-analysis of direct comparisons. *World Psychiatry, 12*(2), 137–148. https://doi.org/10.1002/wps.20038

17   Leucht, S., Hierl, S., Kissling, W., Dold, M., & Davis, J. M. (2012). Putting the efficacy of psychiatric and general medicine medication into perspective: Review of meta-analyses. *The British Journal of Psychiatry, 200*(2), 97–106. https://doi.org/10.1192/bjp.bp.111.096594

18   Witkiewitz, K., Marlatt, G. A., & Walker, D. (2005). Mindfulness-based relapse prevention for alcohol and substance use disorders. *Journal of Cognitive Psychotherapy, 19*(3), 211–228.

19   Brazier, D. (1997). *The feeling Buddha*. London: Constable & Robinson.

20   Bowen, S., Chawla, N., & Marlatt, G. A. (2011). *Mindfulness-based relapse prevention for addictive behaviors: A clinician's guide*. Guilford Press, New York.

21   Bowen, S., Chawla, N., & Marlatt, G. A. (2011). *Mindfulness-based Relapse Prevention for Addictive Behaviors: A Clinician's Guide*. Guilford Press, New York.

22   Grant, S., Colaiaco, B., Motala, A., Shanman, R., Booth, M., Sorbero, M., & Hempel, S. (2017). Mindfulness-based relapse prevention for substance use disorders: A systematic review and meta-analysis. *Journal of Addiction Medicine, 11*(5), 386–396. https://doi.org/10.1097/ADM.0000000000000338

23   Goldberg, S. B., Pace, B., Griskaitis, M., Willutzki, R., Skoetz, N., Thoenes, S., Zgierska, A. E., & Rösner, S. (2021). Mindfulness-based interventions for substance use disorders. *Cochrane Database of Systematic Reviews, 10*, CD011723. . https://doi.org/10.1002/14651858.CD011723.pub2

24   Khoury, B., Lecomte, T., Fortin, G., Masse, M., Therien, P.,
     Bouchard, V., Chapleau, M. A., Paquin, K., & Hofmann, S. G.
     (2013). Mindfulness-based therapy: A comprehensive meta-
     analysis. *Clinical Psychology Review, 33*(6), 763–771. https://doi.
     org/10.1016/j.cpr.2013.05.005

25   Blanck, P., Perleth, S., Heidenreich, T., Kröger, P., Ditzen, B.,
     Bents, H., & Mander, J. (2018). Effects of mindfulness exercises
     as stand-alone intervention on symptoms of anxiety and
     depression: Systematic review and meta-analysis. *Behaviour
     Research and Therapy, 102*, 25–35. https://doi.org/10.1016/
     j.brat.2017.12.002

26   Glasner, S., Mooney, L. J., Ang, A., Garneau, H. C., Hartwell, E.,
     Brecht, M. L., & Rawson, R. A. (2017). Mindfulness-based relapse
     prevention for stimulant dependent adults: A pilot randomized
     clinical trial. *Mindfulness, 8*(1), 126–135.

27   Goodnough, A. (2020). This addiction treatment works. Why is
     it so underused? *The New York Times.* Retrieved from: https://
     www.nytimes.com/2020/10/27/health/meth-addiction-treatm
     ent.html.

28   Petry, N. M., Alessi, S. M., Marx, J., Austin, M., & Tardif, M.
     (2005). Vouchers versus prizes: Contingency management
     treatment of substance abusers in community settings. *Journal of
     Consulting and Clinical Psychology, 73*(6), 1005–1014. https://doi.
     org/10.1037/0022-006X.73.6.1005

29   Prendergast, M., Podus, D., Finney, J., Greenwell, L., & Roll, J.
     (2006). Contingency management for treatment of substance
     use disorders: A meta-analysis. *Addiction, 101*(11), 1546–1560.
     https://doi.org/10.1111/j.1360-0443.2006.01581.x

30   De Crescenzo, F., Ciabattini, M., D'Alò, G. L., De Giorgi, R., Del
     Giovane, C., Cassar, C., Janiri, L., Clark, N., Ostacher, M. J., &
     Cipriani, A. (2018). Comparative efficacy and acceptability of
     psychosocial interventions for individuals with cocaine and
     amphetamine addiction: A systematic review and network
     meta-analysis. *PLoS Medicine, 15*(12), e1002715. https://doi.org/
     10.1371/journal.pmed.1002715

31   Rawson, R. A., McCann, M. J., Flammino, F., Shoptaw, S., Miotto,
     K., Reiber, C., & Ling, W. (2006). A comparison of contingency
     management and cognitive-behavioral approaches for stimulant-
     dependent individuals. *Addiction, 101*(2), 267–274. https://doi.
     org/10.1111/j.1360-0443.2006.01312.x

32 Farrell, M., Martin, N. K., Stockings, E., Bórquez, A., Cepeda, J. A., Degenhardt, L., Ali, R., Tran, L. T., Rehm, J., Torrens, M., Shoptaw, S., & McKetin, R. (2019). Responding to global stimulant use: challenges and opportunities. *Lancet, 394*(10209), 1652–1667. https://doi.org/10.1016/S0140-6736(19)32230-5

33 Petry N. M. (2011). Contingency management: What it is and why psychiatrists should want to use it. *The Psychiatrist, 35*(5), 161–163. https://doi.org/10.1192/pb.bp.110.031831

34 Petry, N. M. (2011). Contingency management: What it is and why psychiatrists should want to use it. *The Psychiatrist, 35*(5), 161–163. https://doi.org/10.1192/pb.bp.110.031831

35 Goodnough, A. (2020). This Addiction Treatment Works. Why Is It So Underused? *The New York Times,* accessed September 17, 2023 at https://www.nytimes.com/2020/10/27/health/meth-addiction-treatment.html

36 Rawson, R. A., Erath, T. G., Chalk, M., Clark, H. W., McDaid, C., Wattenberg, S. A., Roll, J. M., McDonell, M. G., Parent, S., & Freese, T. E. (2023). Contingency management for stimulant use disorder: Progress, challenges, and recommendations. *Journal of Ambulatory Care Management, 46*(2), 152–159. https://doi.org/10.1097/JAC.0000000000000450

37 Ruan, H., Bullock, C. L., & Reger, G. M. (2017). Implementation of contingency management at a large VA addiction treatment center. *Psychiatric Services, 68*(12), 1207–1209. https://doi.org/10.1176/appi.ps.201700242

38 National Public Radio. (2021). To combat meth, California will try a bold treatment: Pay drug users to stop using. Retrieved from: https://www.npr.org/sections/health-shots/2021/09/30/1040412804/to-combat-meth-california-will-try-a-bold-treatment-pay-drug-users-to-stop-using.

39 Substance Abuse and Mental Health Administration. (2013). Family therapy can help. HHS Publication No. (SMA) 13-4784. Retrieved from: https://store.samhsa.gov/sites/default/files/d7/priv/sma13-4784.pdf.

40 Hogue, A., Schumm, J. A., MacLean, A., & Bobek, M. (2022). Couple and family therapy for substance use disorders: Evidence-based update 2010-2019. *Journal of Marital and Family Therapy, 48*(1), 178–203. https://doi.org/10.1111/jmft.12546

41 McCrady, B. S., Wilson, A. D., Muñoz, R. E., Fink, B. C., Fokas, K., & Borders, A. (2016). Alcohol-focused behavioral couple therapy. *Family Process, 55*, 443–459. https://doi.org/10.1111/famp.12231

42 D'Antonio (2022). Lessons learned from the perspective of a dad dealing with his son's addiction. Retrieved from: https://addictionlessons.com.

43 Substance Abuse and Mental Health Services Administration. (2022). Key substance use and mental health indicators in the United States: Results from the 2021 National Survey on Drug Use and Health (HHS Publication No. PEP22-07-01-005, NSDUH Series H-57). Center for Behavioral Health Statistics and Quality, Substance Abuse and Mental Health Services Administration. https://www.samhsa.gov/data/report/2021-nsduh-annual-national-report

44 Donovan, D. M., Ingalsbe, M. H., Benbow, J., & Daley, D. C. (2013). 12-step interventions and mutual support programs for substance use disorders: An overview. *Social Work in Public Health, 28*(3-4), 313–332. https://doi.org/10.1080/19371918.2013.774663

45 Donovan, D. M., Ingalsbe, M. H., Benbow, J., & Daley, D. C. (2013). 12-step interventions and mutual support programs for substance use disorders: An overview. *Social Work in Public Health, 28*(3-4), 313–332. https://doi.org/10.1080/19371918.2013.774663

46 Kelly, J. F., Hoeppner, B., Stout, R. L., & Pagano, M. (2012). Determining the relative importance of the mechanisms of behavior change within Alcoholics Anonymous: A multiple mediator analysis. *Addiction, 107*(2), 289–299.

47 Cloud, R. N., & Kingree, J. B. (2008). Concerns about dose and underutilization of twelve-step programs: Models, scales, and theory that inform treatment planning. *Recent Developments in Alcoholism*, 283–301.

48 Kaskutas, L. A., Ammon, L., Delucchi, K., Room, R., Bond, J., & Weisner, C. (2005). Alcoholics Anonymous careers: Patterns of AA involvement five years after treatment entry. *Alcoholism: Clinical and Experimental Research, 29*(11), 1983–1990.

49 White, W. L. (1998). Slaying the dragon: The history of addiction treatment and recovery in America.

Chapter 12

1 Carroll, K. M., & Weiss, R. D. (2017). The Role of Behavioral Interventions in Buprenorphine Maintenance Treatment: A Review. *American Journal of Psychiatry*, 174, 738–747. https://doi.org/10.1176/appi.ajp.2016.16070792

2 Off-Label Drugs: What You Need to Know. Content last reviewed September 2015. Agency for Healthcare Research and Quality, Rockville, MD. https://www.ahrq.gov/patients-consumers/patient-involvement/off-label-drug-usage.html

3 Smyth, B. P., Barry, J., Keenan, E., & Ducray, K. J. I. M. J. (2010). Lapse and relapse following inpatient treatment of opiate dependence. *The Irish Medical Journal, 103*(6), 176–179.

4 National Institute on Drug Abuse. (2020, September 18). Principles of Effective Treatment. Retrieved from https://www.drugabuse.gov/publications/principles-drug-addiction-treatment-research-based-guide-third-edition/principles-effective-treatment on 2023, June 13.

5 Stead, L. F., Perera, R., Bullen, C., Mant, D., Hartmann-Boyce, J., Cahill, K., & Lancaster, T. (2012). Nicotine replacement therapy for smoking cessation. *Cochrane Database of Systematic Reviews,* (110). https://doi.org/10.1002/14651858.CD000146.pub4

6 Lindson, N., Chepkin, S. C., Ye, W., Fanshawe, T. R., Bullen, C., & Hartmann-Boyce, J. (2019). Different doses, durations and modes of delivery of nicotine replacement therapy for smoking cessation. *Cochrane Database of Systematic Reviews*, (4). https://doi.org/10.1002/14651858.CD013308

7 National Institute on Drug Abuse. (2021, June 9). Tobacco Addiction. Retrieved from https://www.drugabuse.gov/publications/principles-drug-addiction-treatment-research-based-guide-third-edition/evidence-based-approaches-to-drug-addiction-treatment/pharmacotherapies/tobacco-addiction on 2023, June 25.

8 Zhang, B., Cohen, J. E., Bondy, S. J., & Selby, P. (2015). Duration of nicotine replacement therapy use and smoking cessation: a population-based longitudinal study. *American journal of epidemiology, 181*(7), 513–520. https://doi.org/10.1093/aje/kwu292

9 Wadgave, U., & Nagesh, L. (2016). Nicotine replacement therapy: An overview. *International Journal of Health Sciences, 10*(3), 425.

10　Shah, S. D., Wilken, L. A., Winkler, S. R., & Lin, S. J. (2008). Systematic review and meta-analysis of combination therapy for smoking cessation. *Journal of the American Pharmacists Association, 48*(5), 659–665. https://doi.org/10.1331/japha.2008.07063

11　Howes, S., Hartmann-Boyce, J., Livingstone-Banks, J., Hong, B., & Lindson, N. (2020). Antidepressants for smoking cessation. *The Cochrane Database of Systematic Reviews, 4*(4), CD000031. https://doi.org/10.1002/14651858.CD000031.pub5

12　Cryan, J. F., Bruijnzeel, A. W., Skjei, K. L., & Markou, A. (2003). Bupropion enhances brain reward function and reverses the affective and somatic aspects of nicotine withdrawal in the rat. *Psychopharmacology, 168*(3), 347–358. https://doi.org/10.1007/s00213-003-1445-7

13　West, R., Baker, C. L., Cappelleri, J. C., & Bushmakin, A. G. (2008). Effect of varenicline and bupropion SR on craving, nicotine withdrawal symptoms, and rewarding effects of smoking during a quit attempt. *Psychopharmacology, 197*(3), 371–377. https://doi.org/10.1007/s00213-007-1041-3

14　Lerman, C., Niaura, R., Collins, B. N., Wileyto, P., Audrain-McGovern, J., Pinto, A., Hawk, L., & Epstein, L. H. (2004). Effect of bupropion on depression symptoms in a smoking cessation clinical trial. *Psychology of Addictive Behaviors: Journal of the Society of Psychologists in Addictive Behaviors, 18*(4), 362–366. https://doi.org/10.1037/0893-164X.18.4.362

15　Moore, T., Cohen, M., & Furberg, C. (2008). QuarterWatch: 2008 Quarter 1. http://www.ismp.org/QuarterWatch/2008Q1.pdf

16　Nides, M., Glover, E. D., Reus, V. I., Christen, A. G., Make, B. J., Billing, C. B., Jr, & Williams, K. E. (2008). Varenicline versus bupropion SR or placebo for smoking cessation: a pooled analysis. *American Journal of Health Behavior, 32*(6), 664–675. https://doi.org/10.5555/ajhb.2008.32.6.664

17　Mills, E. J., Wu, P., Spurden, D., Ebbert, J. O., & Wilson, K. (2009). Efficacy of pharmacotherapies for short-term smoking abstinence: a systematic review and meta-analysis. *Harm Reduction Journal, 6*, 25. https://doi.org/10.1186/1477-7517-6-25

18　Mills, E. J., Wu, P., Lockhart, I., Thorlund, K., Puhan, M., & Ebbert, J. O. (2012). Comparisons of high-dose and combination nicotine replacement therapy, varenicline, and bupropion for smoking cessation: a systematic review and multiple treatment meta-analysis. *Annals of Medicine*, *44*(6), 588–597. https://doi.org/10.3109/07853890.2012.705016

19 Jordan, C. J., & Xi, Z. X. (2018). Discovery and development of varenicline for smoking cessation. *Expert Opinion on Drug Discovery*, *13*(7), 671–683. https://doi.org/10.1080/17460 441.2018.1458090

20 Cahill, K., Stevens, S., Perera, R., & Lancaster, T. (2013). Pharmacological interventions for smoking cessation: an overview and network meta-analysis. *Cochrane Database of Reviews*, (5).

21 U.S. Food and Drug Administration (2016, December 16). FDA revises description of mental health side effects of the stop-smoking medicines Chantix (varenicline) and Zyban (bupropion) to reflect clinical trial findings. *Drug Safety Communications*, accessed at https://www.fda.gov/media/101633/download

22 Anthenelli, R. M., Benowitz, N. L., West, R., St Aubin, L., McRae, T., Lawrence, D., Ascher, J., Russ, C., Krishen, A., & Evins, A. E. (2016). Neuropsychiatric safety and efficacy of varenicline, bupropion, and nicotine patch in smokers with and without psychiatric disorders (EAGLES): a double-blind, randomised, placebo-controlled clinical trial. *Lancet*, *387*(10037), 2507–2520. https://doi.org/10.1016/S0140-6736(16)30272-0

23 Centers for Disease Control and Prevention. Alcohol-related disease impact (ARDI) application. Atlanta, GA: CDC; 2013: www.cdc.gov/ARDI.

24 Skinner, M. D., Lahmek, P., Pham, H., & Aubin, H. J. (2014). Disulfiram efficacy in the treatment of alcohol dependence: a meta-analysis. *PloS One*, *9*(2), e87366. https://doi.org/10.1371/journal.pone.0087366

25 Ait-Daoud, N., & Johnson, B. A. (2003). Medications for the treatment of alcoholism. In: B. A. Johnson, P. Ruiz, & M. Galanter (Eds.), *Handbook of clinical alcoholism treatment* (pp. ---). Lippincott Williams & Wilkins.

26 Johnson B. A. (2008). Update on neuropharmacological treatments for alcoholism: scientific basis and clinical findings. *Biochemical Pharmacology*, *75*(1), 34–56. https://doi.org/10.1016/j.bcp.2007.08.005

27 O'Malley, S. S., Jaffe, A. J., Chang, G., Schottenfeld, R. S., Meyer, R. E., & Rounsaville, B. (1992). Naltrexone and coping skills therapy for alcohol dependence: A controlled study. *Archives of*

General Psychiatry, 49(11), 881–887. https://doi:10.1001/archp
syc.1992.01820110045007

28   Volpicelli, J. R., Alterman, A. I., Hayashida, M., & O'Brien, C.
P. (1992). Naltrexone in the treatment of alcohol dependence.
Archives of General Psychiatry, 49(11), 876–880. https://
doi:10.1001/archpsyc.1992.01820110040006

29   Kranzler, H. R., & Soyka, M. (2018). Diagnosis and
Pharmacotherapy of Alcohol Use Disorder: A Review. *JAMA,
320*(8), 815–824. https://doi.org/10.1001/jama.2018.11406

30   Monterosso, J. R., Flannery, B. A., Pettinati, H. M., Oslin, D. W.,
Rukstalis, M., O'Brien, C. P., & Volpicelli, J. R. (2001). Predicting
treatment response to naltrexone: the influence of craving and
family history. *The American journal on addictions, 10*(3), 258–268.
https://doi.org/10.1080/105504901750532148

31   King, A. C., Schluger, J., Gunduz, M., Borg, L., Perret, G., Ho,
A., & Kreek, M. J. (2002). Hypothalamic-pituitary-adrenocortical
(HPA) axis response and biotransformation of oral naltrexone:
preliminary examination of relationship to family history of
alcoholism. *Neuropsychopharmacology, 26*(6), 778–788. https://doi.
org/10.1016/S0893-133X(01)00416-X

32   Garbutt, J. C., Kranzler, H. R., O'Malley, S. S., Gastfriend, D.
R., Pettinati, H. M., Silverman, B. L., Loewy, J. W., Ehrich, E.
W., & Vivitrex Study Group (2005). Efficacy and tolerability
of long-acting injectable naltrexone for alcohol dependence: a
randomized controlled trial. *JAMA, 293*(13), 1617–1625. https://
doi.org/10.1001/jama.293.13.1617

33   O'Malley, S. S., Garbutt, J. C., Gastfriend, D. R., Dong, Q., &
Kranzler, H. R. (2007). Efficacy of extended-release naltrexone in
alcohol-dependent patients who are abstinent before treatment.
Journal of Clinical Psychopharmacology, 27(5), 507–512. https://doi.
org/10.1097/jcp.0b013e31814ce50d

34   Pettinati, H. M., Oslin, D. W., Kampman, K. M., Dundon, W.
D., Xie, H., Gallis, T. L., Dackis, C. A., & O'Brien, C. P. (2010).
A double-blind, placebo-controlled trial combining sertraline
and naltrexone for treating co-occurring depression and alcohol
dependence. *American Journal of Psychiatry, 167*(6), 668–675.
https://doi.org/10.1176/appi.ajp.2009.08060852

35   Petrakis, I. L., Ralevski, E., Desai, N., Trevisan, L., Gueorguieva,
R., Rounsaville, B., & Krystal, J. H. (2012). Noradrenergic
vs serotonergic antidepressant with or without naltrexone

for veterans with PTSD and comorbid alcohol dependence. *Neuropsychopharmacology, 37*(4), 996–1004. https://doi.org/10.1038/npp.2011.283

36 Mann, K., Lehert, P., & Morgan, M. Y. (2004). The efficacy of acamprosate in the maintenance of abstinence in alcohol-dependent individuals: Results of a meta-analysis. *Alcoholism, Clinical and Experimental Research, 28*(1), 51–63. https://doi.org/10.1097/01.ALC.0000108656.81563.05

37 Bouza, C., Angeles, M., Muñoz, A., & Amate, J. M. (2004). Efficacy and safety of naltrexone and acamprosate in the treatment of alcohol dependence: A systematic review. *Addiction, 99*(7), 811–828. https://doi.org/10.1111/j.1360-0443.2004.00763.x

38 Mason, B. J., Goodman, A. M., Chabac, S., & Lehert, P. (2006). Effect of oral acamprosate on abstinence in patients with alcohol dependence in a double-blind, placebo-controlled trial: The role of patient motivation. *Journal of Psychiatric Research, 40*(5), 383–393. https://doi.org/10.1016/j.jpsychires.2006.02.002

39 Jonas, D. E., Amick, H. R., Feltner, C., Bobashev, G., Thomas, K., Wines, R., Kim, M. M., Shanahan, E., Gass, C. E., Rowe, C. J., & Garbutt, J. C. (2014). Pharmacotherapy for adults with alcohol use disorders in outpatient settings: A systematic review and meta-analysis. *JAMA, 311*(18), 1889–1900. https://doi.org/10.1001/jama.2014.3628

40 Jonas, D. E., Amick, H. R., Feltner, C., Bobashev, G., Thomas, K., Wines, R., Kim, M. M., Shanahan, E., Gass, C. E., Rowe, C. J., & Garbutt, J. C. (2014). Pharmacotherapy for adults with alcohol use disorders in outpatient settings: A systematic review and meta-analysis. *JAMA, 311*(18), 1889–1900. https://doi.org/10.1001/jama.2014.3628

41 Witkiewitz, K., Litten, R. Z., & Leggio, L. (2019). Advances in the science and treatment of alcohol use disorder. *Science Advances, 5*(9), eaax4043. https://doi.org/10.1126/sciadv.aax4043

42 US Department of Veterans Affairs. (2021). VA/DoD clinical practice guideline for the management of substance use disorders. Retrieved from: https://www.healthquality.va.gov/guidelines/MH/sud/VADoDSUDCPGProviderSummary.pdf

43 American Psychiatric Association. (2017). The American Psychiatric Association practice guidelines for the pharmacological treatment of patients with alcohol use disorder.

Retrieved from: https://psychiatryonline.org/doi/pdf/10.1176/appi.books.9781615371969.

44 Manhapra, A., Chakraborty, A., & Arias, A. J. (2019). Topiramate pharmacotherapy for alcohol use disorder and other addictions: A narrative review. *Journal of Addiction Medicine, 13*(1), 7–22. https://doi:10.1097/ADM.0000000000000443

45 Cheng, H., Kellar, D., Lake, A., Finn, P., Rebec, G. V., Dharmadhikari, S., Dydak, U., & Newman, S. (2018). Effects of alcohol cues on MRS glutamate levels in the anterior cingulate. *Alcohol and Alcoholism, 53*(3), 209–215.

46 Kenna, G. A., Lomastro, T. L., Schiesl, A., Leggio, L., & Swift, R. M. (2009). Review of topiramate: An antiepileptic for the treatment of alcohol dependence. *Current Drug Abuse Reviews, 2*(2), 135–142.

47 Johnson, B. A., & Ait-Daoud, N. (2010). Topiramate in the new generation of drugs: Efficacy in the treatment of alcoholic patients. *Current Pharmaceutical Designs,16,* 2103–2112.

48 Wajid, I., Vega, A., Thornhill, K., Jenkins, J., Merriman, C., Chandler, D., Shekoohi, S., Cornett, E. M., & Kaye, A. D. (2023). Topiramate (Topamax): Evolving role in weight reduction management: A narrative review. *Life (Basel), 13*(9), 1845. https://doi.org/10.3390/life13091845

49 Reus, V. I., Fochtmann, L. J., Bukstein, O., Eyler, A. E., Hilty, D. M., Horvitz-Lennon, M., et. al. (2018). The American Psychiatric Association practice guideline for the pharmacological treatment of patients with alcohol use disorder. *American Journal of Psychiatry, 175*(1), 86–90. https://doi.org/10.1176/appi.ajp.2017.1750101

50 Knapp, C. M., Ciraulo, D. A., Sarid-Segal, O., Richardson, M. A., Devine, E., Streeter, C. C., et. al. (2015). Zonisamide, topiramate, and levetiracetam: Efficacy and neuropsychological effects in alcohol use disorders. *Journal of Clinical Psychopharmacology, 35*(1), 34.

51 Johnson, B. A., Swift, R. M., Addolorato, G., Ciraulo, D. A., & Myrick, H. (2005). Safety and efficacy of GABAergic medications for treating alcoholism. *Alcoholism: Clinical and Experimental Research, 29*(2), 248–254.

52 Mason, B. J., Quello, S., Goodell, V., Shadan, F., Kyle, M., & Begovic, A. (2014). Gabapentin treatment for alcohol dependence: A randomized clinical trial. *JAMA Internal Medicine, 174*(1), 70–77. https://doi.org/10.1001/jamainternmed.2013.11950

53   Falk, D. E., Ryan, M. L., Fertig, J. B., Devine, E. G., Cruz, R., Brown, E. S., et al., & National Institute on Alcohol Abuse and Alcoholism Clinical Investigations Group (NCIG) Study Group. (2019). Gabapentin enacarbil extended-release for alcohol use disorder: A randomized, double-blind, placebo-controlled, multisite trial assessing efficacy and safety. *Alcoholism: Clinical and Experimental Research, 43*(1), 158–169.

54   Kranzler, H. R., Feinn, R., Morris, P., & Hartwell, E. E. (2019). A meta-analysis of the efficacy of gabapentin for treating alcohol use disorder. *Addiction, 114*(9), 1547–1555.

55   Smith, R. V., Havens, J. R., & Walsh, S. L. (2016). Gabapentin misuse, abuse and diversion: A systematic review. *Addiction, 111*(7), 1160–1174. https://doi.org/10.1111/add.13324

56   Agabio, R., Sinclair, J. M., Addolorato, G., Aubin, H. J., Beraha, E. M., Caputo, F., et al. (2018). Baclofen for the treatment of alcohol use disorder: The Cagliari Statement. *Lancet Psychiatry, 5*(12), 957–960.

57   Farokhnia, M., Deschaine, S. L., Sadighi, A., Farinelli, L. A., Lee, M. R., Akhlaghi, F., & Leggio, L. (2021). A deeper insight into how GABA-B receptor agonism via baclofen may affect alcohol seeking and consumption: Lessons learned from a human laboratory investigation. *Molecular Psychiatry, 26*(2), 545–555. https://doi.org/10.1038/s41380-018-0287-y

58   Pierce, M., Sutterland, A., Beraha, E. M., Morley, K., & van den Brink, W. (2018). Efficacy, tolerability, and safety of low-dose and high-dose baclofen in the treatment of alcohol dependence: A systematic review and meta-analysis. *European Neuropsychopharmacology, 28*(7), 795–806. https://doi.org/10.1016/j.euroneuro.2018.03.017

59   Reynaud, M., Aubin, H. J., Trinquet, F., Zakine, B., Dano, C., Dematteis, M., Trojak, B., Paille, F., & Detilleux, M. (2017). A randomized, placebo-controlled study of high-dose baclofen in alcohol-dependent patients—the ALPADIR study. *Alcohol and Alcoholism, 52*(4), 439–446. https://doi.org/10.1093/alcalc/agx030

60   Drobes, D. J., Anton, R. F., Thomas, S. E., & Voronin, K. (2004). Effects of naltrexone and nalmefene on subjective response to alcohol among non-treatment-seeking alcoholics and social drinkers. *Alcoholism: Clinical and Experimental Research, 28*(9), 1362–1370. https://doi.org/10.1097/01.ALC.0000139704.88862.01

61 Gual, A., Bruguera, P., & López-Pelayo, H. (2014). Nalmefene and its use in alcohol dependence. *Drugs of Today (Barcelona), 50*(5), 347–355. https://doi.org/10.1358/dot.2014.50.5.2132323

62 van den Brink, W., Strang, J., Gual, A., Sørensen, P., Jensen, T. J., & Mann, K. (2015). Safety and tolerability of as-needed nalmefene in the treatment of alcohol dependence: Results from the Phase III clinical programme. *Expert Opinion on Drug Safety, 14*(4), 495–504. https://doi.org/10.1517/14740338.2015.1011619

63 Minozzi, S., Saulle, R., De Crescenzo, F., & Amato, L. (2016). Psychosocial interventions for psychostimulant misuse. *Cochrane Database of Systematic Reviews, 9*(9), CD011866. https://doi.org/10.1002/14651858.CD011866.pub2

64 Chan, B., Freeman, M., Kondo, K., Ayers, C., Montgomery, J., Paynter, R., & Kansagara, D. (2019). Pharmacotherapy for methamphetamine/amphetamine use disorder: A systematic review and meta-analysis. *Addiction, 114*(12), 2122–2136. https://doi.org/10.1111/add.14755

65 McCall Jones, C., Baldwin, G. T., & Compton, W. M. (2017). Recent increases in cocaine-related overdose deaths and the role of opioids. *American Journal of Public Health, 107*(3), 430–432. https://doi.org/10.2105/AJPH.2016.303627

66 Degenhardt, L., Randall, D., Hall, W., Law, M., Butler, T., & Burns, L. (2009). Mortality among clients of a state-wide opioid pharmacotherapy program over 20 years: Risk factors and lives saved. *Drug and Alcohol Dependence, 105*(1-2), 9–15.

67 Degenhardt, L., Bucello, C., Mathers, B., Briegleb, C., Ali, H., Hickman, M., & McLaren, J. (2011). Mortality among regular or dependent users of heroin and other opioids: A systematic review and meta-analysis of cohort studies. *Addiction, 106*(1), 32–51.

68 Sordo, L., Barrio, G., Bravo, M. J., Indave, B. I., Degenhardt, L., Wiessing, L., Ferri, M., & Pastor-Barriuso, R. (2017). Mortality risk during and after opioid substitution treatment: Systematic review and meta-analysis of cohort studies. *BMJ, 357.* https://doi.org/10.1136/bmj.j1550

69 US Food and Drug Administration (2017). FDA urges caution about withholding opioid addiction medications from patients taking benzodiazepines or CNS depressants: Careful medication management can reduce risks. *FDA Drug Safety Communication.* Retrieved from: https://www.fda.gov/drugs/drug-saf

ety-and-availability/fda-drug-safety-communication-fda-urges-caution-about-withholding-opioid-addiction-medications.

70   Bawor, M., Bami, H., Dennis, B. B., Plater, C., Worster, A., Varenbut, M., et al. (2015). Testosterone suppression in opioid users: A systematic review and meta-analysis. *Drug and Alcohol Dependence, 149*, 1–9.

71   Andorn, A. C., Haight, B. R., Shinde, S., Fudala, P. J., Zhao, Y., Heidbreder, C., Learned, S. M., Fox, N. L., Nadipelli, V. R., Hassman, D., & Rutrick, D. (2020). Treating opioid use disorder with a monthly subcutaneous buprenorphine depot injection: 12-month safety, tolerability, and efficacy analysis. *Journal of Clinical Psychopharmacology, 40*(3), 231–239. https://doi.org/10.1097/JCP.0000000000001195

72   Haight, B. R., Learned, S. M., Laffont, C. M., Fudala, P. J., Zhao, Y., Garofalo, A. S., Greenwald, M. K., Nadipelli, V. R., Ling, W., Heidbreder, C., & RB-US-13-0001 Study Investigators (2019). Efficacy and safety of a monthly buprenorphine depot injection for opioid use disorder: A multicentre, randomised, double-blind, placebo-controlled, phase 3 trial. *Lancet, 393*(10173), 778–790. https://doi.org/10.1016/S0140-6736(18)32259-1

73   Ling, W., Nadipelli, V. R., Solem, C. T., Ronquest, N. A., Yeh, Y. C., Learned, S. M., Mehra, V., & Heidbreder, C. (2019). Patient-centered outcomes in participants of a buprenorphine monthly depot (BUP-XR) double-blind, placebo-controlled, multicenter, phase 3 study. *Journal of Addiction Medicine, 13*(6), 442–449. https://doi.org/10.1097/ADM.0000000000000517

74   Lofwall, M. R., Walsh, S. L., Nunes, E. V., Bailey, G. L., Sigmon, S. C., Kampman, K. M., Frost, M., Tiberg, F., Linden, M., Sheldon, B., Oosman, S., Peterson, S., Chen, M., & Kim, S. (2018). Weekly and monthly subcutaneous buprenorphine depot formulations vs daily sublingual buprenorphine with naloxone for treatment of opioid use disorder: A randomized clinical trial. *JAMA Internal Medicine, 178*(6), 764–773. https://doi.org/10.1001/jamainternmed.2018.1052

75   Lintzeris N, Dunlop AJ, Haber PS, et al. Patient-reported outcomes of treatment of opioid dependence with weekly and monthly subcutaneous depot vs daily sublingual buprenorphine: A randomized clinical trial. *JAMA Network Open*. 2021;4(5):e219041. doi:10.1001/jamanetworkopen.2021.9041

76 Lee, J. D., Nunes, E. V. Jr., Novo, P., Bachrach, K., Bailey, G. L., Bhatt, S., Farkas, S., Fishman, M., Gauthier, P., Hodgkins, C. C., King, J., Lindblad, R., Liu, D., Matthews, A. G., May, J., Peavy, K. M., Ross, S., Salazar, D., Schkolnik, P., Shmueli-Blumberg, D., . . . & Rotrosen, J. (2018). Comparative effectiveness of extended-release naltrexone versus buprenorphine-naloxone for opioid relapse prevention (X:BOT): A multicentre, open-label, randomised controlled trial. *Lancet*, *391*(10118), 309–318. https://doi.org/10.1016/S0140-6736(17)32812-X

77 Tanum, L., Solli, K. K., Latif, Z. E., Benth, J. Š., Opheim, A., Sharma-Haase, K., Krajci, P., & Kunøe, N. (2017). Effectiveness of injectable extended-release naltrexone vs daily buprenorphine-naloxone for opioid dependence: A randomized clinical noninferiority trial. *JAMA Psychiatry*, *74*(12), 1197–1205. https://doi.org/10.1001/jamapsychiatry.2017.3206

78 Degenhardt, L., Larney, S., Kimber, J., Farrell, M., & Hall, W. (2015). Excess mortality among opioid-using patients treated with oral naltrexone in Australia. *Drug and Alcohol Review*, *34*, 90–96.

79 Jarvis, B. P., Holtyn, A. F., Subramaniam, S., Tompkins, D. A., Oga, E. A., Bigelow, G. E., & Silverman, K. (2018). Extended-release injectable naltrexone for opioid use disorder: A systematic review. *Addiction*, *113*(7), 1188–1209.

80 Sullivan, M., Bisaga, A., Pavlicova, M., Choi, C. J., Mishlen, K., Carpenter, K. M., Levin, F. R., Dakwar, E., Mariani, J. J., & Nunes, E. V. (2017). Long-acting injectable naltrexone induction: A randomized trial of outpatient opioid detoxification with naltrexone versus buprenorphine. *American Journal of Psychiatry*, *174*(5), 459–467. https://doi.org/10.1176/appi.ajp.2016.16050548

81 Fishman, M., Tirado, C., Alam, D., Gullo, K., Clinch, T., & Gorodetzky, C. W. (2019). Safety and efficacy of lofexidine for medically managed opioid withdrawal: A randomized controlled clinical trial. *Journal of Addiction Medicine*, *13*(3), 169. https://doi.org/10.1097%2FADM.0000000000000474

82 Substance Abuse and Mental Health Services Administration. (2020). Key substance use and mental health indicators in the United States: Results from the 2019 National Survey on Drug Use and Health (HHS Publication No. PEP20-07-01-001, NSDUH Series H-55). Rockville, MD: Center for Behavioral Health Statistics and Quality, Substance Abuse and Mental Health Services Administration. Retrieved from https://www.samhsa.gov/data/

83 Schwartz, R. P., Gryczynski, J., O'Grady, K. E., Sharfstein, J. M., Warren, G., Olsen, Y., Mitchell, S. G., & Jaffe, J. H. (2013). Opioid agonist treatments and heroin overdose deaths in Baltimore, Maryland, 1995–2009. *American Journal of Public Health, 103*(5), 917–922.

84 Wakeman, S. E., Larochelle, M. R., Ameli, O., Chaisson, C. E., McPheeters, J. T., Crown, W. H., Azocar, F., & Sanghavi, D. M. (2020). Comparative effectiveness of different treatment pathways for opioid use disorder. *JAMA Network Open, 3*(2), e1920622– e1920622. https://doi:10.1001/jamanetworko pen.2019.20622

85 Volkow, N. D., & Blanco, C. (2020). Medications for opioid use disorders: Clinical and pharmacological considerations. *Journal of Clinical Investigation, 130*(1), 10–13. https://doi.org/10.1172/JCI134708

86 Betty Ford Institute Consensus Panel. (2007). What is recovery? A working definition from the Betty Ford Institute. *Journal of Substance Abuse Treatment, 33*(3), 221–228. https://doi.org/10.1016/j.jsat.2007.06.001

87 Heimer, R., Hawk, K., & Vermund, S. H. (2019). Prevalent misconceptions about opioid use disorders in the United States produce failed policy and public health responses. *Clinical Infectious Diseases, 69*(3), 546–551. https://doi.org/10.1093/cid/ciy977

88 Strang, J., Kelleher, M. J., Best, D., Mayet, S., & Manning, V. (2006). Preventing heroin overdose deaths with emergency naloxone. *British Medical Journal; 333*: 614–615.

89 Bukten, A., Stavseth, M. R., Skurtveit, S., Tverdal, A., Strang, J., & Clausen, T. (2017). High risk of overdose death following release from prison: Variations in mortality during a 15-year observation period. *Addiction, 112*(8), 1432–1439.

90 Mojtabai, R., Mauro, C., Wall, M. M., Barry, C. L., & Olfson, M. (2019). Medication treatment for opioid use disorders in substance use treatment facilities. *Health Affairs (Project Hope), 38*(1), 14–23. https://doi.org/10.1377/hlthaff.2018.05162

91 Schuman-Olivier, Z., Albanese, M., Nelson, S. E., Roland, L., Puopolo, F., Klinker, L., & Shaffer, H. J. (2010). Self-treatment: illicit buprenorphine use by opioid-dependent treatment seekers. *Journal of Substance Abuse Treatment, 39*(1), 41–50. https://doi.org/10.1016/j.jsat.2010.03.014

92 National Institute on Drug Abuse. (2021). What is the treatment need versus the diversion risk for opioid use disorder treatment? Retrieved from: https://www.drugabuse.gov/publications/research-reports/medications-to-treat-opioid-addiction/what-treatment-need-versus-diversion-risk-opioid-use-disorder-treatment.

93 Cicero, T. J., Ellis, M. S., & Chilcoat, H. D. (2018). Understanding the use of diverted buprenorphine. *Drug and Alcohol Dependence*, *193*, 117–123. https://doi.org/10.1016/j.drugalcdep.2018.09.007

94 US Food and Drug Administration. (2023). FDA and kratom. Retrieved from: https://www.fda.gov/news-events/public-health-focus/fda-and-kratom.

95 National Center for Complementary and Integrative Health. (2022). Kratom. Retrieved from: https://www.nccih.nih.gov/health/kratom..

96 Weiss, S. T., & Douglas, H. E. (2021). Treatment of kratom withdrawal and dependence with buprenorphine/naloxone: A case series and systematic literature review. *Journal of Addiction Medicine*, *15*(2), 167–172. https://doi.org/10.1097/adm.0000000000000721

97 Donroe, J. H., & Fiellin, D. A. (2022). A case of kratom use: Implications for managing addiction and addressing comorbidity in overdose survivors, and for the education of clinicians who are not addiction specialists. *Journal of Addiction Medicine*, *16*(2), 138–140. https://doi.org/10.1097/ADM.0000000000000872

98 Dixon, R. B., Waggoner, D., Davis, M., Rembold, K., & Dasgupta, A. (2019). Contamination of some kratom products with salmonella. *Annals of Clinical & Laboratory Science*, *49*(5), 675–677.

99 Alsarraf, E., Myers, J., Culbreth, S., & Fanikos, J. (2019). Kratom from head to toe—case reviews of adverse events and toxicities. *Current Emergency and Hospital Medicine Reports*, *7*(4), 141–168.

100 US Drug Enforcement Agency. (2016). Withdrawal of notice of intent to temporarily place mitragynine and 7-hydroxymitragynine into Schedule I. *Federal Register*, *81*(198), 70652–70654. Retrieved from:https://gpo.gov/fdsys/pkg/FR-2016-10-13/pdf/2016-24659.pdf.

101 Coe, M. A., Pillitteri, J. L., Sembower, M. A., Gerlach, K. K., & Henningfield, J. E. (2019). Kratom as a substitute for opioids: Results from an online survey. *Drug and Alcohol Dependence*, *202*, 24–32.

102 Wilder, C. M., Miller, S. C., Tiffany, E., Winhusen, T., Winstanley, E. L., & Stein, M. D. (2016). Risk factors for opioid overdose and awareness of overdose risk among veterans prescribed chronic opioids for addiction or pain. *Journal of Addictive Diseases, 35*(1), 42–51. https://doi.org/10.1080/10550887.2016.1107264

103 Frank, D., Mateu-Gelabert, P., Guarino, H., Bennett, A., Wendel, T., Jessell, L., & Teper, A. (2015). High risk and little knowledge: overdose experiences and knowledge among young adult nonmedical prescription opioid users. *International Journal on Drug Policy, 26*(1), 84–91. https://doi.org/10.1016/j.dru gpo.2014.07.013

104 American Medical Association. (2018). Surgeon General: Naloxone should be widely prescribed, carried. Retrieved from: https://www.ama-assn.org/print/pdf/node/18286.

105 National Institute on Drug Abuse. (2019). Opioid overdose reversal news: FDA-approved naloxone devices produce substantially higher blood levels of naloxone than improvised nasal spray. Retrieved from: https://www.drugabuse.gov/ news-events/news-releases/2019/03/opioid-overdose-reversal-news-fda-approved-naloxone-devices-produce-substantially-hig her-blood-levels-of-naloxone-than-improvised-nasal-spray.

106 Krieter, P. A., Chiang, C. N., Gyaw, S., & McCann, D. J. (2019). Comparison of the pharmacokinetic properties of naloxone following the use of FDA-approved intranasal and intramuscular devices versus a common improvised nasal naloxone device. *Journal of Clinical Pharmacology, 59*(8), 1078–1084.

107 Barenie, R. E., Gagne, J. J., Kesselheim, A. S., Pawar, A., Tong, A., Luo, J., & Bateman, B. T. (2020). Rates and costs of dispensing naloxone to patients at high risk for opioid overdose in the United States, 2014-2018. *Drug Safety, 43*(7), 669–675. https://doi. org/10.1007/s40264-020-00923-6

108 Belz, D., Lieb, J., Rea, T., & Eisenberg, M. S. (2006). Naloxone use in a tiered-response emergency medical services system. *Prehospital Emergency Care, 10*(4), 468–471.

109 McClellan, C., Lambdin, B. H., Ali, M. M., Mutter, R., Davis, C. S., Wheeler, E., Pemberton, M., & Kral, A. H. (2018). Opioid-overdose laws association with opioid use and overdose mortality. *Addictive Behaviors, 86*, 90–95.

110 Townsend, T., Blostein, F., Doan, T., Madson-Olson, S., Galecki, P., & Hutton, D. W. (2020). Cost-effectiveness analysis of

alternative naloxone distribution strategies: First responder and lay distribution in the United States. *International Journal of Drug Policy, 75*, 102536.

111 Hamilton, L., Davis, C. S., Kravitz-Wirtz, N., Ponicki, W., & Cerdá, M. (2021). Good Samaritan laws and overdose mortality in the United States in the fentanyl era. *International Journal on Drug Policy, 97*, 103294. https://doi.org/10.1016/j.drugpo.2021.103294

112 Sigmon, S. C., C Meyer, A., Hruska, B., Ochalek, T., Rose, G., Badger, G. J., Brooklyn, J. R., Heil, S. H., Higgins, S. T., Moore, B. A., & Schwartz, R. P. (2015). Bridging waitlist delays with interim buprenorphine treatment: Initial feasibility. *Addictive Behaviors, 51*, 136–142. https://doi.org/10.1016/j.addbeh.2015.07.030

113 Ahmad, F. B., Anderson, R. N., Cisewski, J. A., Rossen, L. M., Warner, M., & Sutton, P. (2023). County-level provisional drug overdose death counts. *National Center for Health Statistics.* https://www.cdc.gov/nchs/nvss/vsrr/prov-county-drug-overdose.htm

114 Jones, C. M., Olsen, Y., Ali, M. M., Sherry, T. B., Mcaninch, J., Creedon, T., Juliana, P., Jacobus-Kantor, L., Baillieu, R., Diallo, M. M., Thomas, A., Gandotra, N., Sokolowska, M., Ling, S., & Compton, W. (2023). Characteristics and prescribing patterns of clinicians waivered to prescribe buprenorphine for opioid use disorder before and after release of new practice guidelines. *JAMA Health Forum, 4*(7), e231982. https://doi.org/10.1001/jamahealthforum.2023.1982

115 Lagisetty, P. A., Healy, N., Garpestad, C., Jannausch, M., Tipirneni, R., & Bohnert, A. S. B. (2019). Access to primary care clinics for patients with chronic pain receiving opioids. *JAMA Network Open, 2*(7), e196928. https://doi.org/10.1001/jamanetworkopen.2019.6928

116 Han, B., Compton, W. M., Blanco, C., & Colpe, L. J. (2017). Prevalence, treatment, and unmet treatment needs of US adults with mental health and substance use disorders. *Health Affairs, 36*(10), 1739–1747. https://doi.org/10.1377/hlthaff.2017.0584

117 Ouimette, P., Moos, R. H., & Finney, J. W. (2003). PTSD treatment and 5-year remission among patients with substance use and posttraumatic stress disorders. *Journal of Consulting and Clinical Psychology, 71*(2), 410–414. https://doi.org/10.1037/0022-006x.71.2.410

118   Nunes, E. V., & Levin, F. R. (2004). Treatment of depression
      in patients with alcohol or other drug dependence: a meta-
      analysis. *JAMA, 291*(15), 1887–1896. https://doi.org/10.1001/
      jama.291.15.1887
119   Iqbal, M. N., Levin, C. J., & Levin, F. R. (2019). Treatment for
      substance use disorder with co-occurring mental illness. *Focus,
      17*(2), 88–97. https://doi.org/10.1176/appi.focus.20180042
120   Cornelius, J. R., Salloum, I. M., Ehler, J. G., Jarrett, P. J., Cornelius,
      M. D., Black, A., Perel, J. M., & Thase, M. E. (1997). Double-blind
      fluoxetine in depressed alcoholic smokers. *Psychopharmacology
      Bulletin, 33*(1), 165–170.
121   Moak, D. H., Anton, R. F., Latham, P. K., Voronin, K. E., Waid,
      R. L., & Durazo-Arvizu, R. (2003). Sertraline and cognitive
      behavioral therapy for depressed alcoholics: Results of a
      placebo-controlled trial. *Journal of Clinical Psychopharmacology,
      23*(6), 553–562. https://doi.org/10.1097/01.jcp.0000095
      346.32154.41
122   McKeehan, M. B., & Martin, D. (2002). Assessment and treatment
      of anxiety disorders and co-morbid alcohol/other drug
      dependency. *Alcoholism Treatment Quarterly,20*, 45–59.
123   Bolton, J., Cox, B., Clara, I., & Sareen, J. (2006). Use of alcohol
      and drugs to self-medicate anxiety disorders in a nationally
      representative sample. *Journal of Nervous and Mental Disease,
      194*(11), 818–825. https://doi.org/10.1097/01.nmd.0000244
      481.63148.98
124   Randall, C. L., Thomas, S., & Thevos, A. K. (2001). Concurrent
      alcoholism and social anxiety disorder: a first step toward
      developing effective treatments. *Alcoholism, Clinical and
      Experimental Research, 25*(2), 210–220.
125   Batki, S. L., Pennington, D. L., Lasher, B., Neylan, T. C., Metzler,
      T., Waldrop, A., Delucchi, K., & Herbst, E. (2014). Topiramate
      treatment of alcohol use disorder in veterans with posttraumatic
      stress disorder: a randomized controlled pilot trial. *Alcoholism,
      Clinical and Experimental Research, 38*(8), 2169–2177. https://doi.
      org/10.1111/acer.12496
126   Petrakis, I. L., Poling, J., Levinson, C., Nich, C., Carroll, K.,
      Ralevski, E., & Rounsaville, B. (2006). Naltrexone and disulfiram
      in patients with alcohol dependence and comorbid post-
      traumatic stress disorder. *Biological Psychiatry, 60*(7), 777–783.
      https://doi.org/10.1016/j.biopsych.2006.03.074

127 Satre, D. D., Iturralde, E., Ghadiali, M., Young-Wolff, K. C., Campbell, C. I., Leibowitz, A. S., & Sterling, S. A. (2020). Treatment for anxiety and substance use disorders during the COVID-19 pandemic: Challenges and strategies. *Journal of Addiction Medicine, 14*(6), e293–e296. https://doi.org/10.1097/ADM.0000000000000755

128 Najavits L. M., & Hien D. (2013). Helping vulnerable populations: A comprehensive review of the treatment outcome literature on substance use disorder and PTSD. *Journal of Clinical Psychology, 69*, 433–479. https://doi.org/10.1002/jclp.21980

129 Back, S. E., Foa, E. B., Killeen, T. K., Brady, K. T., Schwandt, M. L., Heilig, M., & Magnusson, A. (2015). *Concurrent treatment of PTSD and substance use disorders using prolonged exposure (COPE) therapist guide.* New York: Oxford University Press.

130 Roos, C. R., Bowen, S., & Witkiewitz, K. (2017). Baseline patterns of substance use disorder severity and depression and anxiety symptoms moderate the efficacy of mindfulness-based relapse prevention. *Journal of Consulting and Clinical Psychology, 85*(11), 1041–1051. https://doi.org/10.1037/ccp0000249

131 Glasner-Edwards, S., Mooney, L. J., Ang, A., Garneau, H. C., Hartwell, E., Brecht, M. L., & Rawson, R. A. (2017). Mindfulness based relapse prevention for stimulant dependent adults: A pilot randomized clinical trial. *Mindfulness, 8*(1), 126–135. https://doi.org/10.1007/s12671-016-0586-9

132 Wolitzky-Taylor, K., Krull, J., Rawson, R., Roy-Byrne, P., Ries, R., & Craske, M. G. (2018). Randomized clinical trial evaluating the preliminary effectiveness of an integrated anxiety disorder treatment in substance use disorder specialty clinics. *Journal of Consulting and Clinical Psychology, 86*(1), 81–88. https://doi.org/10.1037/ccp0000276

133 Notzon, D. P., Pavlicova, M., Glass, A., Mariani, J. J., Mahony, A. L., Brooks, D. J., & Levin, F. R. (2020). ADHD is highly prevalent in patients seeking treatment for cannabis use disorders. *Journal of Attention Disorders, 24*(11), 1487–1492. https://doi.org/10.1177/1087054716640109

134 van de Glind, G., Konstenius, M., Koeter, M. W. J., van Emmerik-van Oortmerssen, K., Carpentier, P. J., Kaye, S., Degenhardt, L., Skutle, A., Franck, J., Bu, E. T., Moggi, F., Dom, G., Verspreet, S.,

Demetrovics, Z., Kapitány-Fövény, M., Fatséas, M., Auriacombe, M., Schillinger, A., Møller, M., Johnson, B., . . . & van den Brink, W. (2014). Variability in the prevalence of adult ADHD in treatment seeking substance use disorder patients: Results from an international multi-center study exploring DSM-IV and DSM-5 criteria. *Drug and Alcohol Dependence, 134*, 158–166. https://doi.org/10.1016/j.drugalcdep.2013.09.026

135 Levin, F. R., Mariani, J. J., Specker, S., Mooney, M., Mahony, A., Brooks, D. J., Babb, D., Bai, Y., Eberly, L. E., Nunes, E. V., & Grabowski, J. (2015). Extended-release mixed amphetamine salts vs placebo for comorbid adult attention-deficit/hyperactivity disorder and cocaine use disorder: A randomized clinical trial. *JAMA Psychiatry, 72*(6), 593–602. https://doi.org/10.1001/jamapsychiatry.2015.41

136 Wilens, T. E., Faraone, S. V., Biederman, J., & Gunawardene, S. (2003). Does stimulant therapy of attention-deficit/hyperactivity disorder beget later substance abuse? A meta-analytic review of the literature. *Pediatrics, 111*(1), 179–185. https://doi.org/10.1542/peds.111.1.179

137 Cassidy, T. A., Varughese, S., Russo, L., Budman, S. H., Eaton, T. A., & Butler, S. F. (2015). Nonmedical use and diversion of ADHD stimulants among U.S. Adults ages 18-49: A national internet survey. *Journal of Attention Disorders, 19*(7), 630–640. https://doi.org/10.1177/1087054712468486

Chapter 13

1 Glasner, S., Kalichman, S., Cowie, K., Garcia, M., Michero, D., Moore, D. J., Lee, A. B., Beckwith, M., Cushman, C., & Montoya, J. (2022). Stigma experiences related to opioid use disorder and mental health among adults initiating treatment with buprenorphine. *Paper presented at the NIH Helping End Addiction Long-Term (HEAL) Investigators Meeting*, April 11–12, 2022.

2 Bartram, A., Eliott, J. A., & Crabb, S. (2017). "Why can't I just not drink?" A qualitative study of adults' social experiences of stopping or reducing alcohol consumption. *Drug and Alcohol Review, 36*, 449–455.

3 Advocat, J., & Lindsay, J. (2015). To drink or not to drink? Young Australians negotiating the social imperative to drink to intoxication. *Journal of Sociology, 51*, 139–153.

4 Warren, J. I., Stein, J. A., & Grella, C. E. (2007). Role of social support and self-efficacy in treatment outcomes among clients with co-occurring disorders. *Drug and Alcohol Dependence, 89*(2-3), 267–274. https://doi.org/10.1016/j.drugalcdep.2007.01.009

Chapter 14

1 Kelly, J. F., Bergman, B., Hoeppner, B. B., Vilsaint, C., & White, W. L. (2017). Prevalence and pathways of recovery from drug and alcohol problems in the United States population: Implications for practice, research, and policy. *Drug and Alcohol Dependence, 181*, 162–169. https://doi.org/10.1016/j.drugalc dep.2017.09.028

2 Jones, C. M., Noonan, R. K., & Compton, W. M. (2020). Prevalence and correlates of ever having a substance use problem and substance use recovery status among adults in the United States, 2018. *Drug and Alcohol Dependence, 214*, 108169. https://doi.org/10.1016/j.drugalcdep.2020.108169

3 Jones, C. M., Shoff, C., Hodges, K., Blanco, C., Losby, J. L., Ling, S. M., & Compton, W. M. (2022). Receipt of Telehealth Services, Receipt and Retention of Medications for Opioid Use Disorder, and Medically Treated Overdose Among Medicare Beneficiaries Before and During the COVID-19 Pandemic. *JAMA psychiatry, 79*(10), 981–992. https://doi.org/10.1001/jamapsychia try.2022.2284

4 McLellan, A. T., Lewis, D. C., O'Brien, C. P., & Kleber, H. D. (2000). Drug dependence, a chronic medical illness: implications for treatment, insurance, and outcomes evaluation. *JAMA, 284*(13), 1689–1695. https://doi.org/10.1001/jama.284.13.1689

5 Witkiewitz, K., Heather, N., Falk, D. E., Litten, R. Z., Hasin, D. S., Kranzler, H. R., Mann, K. F., O'Malley, S. S., & Anton, R. F. (2020). World Health Organization risk drinking level reductions are associated with improved functioning and are sustained among patients with mild, moderate and severe alcohol dependence in clinical trials in the United States and United Kingdom. *Addiction, 115*(9), 1668–1680. https://doi.org/10.1111/add.15011

6 Hasin, D., Paykin, A., & Endicott, J. (2001). Course of DSM-IV alcohol dependence in a community sample: Effects of parental history and binge drinking. *Alcoholism: Clinical and Experimental*

Research, 25(3), 411–414. https://doi.org/10.1111/j.1530-0277.2001.tb02228.x

7 White, W. L. (2012). *Recovery/remission from substance use disorders: An analysis of reported outcomes in 415 scientific reports, 1868-2011.* Philadelphia: Philadelphia Department of Behavioral Health and Intellectual Disability Services and the Great Lakes Addiction Technology Transfer Center.

8 Maisto, S. A., & Connors, G. J. (2006). Relapse in the addictive behaviors: integration and future directions. *Clinical Psychology Review, 26*(2), 229–231. https://doi.org/10.1016/j.cpr.2005.11.009

9 Vaillant, G. E. (2003). A 60-year follow-up of alcoholic men. *Addiction, 98*(8), 1043–1051. https://doi.org/10.1046/j.1360-0443.2003.00422.x

10 Moos, R. H., & Moos, B. S. (2006). Rates and predictors of relapse after natural and treated remission from alcohol use disorders. *Addiction, 101*(2), 212–222. https://doi.org/10.1111/j.1360-0443.2006.01310.x

11 Vaillant, G. E., & Hiller-Sturmhöfel, S. (1996). The natural history of alcoholism. *Alcohol Health and Research World, 20*(3), 152–161.

12 Vaillant, G. E. (2003). A 60-year follow-up of alcoholic men. *Addiction, 98*(8), 1043–1051. https://doi.org/10.1046/j.1360-0443.2003.00422.x

13 Flynn, P. M., Joe, G. W., Broome, K. M., Simpson, D. D., & Brown, B. S. (2003). Recovery from opioid addiction in DATOS. *Journal of Substance Abuse Treatment, 25*(3), 177–186. https://doi.org/10.1016/s0740-5472(03)00125-9

14 McQuaid, R. J., Malik, A., Morrisey, M., & Baydack, N. (2017) *Life in Recovery From Addiction in Canada,* in series: "Life in Recovery from Addiction in Canada." Ottawa, ON: Canadian Centre on Substance Abuse. Retrieved from https://www.ccsa.ca/sites/default/files/2019-04/CCSA-Life-in-Recovery-from-Addiction-Report-2017-en.pdf

15 Kelly, J. F., Greene, M. C., Bergman, B. G., White, W. L., & Hoeppner, B. B. (2019). How many recovery attempts does it take to successfully resolve an alcohol or drug problem? Estimates and correlates from a national study of recovering U.S. adults. *Alcoholism, Clinical and Experimental Research, 43*(7), 1533–1544. https://doi.org/10.1111/acer.14067

16 McCabe, S. E., West, B. T., Strobbe, S., & Boyd, C. J. (2018).
    Persistence/recurrence of and remission from DSM-5 substance
    use disorders in the United States: Substance-specific and
    substance-aggregated correlates. *Journal of Substance Abuse
    Treatment, 93*, 38–48. https://doi.org/10.1016/j.jsat.2018.07.012
17 Glasner-Edwards, S. (2015). *The Addiction Recovery Skills
    Workbook.* New Harbinger, San Francisco, CA.
18 Larimer, M. E., Palmer, R. S., & Marlatt, G. A. (1999). Relapse
    prevention. An overview of Marlatt's cognitive-behavioral
    model. *Alcohol Research & Health, 23*(2), 151–160.

INDEX

For the benefit of digital users, indexed terms that span two pages (e.g., 52–53) may, on occasion, appear on only one of those pages.

Tables and figures are indicated by an italic *t* and *f* following the page/paragraph number.